1993

New Approaches to Mental Health from Birth to Adolescence

EDITED BY

COLETTE CHILAND, M. D., Ph. D.

J. GERALD YOUNG, M. D.

Translation of the French chapters by Maev-Ann de la Guardia

Yale University Press   New Haven & London

Published with assistance from the foundation established in memory of Philip Hamilton McMillan of the Class of 1894, Yale College.

This work was supported by a grant from the Medical Fellows Program of the Office of Mental Retardation and Developmental Disabilities, State of New York.

Set in Primer type by The Composing Room of Michigan, Inc. Grand Rapids, Michigan
Printed in the United States of America by Edwards Brothers, Inc., Ann Arbor, Michigan

International Standard Serial Number: 0277-6790
International Standard Book Number: 0-300-04438-0

The paper in this book meets the guidelines for permanence and durability of the Committee on Production Guidelines for Book Longevity of the Council on Library Resources.

10 9 8 7 6 5 4 3 2 1

CONTRIBUTORS

Anne-Marie Ambert, Ph.D., Department of Sociology, York University, Downsview, Ontario, Canada

Hillevi M. Aro, M.D., Department of Public Health, University of Tampere, Tampere, Finland

Ralph Barocas, Ph.D., Professor of Psychology, George Mason, University, Fairfax, Va., United States

Magda Campbell, M.D., Professor of Psychiatry, New York University Medical Center, New York, N.Y., United States

Marianne Cederblad, M.D., Professor of Child and Youth Psychiatry, University of Lund, Lund, Sweden

Colette Chiland, M.D., Ph.D., Professor of Clinical Psychology, René Descartes University, Paris, France

Donald J. Cohen, M.D., Professor of Child Psychiatry, Psychology, and Pediatrics, Yale University School of Medicine, New Haven, Conn., United States

Helen Margaret Connell, Associate Professor of Child Psychiatry, University of Queensland, Department of Child Health, Royal Brisbane Children's Hospital, Herston, Australia

René Diatkine, M.D., formerly Professor, School of Medicine of Geneva; Assistant Executive Director, Mental Health Association, Alfred Binet Center, Paris, France

Michel Dugas, M.D., Professor of Child Psychiatry, Child and Adolescent Psychopathology Service, Herold Hospital, France

Gunther Esser, Ph.D., Child and Adolescent Psychiatry Clinic, Central Institute for Mental Health, Manheim, Germany

Tilman H. Furniss, M.D., M.Phil., M.R.C.Psych., Senior Registrar, Department of Child, Adolescent, and Family Psychiatry, University College Hospital, Middlesex Hospital, London, United Kingdom

Eleanor Galenson, M.D., Clinical Professor of Psychiatry, Mount Sinai School of Medicine, New York, N.Y., United States

Christophe Gérard, M.D., Child and Adolescent Psychopathology Service, Herold Hospital, Paris, France

Bernard Gibello, M.D., Ph.D., Professor of Clinical Psychology and Psychopathology, Bourgogne University, Dijon, France

Philip J. Graham, M.D., Professor of Child Psychiatry, Institute for Mental Health, Hospital for Sick Children, London, United Kingdom

Stanley Greenspan, M.D., Clinical Associate Professor of Psychiatry, George Washington University, Washington, D.C., United States

Lionel Hersov, M.D., F.R.C.P., F.R.C.Psych., D.P.M., Professor of Psychiatry and Pediatrics, University of Massachusetts Medical School, Worcester, Mass., United States

Jill Hodges, Anna Freud Centre, 21 Maresfield Gardens, London, United Kingdom

Johji Inomata, M.D., Department of Psychiatry, Tokai University, Kanagawa, Japan

Philippe Jeammet, M.D., Professor of Psychiatry, Pierre and Marie Curie University,

International University Hospital, Paris, France

R. Olukayode Jegede, M.D., Professor of Psychiatry, University College Hospital, Ibadan, Nigeria

Ryuji Kobayashi, M.D., Department of Psychiatry, School of Medicine, Fukuoka University, Fukuoka, Japan

François Ladame, M.D., Privat Dozent, School of Medicine of Geneva, Geneva, Switzerland

Roland Lazarovici, M.D., Trousseau Hospital, Paris, France

Serge Lebovici, M.D., Emeritus Professor of Child Psychiatry, University of Paris–Nord, Psychopathology Department, UFR Health, Medicine, Human Biology, Bobigny, France

James F. Leckman, M.D., Associate Professor of Pediatrics and Psychiatry, Yale University School of Medicine, New Haven, Conn., United States

John Alex Mackenzie, Tokyo University of Fisheries, Tokyo, Japan

Kiyoshi Makita, M.D., Department of Psychiatry, Tokai University, Kanagawa, Japan

Frances Marton, Anna Freud Centre, 21 Maresfield Gardens, London, United Kingdom

Guy Michael McClure, M.D., Consultant and Senior Lecturer, Riverside Department of Child and Family Psychiatry, Westminster Children's Hospital, London, United Kingdom

Blanche Méliarenne, Psychologist, Trousseau Hospital, Paris, France

Roger Misès, M.D., Professor of Child Psychiatry, University of Paris, Vallée Foundation, Gentilly, France

Toyohisa Murata, M.D., Department of Psychiatry, School of Medicine, Fukuoka University, Fukuoka, Japan

Anula Nikapota, M.D., Senior Lecturer in Child Psychiatry, Department of Psychiatry, Colombo, Sri Lanka

Marika Nosten, Ph.D., Genetics, Neurogenetics, and Behavior Unit, René Descartes University, Paris, France

Richard Perry, M.D., Clinical Assistant Professor of Psychiatry, New York University Medical Center, New York, N.Y., United States

Païvi Kristina Rantanen, M.D., Department of Public Health, University of Tampere, Tampere, Finland

Pierre Roubertoux, Ph.D., Professor of Psychophysiology, René Descartes University, Paris, France

Michael Rutter, M.D., Honorary Director, MRC Child Psychiatry Unit, London, United Kingdom

Arnold J. Sameroff, Ph.D., Professor of Psychiatry and Human Behavior, Brown University, Bradley Hospital, East Providence, R.I., United States

Juan M. Sauceda, M.D., Assistant Director, National Institute of Mental Health, Mexico, DF, Mexico

Jean-François Saucier, M.D., Ph.D., Department of Psychiatry, University of Montreal, Montreal, Quebec, Canada

Lore Schacht, M.D., Hoechtestrabe 38, D-7831 Sexau, RFA

Martin H. Schmidt, M.D., Professor of Child and Adolescent Psychiatry, Central Institute for Mental Health, Manheim, Germany

Ronald Seifer, Ph.D., Assistant Professor of Psychiatry and Human Behavior, Brown University, Providence, R.I., United States

Arthur M. Small, M.D., Clinical Professor of Psychiatry, New York University Medical Center, New York, N.Y., United States

Liliane Spector-Dunsky, Ph.D., University of Montreal, Educational Sciences, Montreal, Quebec, Canada

Robert J. Stoller, M.D., late Professor of Psychiatry, University of Calif. School of Medicine, Los Angeles, Calif., United States

Tao Kuo-tai, M.D., Nanjing Child Mental Health Research Center, People's Republic of China

Barbara Tizard, Professor, Thomas Coram Research Unit, London, United Kingdom

Kenneth E. Towbin, M.D., Assistant Clinical Professor of Pediatrics and Psychiatry, Yale University School of Medicine, New Haven, Conn., United States

Kosuke Yamazaki, M.D., Department of Psychiatry, Tokai University, Bosedai, Kanagawa, Japan

J. Gerald Young, M.D., Professor of Psychiatry, New York University Medical Center, New York, N.Y., United States

Melvin Zax, Ph.D., Professor of Psychology, University of Rochester, Rochester, N.Y., United States

CONTENTS

Part XI: Conclusion

PREFACE

This book stems from the Eleventh International Congress of Child and Adolescent Psychiatry and Allied Professions, held in Paris 21–25 July 1986. More than seven hundred papers were presented.

The Congress was organized along lines roughly comparable to the meridians of the earth. Themes were fitted together like a series of intersecting circles in such a way that participants could follow the lines of their own particular interests throughout. Biological, psychoanalytic, and cognitive approaches; classification; infant psychiatry; adolescent psychiatry; the relationship between our own disciplines and pediatrics; mental retardation, developmental disabilities, and autism; the effects of violence and death upon children; the family approach; cross-cultural studies; epistemology; school and mental health; and various therapeutic approaches were among the themes represented.

The need to ensure the overall unity of the book made it impossible to include all these subjects, despite their importance. Our concern was to present information on approaches that inject fresh elements into day-to-day clinical work and research in our fields of activity.

The contribution of *The Yearbook of the International Association for Child and Adolescent Psychiatry and Allied Professions* is that it provides a view of what is being done in various countries as well as a forum for dialogue among colleagues working with different outlooks. The present volume gives rather more emphasis to work done by French-speaking psychiatrists than has been the case in previous volumes because the Congress took place in Paris.

We wish to thank all those—so many that we are unable to mention individual names—who helped make the Paris Congress and this book possible.

The editorial team responsible for this yearbook, Colette Chiland and J. Gerald Young, express their appreciation for the dedicated work accomplished by E. James Anthony in editing the first eight volumes.

Colette Chiland
J. Gerald Young

I

Mental Health: General Issues

1

Introduction

COLETTE CHILAND

The terms *psychiatrist* and *psychiatry* appeared in the nineteenth century, with the emergence of a medical approach to mental disturbances. Child psychiatry did not develop until the late nineteenth century and was initially a matter of looking for early forms of mental illnesses as they had become known in adult cases. It was gradually recognized that mental disturbances in children have their own specific characteristics and that it is only toward adolescence that the pathology presents the forms found in adults.

Concern for mental health (in other words, prevention of mental disturbances) and for identifying conditions conducive to the most favorable development possible did not arise until the twentieth century.

In the next chapter of Part I, Colette Chiland attempts to define the concept of mental health. One possible definition is the *absence* of mental illness, but the concept of mental illness itself is perceived from two major divergent viewpoints. According to one line of thinking, it is similar in every respect to physical illness, and only research relating to organic factors is accepted as valid; the other standpoint underlines the particular characteristics of mental disorders, whose expression varies among different cultures, and emphasizes the interactions between biological determinants and environment. We are inevitably led to consider the notion of normality and its various connotations—statistical, normative, and ideal—and to inquire whether happiness and mental health necessarily go hand in hand. With the development of knowledge and techniques, new problems arise, and new approaches are required to deal with them. This is the case as regards our knowledge concerning infants, new forms or increased frequency of familiar adolescent disturbances such as drug addiction, suicide, and anorexia, and new techniques in medically assisted procreation and "sex change" made possible by advances in endocrinology and surgery. It is essential to examine the ethical aspects of these developments, but it is no easy matter to make a clear distinction between preconceptions and wisdom in this respect.

What are we heading for? The year 2000 does not have the resplendent aura of the year 1000. No one is expecting mysterious and disquieting phenomena to burst upon us, nor are we awaiting a universal upheaval. This round figure provokes reflection on the immediate future as it appears from the evolution that has taken place in our field in recent years. Chapters 3 and 4 deal with this subject, with particular attention being given in chapter 4 to the situation in developing countries.

It is interesting to note that authors Serge Lebovici (chapter 3) and Anula Nikapota and Philip Graham (chapter 4) concur in their conception of an overall approach to health, in which physical and mental health are not dissociated from each other. They remark upon the frequency of somatic manifestations of disorders arising from psychological sources and agree on the principle of promoting an overall policy of public health based on epidemiological studies. They underline the importance of helping families subjected to particularly adverse and stressful circumstances.

Using the example of what has been achieved in Sri Lanka, Nikapota and Graham demonstrate the possibility of efficient action in developing countries, where there are extremely few, if any, specialists. In addition to the disturbances experienced by children in developed countries, such disorders as mental retardation, epilepsy, and cerebral palsy are especially prevalent in developing areas. In both groups of countries, it is particularly important to encourage behavior conducive to health and to fight against health-damaging behavior, including violence, the use of tobacco, drug taking, and overconsumption of alcohol and medicines.

The authors of this chapter outline how all those dealing with primary health care can and should be trained to ensure that they can contribute efficiently to the prevention of psychological disorders and to enable them to treat some of these disturbances.

Serge Lebovici is concerned here with the development of therapeutic consultations at all ages, particularly for infants, as well as with more clearly defined guidelines regarding long-term psychotherapies, the family approach, and part-time care units as an alternative to the full-time institutionalization. While he emphasizes that psychiatry should not be divorced from medicine, he expresses some anxiety at seeing infantile autism being reduced to a handicap or Tourette's syndrome being defined as an exclusively neurological disorder.

In chapter 5, Lionel Hersov selects the example of school refusal to illustrate how a retrospective and prospective study in child psychiatry is carried out. He outlines a series of stages that open up many possible directions for research:

1. School refusal appeared as a psychological disorder only when school attendance became compulsory for all children.
2. In 1932 Broadwin described this disorder in clear and vivid terms. Influenced by psychoanalytic theory, he concluded that it is not a matter of common truancy.
3. In 1941 Adelaide Johnson and her colleagues called the disorder school phobia.
4. Toward the end of the 1950s, the disturbance was linked to separation anxiety.
5. In the 1960s the whole context of school refusal came under study, and a clear distinction was made between this disorder and truancy, which is accompanied by conduct disorders.
6. Learning theory and behavior therapy were both applied to school refusal during the 1960s.
7. The family approach was also adopted in the late 1960s. An *epidemiological study* carried out during this period by Michael Rutter and his colleagues provides data concerning the frequency of the disorder, particularly in adolescents, its seriousness, and the incidence of associated depressive disorders.
8. Medication was introduced in the 1960s, and drugs, especially imipramine, were used from then onward with increasing frequency.
9. Uniform diagnostic criteria were defined with the development of classifications such as multiaxial classification and D.S.M. III.
10. The relationship between school refusal and adult disorder is also examined.

The example of school refusal is used to introduce the growth of various approaches marking the recent history of child psychiatry, which has been important in developed countries and virtually nonexistent in developing countries.

This disorder underlines a striking contrast between the developed countries, where school refusal and all the educational attainment disorders, including dyslexia, emerged only when school became compulsory for all children, and in developing countries, where it has yet to become possible for all children to go to school, and often they do not even manage to survive long enough to get to school in the first place.

2

The Concept of Mental Health

COLETTE CHILAND

This book deals with new approaches to mental health as a concept whose application covers an area far wider than psychiatry.

Those who fear and distrust psychiatry see it as medicine for the mad and, implicitly, as medicine practiced by lunatics. One has to be crazy oneself to look after lunatics, and if this is not so at the outset it will be in the end, through contamination by what is seen as the AIDS of the soul. In fact, the word *psychiatry* should be read as *medicine for the soul.*

What we call *lunatics* in the vernacular are referred to as the *mentally ill* in scientific terminology. Dealing with mental health obviously involves caring for the mentally ill. This is not simply a question of preventing them from being a danger to society—a notion reflected in the 1838 French law specifying as a requirement for psychiatric internment that the subject be "a danger to himself and to others"—but also of providing care and treatment for them. And as child psychiatrists have discovered, the sooner this is done, the greater the chances of success. It is also generally accepted in all fields of medicine that prevention is better than cure, which takes us beyond the area of care into primary prevention. Our concern cannot be restricted exclusively to the clinic or the psychiatric hospital; we have to take an interest in the overall environment—what goes on in the family, at school, in the general hospital, from the maternity ward to the pediatric services, as well as in the community at large—even at the risk of being accused of turning everything into a psychiatric problem.

The word *interest* is used deliberately, to exclude the idea of "controlling," or even any claim to be able to control. In most cases all we can do is raise questions, and in some instances provide answers. Psychiatrists, psychologists, social workers, nurses, teachers, speech therapists, pediatricians, lawyers, and sociologists working in our field all share a passionate concern for "the best interests of the child," to quote Albert Solnit. We shall see, however, that not only do our answers to the questions differ, but we have different ways of putting the questions themselves.

Our differences of opinion are welcomed by the mass media, which, shaped by the particular biases of one journalist or another, oversimplify our positions, give only a rough approximation of the issues, and aggravate the conflicts. What benefit can be gained from this, either by the psychiatric professions or by the public? Working in a field where inquiry and reflection are difficult and where it is hard to bring clear evidence or even tentative proof to back up our views, it is no easy matter to understand one another.

TOWARD A DEFINITION OF MENTAL HEALTH

I have been working for more than twenty years at the Alfred Binet Center, the children's department of the Mental Health Association in the thirteenth district of Paris. This psychiatric service, whose activity is entirely centered on mental health, was a pilot experiment in catchment-area psychiatry.

In contrast, textbooks on the history of psychiatry give minimal consideration to the concept of mental health. The term is mentioned fewer than ten times in major works, and even these occasional references are due to the existence of the National Institute of Mental Health in the United States (see Alexander and Selesnick's *The History of Psychiatry*) and the Thirteenth District Mental Health Association in Paris (referred to in Postel and Quétel's *Nouvelle histoire de la pyschiatrie*). Since child psychiatry takes up less than 4 percent of the former work and scarcely more than 2 percent of the latter, it is not surprising to find that child mental health is not mentioned at all.

I invited several historians to address the Paris Congress on the History of Child Mental Health. Not one accepted the invitation. The fact is that there has been no research and nothing published on the subject. Everything still remains to be done in this field.

In his book *La santé mentale* (1966), François Cloutier, former president of the World Federation for Mental Health, outlines three possible ways of defining mental health: (1) as the absence of mental illness;

(2) as normality, and (3) by reference to the subjective criteria of well-being, happiness, and satisfaction. He also quotes (p. 15) the two-point definition given in 1948 by the Preparatory Commission of the Third International Mental Health Congress, according to which (1) mental health is a condition allowing the optimal physical, intellectual, and emotional development of the individual as far as it is compatible with the mental health of others, and (2) a good society is one that permits its members such development, at the same time ensuring its own development and showing tolerance toward other societies.

A vast program indeed!

MENTAL HEALTH AND THE ABSENCE OF MENTAL ILLNESS

Any discussion of the absence of mental illness requires first of all a definition of mental illness, and this is where our paths begin to diverge.

Medicine entered the field of science with the anatomical-clinical method in the nineteenth century, but Bayle's disease, or general paralysis, remained an isolated instance of success in the application of this method to mental pathology. The method identified a specific agent, evidence of specific damage, a precise symptomatology, and specific treatment.

Should we adopt the hypothesis that this or a similar pattern can be made to apply to all mental diseases? There are psychiatrists who not only do so but for whom the idea is sometimes more than a working hypothesis—it becomes a matter of conviction and dogma. Others feel that this exclusively biological approach shows a fundamental misunderstanding of the very nature of mental illness. This point merits closer examination.

The search for an organic etiology of mental deficiency has indeed revealed the presence of metabolic diseases and chromosomal abnormalities. For metabolic diseases there are some extremely valuable therapeutic possibilities, such as the use of a phenylalanine-free diet in phenylketonuria. As far as chromosomal abnormalities are concerned, however, the only solution is to prevent the birth of damaged children, through genetic counseling, amniocentesis, karyotyping and interruption of pregnancy. In the case of Down's syndrome there is invariably a trisomy 21, even where this is only one of many factors. Brain damage can certainly be found in children with cerebral palsy, but there is a disconcerting lack of correlation between the extent of the cerebral lesion and the degree of mental deficiency.

Where there is no heavy damage with obvious organic signs, such as paralysis, for example, psychiatrists who think along these lines tend to assume the existence of minimal brain damage—an assumption that frequently becomes a dogmatic assertion. The only neurological signs found are "soft" ones. The word is also used in relation to "soft," or nonalcoholic, drinks and "soft" toys, which are noncontusive and cuddly; "soft" here implies mildness, pliability, and absence of danger. We also speak of computer "software," or programs, as opposed to "hardware," which refers to material structure. The word *soft* has come to lose these connotations through being translated as "minor," whereas a more accurate rendering could have been given by "slight, attenuated, unstable, variable."

The presence of "soft neurological signs" inevitably leads from the assumption of minimal brain damage to minimal brain dysfunction. The continuity of the approach is more obvious in English than it is in French: the abbreviation MBD is used for both "minimal brain damage" and "minimal brain dysfunction." Evidence of it is sought for in perinatal antecedents. Retrospective studies show a higher incidence of prematurity, postmaturity, and difficult deliveries among a group of children with what the DSM III calls attention deficit disorder, hyperactivity, and academic difficulties, particularly problems relating to developmental reading disorder. In prospective studies it emerges that not all premature, postmature, or difficult-delivery children have these disorders.

Proponents of an updated anatomical-clinical model emphasize the statistical data given in the retrospective studies and go from there straight into consideration of causes, with no reflection on concomitant events. Others who have a different view of mental illness put the emphasis on the differences shown in the prospective studies between the children who turned out to be disturbed and those who did not. What differences were there in the history of their interactions with the environment? Conclusions drawn from this can determine what measures should be taken to forestall disorders among children at risk.

Similar problems occur with regard to infantile autism. Obviously, in this day and age macroscopic damage is no longer the only factor taken into account. In fact, the very idea of lesion, even microscopic, has been discarded. The updated anatomical-clinical model has become an anatomical-physiological-clinical model supported by clinical studies on genes, neurotransmitters, and so forth. The line of thought nonetheless remains unchanged, and efforts are all directed at finding some organic etiological disorder.

Mental illnesses are not identical to physical diseases in every respect. Their expression varies from one culture to another and according to their social and historical settings. They belong to a whole series of phenomena that, though not necessarily exclusive to humankind, are far more prevalent in human beings than in the rest of the animal world.

One of these is language. The ability to speak requires intact genetic potential as well as an intact brain and phonatory apparatus. In addition, the child must have other people around in order either to learn an existing language or to invent a cryptophasia such as the secret language sometimes used between twins. On this subject reference is always made to the experiment carried out by Emperor Frederic II. Curious to find out which was the first language used by human beings, he had a number of children brought up by nurses who were strictly forbidden to talk to them. The result was that the children did not speak Hebrew, Greek, or Latin, nor high or low German either. In fact, not only did they not speak at all; they died.

Children do not speak a genetically programmed language—they speak the language they hear spoken to them. Even though this potential is inherent in the human psychobiological makeup, it can be developed only through a process of interaction. Why should this not be true also of other potentialities and the vicissitudes affecting their actualization?

The human being is shaped by two inherited circumstances: biological characteristics, or heredity, and a social heritage, comprising the family, the social environment, the country, and the time of birth. These two sets of factors are not separate and independent but work in interaction with each other, and their respective importance and influence can vary with the individual.

Nobody—not even Freud, contrary to common belief—has supported the hypothesis of pure psychogenesis. Freud did speak of an etiological equation (cf. Chiland and Roubertoux, 1976), whereby to produce a given disorder fewer events were necessary in cases where there were weighty hereditary factors, whereas a greater number of events had to occur when hereditary factors were minimal.

In modern genetics "the hypothesis of isomorphism of genetic and psychological structures is no more tenable than that of isomorphism between neurological and behavioral structures" (Roubertoux and Carlier, 1985, p. 85). Four types of facts have to be taken into account:

(1) the diversity of the genotypes associated with character; (2) the epistatic effects—"a given gene has a different effect according to the succession of genes on the same chromosome" (p. 87); (3) genotype-environment interaction; and (4) the pleiotropic effects or multiple-phenotypic effects of a single gene.

"On the level of individual prediction, while the appearance of a characteristic is determined by its genetic substratum, it also depends on the genetic context and a number of environmental factors. At the population level, the statistical prediction of a disorder, the evaluation of its intensity and the extent of the clinical picture also depend on the genetic structure of the population and on environmental, biological and social factors" (p. 90).

No psychologist (parapsychologists are excluded)—and especially not Freud—thinks that anything can occur without the brain's being involved. I often quote Julian de Ajuriaguerra's comment that "everything goes through the brain, nothing through the halo."

The second working hypothesis, however, does not postulate a simple linear causality between the brain and the complex behavior involved in daily life. The importance attributed to interactions and their concatenation means that the history of the individual has to be taken into consideration as a contributing factor in the genesis of a disorder.

MENTAL HEALTH AND NORMALITY

The second guideline proposed by François Cloutier for defining mental health refers to the idea of normality. Can *healthy* be considered synonymous with *normal*?

Without reopening a discussion as to what constitutes normality, which has already been the subject of considerable attention (see Chiland, 1971, 1972), we can say that the concept is linked to several elements: statistics; rules; "normative" capacity, or the ability to establish norms; and an ideal.

Since there is no such thing as identical behavior among individuals in any population, normal behavior can be taken as that shown by the majority, a given percentage (a particular test item is considered to be characteristic of a specific age group if 75 percent of children of that chronological age succeed in it), or the average (intelligence is considered normal if it corresponds to an average intelligence, which is an I.Q. of 100; however, while this level would be considered normal if it related to anonymous individuals in a population being used for standardization purposes, it would be below our expectations as far as our own individual children are concerned).

The notion of normality also depends on the demands imposed by society. This is of little help in reaching a definition of mental health. Hardly anyone would stipulate blind respect for every rule and prescription—there are rules that every sensible individual has to comply with and others that he simply cannot and should not follow, even at the risk of his life. The social injunction is variable: "Thou shalt not kill—except in case of war."

Georges Canguilhem is someone who is often quoted in France on what is normal and what is pathological. Although he does not go into problems that strictly concern mental health, he nevertheless concludes with the idea of the normative capacity—in other words, the notion that a healthy individual is one who can fall sick and recover, who is capable of establishing new functional norms in different contexts.

This line of thought discards the absence of illness and low occurrence of particular symptoms as criteria in the definition of mental health and refers rather to the characteristics of mental functioning as a whole. Although this approach is a familiar one in France, it seems to surprise our Anglo-Saxon colleagues and others with a predominantly Anglo-Saxon orientation.

Such an attitude leads to a global consideration of the overall psychosomatic economy, as illustrated in particular by a study carried out by the Paris Psychosomatic Institute. Conflicts and traumas occurring in life events are metabolized on three levels: in the body, in behavior, and in mental life as such. The capacity for mental elaboration, even in the symptomatic form, appears to play a protective role against severe somatic disorganization.

AN IDEAL: MENTAL HEALTH AND HAPPINESS

"Purely subjective criteria" constitutes the third line of reflection suggested by François Cloutier.

Can one be mentally healthy and not be happy? Bipolar patients feel that they are happy only during their manic phases, whatever the price they must pay for that. These are the only times they have the impression of being able to transcend the usual limitations and constraints of their lives, and this makes them accept more readily the idea that someone in a state of depression is not in a state of health.

There is often only a fine distinction between depression and a lucid awareness of the limitations of human existence, in view of our impotence in the face of natural catastrophes, violence between human beings and the tragedies it engenders, and our powerlessness against death. Seen in the light of our definition of satisfactory mental functioning, people who claim that they are never prey to anxiety and have no psychological problems give us more cause for concern than for reassurance.

It is difficult to avoid reference to an ideal when discussing health or norms.

The concept of mental health belongs to the twentieth century. No mention of it is to be found in nineteenth-century works; medical dictionaries of that period refer to *hygiene* rather than *health* (Hygeia was the Greek goddess of health). Nysten, Littre, and Robin's 1858 medical dictionary discusses military, naval, public, and rural hygiene, and in 1877 Dechambre includes entries on intellectual, moral, and pedagogical hygiene, but nowhere is "mental hygiene" mentioned. Panckoucke (1812) defines health—but not mental health—as "the free, easy, regular and pleasant exercise of all the functions of animal economy." This comes close to the notion of happy and harmonious functioning, as well as optimal development. It is an asymptotic ideal.

Even though the term *mental health* does not appear in these works, the idea nonetheless was beginning to take shape in the nineteenth century, at much the same time as the emergence of psychiatry. The word *psychiatre* (psychiatrist) came into the French language in 1802, and *psychiatrie* (psychiatry) in 1842 (Swain, 1977, p. 25). "Medicine of the soul" appears at the point where the soul becomes secularized, so to speak, and escapes from the monopoly of religion. Until then, mental disorders were considered in the Christian world the result of sin, possession by the Devil, and so on. Lack of *sanctitas* rather than *sanitas*— the absence of holiness rather than of health—was at the root of the evil.

Child psychiatry did not develop until the end of the nineteenth century, as Lionel Hersov discusses in chapter 5. Although for centuries no attention was given to the issue of children's mental health, their education was attended to in conjunction with their religious and moral instruction. At various times, children of certain classes were refused education, and girls were sometimes excluded. Concern for the mental health of the individual child could acquire the importance it has today only when the children managed to survive in the first place—and there are still countries where survival itself is a priority issue. Present-day concern grew out of a sequence of events. The Renaissance saw a return to the idea of *mens sana in corpore sano;* the Reformation brought individual conscience to the fore; and a need for the development of individual capacities evolved with the advent of the modern world.

Is this effort to identify and describe what is new in the field an attempt to show how up to date we are? And is everything described here actually new? Knowledge that has come to light within the past twenty years has to some extent led to the individualization of *la psychiatrie du nourisson*—literally, "psychiatry of the breast-fed child." But the term is not a very satisfactory equivalent for "infant psychiatry," nor does it make clear that it refers to children up to the age of three.

A similar individualization has taken place in adolescent psychiatry in order to cope with new adolescent problems. Adolescents today are caught between a longer period of education and later assumption of full responsibility in life, on the one hand, and authorized or tolerated precocious sexual activity, on the other. Tension between the innumerable stimulations of modern life and hidden or manifest depression leads them to drugs and suicide, and anorexia nervosa thrives alongside an abundance of food. The family unit has withered away from the extended family to the nuclear family, and nowadays to single parenthood (can a "single-parent family" still be called a family?). Yet never has the family been so greatly emphasized in etiology, diagnosis, and treatment. New approaches, then, are necessary because we are confronted with new problems, even though it would be easy to give in to the temptation of supplying hasty answers based on our customary way of thinking and personal ideological biases without first submitting them to the test of factual proof.

The headlong development of procreative techniques has perhaps come as a surprise. No longer are we dealing only with birth control, family planning, and abortion; we also deal with artificial insemination by spouse or other donor, in vitro fertilization, frozen embryos, surrogate mothers, and so on.

We are also taken aback by the consequences of the greater incidence of phenomena of which we might theoretically approve, such as divorce. We view the increased frequency of divorce and the single-parent family with some alarm, but we have to ask ourselves if our concern is based on a true understanding of the needs of the children whose interests we are trying to defend or if it is really determined by cultural influences on our thinking. Was patrilineal or bilateral filiation conceivable in a society with a matrilineal filiation system? Today matrilineal filiation is once again becoming a more frequent occurrence for children born out of wedlock. It is marriage that ensures protection of the rights of the father, and it is in decline or even on the verge of disappearing altogether.

To compensate for our lack of imagination, social anthropology offers us a variety of cultural patterns to choose from. But they all show that through one unconscious combinative choice or another, the group establishes rules that ensure its survival. Many of the requests expressed invoke the rights of the individual as opposed to the survival of the group.

Although individuals cannot develop their human potentialities in isolation from the group, they sometimes feel overwhelmed by the group. The individual delegates his powers by voting for an elected representative, but he then runs the risk of being crushed by those he has brought to power—a less optimistic version of the "social contract" than Jean-Jacques Rousseau proposed. It should be borne in mind that Adolf Hitler rose to power legally, with devastating results within twelve years: Nazi Germany demanded its "vital space." The group seeks to ensure its survival, and marginality can be tolerated only to the extent that it remains marginal. If exclusive homosexuality were to become generalized, for example, it would mean the death of the social group—unless, of course, it were to go beyond test-tube fertilization and carry out the complete process of procreation in vitro, as in Aldous Huxley's *Brave New World*. With writers, imagination takes over: Jules Verne even made the journey from earth to the moon.

Biological considerations are useful aids in dealing with other problems. The human race is by nature divided into two sexes, but it is also inherent in humankind to have a cultural tendency to modify nature. It is not yet possible to graft a uterus or a penis, but the administering of hormones and surgery can produce what on the surface appears to be a sex change. Should we encourage or oppose the surgical intervention and change of civil status demanded by transsexuals? Are our hesitations due to difficulty in getting away from ingrained attitudes?

I would only say that for a woman psychoanalyst it is curious to hear a biologically male transsexual explain that the penis is an ugly outgrowth of flesh that is regrettably not attached with snap fasteners; when "she" was "he," he tried to remove it by pulling, but it would never come off (what an affront to Freud, to phallic primacy and penis envy!). Further, being a woman is wonderful; she ("he" is now "she," so I shall refer to her as such) has become physically and legally what she truly feels herself to be in her soul. She will wait for her husband at home, do the cooking, and push her adopted baby in the pram in the street, because that is what "real" women do (what an outrage to feminism—generations of women have fought and suffered to escape from these very limitations and to no longer be defined by such life activities!).

To conclude, what we hear from all our patients, transsexual or otherwise, is the expression of suffering.

But "Fluctuat nec mergitur"—to quote the motto of the city of Paris: like a boat, "It floats but does not sink." Let us hope that we can guide our own bark safely between the Scylla of being behind the times and the Charybdis of losing our way.

REFERENCES

Alexander, F. G., and Selesnick, S. T. (1966). *The History of Psychiatry: An Evaluation of Psychiatric Thought and Practice from Prehistoric Times to the Present.* New York: Harper and Row.
Chiland, C. (1971). *L'enfant de six ans et son avenir.* Paris: P.U.F.
————— (1972). "Des apories de toute réflexion sur la normalité." *Revue française de psychanalyse* 36, no. 3:411–419.
————— (1987). "Minimal Brain Dysfunction: Factor or Fiction?" In E. J. Anthony and C. Chiland, *Perilous Development: Child Raising and Identity Formation under Stress.* New York: Wiley.
Chiland, C., and Roubertoux, P. (1976). "Freud et l'hérédité." *Bulletin de psychologie,* no. 321, 29/4–7:337–343.
Cloutier, F. (1966). *La santé mentale.* Paris: PUF.
Dechambre. (1875). *Dictionnaire encyclopédique des sciences médicales.* Paris: Asselin and Masson.
Nysten, P. H., Littre, E., and Robin, C. (1858). *Dictionnaire de médecine, de chirurgie, de pharmacie, des sciences accessoires et de l'art vétérinaire.* 11th ed. Paris: J-B Baillière.
Panckoucke. (1812). *Dictionnaire des sciences médicales.* Paris: C.L.F. Editeur.
Roubertoux, P., and Carlier, M. (1985). "Apports de la génétique à la psychiatrie de l'enfant." In S. Lebovici, R. Diatkine, and M. Soule, *Traité de psychiatrie de l'enfant et de l'adolescent.* Paris: P.U.F., 1:83–111.
Swain, G. (1977). *Le sujet de la folie: Naissance de la psychiatrie.* Toulouse: Privat.

3

Mental Health in the Year 2000

SERGE LEBOVICI

*For a very long time to come, imagination will continue to
be the most powerful reality in the existence of mankind.*
—*Barbey d'Aurevilly, "L'Ensorcelée"*

The year 1000 brought wild expectations and terrifying
fears, at least among the peoples of the world who shared our calendar.
This serves to remind us that our predictions are not universal but apply
only within a given cultural area, and that we have to be careful to avoid
unwarranted simplification, as though the next century were going to
start off with dramatic changes.

In any case, geneticists are well aware that the evolution and mutations of human genetic inheritance are remarkably slow, whereas cultural changes occur at an extremely fast rate, alongside rapid technological progress in developed countries (Jacquard and Tomkiewicz,
1987).

This contradiction obviously has repercussions for physical and mental health. It should also remind us, however, that human mental functioning changes very little and very slowly, and that whatever form the
expression of mental illness takes, its nature and evolution are unlikely
to undergo any real modifications, whatever the cultural circumstances.

Will the concept of mental health be valid for very much longer? A
monistic approach to health and sickness, which is called for in psychiatry, at any rate assumes that physical health and mental illness should

not be set on opposing planes. Somato-psychic and psycho-somatic interactions are the general rule in all illnesses—if not in their genesis, then at least in their evolution. Formerly, "mental hygiene" was the term used, the implication being that each individual should lead as physically healthy a life as possible in order to ensure solid mental health as well. It was only a short step from mental hygiene programs to recommending a well-balanced and moderate life to justify the adage *mens sana in corpore sano*. Toward the close of this century, cultivation of the body has become a requirement and an ideal. But it might justifiably be said that the excesses seen in contemporary sport could reflect idealization of the body alongside denial of the power of the psyche. Various types of body therapy, jogging, marathons, and so forth force many people who practice them to exploit their bodies to the point of contempt by denying their needs, as anorexics do.

Everything seems to indicate that the concept of mental health should be replaced by the idea of overall health, for the following reasons:

1. Psychiatry should not be dissociated from medicine. Indeed, many primary-care physicians find themselves dealing with mental disorders, in adults as well as children.

2. Psychiatry represents a model of an overall approach to health; its practice is based on more flexible semiological and nosographic guidelines than is the case in other branches of medicine. Classifying disorders according to criteria-based behavioral categories makes it possible to establish a good comparison of medicinal and therapeutic actions, but it does not measure the importance of mental life or the individual's place in family structures whose organization reflects interactive and retroactive systems. Nor does it take into account the way in which stressful events and transgenerational mandates later acquire a significance that transforms the sterile repetitions of human behavior into a history.

3. The mental disorders described represent only a small proportion of accidents to health. A great many mental disturbances can be masked by functional disorders expressed in somatic form. Symptoms considered neurotic in the adult must often be interpreted as normal developmental features in a child. It is well known that children and adolescents are rarely brought to a psychiatrist because of clearly psychiatric disorders, but much more frequently for behavior problems that interfere with their adaptation to the social environment. Their mental health problems are expressed indirectly. This means that when their particular discipline is in fashion, psychiatrists receive a great many cases that

do not necessarily fall within their field of competence. What they are really asked to do is to put a stop to what is called maladjustment.

This is what happened in the 1950s, when language-learning difficulties were labeled dyslexia, without considering the possibility of inadequate teaching methods, the pedagogical incompetence of teachers, or inequality of opportunity linked to cultural injustice. The surge in the number of cases contributed to the segregation of children who were too readily sent for psychiatric treatment and were stigmatized as a result. It also influenced to some extent the development of a number of psychiatric centers.

In France the tendency was reversed in 1975 by the "Social law," whereby mental disorders were declared a handicap. Education and reeducation were to be revalued, and school was to be the place where children should be accepted and helped.

The activity of psychiatric centers cannot be considered a reliable basis for measuring epidemiological research on mental health. The multiprofessional association responsible for this yearbook is clear proof of that. As far as public health and clear identification of needs are concerned, research has to go well beyond the bounds of psychiatry and medicine.

The notion of needs is not a sufficient basis for deciding what efforts should be made toward the improvement of mental health. Assessment of requirements depends first of all on the satisfaction of the most elementary needs, starting with food, and this is far from being accomplished everywhere. Toward the end of the twentieth century, huge numbers of children are still dying of starvation. Many who are not killed by famine are prevented from developing by malnutrition, especially through protein deficiency. The idea of needs also depends on the means of action available to pressure groups representing different categories of children with greater or lesser handicaps.

The life-style and the family organization of some children assign them to high-risk communities. It is recognized, however, that the very act of identification of vulnerability leads to the stigmatizing of certain sectors of the population who have no way of escape. This means that even less vulnerable subjects are unable to avoid a fate determined in advance by the computerization of the sociocultural ghetto that confines these families.

Experience shows that certain families will be identified because of the exclusion to which they are condemned—because of their abject poverty in the first place, but also because of innumerable social problems that beleaguer them. Here it is not just the normal risk factors that are noticed; the social or health worker is also struck by certain lateral "warning signals" that draw attention (Noel and Soule, 1985)—for example, the young women who refuse to declare their pregnancy or fail to take advantage of prenatal care to which they have access.

Crises also can upset the equilibrium of children and their families; sometimes, as in the following example, these are crises on a national level, such as war, civil war, or natural catastrophes:

The family is disrupted. Parents are forced to become political refugees who not only have to confront the desperate problems of exile but also are often viewed with contempt by their children, who have witnessed their arrest and humiliation. The children deidealize the parents and at the same time undergo severe problems of identification in their adoptive country.

Family crises, mainly divorce, are an increasingly weighty factor in child problems: children in the United States have only one chance in two of still living with both parents by the time they reach fifteen years of age. And it must be pointed out that individual crises linked to the illness, professional or accidental incapacity, or death of one of the parents have far more intense effects in the nuclear family of a Western megalopolis than they would in more supportive cultures.

In the final analysis, improvement in mental health requires a global approach to health, a study of needs based on epidemiological public health research, identification of risk factors outside the pathology, and assistance for children and their families when under heavy stress.

HEALTH FOR ALL BY THE YEAR 2000

This slogan encapsulates the idea of enabling every child to have access to all means available for preserving or improving health. But the principles defining this aspiration are especially difficult to apply to problems of mental health, for mental disorders have a particularly chronic evolution that requires great perseverance. These remarks point to the inequalities in this field according to the geographical area involved. But inequalities are great even in developed countries, as we shall see.

The likelihood that advances brought about by psychiatric practices developed over the past few decades will continue is indicated by the sustained trend of progress shown in recent years. These advances relate to the following:

1. The light thrown on psychopathology by psychoanalysis, which has made possible the widespread application of various psychotherapies. Their effectiveness, however, depends on how valid their prescription is and on the quality of the child psychoanalyst's training. Everything indicates that there will be a more rigorous selection of cases for treatment. Different interventions aimed at short-term or focused psychotherapies and therapeutic consultations allow considerable flexibility in action taken to help children and their families (Lebovici, 1986).

2. The use of family therapy. Many families have complained—often rightly—that certain services view parents as patients requiring treatment. It goes without saying that a child's difficulties reflect something wrong in the family. The work of family systems therapists has correctly drawn attention to the fact that a sick child, or one who is presented as such, forms part of the equilibrium of that system. In some cases this child also bears the burden of the transmission of certain events through several generations. It is fortunate that some psychoanalysts are interested in the family approach and take into consideration the personal conflicts it reveals.

3. Community psychiatry. Developed during the 1960s, community psychiatry broke away from the isolated practice of medical consultation and opposed placing patients in institutions or hospitals. Key figures in the community will increasingly be called upon to help in the solution of family crises. A policy of integration will be developed, except where there is a risk that it will be detrimental to the well-being of children in schools. Costly full-time institutions will be replaced by self-managed part-time units that function in a flexible way and are as unconfining as possible. The parents of children attending these units will be involved in the accommodations and catering arrangements and even in the technical-management side. In every family, home observation of children under treatment can be valuable.

With regard to child mental health, recent developments concern the understanding of the disorders observed, emphasis on the role of the family, and the reactivation of community psychiatry. These different approaches have achieved considerable progress in a few decades, and their underlying principles should be evaluated; this will undoubtedly lead to some measure of revision and call many things into question. There is good reason to think that present economic problems preclude further anarchical growth.

A review of events of this period illuminates theoretical conflicts that are likely to have a great influence on the evolution of techniques applied since the last world war. This prediction is supported by the examples of infantile autism and of Tourette's syndrome. Most psychopathologists consider infantile autism, which was described by L. Kanner in 1943, as a form of psychosis. But the presence of certain characteristic cognitive problems has led some psychiatrists, particularly in the Anglo-Saxon framework, to regard it as a physical handicap rather than a mental illness. This tendency was endorsed by many parents, who preferred the idea of education rather than treatment. As a result, the notion of child psychosis has gradually faded to the extent that the autistic syndrome in some situations eludes the field of psychiatry and mental health.

An information bulletin of the Tourette's Syndrome Association, issued in 1986, included a question-and-answer section encouraging people to join. The following is representative of its contents:

Question: Is Tourette's Syndrome a psychiatric disorder? Answer: No, Tourette's Syndrome is a *neurological* disorder. However, secondary psychological problems can arise from the persistent difficulties involved in adjusting to the disorder and social reactions to it. The syndrome can include some behavioral problems, such as attention disorders, compulsivity, hyperactivity and so on, which can cause significant difficulties in adjustment.

In some cases, psychological guidance can further the adaptation of people suffering from Tourette's Syndrome and help them to find ways of coping.

These two examples show how greatly some people would like to reduce the role of psychiatry within the area of mental health. Such a trend is no doubt the result of two converging factors: the persistent shame associated with having to see a psychiatrist, and the artificial opposition set up between neurobiology and its applications in the cognitive field, on the one hand, and knowledge of unconscious conflicts, on the other.

Fundamental research in the neurobiological sciences has led to considerable progress in our understanding of the neurobiological mechanisms of behavior in animals and humans. However, one cannot deny that the mental life of human beings is affected by desires and the intensity of the underlying fantasies within dissimilar cultural and social systems.

A cross-disciplinary outlook and practice would make a global approach to problems of mental health possible, although this does not mean scrambling to bridge the gap between psychophysiologists and clinical psychopathologists. Although analogical reasoning and risky metaphors can sometimes be helpful within the therapeutic approach, they are of no use as far as scientific research is concerned.

Nonetheless, some of the principles generally accepted by present-day science should be borne in mind:

1. The innate/acquired conflict is completely outdated.
2. The organization of the nervous system can become self-structured only through a facilitation of neuronal links, which depends largely on postnatal events.
3. Animal models used in the study of the nervous system can be applied to human beings only if caution is exercised. Otherwise the study of animal behavior can provide nothing more than a metaphorical reference.

Respect for the views of related disciplines also rests on the assumption that the working hypotheses used are actually applicable. Let us take learning difficulties as an example.

In the postwar years the idea of isolated instrumental disorders was very much in favor, and dyslexia (developmental reading disorder) and/or dysorthography (developmental expressive writing disorder) were constantly brought up to define disturbances in written-language learning. This was a working outlook based on the idea of an underlying functional disturbance and resulted in a great increase in various forms of specialized reeducation and the development of medico- or psycho-educational centers in France.

During the 1960s this point of view was criticized from two standpoints. One of these attacks was from the pedagogical and sociological direction, deploring the effects of educational mishandling and social inequalities. Children's reading improved if they enjoyed it, which depended to a great extent on the quality of verbal exchanges within the family. The other, which came from psychoanalytic circles, pointed out that these supposedly specific disorders were found in children who were passive and neurotic, and that the effectiveness of their reeducation could well be due to its psychotherapeutic virtues.

Handicaps became the subject of increasing attention. In some respects there was a return to the ideas that led to the selection of so-called retarded children by means of tests, according to the method invented by Binet and Simon at the beginning of the century. But above all, the remarkable work on the specialization of the cerebral hemispheres demonstrated the existence of highly significant specific neuropsycho-logical difficulties.

Does this imply that delicate neuropsychological research should be undertaken in every case of apparent dyslexia or dysorthography? Even though the causes of inadequate cultural and educational supports per-sist and the child's family difficulties and neurotic problems can be expressed through these learning disorders?

This is not just an economic problem but a real epistemological di-lemma. Critical examination of pathogenic factors is interesting from the point of view of possible consequences for reeducation, therapy, and prevention. Causative factors cannot be isolated, however, for they are organized in interacting sequences that are difficult to separate in chil-dren.

As far as the neurological sciences are concerned, new knowledge has been achieved concerning neurotransmitters, molecular messengers that define neural function in the nervous system and the hormonal neuroregulator systems. This has brought to light complex mecha-nisms, albeit elementary, of human behavior and will continue to reveal others. The beneficial effects of certain drugs on particular disorders leads to suggestions of specific target neuronal systems but does not yet give grounds for inferring direct connection between action at these sites and the nature of the disorders observed.

On the other hand, though some psychoanalysts' insistence on work-ing only on psychoanalytic material is understandable, this preoccupa-tion does not fully answer requirements for mental health. Psycho-analysts are well aware that they have to take into account the reality of personal conflicts, data arising from observation of the child, and recent studies on early interactions. Freud—the "biologist of the mind," as F. Sulloway called him in 1975—was a neuropsychologist who always placed psychoanalysis among the natural sciences, not the behavioral sciences. Instead of bothering about the achievements of neurobiology in understanding mental processes and behavior, psychoanalysts would sometimes do well to take a good look at their theory.

Psychoanalytic theory remains essential to understanding the genesis of mental images, the significance of object relationships and of the differences between sexual roles, the world of fantasies and desires and of intrapsychic conflicts. These are the psychological elements re-lated to the biological study of children and adults (Cooper, 1985). Eric Kandel was evoking the foreseeable future when he wrote in 1983 that "the emergence of an empirical neuropsychology of cognition . . . can produce a renascence of scientific psychoanalysis." This form of psycho-analysis can be based on theoretical hypotheses more modest than those advanced so far, because they are better authenticated vis-à-vis experimental research.

Unless the efforts described above are put into action, the field of mental health runs the risk of being split into two tendencies. One, influenced by neurobiological research, will result in the development of neuropsychology, whose applications will be narrow in relation to the immensity of the needs involved, as was the case with learning disorders. The other will concentrate on reeducation for the handicapped, within the sole perspective of reeducation.

In this event, neuropsychology would conserve the patent of nobility accruing to basic research in highly technical university services. Disability services would lead to integration of care along lines determined by the desires of parents. Their wishes would bear more weight because the largely demedicalized assistance provided would enable them to find reeducation institutions that would suit them, even if they do not offer the most favorable prospects for ensuring the child's fullest development.

Such a split, which would be most unfortunate for children over the long term, can be avoided only if research is developed in several directions, including basic neurobiological research, social-epidemiological research, and clinical research.

Clinical research must be developed within the perspective of psycho-pathological studies that are comparable without being reductive. It is as essential as the other two for establishing acceptable mental health policies.

MENTAL HEALTH: NEW PATHOLOGIES AND ACTION

The very uneven development found in human societies at the end of the twentieth century means that policies must necessarily vary. We shall be dealing here only with the new needs that have emerged in postindustrial Western society.

In defining these needs, the stereotyped and often dramatized views presented by the mass media have to be avoided; their methods of information can be harmful to mental equilibrium unless they obey a certain ethic, which merits attention. It is a matter not of applying censorship but of ensuring complete information by providing the elements necessary for forming a judgment.

There is little likelihood that the economic crisis will be solved. Adolescents are caught between the need for highly qualified technical training and the claims of their surrounding milieu, and they are condemned to unemployment unless they manage to obtain diplomas. The danger of marginalization, violence, and drug consumption will therefore remain at the forefront. With the ageing of the population, younger people will also have to bear the responsibility of ensuring retirement pensions for earlier generations. This could be too great a burden, and the situation could be bluntly expressed in terms such as "The older generation stop us from getting into active life. If we do manage to do so, it's to enable them to survive."

The problems threatening these adolescents will be forestalled only through improved education from an early age and by training them toward moderation in their treatment of the body and their use of stimulants, drugs, alcohol, and tobacco. If this is to be achieved, parents will have to avoid aping their children, whom they envy for enjoying—at least in appearance—greater freedom than they did themselves.

Industrial societies have come to depend on migrants whose families frequently hope to return eventually to their native country. These families constitute a subproletariat whose struggle against unfavorable living conditions is helped along by their attachment to their native culture. This is not necessarily shared by their offspring, who are second-generation immigrants. These children are a group threatened by rejection and lack of culture. It could be argued that in their case biculturalism offers the most favorable ground for identification.

Mental health is and will continue to be a factor in achieving the standard of comfort commonly desired. Being better equipped means being better qualified, and therefore being in a position to become qualified. Being a parent means being one when one so desires and having attractive, intelligent, successful children. The issue is no longer simply that of reducing the handicaps associated with disabilities but also of offering the possibility of achieving what each individual sees as happiness. Low-fertility couples must be enabled to have children at the right time: apparent sterilities may be of psychogenic origin, but assisted procreation techniques do not preclude the need of help for those who are absolutely determined to obtain results from them.

This example of difficulties linked to technical advances in medicine, which are not always applied on the basis of judgment, leads to consideration of the requirements for assistance to children and families in distress.

Many children in pediatric hospitals are afflicted by extremely serious illnesses. Although these can be fatal, there is an increasingly frequent incidence of recovery at the cost of appalling mutilation, relapses leading to repeated hospitalizations, and so on.

Advanced technology sometimes increases the distress of those who can be helped by it. Staff in the departments where these techniques are applied are often aware of this, but they tend to leave the psychological side of care to mental health specialists. This is not necessarily the best approach, and here as in many other respects, one might wish that medical care staff could be more directly interested and involved in these problems.

Experience has shown, for example, that the very young cancer patient hardly ever complains of pain; it goes unrecognized and is even denied, and therefore receives no treatment (Piquard-Gauvin, 1985). Pain is the source of a depression that is also difficult to bring to light. Where the correlation between these two affects is recognized, it can lead to therapeutic interventions, the prescription of analgesics, and institutional arrangements such as parental participation in attending to the child on the level of everyday care rather than on the technical side.

The importance of the care that has to be given to small babies indicates that mental health services developed for children in the latency period and for adolescents have to include training to understand babies and their interactions with the adults who take care of them (Lebovici, 1983). This orientation will be all the more decisive in coming years because it falls within the general outlook of global health, where mental health workers intervene within a framework of preventive action in cooperation with those responsible for supervising the health of the baby and its family.

These predictions take into account the changes we observe and participate in. But using them as a basis for any attempt to foresee the necessary changes and inevitable revisions would mean ignoring the fact that the advance of science and its applications is influenced by unforeseen events and is determined by disasters that befall it.

Individual drama will nonetheless go on belonging to the inner realm of the imaginary, the history that creates this, and the capacity for response to it that our organism permits or refuses to allow.

REFERENCES

Cooper, A. (1985). "Will Neurobiology Influence Psychoanalysis?" *Am. J. Psychiatry* 12, no. 12:1395–1402.

Jacquard, A., and Tomkiewicz, S. (1987). "Génétique et développement: Les aspects épidémiologiques, somatiques, sociaux et psychologiques de la santé de l'enfant." In M. Manciaux and S. Lebovici, *L'enfant et sa santé*. Paris: Doin.

Kandel, E. R. (1983). "From Metapsychology to Molecular Biology: Explorations into the Nature of Anxiety." *Am. J. Psychiatry* 140:1277–1284.

Lebovici, S. (1983). *Le nourrisson, la mère et le psychanalyste*. Paris: Le Centurion.

——— (1986). "A propos des consultations thérapeutiques chez l'enfant." *Journal de la psychanalyse de l'enfant* 1:135–152.

Noel, J., and Soule, M. (1985). "L'enfant cas social." In S. Lebovici, R. Diatkine, and M. Soulé, eds., *Traité de psychiatrie*. Paris: P.U.F.

Piquard-Gauvain, A. (1985). *La douleur de l'enfant cancéreux de 2 à 6 ans, mémoire du CES de psychiatrie*. Bobigny.

Sulloway, F. (1975). *Freud, Biologist of the Mind. Freud, biologiste de l'esprit*. Trad. franc. Paris: Arthème Fayard, 1981.

4

Child Mental Health in the Year 2000 in Developing Countries

ANULA NIKAPOTA

PHILIP J. GRAHAM

About three-quarters of the world's children live in countries where the gross national product is less than one thousand dollars per head of family a year. In these countries it is common for fewer than half the child population to have the opportunity for schooling beyond the age of twelve years, and literacy levels are low. In many of these countries more than 100 of every 1,000 children die before the age of one year (in contrast to less than 25 per 1,000 in developed countries). Trained mental health professionals working with children are rarely found. Some of these countries have no child psychologists or psychiatrists at all, and many of them have at most only one or two such professionals per million children—a proportion that would be unacceptable in developed countries.

Yet the levels of mental health problems are at least as high in developing countries as in the more economically developed countries of the world. Those of us who work in complex industrial societies with nuclear families living in overcrowded circumstances may have a fantasy that in developing countries children living in extended families with many aunts, uncles, and grandparents to look after them do not show psychiatric disorders or show them only infrequently. But all the evidence is that children living in families with many adult relatives have just as many problems as those living with their parents only (Graham, 1980). Further, as far as many organically determined mental health problems are concerned, it is likely that rates in developing countries are higher than elsewhere. Because of the high prevalence of malnutrition and infectious disease affecting brain tissue, the rates of mental retardation and epilepsy may well be higher in such countries, and indeed there is evidence that this is the case.

There is therefore good reason for the mental health problems of children in developing countries being given prominence in this book, and it is particularly appropriate that such discussion should have occurred at an international meeting held in Paris. France has always taken a strong interest in UNICEF, the U.N. agency primarily responsible for international aid for the welfare of children, and it was in Paris that UNICEF established the Centre International de l'Enfance (International Centre for Children), which has taken such an important role in disseminating information about the welfare of children in third world countries and training workers in the field.

Many things have changed since UNICEF was created, and one important change for the better is that it is no longer considered appropriate for someone from a developed country to pose as an expert on problems of developing countries. In line with this philosophy, Anula Nikapota, who has been responsible for pioneering work in this field in Sri Lanka, agreed to be co-author of this chapter. One section concerns her experience in the delivery of child mental health care in a country relatively poor in economic resources, though, like many such countries, rich in its culture.

Let us first consider what we currently mean by child mental health (WHO, 1977), a concept that has changed and broadened over the years. Many of us, whether psychologists, psychiatrists, or members of other professions, who are particularly concerned with the prevention, assessment, and treatment of emotional and behavioral problems, tend to distinguish them rather sharply from physical health problems, acute and chronic medical disorders. But it is important to remember that many children with physical symptoms are showing signs of emotional distress and do not have a physical basis for their symptomatology, even though there may be physiological reasons for their showing physical symptoms when under stress rather than reacting in other purely behavioral ways. Thus about 90 percent of children brought to doctors with symptoms of headache and stomachache have no identifiable physical cause for their symptoms. Even the highly specialized pediatricians in the United Kingdom (U.K.) reckon that about a third of the children they see do not have a physical cause to explain their symptomatology. Yet very few of these children come to them displaying behavioral or emotional symptoms.

A second concern of child mental health professionals lies in the prevention, detection, and remediation of developmental delays or mental retardation. In developing countries, these professionals spend at least as much time assessing such children and counseling parents as they spend with parents of emotionally disturbed children. The severely retarded child would always have been problematic in these countries, but with improved survival rates, the burden they place on families has increased. The more mildly retarded have not posed problems in the past because in rural communities (until recent times, 80 percent of the population of developing countries lived in such areas), they were able to carry out simple tasks and were gainfully employed. Now, they are cause for concern because they are increasingly expected to attend school (where they fail) and, in cities, to fit into a complex society that makes more demands of them than they can meet. Specialist educational provision for retarded children is nearly always lacking in developing countries, an understandable situation when universal education is not available even for children of normal ability.

The third concern of mental health professionals in developing countries is the chronic neurological disorders, especially epilepsy and cerebral palsy. The fact that these are seen as *mental* health problems may be surprising to many who work in economically developed countries, but traditionally, in developing countries (as in many Eastern European countries) such disorders are often seen as the responsibility of psychiatrists.

The last area of concern of the mental health professional we shall discuss is relatively new to both developed and developing countries, but it is becoming more important. This is the promotion of behavior that is beneficial to physical health and the discouragement of harmful behavior. Individuals are encouraged to take regular exercise and to eat a balanced diet, avoiding foods that lead to obesity or vascular or cerebrovascular disease. There is a longer list of behaviors that are damaging to physical health. These include, especially, tobacco smoking at any level, excessive intake of alcohol, excessive consumption of other drugs such as cannabis, use at any level of heroin and cocaine, and the intake of psychoactive drugs such as the benzodiazepines, which have been grossly overprescribed in recent decades. Health-damaging behavior also includes physical violence, especially child abuse and wife battering. Behavior resulting in so-called accidental physical injury (e.g., failure to take safeguards with agricultural implements and machinery, or to wear seatbelts in automobiles) can also be seen as health-damaging behavior. In developed countries, injuries are the commonest cause of death among one-to-fourteen-year-olds, and for every child who dies, between two hundred and nine hundred are injured. In all industrialized countries, injury ranks among the top three causes of death in children, and even in developing countries where death from malnutrition and infection is common, injuries still rank in the top ten causes of death and produce high levels of disability.

Failure to take advantage of immunization programs is another risky behavior. Senturia (1986) has estimated that failure to achieve optimal levels of immunization for pertussis will result in over 450,000 children incurring avoidable neurological disorders over a given year. Over 200,000 cases of lameness from avoidable poliomyelitis will occur. In all, some 1.5 million children became mentally or physically handicapped in 1987 because of avoidable infectious diseases. Certain sexual behavior can also lead to avoidable disease, as can perinatal care that interferes with the development of the early mother-child relationship. When food resources are limited, a mother who fails to develop a strong and caring attachment to her child may place the youngster at special risk for malnutrition.

It is not difficult to see that the links between behavior and physical health are important and far-reaching. But unfortunately there is a paucity of information, especially in developing countries, on the extent to which some of these problems occur, as well as a lack of techniques for dealing with them. To address this problem, the World Health Organization (WHO) advisory committee on medical research established a subcommittee to develop a program of research and training: the so-called biobehavioral sciences and mental health. The group agreed upon a program, but has obtained only limited resources to support it. Priority has been given to research in the following areas:

1. Population studies of injuries sustained by children aged one to four years. We know too little of the extent and causes of such injuries.
2. Assessment of the effects of different types of perinatal care.
3. The development of methods of assessment and community intervention to alter life-styles adversely affecting health.
4. Studies to assess the impact of sociotechnical change on family life.
5. Evaluation of psychosocial stimulation and health promotion programs for preschool children.

Some of the limited amount of funding secured to develop this program of research has been used to promote research activity at a national level through workshops, seminars, and so on.

Although the scope for a program to achieve mental health for all by the year 2000 is wide, the success of such a program will not be the result of WHO action. The organization can only guide, perhaps inspire, policies; it cannot implement them. How can policy be turned into action? Here specific national examples such as Nikapota's experience in Sri Lanka can be instructive. Her experience offers steps to be taken in the development of an effective policy in this field (Nikapota, 1983, 1984).

Sri Lanka is a developing country in which 37 percent of the 14.9 million citizens are aged under fifteen years. The population is predominantly rural and poor. As is typical in developing countries, the main issues that preoccupy child health planners are diarrhea, respiratory infections, and malnutrition.

Nikapota, the only trained child psychiatrist in Sri Lanka, was directly involved in the work to be described; she joined with child health planners in the late 1970s and early 1980s in considering how child mental health could best be promoted. She was assisted by three factors. First, a reconsideration of the function of the primary health care services was already under way, stimulated by WHO's Health for All policy. Second, because specialized child psychiatric services had hardly developed, there were no existing prejudices to overcome about the role of the child psychiatric team in dealing only with mental disorders. Third, Nikapota had joined with child health planners in the preparation of a national case study, coordinated by Philip Graham, a WHO consultant. The preparation of this study had involved identifying existing knowledge concerning the prevalence of child mental health problems, the background factors affecting child mental health, available resources to deal with mental health problems, and the existing training of relevant health and non–health professional in child mental health.

With assistance from WHO, two pilot projects were undertaken in a small number of districts. The first examined the impact of training in child mental health needs and in simple home-based interventions on the work performance of primary health care (PHC) workers. In the second, the impact of teaching PHC workers to intervene with home-based training of developmentally slow or retarded children was examined. The results of these pilot projects were encouraging. The UNICEF organization agreed to support the work and its monitoring at a national level, and at least some health care planners, persuaded of the value of the approach, began to talk in terms of children's mental health needs as well as physical needs. Following a meeting of top administrators and professionals it was agreed that, as a matter of national policy, child mental health needs should be considered an appropriate focus for PHC workers who, consequently, would need training.

Currently senior staff are trained centrally to act as supervisors for core groups of locally based trainers. These, in turn, train field staff, who include health care workers, especially nurses, teachers, and child care staff. The training, which is highly practical and task-oriented, has been assisted by the availability of WHO manuals, which Nikapota and Graham helped prepare (WHO, 1983).

To ensure continuing awareness of child mental health needs among PHC staff, it was decided that developmental milestones as well as home risk factors would be incorporated into children's growth cards. Some administrators worried that the need to collect such information might deflect the PHC worker from the all-important task of recording the child's weight, but fieldwork has allayed these anxieties. The home risk factors the PHC worker is asked to note include the age of the mother, the number of young children, the mother's ability to understand health messages, her interest in the child, the presence of marital friction, parental mental health problems such as alcoholism, and the presence of abject poverty. Criteria to rate these reliably were developed in a pilot project. A WHO project has attempted to identify a wider range of indicators of healthy development in a number of Southeast Asian countries.

All twenty-two Sri Lankan health districts now conduct health education programs concerning children's psychological needs and the range of normal development, as well as home risk factor monitoring. Workers are trained to undertake home-based assessments and, when mental health problems are identified, to intervene. In five districts the full multisectoral program involving teachers and welfare workers, as well as health workers, has continued, and with the help of UNICEF, monitoring of the program is ongoing. It has been shown that slow, neglected, and retarded children are being identified earlier. The parents of such children are advised by trained health workers in aspects of home-based stimulation and play, and the results have been good. In some instances, inspired by the program, volunteers have begun play groups for the children. The PHC workers are encouraged to refer children to medical officers for diagnosis if developmental delay persists after the child reaches the age of three years.

A few examples of interventions with nonretarded children may be of interest. A mother consulted the health worker regarding her three-year-old. The child had been sent to live with her grandmother after the birth of a sister, and she had become irritable and had begun demanding the breast from the grandmother. The mother, concerned regarding the physical effects of this habit, had not realized that the child felt rejected by her until this was pointed out. The problem was resolved by the mother taking the child home, leaving her with grandmother only during the day.

A four-year-old was failing to thrive and had chronic diarrhea. The health worker during a home visit noted that the child was spoken to very roughly by the grandmother. (The child and mother had returned to grandparents after the child's father had deserted them.) The health worker, while offering advice on nutrition and prevention of gastrointestinal infection, also discussed with mother and grandmother the child's needs for play and stimulation, and arranged that the child attend a play group in the village.

A schoolteacher and a health worker joined forces to advise the parents of a nine-year-old boy who had begun talking unintelligibly at home, raising fears that he was possessed or going mad. His behavior in school was normal, however, and the problem was resolved after his parents were induced to put less pressure on him regarding schoolwork and to relax a rule that he speak to his parents only in English and not in his mother tongue.

Use of the home risk factors has also helped in the identification of a picture of need and the direction health intervention should take. Some villages with a large number of young, educated couples have a low percentage of homes with a risk factor; in others, 20 to 30 percent of the homes may have risk factors. One village may have a large number of families with many children and widespread noncompliance with health care. In others, a high percentage of homes may be afflicted with disorganization, alcoholism, or abject poverty. It is felt that this form of health care has helped direct attention to a particularly important issue in developing countries—the identification of coping and noncoping families so that workers can focus on intervention for families at particular risk. This is a mental health issue of great relevance for overall health compliance, especially in view of the widespread poverty that is almost commonplace in developing countries. In Sir Lanka it is noticeable that, in districts where home risk monitoring is done, and health workers are trained in utilizing community resources, they are becoming more involved in helping families. Indeed, their initiatives have resulted in improvements on the training they received. Program planners now utilize the innovative approaches developed by field staff for training of other staff.

This description of the organization of a child mental health service in a developing country seems to us to have implications for similar work carried out in developed countries. Let us consider these implications in turn.

First, there is an emphasis on primary health in the delivery of most of the service. This is, in fact, already happening in developed countries, although it is not generally realized (Graham, 1982). For example, in the U.K., there are about 30,000 general practitioners or family doctors, virtually none of whom receive more than some six to ten hours training in child psychiatry and psychology during their medical studies. Yet about a fifth of their work (the equivalent of 6,000 full-time doctors) concerns children, and about a third of their work with children (the equivalent of about 2,000 full-time doctors) is of a psychosocial nature. Contrast this with the equivalent of roughly 330 full-time child psychiatrists, and you can readily see that general practitioners do about six times more child psychiatry (work for which they are relatively untrained) than do child psychiatrists. Add to the general practitioners community nurses (nearly 10,000 health visitors, much of whose work concerns children), 2,600 school nurses, and 500 pediatricians (who reckon that about a third of their work is of a psychosocial nature; Graham and Jenkins, 1985), and you can see that the work of non–mental health professionals far outweighs the work of mental health professionals. But there is no need to change the balance of work in terms of specialist and nonspecialist delivery; what is needed is to ensure that those who do the work work together and, above all, are better trained.

Family doctors, pediatricians, and nurses are not going to have a great deal of time to devote to each child and family. Family doctors, for example, average ten minutes for each consultation (because some of their work involves very brief intervention, they are able to spend a little more time on complex problems). Consequently, the forms of assessment and intervention available to them for child mental health problems should be brief as well as effective. On the other hand, primary care workers often have one tremendous advantage over specialist mental health workers—they see children and families over long periods of time. They often already know a great deal about the family background when a problem comes up, and they may have a positive relationship with the family arising from previous helpful interventions. They do not need as much time to build a relationship or to assess a problem as do specialist workers.

What should the content of training for primary health care workers in developed countries consist of? It would not be appropriate to provide a detailed curriculum, but certainly a basic knowledge of normal emotional and cognitive development is required. Some understanding of situations found stressful and the variety of reactions children show, as well as their normal coping and adaptive mechanisms, is essential. As far as intervention is concerned, practitioners should be aware, first, that interventions of all types—whether based on behavioral, psychoanalytic, or family interactional theories—are very modest in their effects, and that time, maturation, and the ordinary experiences children undergo in their everyday lives are usually more important than specific professional interventions. Of course, the latter can make a difference, but primary care professionals should be discouraged from the view that mental health professionals, however charismatic they may be, have solutions that produce dramatic effects. On the other hand, they are able to achieve some definite, if limited improvements, and there is no reason primary care workers cannot do the same. Second, interventions should increase the sense of power that parents and children have over their own fate rather than take power away. Too many psychological treatments (of whatever kind) are practiced in a way that reduces rather than enhances a sense of competence. Third, it should be emphasized that interventions of any type are likely to be effective only if the therapist allies himself or herself with the family and is able to share or at least accept their distress. Unpleasant emotional experiences, especially depression, anxiety, and anger, are more supportable if they are shared. Probably the most promising cost-effective methods of brief intervention are those of the behavioral type, but these are unlikely to be helpful unless they are carried out by someone the family members feel understands and accepts them. For this to happen, some degree of psychodynamic understanding is of great help. Further, interventions are most likely to work if all those likely to be affected by them—both parents and child—are present when they are suggested, so that all can comment about them and provide ideas and reactions. Thus, some knowledge of behavioral, psychodynamic, and family interactional processes, at least at a basic level, is helpful to primary health care workers.

How is such training to be delivered? A natural assumption is that schools should enlist the aid of child psychiatrists and psychologists, and certainly there is a need for a greater input of child mental health matters into medical student and nursing student curricula. Mental health professionals should spend a greater part of their time in under-graduate and postgraduate teaching of doctors and nurses.

But a further desirable development would be the involvement of academic primary health care teachers themselves in this activity. In the U.K., there is an increasing number of academic departments of family medicine, headed by professors of general practice. Most of the medical schools now possess such a department. The teachers work partly in the university medical schools and partly in the community functioning as family doctors. It is these academics and their counterparts in nursing schools who are perhaps best fitted to develop and teach brief assessment and intervention methods that can be used in the community. It is unlikely that psychiatrists and psychologists, used to spending one or two hours with a family they have never met before, will be skilled in teaching methods of dealing in ten minutes with a problem in a child whose family has been known since he was born.

We put much emphasis on multidisciplinary work. Too many families in developed countries receive uncoordinated, duplicated, or even tripli-cated services, with each service deliverer not knowing or understand-ing what the others are trying to do. Even more common are children and families with serious difficulties who receive no help at all because the various services are not organized well enough to ensure they are identified. If a truly multidisciplinary service is to be achieved, it is probably necessary that at least some of the training be multidisciplin-ary. At the Institute of Child Health, London, where one of us works, we have given such courses on subjects like sexual abuse, legal aspects of child care, and behavioral management techniques. We have found that the multidisciplinary nature of these courses is useful and that people develop through them an appreciation of the role of agencies other than their own.

Mental health for all by the year 2000 will be an empty phrase unless we specify what we meant by it, so that we can know whether we have achieved it when that year arrives. In the field of child mental health, many criteria relating to physical health are relevant. Achievement of 100 percent immunization rates against the six common immunizable diseases, for example, would have a major impact on brain dysfunction and mental health. Literacy rates of 90 percent in all countries of the world would ensure that the great majority would have at least the opportunity to participate in an increasingly complex society. Integrat-ing mental health care into primary health care and including a compo-nent of child mental health training in 80 percent of the curricula of general health workers would constitute major advances. This would enable most parents to receive advice on the promotion of optimum development and give them access to sensible assessment and management procedures if their children developed psychological problems. Is such an advance possible? The Sri Lankan experience suggests it might be.

REFERENCES

Graham, P. (1980). "Epidemiological Approaches to Child Mental Health in Developing Countries." In E. F. Purcell, ed., *Psychopathology of Children and Youth: A Cross-Cultural Perspective*. New York: Josiah Macy, Jr., Foundation.

——— (1982). "Child Psychiatry in Relation to Primary Healthy Care." *Social Psychiatry* 17:109–116.

Graham, P., and Jenkins, J. (1985). "Training of Pediatricians for Psychosocial Aspects of Their Work." *Arch. Disease in Childhood* 60:777–780.

Nikapota, A. (1983). "Development of Child Mental Health Services in Sri Lanka." *J. Trop. Ped.* 29:302–305.

——— (1984). "Contributions of Integrated Mental Health Services to Child Mental Health." *Int. J. Mental Health* 12:77–95.

Senturia, Y. (1986). "The Impact of EPI on Neurological Disorders and Psychosocial Development." Unpublished paper.

World Health Organization. (1977). *Child Mental Health and Psychosocial Development*. Technical Report no. 613. Geneva: World Health Organization.

World Health Organization. (1983). *Manuals in Child Mental Health*. Delhi, India: World Health Organization.

5

Child Psychiatry: The State of the Art, Retrospect and Prospect

LIONEL HERSOV

Leo Kanner, in a paper published over twenty-five years ago, ventured to predict the future:

> I am pleased to be in a position to foresee an internationally oriented child psychiatry as a medical specialty on its own footing, with a diminution and eventual cessation of fraternal strife, a truly scientific respect for data of observation, an integrated occupation with all aspects of child development and behavior, and the persistent goal of trying to improve our methods of prevention and treatment. (Kanner, 1964)

He also wrote forcefully of "an era in which hypotheses will be submitted to the tests of their own validity, in which dogmatism of any kind will be abandoned" (pp. 280–89).

It is tempting to see which of his predictions have been fulfilled and which are still beyond our reach, but to compress a discussion of all the issues he raised into a limited number of pages would be tedious. I will return to his predictions in my conclusion, but first I want to tell the story of children who do not attend school, originally an educational problem that in time became a clinical disorder treated by mental health professionals. It provides a useful framework for presenting changes in thinking about childhood psychiatric disorders since the early part of this century. It also permits me to address some of the issues raised by Kanner, such as the value of adopting a developmental approach and of testing hypotheses, in the unfolding of child and adolescent psychiatry as a clinical and scientific discipline.

I have been immersed in nonattendance at school for over thirty years now and have watched with interest as changing concepts of disorder and treatment were applied to the problems of absence from school (Hersov, 1985).

Nonattendance was originally an educational problem. How did it become a clinical disorder of interest to psychiatrists, psychoanalysts, psychologists, social workers, school counselors, family therapists, epidemiologists, psychopharmacologists, categorizers, and more recently adult psychiatrists in many countries around the world? "School phobia," the term introduced in the 1940s, was described by Eisenberg (1958) as "a paradigm of neurotic disorders in children for it illustrates with special clarity the relation between symptoms in the child and the psychological structure of the family." This interaction is the quintessence of clinical practice in most emotional disorders in childhood.

Telling the story of nonattendance requires the mingling of historical, clinical, and research data, and I hope this proves diverting. I have taken as my guide the legal historian Francis Maitland, who said, "The essential matter of history is not what happened but what people thought and said about it."

What happened to bring the educational problem of persistent nonattendance at school from the classroom into the clinician's office was the introduction of compulsory education in the great modern states at the end of the nineteenth century. What mental health professionals of all disciplines and the families of the afflicted children thought and said about nonattendance is the story of truancy and school phobia/school refusal.

Reluctance to go to school was certainly not a new phenomenon, for Shakespeare had already immortalized it as one of the Seven Ages of Man in *As You Like It* (II, vii, 139):

And then,
The whining schoolboy with his satchel,
And shining morning face,
Creeping like a snail,
Unwillingly to school.

In Shakespeare's time schooling was mainly, if not entirely, for the children of the wealthier classes. It was voluntary and required the paying of fees. We now take it for granted that all children should have appropriate free education, and by law it is the parent's responsibility to ensure that they receive it, most often by regular attendance at school. This was not always so, although as early as the fifth century B.C. the sage Solon proclaimed in his Constitution that it was every father's duty to provide the necessary education for his sons. Daughters were not as important in those days.

TEN SIGNPOSTS IN THE STORY OF SCHOOL REFUSAL

Enactment of School Attendance Laws

It was only with the introduction of compulsory common education—that is, open to all—that nonattendance became an educational problem. The first signpost in the story of what we today call truancy and school phobia/refusal is the result of the laws enacted in Europe and the United States at the end of the nineteenth century (Debiesse, 1951; Lester-Smith, 1951). A variety of motives lay behind the legislation besides the provision of education, and these were mostly in the child's best interests. Not surprisingly, working-class families reacted with anger and opposition to these measures: their children were often a source of income and support and their parents could see little or no benefit in the compulsory education that they had not experienced themselves. Families in rural areas still kept their children at home to help with the harvest, and urban families stoned the attendance officers who came to take their children to school.

At first all nonattenders were called "truants," from an Old French and Middle English word meaning "an assemblage of beggars." There were originally associations among truancy, idleness, and vagabondage, but in the sixteenth and seventeenth centuries *truant* was increasingly used to describe "a lazy idle person, especially a boy who absents himself from school attendance without leave" (Murray, Bradley, Craigie, and Onions, 1926).

The early studies of behavior disorders and delinquency by such pioneers as Healy (1915) and Burt (1929) linked truancy with adverse social and economic conditions, marital breakdown, physical punishment at home, and poor progress at school. Today truancy still occurs most often against a similar background of adversity and is usually regarded as a manifestation of a conduct disorder, along with other antisocial behavior. It carries with it a high risk of delinquency and later of lower-status jobs, unstable work history, more serious antisocial behavior, and a likelihood of conviction. Not all truants, however, become delinquent (Hersov and Berg, 1980).

But what of those children coming from different, more stable home backgrounds who are not antisocial, do not become delinquent, yet appear to show on the surface a similar pattern of persistent nonattendance at school? They do not wander about the streets alone or in the company of other truants, but remain at home in close proximity to one or both parents, usually the mother. This form of neurotic refusal to go to school was early remarked upon in passing by Jung in 1913 and Melanie Klein in 1923 in descriptions of analytic treatment of anxious children with other manifestations of neurosis.

A Variant of Truancy

In 1932 I. T. Broadwin, an American psychoanalyst, described a type of nonattendance at school that he maintained differed from the usual pattern of truancy. His description remains a classic of clarity and vividness and is the second signpost in the story:

> The child is absent from school for periods varying from several months to a year. The absence is consistent. At all times the parents know where the child is. It is with the mother or near the home. The reason for truancy is incomprehensible to the parents and the school. The child may say that it is afraid to go to school, afraid of the teacher or say that it does not know why it will not go to school. When at home it is happy and apparently carefree. When dragged to school it is miserable, fearful and at the first opportunity runs home despite the certainty of corporal punishment. The onset is generally sudden. The previous school work had been fair.

Later clinical descriptions of school refusal have included most if not all of the behaviors he described, but other features have since been added, such as somatic symptoms. The reasons for the behavior that emerged in psychotherapy were mainly a fear of something terrible happening to the mother, which made the child run home from school for reassurance. Broadwin also put forward the formulation that such behavior occurred in children with a deep-seated obsessional neurosis or a neurotic character of the obsessional type and many other personality difficulties. He suggested that strong infantile love attachments with intense hostile or sadistic attitudes lay behind the child's overt behavior.

Broadwin naturally turned to the psychoanalytic formulations of the time to describe the psychopathology of the children's behavior. Similar formulations can be found in many studies over the next three decades and reflect the strong influence of psychoanalytic theory and practice on child psychiatry in the United States. Child analysts had gone there from Europe, and the principles they taught were seen as valuable tools for making sense of apparently inexplicable behavior and restoring it to normal.

This clear description of a variant of common truancy was the forerunner of what would later be called "school phobia" and "school refusal." It is also an interesting early example of the continuing effort in child psychiatry to delineate clinical syndromes according to rational principles, with an etiology, phenomenology, psychopathology, prognosis, and treatment. Other examples around that time were Potter's description of childhood schizophrenia and Kanner's 1943 description of childhood autism, an original set of observations that are valid today.

Broadwin's early paper set the stage for many subsequent publications mostly in the United States but also in Britain and later in Europe. The hypothesis that gradually took precedence was that fear of going to school was really a fear of leaving home and mother, called "separation anxiety." Separation anxiety, although mentioned, was not given much prominence in the psychoanalytic writings of the time for it was the imaginative work of John Bowlby (1973) that later gave it a firm place in the psychopathology of child and adult neurosis and generated so much research into attachment theory.

School Phobia

The third signpost in the story is the coining of the term *school phobia* by Adelaide Johnson and her colleagues (1941) to describe a particular form of nonattendance, again differentiated from truancy and favoring the explanatory mechanism of phobic projection onto school or teacher. Again there is mention of obsessive neurotic patterns with phobic and hysteric features, but a well-founded reluctance to call school phobia a clinical entity. Early abortive forms of school phobia that cleared rapidly were mentioned, and they remark for the first time on a thirty-one-year-old female with severe untreated school phobia that later developed into a crippling, widespread, chronic phobic state resisting all forms of analytic treatment.

Precipitants of school phobia, such as illness, a promotion at school, or marital disharmony with maternal anxiety, were also listed. It was hypothesized that the anxiety generated by such events bound mother and affected child closer together or accentuated existing mutual dependence. This was an advance on earlier views for it stressed interpersonal as well as intrapsychic aspects, thus broadening the thinking about and the treatment of the disorder. Virtually all psychodynamic formulations since then have emphasized the mutually dependent hostile relationship between child and mother as central to school refusal, and treatment has included both mother and child.

Later papers in the forties and fifties (E. Klein, 1945; Estes, Haylett, and Johnson, 1956) delineated fear of school into fear of teacher, fear of other pupils, and fear of schoolwork arising from expectation of failure. Fear of separation from a parent was said to arise when the mother threatened to leave home because of marital conflict or attempted to control the child's refusal to comply by threats to depart or to harm herself. These interesting observations were not followed up in much detail at the time, although fear of actual people and situations in school was later to become a focus of treatment by behavior therapists (Yule, Hersov, and Treseder, 1980).

Separation Anxiety

Toward the end of the 1950s and early 1960s the fourth signpost was the hypothesis that "anxiety about separation" was *the* primary psychopathology in all cases. The hitherto prevailing view had been that of repressed hostility to a parent with projection onto teacher or school and consequent avoidance of both. Some studies emphasized that anxiety about separation did not explain the behavior of children who had attended school regularly for long periods before developing symptoms and also noted that separation anxiety seemed to apply more readily to younger children. The peak prevalence at eleven years, following change of school, did not support the separation anxiety hypothesis and suggested there might be other factors such as the stresses of school transitions (Blyth and Simmons, 1983).

Even in the 1950s there were those who were skeptical of a single psychopathology to explain every case of school refusal that seemed, after all, to occur at any school age and in different circumstances across a time span of twelve to thirteen years. All this time the child is rapidly developing in the biological, cognitive, affective, and interpersonal fields, and it seemed unlikely that the same psychopathology could apply equally to a five-year-old and a seventeen-year-old if the emerging data on child development were to be believed. The distinction between truancy and school refusal was also accepted uncritically without any empirical study of possible similarities and differences.

Many argued that the time had come to carry out studies of large samples, reflecting growing skepticism of the generalizations made from single-case or small-sample studies without comparison groups or controls. Child psychiatrists were being heavily criticized by other psychiatrists and physicians for their unscientific approach and lack of proper studies, and the pressure was mounting to do controlled research and epidemiological studies.

Current thinking also did not take into account many important psychosocial and environmental factors or social class and ethnic influences in school refusal. Some authorities, for example, remarked on the apparent absence of school refusal among black children in Britain and the United States (Hersov, 1985).

Empirical Studies

The fifth signpost, in the 1960s, was the execution of empirical studies with comparisons among truants, school refusers, and other neurotic children in terms of diagnostic categories, socioeconomic background, parental attitudes and methods of discipline, children's intelligence and attainments, influence of school transitions, expressed fears of school, separation anxiety, and family mental disorder. Significant differences were found between groups including differences in separation experience and the rarity of conduct disorder in school refusal. Anxiety about separating from mother was often found in school refusal but not exclusively so, and more so in younger children. It was also shown that there were markedly different patterns of parental and parent-child relationships over the issue of discipline and obedience generally, but particularly in relation to going to school, which led to different methods of home management. The rather leisurely psychotherapeutic approach of that era of waiting for insight to dawn was also criticized by others who viewed early return to school as the main goal of treatment, with or without insight.

Since the original empirical studies in the 1960s there has been a continuing stream of similar research in the United States, Japan, Finland, and especially Britain. The distinction between truancy and school refusal has been supported repeatedly, and the association of truancy and conduct disorder is now accepted as an important difference from school refusal. The overdependence of school-refusing children on their mothers has also been empirically demonstrated. There have been attempts to subdivide school refusal as a unitary concept in terms of the extent of the disorder (Kennedy, 1965). In the type labeled neurotic, or Type 1, the children have problems over school attendance, but their development and peer relationships are otherwise normal. The characterological, or Type 2, have fear of school as only one feature in a pervasive disorder with a general fear of the outside world and a constricted life limited to the household—like the fifteen-year-old boy who said during his treatment that the only place he might conceivably feel safe would be in the vaults of the Bank of England. Not surprisingly some have said that school refusal with onset in adolescence appears to be a more severe disorder with a worse prognosis.

Since school refusal was first described, there has also been a continuing debate about whether it is a single syndrome, a clinical entity that presents with a variety of symptoms, or, instead, a variety of syndromes with a common presenting symptom. Matters were further complicated in that school refusal can also present with what has been called the "somatic disguise"—physical complaints of abdominal pain, nausea, vomiting, urinary frequency, diarrhea, and headache with no overt display of anxiety about going to school (Eisenberg, 1958). Such children are usually first seen by family doctors and pediatricians, and no doubt many are helped to return to school. The pattern of child-parent relationship and the child's psychopathology is very similar to those with the usual presentation of expressed fear, but there are other factors that determine to whom the parents first turn for help.

The emphasis on examining family factors, relationships, and psychodynamic formulations, rather than studying educational and social factors, led to criticism of what was called the "medicalization" of nonattendance at school. Many school and clinical psychologists, particularly those with a behavioral orientation, began to develop models of phobic symptom formation based on learning theory, as well as treatment methods. Very simply, phobias are seen as learned responses to stimuli that have become linked with fear-producing experiences. A distinction was also drawn between fear of leaving mother and fear of school in itself. Many of the case studies published on these lines also produced data that were quite compatible with psychodynamic formulations, and it seems clear that the differences were often of focus rather than substance (Yule, Hersov, and Treseder, 1980).

There were some important differences from the psychodynamic view, such as an emphasis on fear of failure and loss of self-esteem, and of *going to* school, labeled anticipatory anxiety, instead of separation anxiety. These differences are important for defining the focus of treatment, whether it be the family dynamics or an actual situation at school, or a combination of both.

Learning Theory and Behavior Therapy

The 1960s also marked the application of learning theory and its offshoot, behavior modification, to the understanding and treatment of school refusal, the sixth signpost in the story. Functional analysis of the circumstances in which the school refusal first occurred, and was later maintained by reinforcing factors in the family, was considered more helpful in planning treatment than psychopathological formulations. The child who learns (adaptively) by classical and instrumental conditioning to avoid dangerous situations can learn in the same way (maladaptively) to avoid school and other social gatherings, and a parent may unwittingly reinforce the avoidance behavior by colluding with it.

Others have taken a developmental approach. It is assumed that almost all children will experience some anxiety about coping with impersonal school demands at some time in their school career, particularly at the beginning. Most children master this through succeeding in their schoolwork, enjoying peer relationships and games, and pleasing teachers and parents, all features that enhance confidence and self-esteem. Other more vulnerable children from close-knit socially isolated families with parental psychiatric disorder may have fewer or no positive experiences. Those they do have may not counteract the anxiety provoked by the more stressful and less rewarding events (Hersov, 1985).

If there is already a past history of anxiety about separating from home and parents, then criticisms by a teacher, bullying by peers, or the loss of a supportive friendship may cause greater anxiety and lead to school refusal, which mother responds to in predictably overprotective fashion. This simpler formulation may make more sense to a teacher than more recondite psychopathology, thus enabling them to cooperate in a systematic plan to get the child back to school. Not surprisingly, teachers do not like to be called phobic objects.

Family Therapy

The seventh signpost, again appearing in the late 1960s and early 1970s, was an increasing interest in family approaches to the treatment of a number of child psychiatric disorders. Many psychiatrists reacted negatively at first to the claims of exponents of family therapy, saying it had nothing new to offer and had always been practiced because parents were also interviewed. Modern family therapy, however, draws on systems theory and concepts of whole-family function and dysfunction, and entire families are seen. Because school refusal usually arises in settings of obvious family dysfunction, it was predicted that family therapy would be of value.

"School refusal" is considered a more appropriate description of the child's behavior than "school phobia" by many clinicians and family therapists, because it does not imply a commitment to a particular theory of psychopathology such as the origin of phobias, nor does it assume that we are dealing with a unitary homogeneous disorder. Family therapists believe the origins of the child's anxiety lie mainly within the family. From the systemic point of view "refusal," rather than "phobia," points more clearly to the interpersonal rather than the intrapsychic sources of the fear of school, whether it be separation or anticipatory anxiety. According to the concept of family homeostasis, symptomatic behavior has a stabilizing family function and attempts to solve underlying family conflict and stress, albeit in a dysfunctional way. Family members try to preserve the family rules and resist change. It is believed that such families overestimate the "power" of the symptomatic child and support the child's self-image by emphasizing abilities, while also protecting them from experiences that might threaten their own or the family's self-image. Going to school exposes the child to the risk of failure in scholastic and interpersonal terms and therefore must be avoided.

Treatment has to take into account family defiance, and the therapist must assess power within the family and mobilize resources that will overcome the child's resistance to going to school. This may require a paradoxical strategy (Hawkes, 1981); at other times a structural and strategic view is taken, placing school phobia and school refusal at the two ends of a continuum of progression from "involuntary" symptoms at one end, such as separation anxiety, phobic avoidance, and somatic disguise, to willful "refusal" at the other. In the later stages of school refusal the behavior has often changed from a simple fear response to a more complex protective function for the whole family. From the point of view of treatment, straightforward fear-reduction techniques are useful in the acute stages of the disorder; in the more chronic cases, however, a family systems approach may generate more effective treatment strategies, in which a proper family hierarchy is established with the parents in control and boundaries defined (Hsia, 1984).

The 1960s also saw, on the Isle of Wight, the first major epidemiological study of child psychiatric disorders (Rutter, Tizard, and Whitmore, 1970), an important step in the history of child psychiatry, as well as the study of school refusal. For the first time an accurate figure of prevalence of disorders in late childhood and adolescence was available, instead of widely different estimates from different clinical populations. Far more cases of school refusal were diagnosed in the adolescent school population than were diagnosed at the age of ten to eleven years, a most important finding from two points of view. It supported other clinical findings that school refusal is a more frequent and serious disorder in adolescence, with a less hopeful prognosis requiring more extensive treatment and possibly admission to a psychiatric unit. A higher incidence of depressive disorder was also found in adolescence than before puberty, and this has become an important link with school refusal.

Pharmacotherapy

The eighth signpost in the story of school refusal and child psychiatry was the introduction of medication in the 1960s and its use on a much larger scale in the 1970s and 1980s. This was initiated by the use of psychotropic drugs such as chlorpromazine for adult disorders, but then, as more drugs were put on the market, they began to be used with children and adolescents. Amphetamines had been used for hyperkinetic children as early as 1936, and sedatives of different kinds were prescribed for anxious or agitated youngsters. With school refusal, phenobarbital and benzodiazepines were tried for anxiety in the mornings before school without much success. There were no systematic studies, mostly open trials with small case numbers from which little definite could be inferred.

During the 1970s the first systematic studies of the use of imipramine in school refusal were carried out by the Kleins in New York (Gittelman-Klein and Klein, 1980). Donald Klein had earlier found that imipramine regularly blocked adult agoraphobics' apparently spontaneous panic attacks, which he believed were a pathological variant of normal separation anxiety. He had found that adult agoraphobics had a 50 percent frequency of school refusal and separation anxiety in childhood, looked at retrospectively. He therefore predicted that imipramine would be effective in children with handicapping separation anxiety and selected school-phobic children to test his hypothesis because they showed a clear, objectively quantifiable behavioral sequel, namely school phobia, to the primary pathological separation anxiety.

An initial trial was promising, leading to a double-blind trial that demonstrated the effectiveness of imipramine in aiding the return to school. Predictably, the effects of the medication could not be easily separated from the results of other psychosocial methods applied at the same time. The conclusion was that medication does not ensure return to school automatically, but improves the affective state sufficiently to enable return to school with the help of desensitization and other supportive techniques. The Kleins claimed that they did not find evidence of depressive disorder in the children, but they did not apply any systematic criteria, so there is the possibility that the positive effect of the imipramine may have been on depression rather than anxiety. A replication study in Britain (Berney et al., 1981) did not support the therapeutic effect of similar medication in what many considered too small a dose. The current view seems to be that psychosocial and behavioral methods are still central to treatment, with antidepressants as a valuable adjunct.

School Refusal: Anxiety Disorder or Depressive Disorder?

Our ninth signpost was the introduction of agreed diagnostic categories into child psychiatry practice and research in the 1970s and 1980s. The advent of multiaxial classifications (Rutter, Shaffer, and Sturge, 1975) and D.S.M. III meant that uniform diagnostic criteria could now be applied, with the hope that this would lead to valid comparisons between different studies of the same disorder and between different treatments and outcomes in the same study. The category of separation anxiety disorder was introduced by D.S.M. III, with school refusal as one of the items required to make the diagnosis. This has remained unchanged in the current revision of D.S.M. III and has been introduced among the provisional list of categories in the recent revision of *The International Classification of Diseases.* These moves may end the controversy about school refusal being either a unitary or a heterogeneous disorder. Clinical experience has also shown that school refusal can occur without apparent separation anxiety and can present as phobic avoidance of school that can be diagnosed as *true* school phobia.

This brings me to the question of depressive disorder in childhood with school refusal as its manifestation. My own empirical study in the 1960s showed that this did occur, a conclusion supported by other case studies. The issue has recently been put to the test (Bernstein and Garfinkel, 1986) using structured interviews, depression scales, and anxiety scales in adolescent school refusal with at least a two-year history. The findings are that as many cases meet criteria for depression as do for anxiety disorder, with a fair number showing both diagnoses, these being more severely affected, with higher scores all round. The distinction between severe anxiety and depressive disorder in adolescence is often difficult to make clinically, and the study bears this out. The findings have important implications for different kinds of treatment, including medication, and there are currently trials of antidepressant and anti-anxiety medications going on in the United States.

Relationship between School Refusal and Adult Disorder

The tenth and last signpost points to the current interest in the links between childhood and adult psychiatric disorder. Outcome studies of school refusal show that at least one-third continue to exhibit psychiatric dysfunction, some with phobic disorders. The occurrence of school refusal in adult psychiatric patients has been found significantly more often than in controls. Past school phobia predicts an earlier onset of adult agoraphobia but is followed by agoraphobia in only a small portion of cases. School refusal also occurs more often in children of agoraphobic mothers. And, too, there is a continuity between depressive syndromes in childhood with or without school refusal and adult depressive disorder, although most depressed adults do not have a history of psychiatric problems in childhood. There are also links between anxiety and depressive disorders in parents and disorders in children (Weissman et al., 1984). For example, panic disorders in parents conferred more than a threefold increased risk of separation anxiety in their children.

CONCLUSION

In conclusion, I would like to return to Kanner's forecast and consider how it stands today. As to his first point, child and adolescent psychiatry is now fully recognized as a specialty of psychiatry and medicine on its own footing in most places. Although a relatively young discipline, it has outstanding clinicians, teachers, and researchers whose work is respected and who have contributed to advances in conceptualization and treatment in other disciplines as well.

The second point is that fraternal strife of the kind that Kanner experienced at the time he was writing has markedly receded. The hidden agenda, at least in the United States, in difficult discussions among psychiatrists, psychologists, and social workers dealing with children and families has to do with territory and reimbursement and the fact that they share common therapeutic skills. Interdisciplinary collaboration is still a major feature of clinical work, however, and effective research today is most often multidisciplinary. This is not surprising given the multifactorial etiology of so many disorders in childhood and adolescence, so that practice and research require knowledge derived from the basic sciences, neurobiology, sociology, child development, and statistics, to name but a few. The interdisciplinary research of today is the clinical practice of tomorrow.

The third point is that nowadays data from child development and behavior research make a crucial contribution to clinical practice. *The understanding of developmental processes is to child psychiatry what physiology is to general medicine.* As pointed out by Rutter and Garmezy (1983), development is not merely a focus on early life experience alone. Looked at in isolation, it gives an unbalanced view of developmental influences, for experiences throughout a lifetime are important. We clearly have much to gain from studies in developmental biology, psychology, and psychopathology.

The fourth point is that empirical methods of study are the order of the day, including putting hypotheses to the test. This is shown in the range and quality of research work now appearing in some journals. One hopes the present generation of child psychiatrists will forsake dogmatism and appreciate the virtues of informed skepticism, for as Nietzsche said, "The surest way to corrupt a young man is to teach him to esteem more highly those who think alike than those who think differently."

The fifth point is that studies for improving and evaluating methods of prevention and treatment still lag behind, for the work is difficult. Double-blind trials are now obligatory in testing the efficacy of medication, but comparisons among the different forms of individual psychotherapy, group therapy, and family therapy, and among outpatient, day-patient, and inpatient therapies are still all too rare (Kolvin et al., 1981).

Much has been written on prevention, both in articles and books, but there are few studies with well-established findings. Distinguishing between primary and secondary prevention in child psychiatry is difficult because of problems of definition and measurement. This may become easier as classification systems become more precise. It has been said that true primary prevention is impossible until we know the cause of each specific disorder, but it is unlikely that a specific cause will be identified for the many conditions listed in D.S.M. III-R and I.C.D. 10. It has also been said that mental disorders are not illnesses and diseases with a specific etiology, so that the public health model of prevention is not easy to apply.

There is, however, much to be said for primary prevention if possible, especially the prevention of unnecessary suffering before treatment is initiated. Those most in need of help are often the last to receive it because of the way services are provided in terms of both availability and selection for treatment. I refer, of course, to the conduct disorders, because of their frequency and poor long-term outcome. Preventive programs aimed at reducing the incidence of brain damage by disease or injury are valuable, as they lessen the number of children at risk for childhood psychiatric disorder. Claims have been made that programs aimed at diminishing stress, strengthening coping skills, improving social competence, enhancing self-esteem, and providing support groups will have a preventive effect, but these need to be put to the test (Rutter, 1978).

My final point is Kanner's reference to child and adolescent psychiatry as an internationally oriented discipline. Although the association has worked to foster this over the years, the reality still is that much of adult and child psychiatry is based on only 15 percent of the world's population—those in Western society. We are only just beginning to appreciate the importance of ethnic and sociocultural influences on the presentation and course of psychiatric disorders in different societies. From a developmental point of view the individualistic orientation of Western and particularly Anglo-American cultures differs markedly from the dominant family orientation in many non-Western societies (Kleinman, 1986).

The displacement of numbers of people from their native homes, because of poverty, persecution, or war, to other countries with better opportunities but different traditions and beliefs about psychiatric disorder impinges on the training and practice of mental health professionals working with children and families. Kleinman and Good (1985), who are both psychiatrists and anthropologists, have argued cogently for an appreciation of the differences: "When culture is treated as a constant . . . it is relatively easy to view depression as a biological disorder triggered by social stresses in the presence of ineffective support and reflected in a set of symptoms and complaints that map back on to the biological substrate of the disorders. . . . Depressive illness and dysphoria are thus not only interpreted differently in non-Western societies and across cultures; they are constituted as fundamentally different forms of social reality."

We need to listen more carefully to our colleagues from other continents, to give credit to their observations and explanations of childhood disorders, rather than overwhelm them with beliefs and opinions derived from training and practice in Western societies. It is for them to write the next signpost and for us to draw on their experience in assembling a truly international body of knowledge in child and adolescent psychiatry to apply to the increasingly complex work in the decades ahead.

REFERENCES

Berney, T.; Kolvin, I.; Bhate, S.; Garside, T.; Jeans, B.; Kay, B.; and Scarth, L.
(1981). "School Phobia: A Therapeutic Trial with Clomipramine and Short-
Term Outcome." *British Journal of Psychiatry* 138:110–118.

Bernstein, G. A., and Garfinkel, B. D. (1986). "School Phobia: The Overlap of
Affective and Anxiety Disorder." *Journal of the American Academy of
Child Psychiatry* 25:235–241.

Blyth, D. A., and Simmons, R. G. (1983). "The Adjustments of Early
Adolescents to School Transitions." *Journal of Early Adolescence* 3:105–
120.

Bowlby, J. (1973). *Attachment and Loss*. Vol. 2, *Separation Anxiety and
Anger*. London: Hogarth Press.

Broadwin, I. T. (1932). "A Contribution to the Study of Truancy." *American
Journal of Orthopsychiatry* 2:253–259.

Burt, C. (1929). *The Young Delinquent*. New York: D. Appleton.

Debiesse, J. (1951). *Compulsory Education in France*. Paris: UNESCO.

Eisenberg, L. (1958). "School Phobia: Diagnosis, Genesis and Clinical
Management." *Paediatric Clinics of North America* 5:645–660.

Estes, H. R., Haylett, C., and Johnson, A. (1956). "Separation Anxiety."
American Journal of Psychotherapy 10:682–695.

Gittelman-Klein, R., and Klein, D. F. (1980). "Separation Anxiety in School
Refusal and Its Treatment with Drugs." In L. Hersov and I. Berg, eds., *Out
of School: Modern Perspectives in School Refusal and Truancy*.
Chichester: Wiley, 321–341.

Hawkes, R. (1981). "Paradox and a Systems Approach to a Case of Severe
School Phobia." *Australian Journal of Family Therapy* 2:56–62.

Healy, W. (1915). *The Individual Delinquent*. Cambridge, Mass.: Harvard
University Press.

Hersov, L. (1985). "School Refusal." In M. Rutter and L. Hersov, eds., *Child
and Adolescent Psychiatry: Modern Perspectives*. 2nd ed. Oxford:
Blackwell, 382–399.

Hersov, L., and Berg, I., eds. (1980). *Out of School: Modern Perspectives in
School Refusal and Truancy*. Chichester: Wiley.

Hsia, H. (1984). "Structural and Strategic Approach to School Phobia/School
Refusal." *Psychology in the Schools* 21:360–367.

Johnson, A. L.; Falstein, E. I.; Szurek, S. A.; and Svendsen, M. (1941).
"School Phobia." *American Journal of Orthopsychiatry* 11:702–711.

Jung, C. G. (1913). "A Case of Neurosis in a Child." In *The Collected Works
of C. G. Jung*. Vol. 4. New York: Basic Books, 1961.

Kanner, L. (1935). *Child Psychiatry*. Springfield, Ill., Charles C. Thomas.

——— (1943). "Autistic Disturbances of Affective Contact." *Nervous Child*
2:217–250.

—— (1964). "The Future of Child Psychiatry." In D. Arn Van Krevelen, ed., *Child Psychiatry and Prevention*. Proceedings of the Fifth International Congress of Child Psychiatry. Bern: Verlag Hans Huber.

Kennedy, W. A. (1965). "School Phobia: Rapid Treatment of Fifty Cases." *Journal of Abnormal Psychology* 70:285–289.

Klein, E. (1945). "The Reluctance to Go to School." *Psychoanalytic Study of the Child* 1:263–279.

Klein, M. (1923). "The Role of the School in the Libidinal Development of the Child." *International Zeitschrift for Psychoanalyse* 9:312.

Kleinman, A. (1986). Personal communication.

Kleinman, A., and Good, B. eds. (1985). *Culture and Depression; Studies in the Anthropology and Cross-Cultural Psychiatry of Affect and Disorder*. Berkeley: University of California Press.

Kolvin, I.; Garside, R. G.; Nicol, A. R.; MacMillan, A.; Wolstenholme, F.; and Leitch, I. M. (1981). *Help Starts Here: The Maladjusted Child in the Ordinary School*. London: Tavistock.

Lester-Smith, W. O. (1951). *Compulsory Education in England*. Paris: UNESCO.

Murray, J. A. H.; Bradley, H.; Craigie, W. H.; and Onions, C. T. (1926). *A New English Dictionary*. Vol. 10. Oxford: Clarendon Press.

Potter, H. W. (1933). "Schizophrenia in Children." *American Journal of Psychiatry* 89:1253–1270.

Rutter, M. L. (1978). "Research into Prevention of Psychosocial Disorders in Childhood." In J. Barnes and M. Connelly, eds., *Social Care Research*. London: Bedford Square Press, 104–117.

Rutter, M., and Garmezy, N. (1983). "Developmental Psychopathology." In E. M. Hetherington, ed., *Socialization, Personality and Social Development*. Vol. 4, *Handbook of Child Psychology*. 4th ed. New York: Wiley, 77–99.

Rutter, M., Shaffer, D., and Sturge, C. (1975). *A Multiaxial Classification of Child Psychiatric Disorders*. Geneva: World Health Organization.

Rutter, M., Tizard, J., and Whitmore, K. (1970). *Education, Health and Behavior*. London: Longman. Reprint, Huntington, N.Y.: Krieger, 1981.

Weissman, M. M.; Leckman, J. F.; Merikangas, K. R.; Gammon, G. D.; and Prusoff, B. A. (1984). "Depression and Anxiety Disorders in Parents and Children." *Archives of General Psychiatry* 47:845–852.

Yule, W., Hersov, L., and Treseder, J. (1980). "Behavioral Treatments of School Refusal." In L. Hersov and I. Berg, eds., *Out of School: Modern Perspectives in School Refusal and Truancy*. Chichester: Wiley, 267–301.

II

Psychobiological Endowment and Developmental Interactions

6

Introduction

J. GERALD YOUNG

Debate about the meaning of mental health invariably stimulates questions about the endowment of the child and the effects of environmental nurturance or interference. This reflects Freud's concepts of the etiological equation and the complemental series, the balance between heredity and life events in the genesis of illness (chap. 2). Specification of causative factors arrayed between these poles is essential for the development of improved treatments. Environmental influences were extensively explored in recent decades, but clinical investigators were unable to delineate Freud's "constitution," the genetic endowment. Genetic methods now supply tools to better achieve these aims, however, and clinical scientists have begun to expose hereditary causes of childhood neuropsychiatric disorders. The unraveling of the heritability and mode of transmission of Gilles de la Tourette's disorder is a recent example of this progress (chap. 12). For most clinical investigators, the genetic contribution is respected as a strong influence but is conceptualized in a simplified form. Chapter 7, by Roubertoux and Nosten, considers the limitations of a simple linear model of genetic effects on behavior and outlines more complex genetic influences and experimental evidence supporting them.

Analysis of genetic effects can follow a path starting with a specific behavior and leading to the gene, a direction attractive to clinicians. Roubertoux and Nosten caution us that this is a more difficult route and describe experiments proceeding from an identifiable genetic origin to observable behaviors. They concede that the intervening physiological events governed by the genes are poorly understood. Nevertheless, there are approaches available to establish whether the relationship between gene and behavior is linear or nonlinear.

These investigators emphasize that genotype-environment interactions are not necessarily the general rule but depend upon such factors as the genetic strain of the offspring or the foster mothers in experiments, the phenotypic behavior observed, and the age at which it is examined. It is likely that there are variations in sensitivity of the genotype to the environment, and identification of critical or sensitive periods (times of maximal receptivity to environmental influences) may be essential to understanding these events. Critical periods may also be useful markers for specific physiological mechanisms associated with genotype-environment interactions. It should be possible to identify physiological events that correspond to the timing of these sensitive periods; the maturation of cell receptors, the formation of synaptic connections, and regressive phenomena (normal cell death or neuronal process elimination) are among the events likely to be involved. The specification of multiple sensitive periods, each related to specific genetic mechanisms and associated with particular physiological events, will be accomplished through systematic research, and targeted treatments will be designed accordingly. This is a broad and encouraging prospect for the future, but a great deal of research effort will be required (see chap. 7).

Some steps toward this understanding have been taken already. Perhaps the genetic predisposition to environmental influences can be seen with greatest clarity by a review of this interaction in well-studied physical disorders. For example, the effects of environmental factors on the expression of genetically determined phenotypic abnormalities are evident in McArdle's disease. This defect in muscle phosphorylase is transmitted as an autosomal recessive pattern, and in the resting individual no symptoms are observed. By the second decade of life, however, the onset of exercise leads to severe muscle pain, stiffness, and weakness, with eventual muscle necrosis (Antel and Arnason, 1983; Felig, 1980). In another autosomal recessive disorder the patient has a remarkable and potentially lethal response to a particular drug but is quite normal if he does not encounter it in the environment. Plasma cholinesterase degrades succinylcholine, a neuromuscular blocking agent. A manifest abnormality in plasma cholinesterase occurs in one of three thousand individuals (the prevalence of the gene is 2/100) and leads to a hydrolysis of succinylcholine one hundred times slower than normal. Administration of this drug to a genetically vulnerable individual leads to muscle relaxation and apnea lasting for several hours. In this example, a normally inconsequential alteration in a gene product can have a lethal effect in certain environmental circumstances (Antel and Arnason, 1983).

Most developmentalists are aware of the classic example of dietary factors as environmental influences: phenylketonuria, in which failure to restrict phenylalanine in the diet from the earliest months of life leads to severe neurological impairment. Proper dietary restriction can prevent retardation in this autosomal recessive condition, another example of the interaction of genes and environment in the determination of phenotype. Extensions of this concept clarify the role of genes in the regulation of susceptibility or resistance to environmentally determined diseases. Examples are genetic factors underlying a susceptibility to the thiamine deficiency of Wernicke-Korsakoff's syndrome or the toxic effects of the drug isoniazid in patients with a genetically determined reduction in liver acetyl transferase (Antel and Arnason, 1983). Finally, the genetic determination of immunological factors has a profound effect on the susceptibility of individuals to specific illnesses. Only recently have the interacting effects of the brain and immune system been the subject of programmatic research (Stein, Keller, and Schleifer, 1985), and these concepts are now being applied to our understanding of psychiatric disorders and their development during childhood (Schliefer et al., 1986).

Clinicians struggle to objectify the psychobiological endowment derived from the genetic-prenatal matrix, using concepts that are never entirely satisfactory, such as temperament. This matrix is the starting point for complex developmental interactions, and we artificially separate genetic and developmental influences. One sector of clinical research in which these efforts have been particularly enlightening has been the investigation of gender identity and its disorders.

As we turn to the development of gender identity, it is useful to recall that, however complex the interaction of genotype and environment in animals, there is an additional complication inherent in the study of human development. The capacity for self-consciousness makes the individual's inner life available as an additional index to understand the effects of endowment and environment; it also raises a question concerning the influence of internal mental life on the further development of the individual. However much predetermined by genes and environment, does this evolving inner map of a child alter his further response to the environment? Does the genotype have recognizable effects on how this internal mental life affects sensitivity to environmental events? The development of gender identity has especially favorable features available for sorting out these interwoven components.

The elements of the genotype-environment interaction in the development of gender identity have been established and are agreed upon: the chromosomal basis for the sex of the individual and the development of the gonads and internal sexual apparatus, external genitalia, and secondary sex characteristics; the secretion of sex hormones and resultant prenatal organization of brain centers regulating erotic and gender behaviors and other postnatal developmental changes; and the familial and cultural influences bearing upon the child and his maturing body as his gender identity begins to form. Our conceptualization of genotype-environment interactions is enriched by Stoller's description in chapter 8 of the development of gender identity, as he identifies the biological-genetic substrate, but then moves to behavioral learning and psychodynamic descriptions of environmental influences. The power of the developing inner life and its choices and conflicts is both startling (in its ability to override apparent genetic-prenatal endowment, which is actually better considered as potential) and discouraging (in its relative immutability after childhood). In this instance, the postnatal influences of the maternal and paternal environment (in relation to the individual's specific phenotype and the timing of its development) are emphasized in the genotype-environment interaction, but research may eventually uncover evidence for genetic heterogeneity, epistasis, and prenatal maternal effects in the development of gender identity. Stoller's elegant and lucid description of the concepts, vocabulary, and sequence of events intrinsic to the development of gender identity will facilitate strategies for this research.

Developments in genetics do not alter the fundamental importance of environmental influences on the developing child, so the search for crucial sources of facilitation and interference continues. The behaviors most intensively studied for their hypothesized effects on later symptoms and psychic structure are those grouped around the concept of attachment.

Early hypotheses postulated links between interference with mother-infant attachment and later psychic conflict and symptom formation. Confounding factors have made research validating these concepts difficult to carry out, however, and investigators have reported contradictory results (Rutter, 1972). It has been difficult to identify environmental circumstances that are "specifically" detrimental to attachment processes (not confounded by too many other influences), so that children affected by these circumstances can serve as primary subject groups for comparisons to distinguish long-term effects of impaired attachment in infants. But longitudinal studies of infants separated from caretakers, examining outcome in childhood and adolescence, have been useful. Another illuminating effort to clarify effects of impaired attachment on development and adolescent outcome is described in chapter 9 by Hodges and Tizard. This research does not provide final answers to the nature-nurture questions at the root of child development research, but it is an important guide for further research on the complexities of genetic-environmental interactions, incorporating the special responsivity to the environment of the earliest period of the child's development.

REFERENCES

Antel, J. P., and Arnason, B. G. W. (1983). "Genetic Predisposition to Environmental Factors." In S. S. Kety, L. P. Rowland, R. L. Sidman, and S. W. Matthysse, eds., *Genetics of Neurological and Psychiatric Disorders.* New York: Raven Press, 255–271.

Felig, P. (1980). "Disorders of Carbohydrate Metabolism." In P. K. Bondy and L. E. Rosenberg, eds., *Metabolic Control and Disease.* 8th ed. Philadelphia: W. B. Saunders, 276–392.

Rutter, M. (1972). *Maternal Deprivation Reassessed.* Baltimore: Penguin.

Schleifer, S. J.; Scott, B.; Stein, M. and Keller, S. E. (1986). "Behavioral and Developmental Aspects of Immunity." *Journal of the American Academy of Child Psychiatry* 26:751–763.

Stein, M.; Keller, S. E.; and Schleifer, S. J. (1985). "Stress and Immunomodulation: The Role of Depression and Neuroendocrine Function." *Journal of Immunology* 135:827s–833s.

7

Toward a Nonlinear Conception of Gene-Behavior Relationships

PIERRE ROUBERTOUX

MARIKA NOSTEN

Genotypic variation can be observed and measured by techniques such as electrophoresis, and manipulated by mutagenesis. These tangible variations of genetic information may be associated with variation in behavioral traits. Clearly identified genes can modify the behavioral phenotype by altering triggering mechanisms or in some cases by suppressing outcome behaviors entirely. Genetic correlates of behaviors have been demonstrated for a number of species, including humans. Thus the field or research the geneticist deals with when investigating behavior does not cover the one that objectivist ethology classified as nature-nurture; neither does it refer to what outdated developmental psychology termed the heredity-environment controversy. We have gone beyond the stage of attempting to define whether nature or nurture is the major mover in the heredity-environment debate and prefer to leave these questions to theologians or philosophers. Our true purpose is the discovery of genes and the description of the physiological mechanisms by which they act on behavioral sequences.

We will be dealing with two main points in this chapter: first we will argue that there are genetic correlates to behavior. By genetic correlates, we mean genes that can be "found, caught, and kept"—in other words, genes that have an effect on normal as well as pathological behav-

Research reported in this chapter was supported by C.N.R.S. (U.A. 656, A.T.P. Développement Sensoriel et Moteur to M. Carlier), M.E.N. (Université Paris V: U.E.R. de Psychologie and U.E.R. Biomédicale; A.T.P. Biologie 84 to P. Roubertoux), Fondation pour la Recherche Médicale (grants to P. Roubertoux), and M.A.S. (grant to M. Nosten).

ioral variation, that can be located on the chromosome, and that can be maintained over generations. Second, we will attempt to show that, despite certain suggestions to the contrary, genes do not act in a linear fashion on behavioral, morphological, or physiological traits.

GENETIC CORRELATES OF BEHAVIORAL TRAITS

There are several ways of demonstrating the existence of genetic correlates of behavior. The first consists of examining mutations that have been cataloged for their effects on morphology or on the functioning of the nervous system. The method involves identifying the behavioral correlates for the disorders produced by these genes. In the mouse, more than fifty neurological mutants have been identified (Green, 1981).

Identification of the effects of a mutation is facilitated when working on species where there are coisogenic and congenic strains. Two strains are said to be coisogenic when they differ at only one locus, resulting, for example, from a mutation. Strains are said to be congenic when they differ only in a short fragment of a chromosome transferred from another strain. Some behavioral correlates of the mutations are, in fact, purely trivial expressions of these genes. The staggerer mutation in the mouse results, among other things, from an alteration in the Purkinje cells, which are located in the cerebellum. A disorder of this type negatively affects equilibrium and motility in the mouse, and it is not surprising to find alterations in pup care behavior in female mice that exhibit this disorder, particularly as regards the ability to take the pup in the mouth and to retrieve pups outside the nest.

Mutations that affect neurosensory functions are more revealing. The identification of behavioral correlates for sensory mutations provides two types of information: (1) it indicates how information is processed in this behavioral sequence, and (2) it reveals the presence of a genetic mechanism that may be behind the alteration of the behavioral sequence.

A third and more difficult way of proceeding is to investigate behaviors to discover genes. In our laboratory we have used this method to study several behavioral phenotypes, and in particular the rooting response, a motor response that is present at birth and disappears between the ages of seven and thirteen days (depending on the strain of mice). We have demonstrated that the age of disappearance of the rooting response is linked to one gene. We employed several independent methods, which indicated that this gene was located on chromosome IV at 4 centi-Morgans (recombination units) from the H-21 locus toward the telomeric end (Roubertoux et al., 1985, 1987). Other authors have shown that the fact that female mice are able to recognize male partners is linked to differences in genetic information carried on the T locus (Lenington and Egid, 1985) and on the H-2 system (Yamazaki et al., 1983).

One of the major issues facing biologists today is how to identify the target of a gene and thereby characterize the physiological mechanisms it governs. The study of the physiological pathways between genes and behavior remains, however, the area where the least is known. Progress here is difficult and slow. For example, as regards the rooting response, several unpublished experimental findings suggest that the age at disappearance of this response depends upon the rate of maturation of the olfactory system of the mouse pup. Current advances in techniques and the use of new methods have accelerated the discovery of genes affecting behavior.

What can be said for chromosome mapping of genes linked to behaviors in other species? We will restrict ourselves here to the human species and to psychiatric disorders. With respect to affective bipolar illness, Mendlewicz's work has suggested that the disease is dominant and X-linked. Roubertoux (1983) has dealt in detail with the question of whether these results can be extended to all cases of affective bipolar illness. He has suggested that this mode of transmission is restricted to a small number of families. In cases where the mapping of the gene associated with the disorder has been accomplished by using markers on the X-chromosome, the results show that the gene is near loci involved in color vision and G6PD (an electrophoretic variant). We will come back to the interpretation of these results later.

The fact that genetic correlates of behavior have been identified or even mapped on chromosomes will, in the future, lead to isolating these genes and cloning them. Does this type of result and these perspectives justify considering the relationship between genes and behavior as linear?

THE RELATIONSHIPS BETWEEN GENES AND BEHAVIOR

There are at least two arguments to support the point of view that the relationships between genes and behavior are nonlinear: a given morphological or behavioral trait is governed by different genetic mechanisms; and the effect of a gene may interact with the genotypic background and the environment.

Heterogeneity of Genetic Correlates for a Given Trait

The introduction of the anatomic-pathological approach in psychology postulates that there is a linear relationship between genes and behavior. According to this line of reasoning, a given gene is thought to govern one behavior or behavioral disorder. Thus, conversely, the identification of a disorder would provide a means of identifying the gene. We will refer to experimental findings demonstrating that this is not the case.

Attacking behavior in male mice has been analyzed from a genetic point of view in several inbred strains. The findings show that the "number of attacks" has either a genetic or a nongenetic basis, depending upon the genetic structure of the population (Carlier, 1985). The findings indicate that the segregating units involved vary as a function of the genetic pool of the population. Observed variation between NZB and CBA/H and between DBA/1J and C57BL/10By involve Y-chromosome differences. The differences between C57BL/6 and BALB/CBy involve autosomal genes.

A trait governed by a gene can be identified within a population and can be modified by the postnatal maternal environment in another population. The rooting response is controlled by a single gene in C57BL/6By and BALB/CBy and their recombinant inbred strains (Roubertoux et al., 1985, 1986), but the trait is modified by the postnatal maternal environment of other strains such as NZB and CBA/H (Carlier and Roubertoux, 1986), and XLII and C57BL/6 (Carlier and Roubertoux, 1985).

Let us now turn to the human species. The literature on psychiatric disorders clearly shows that there is a heterogeneous etiology for the majority of disorders as Freud suggested at the beginning of the century (Chiland and Roubertoux, 1976). Twin studies have demonstrated that there is a greater resemblance between monozygotes than between dizygotes, which suggests the presence of genetic components in the etiology. But the degree of resemblance of genetically identical individuals—the definition of monozygotes—is far below the 100 percent it should be if a purely genetic etiology were operant. For example, the rate of concordance for autistic monozygotic twins is over 90 percent in Ritvo's studies, whereas it is under 40 percent for Folstein and Rutter (1977). The rate of concordance for monozygotes exhibiting affective psychoses is below 67 percent (Roubertoux, 1983) against 17 percent for dizygotes. For some authors, the deviation from 100 percent is due to a variability of phenotypes related to gene expression. This argument, however, presupposes accepting the fact that there is a genetic basis to these disorders, whereas the twin method is designed precisely to test this eventuality. This is, thus, a case of circular reasoning that can be avoided only by adhering to the notion of an etiological heterogeneity for these disorders.

With respect to autism, it is likely that some cases have a genetic etiology. Other forms most probably have a nongenetic basis. As concerns the genetic etiologies, Spence et al. (1985) have provided extensive evidence for heterogeneous transmission. This is also the case for affective bipolar psychoses, where Roubertoux (1983) has pointed out that the hypothesis of an X-linked gene was incompatible with the transmission of the illness in certain families. Similarly, Comings (1979) showed that there is a linkage disequilibrium between affective bipolar psychoses and the Pc1A autosomal locus.

The idea of heterogeneity of the etiology of a given psychiatric disorder is in perfect agreement with what we have learned from the study of metabolic diseases, which is not surprising for the geneticist (Lamy et al., 1968). Thus, we have a system where identical effects are produced by different causes. This reasoning could be extended one step further: if the genes correlated with a given disorder are different, the physiological mechanisms underlying these disorders must be different as well.

Gene Interactions (Epistasis)

A given gene has different effects, depending upon the genetic context in which it is found. Plant genetics provides a multitude of examples of this type, and in the behavioral sciences the examples are equally abundant. What is termed epistasis corresponds to the fact that the effect of a given gene is modified by the effect of another gene. This concept covers a variety of mechanisms. To date, as regards behavior or the functioning of the nervous system, studies have been restricted to the identification of these effects, whereas their underlying mechanisms remain unknown. Several examples of behavioral epistasis will be given here.

Michard and Roubertoux (1985) obtained clear evidence, using a biometric method, that there is an interaction between homozygotic loci and heterozygotic loci for latency of retrieval of mouse pups by the female. A more direct demonstration is provided by Carlier for the analysis of attacking behavior in inbred strains of mice CBA/H(H) and

NZB(N). In generations produced by reciprocal backcrosses between H females and HNF1 males, the offspring differ only for the Y chromosome. The results show (Roubertoux and Carlier, 1984) that males with a Y chromosome from the N strain attack a standard opponent more often than those with the Y chromosome from the H strain. There is unquestionably a Y chromosome effect on aggressive behavior in male mice. Carlier (1985) bred special strains where the YN chromosome was transferred to a CBA/H background. The males in this new strain did not attack more than the CBA/H. This clearly illustrates that the YN chromosome effects on attacking behavior are not expressed in the absence of N autosomal genes. Comparing this result with findings for the reciprocal backcross shows that autosomal information from N can be present in a heterozygotic state.

Thus, epistasis forms an additional argument in favor of a nonlinear conception of the relationships between genes and behavior.

Genotypes and Maternal Environment

Given the length of time the maternal environment has an effect, especially among mammalian species of which we are one, the maternal environment plays a critical role. It is not only a buffer that filters and transforms information from the outside world, but it is the milieu in which and through which the genotype is expressed. This is why we will be concentrating, although not exclusively, upon additive and interactive effects between gene effects and this kind of environment.

Genes and environment: additive and interactive effects on behavioral phenotypes. There is interaction, in the strict sense of the word, when the association between the phenotypic variance and the genotype depends on the variance of the environments. The term *interaction* is rarely employed in this narrow sense by nongeneticists. Consequently, genotype-environment interaction is both the worst and the best concept that genetics has produced: the worst, in that it can be used artificially to squeeze the data to fit a model of genetic transmission; the best because it can be one of the most useful tools we possess when it is used with the purpose of increasing our knowledge of the mechanisms through which a gene or a set of gene effects are modified. This clearly implies that no one can speak seriously about G × E interaction without first having defined the gene and being in a position to measure its effects in different environments. Thus, genotype-environment interaction effects are difficult to demonstrate in species such as ours, where ethics prevent experimental manipulations of this type. Nonetheless, findings on different treatments used to combat metabolic disorders are good examples of this form of interaction.

Psychologists often tend to pay exclusive attention to socioaffective environmental parameters. The environment, however, is biological before being social. And the environment is first and foremost prenatal. Two components of the prenatal maternal effect—namely, the uterine component and the cytoplasmic component—must be defined in particular when investigating prenatal effects in mammals. The cytoplasmic effect itself can be broken down into the environmental cytoplasmic effect and the genetic cytoplasmic effect. In mammals, the embryo has a relatively long uterine existence and differences between uterine environments may have an effect on the development of the embryo and later on the development of a certain number of traits, whether these are behavioral or not. The environment begins in the cytoplasm, at the nuclear membrane.

It has been demonstrated that differences between cytoplasms may be related to differences in progeny phenotypes. A prenatal effect of this type can be considered as environmental because it arises from the egg cytoplasm (even if the cytoplasm is influenced by nuclear genes). Finally, a cytoplasmic effect can be due to extranuclear inheritance, so termed because the genetic information is located outside the nuclear chromosomes: mitrochondrial DNA has been identified in eucaryotes, although its effects are not well known.

Postnatal maternal influence is the other source of environmental variance that can influence offspring phenotypic development, especially in mammals. It can be divided into several factors, including nutrition and caregiving. These different components, and their additive or interactive effects on gene expression, can clearly be identified and experimentally manipulated in mice. The examples of interactive effects we will be presenting will serve as a basis for a demonstration of the nonlinearity of gene-behavior relationships. The effect of the components of the maternal environment has been demonstrated for behavioral phenotypes either singly or in conjunction with the effect of the genotypes (additive or interactive effects). Carlier and Roubertoux (1986) have reviewed the literature in this field, but we will limit ourselves here to a few illustrations.

Cytoplasmic effects have seldom been reported for animal species and are even more rare for mammals. This is a natural consequence of the technical obstacles encountered in experimentation of this type. But with an adequate technique (ovary transplant in situ and appropriate crosses) it is possible to demonstrate cytoplasmic effects for sensory-motor development in pre-weaned mice (Nosten and Roubertoux, 1985).

Controversy surrounds the presence of prenatal maternal effects on behavioral phenotypes since they are extremely difficult to demonstrate. One successful procedure is the joint use of ovary transplants in situ and cross-fostering methods. This combination of techniques serves to produce subjects carried in different uterine environments, while keeping the effects of the postnatal maternal environment constant. The results have led us to the following conclusions:

- The uterine environment acts upon behavioral phenotypes observed either during development or during adulthood (e.g., aggressive behavior; Roubertoux and Carlier, 1984).
- The uterine environment has different effects as a function of the phenotype exposed to it.

The cross-fostering method has clearly demonstrated, as regards the maternal postnatal environment, that the same phenotype can develop at different rates in different postnatal maternal environments. The most interesting result is that two different genotypes react entirely differently to the same maternal postnatal environment.

For example, in a cross-fostering experiment, we have shown an effect for age at eye opening. NZB pups reared by NZB mothers open their eyes at 17.5 days, but at 14.5 days when they are reared by CBA/H mothers. CBA/H pups are not affected by cross fostering for the trait.

The following conclusions can be drawn as concerns the data on genotype-environment interactions:

1. Interactions are not the general rule.

2. Interactions have varying effects depending upon the type of behavior observed. For strains N and H, for example, sensory-motor development and aggression are affected by variation in early environment, whereas, as regards the production of ultrasounds, parental behavior is entirely under genetic control.

3. Genotype × early maternal environment interactions have varying effects depending upon the age at which the behavior is observed. Some effects can still be seen in adult subjects (number of attacks and ethanol absorption). Others disappear with age. For example, in a cross-fostering experiment using two strains of mice (NZB and CBA/H) we measured weight from weaning to forty-two days. At weaning the effect of the adoptive strain is significant, but this effect disappears with age: at forty-two days only the genotype has an effect.

4. It seems likely that interaction effects depend on the population

under consideration. A battery of sensory-motor tests was used with different strains of mice observed with their own mothers or with foster mothers. The results vary as a function of the strain of the foster mothers—in other words, as a function of the nature of the postnatal maternal environment. Interaction also depends upon the strain of the pups. This leads us to suspect a variation in sensitivity to environmental effects. We will return to this point when discussing the physiological mechanisms underlying interaction.

5. It is highly probable that gene × environment interaction is dependent upon the time when changes in the environment occur. Thus, studies on G × E interactions must also take the presence of a critical period into account. We will deal with this point later as well.

Physiological mechanisms underlying G × E interactions. Certain authors have attempted to characterize strains in terms of their sensitivity or lack of sensitivity to the environment. In 1981, Roubertoux suggested that there were genetic correlates to this sensitivity. Christine Michard (1984, 1986) has been able to show the relevance of this hypothesis via a more general paradigm based on the hypothesis that an early injection of male steroids would produce a masculinization of female behavior, in particular attacking behavior in females in response to males attempting to mate. The protocol was the following: the animals, aged seventy-two hours, were injected with a 1 mg solution of testosterone. After weaning, the females were isolated and then tested at the age of about two months, during attempted mating by one male. The females that had received testosterone showed a high frequency of attacking behavior. The identical protocol was used first by Vale, Ray, and Ray (1972) and then by Michard on two strains: BALB/C and C57BL/6. The findings of both studies are consistent: B6 mice do not react to treatment, whereas BALB/C do. Several experiments have shown that this sensitivity difference was due to genetic factors.

The identification of genetic factors in differences in reactivity to early androgenization in BALB/C and C57BL/6 is the first step toward an investigation of the physiological targets of these genetic components. In other words, which physiological mechanisms reveal an interaction between genotype and environment as regards early exposure to testosterone? The most likely explanation is that there is an early critical period of sensitivity to testosterone that presents different characteristics in BALB/C and C57BL/6.

Undeniably, treatments used to correct metabolic disorders, as well as the effects of neurological mutations in animals, are only effective if they are administered at a specific moment of their existence, often at a very early age. Take, for example, the case of PKU in humans. This is a recessive autosomal disorder, which is accompanied by mental disability. A treatment, however, is known: change in diet modifies I.Q., and figures clearly show that I.Q. decreases if the onset of the treatment takes place too late. Treatment that starts two years after birth has no effect. Other examples from the field of metabolic disorders have led to similar conclusions. Does this mean that there is a single critical period? We personally do not think so. Rather, we believe that there is a critical period for a given treatment for a given disorder. Thus, there are numerous critical periods.

Let us turn now to nonpathological development. In a genetic analysis of sensory-motor development in the mouse, we have shown that responses obey different determinisms and those for which we identified the genetic determinisms arose in fact from different genetic mechanisms. Thus there is no one general genetic factor of development. If the underlying genotypic mechanisms differ, the physiological targets affected are also different. Consequently, the way neuronal maturation is affected and the way the nervous system structures are formed differ according to responses. Thus, it can be stated that each response would correspond to a different treatment and that the critical period for this treatment also differs.

CONCLUSIONS

Genes are related to behavior. We have deliberately chosen to limit this presentation to identified genetic correlates of behavior, eliminating reference to the numerous cases in which these correlations are nothing more than the outcome of convergent suppositions, in order not to weaken the demonstration.

We have stressed that gene-behavior relationships are nonlinear. Three major facts support this point of view:

1. Several genes can produce the same behavioral phenotype independently.
2. An identified gene may interact with other genes to produce a given behavioral phenotype.
3. A given gene may interact with several components of the maternal environment, beginning in the first instants after gametic fusion.

REFERENCES

Carlier, M. (1985). "Differences between NZB and CBA/H Mice on Intermale Aggression: Test of Y Chromosome Effect through use of Congenic Strains CBA/H-YN and NZB-YH." *Behavior Genetics* 15, no. 6:586–587.

Carlier, M., and Roubertoux, P. (1985). "Motor Development of Newborn Mice: Genetic-Analysis." In C. J. Brainerd, V. F. Reyna, eds., *Developmental Psychology.* Amsterdam: Elsevier/North-Holland.

Carlier, M., and Roubertoux, P. (1986). "Le développement des comportements: Effets des interactions entre le génotype et l'environnement maternel." *Confrontations psychiatriques* 1:52–76.

Chiland, C., and Roubertoux, P. (1976). "Freud et l'hérédité." *Bulletin de psychologie* 29:337–343.

Comings, D. E. (1979). "Pc1 Duarte: A Common Polymorphism of Human Brain Protein and Its Relationship to Depressive Disease and Multiple Sclerosis." *Nature* 277:28–32.

Folstein, S., and Rutter, M. (1977). "Infantile Autism: A Genetic Study of 21 Twin Pairs." *J. Child Psychol. Psychiatry* 18:297–331.

Green, M. C. (1981). *Genetic Variants and Strains of the Laboratory Mouse.* Stuttgart: Fisher.

Lamy, M.; Royer, P.; Frezal, J., and Rey, J. (1968). *Maladies héréditaires du métabolisme.* Paris: Masson.

Lenington, S., and Egid, K. (1985). "Female Discrimination of Male Odors Correlated with Male Genotype at the T Locus: Response to the T Locus or H-2 Variability." *Behavior Genetics* 15:53–68.

Michard, C. (1984). "Strain X Early Androgen Exposure on Aggressive Behavior in Female Mice." *Behavior Genetics* 14:610.

Michard, C., and Roubertoux, P. (1985). "Application des modèles mendéliens à la transmission de caractères comportementaux dans le cas particulier de souches consanguines." In R. Ghiglione, ed., *Comprendre l'homme, construire des modèles.* Paris: CNRS, Comportements, 131–140.

Michard-Vanhee, C. (1988). "Aggressive Behavior Induced in Female Mice by an Early Single Injection of Testosterone Is Genotype Dependent." *Behavior Genetics* 18:1–12.

Nosten, M., and Roubertoux, P. (1985). "Early Sensory Motor Development in NZB and CBA/H Mice." *Behavior Genetics* 15:603.

Roubertoux, P. (1983). "Application de l'analyse génétique aux psychoses affectives." In H. Cuche, A. Gerard, H. Loo, and E. Zarifian, eds., *Psychiatrie biologique.* Paris: Pharmuka, 17–28.

Roubertoux, P., and Carlier, M. (1984). "Differences between NZB and CBAZ/H on Intermale Aggression: Maternal Effect and/or Y-Chromosome Effect?" *Behavior Genetics* 14, no. 6:614.

Roubertoux, P.; Baumann, L.; Ragueneau, S.; and Semal, C. (1987). "Early

Development in Mice. IV, Age at Disappearance of the Rooting Response; Genetic Analysis in Newborn Mice." *Behavior Genetics* 17:453–464.

Roubertoux, P.; Semal, C.; and Ragueneau, S. (1985). "Early Development in Mice: II, Sensory Motor Behavior and Genetic Analysis." *Physiology and Behavior* 35:659–666.

Spence, A. M.; Ritvo, E. R.; Marazita, M. L.; Funderbunk, S. J., Sparkes, R. S., and Freeman, B. J. (1985). "Gene Mapping Studies with the Syndrome of Autism." *Behavior Genetics* 15:1–14.

Vale, J. R., Ray, D., and Ray, C. A. (1972). "The Interaction of Genotype and Exogenous Neonatal Androgen: Agonistic Behavior in Female Mice." *Behavioral Biology* 7:321–334.

Yamazaki, K.; Beauchamp, G. K.; Wysocki, C. J.; Bard, J.; Thomas, L.; and Boyse, F. A. (1983). "Recognition of H-2 Type in Relation to the Blocking of Pregnancy in Mice." *Science* 221:186–188.

8

Gender Identity Development and Prognosis: A Summary

ROBERT J. STOLLER

Let me begin with a vocabulary review. *Gender identity* refers to a complex system of beliefs about oneself: a sense of one's masculinity and femininity. It implies nothing about the origins of that sense (e.g., whether the person is male or female). It has, then, psychologic connotations only: one's subjective state. I find it preferable to *sexual identity,* a term that leaves unclear whether *sexual* is a synonym for "erotic," "biologic sex," "masculinity and femininity," or a combination of all (meanings that one or another author has given to *sexual identity*).

By *sex* I mean "male" and "female," with the criteria for definition being purely biologic: chromosomes and their genes, external genitals, internal sexual apparatuses (e.g., prostate, uterus), gonads, secondary sex characteristics and sex hormonal state, and brain.

By *masculinity* and *femininity* I mean only what the person, as a result of development and of his or her being the repository of a culture's definitions, believes are masculinity and femininity.

By *core gender identity* I mean the sense we have of the sex to which we belong: that we feel we are a male or female (regardless of whether we feel we are competently male or female) or, in the rare case, a sense of being either both male and female or neither male nor female (hermaphroditic identity). This mental "structure" (in fact a set of permanent beliefs) is the first part of gender identity to develop and is pretty much unalterable after age four or five.

Sex assignment is the societal act performed at birth when, after inspection of the external genitals, parents are told—and confirm for themselves—that their infant is a male, a female, or in the rare case, a hermaphrodite.

DEVELOPMENT

Three theories serve at present to explain how gender identity develops; each has findings to support its position. Let me summarize them, at first ignoring that theorists may use combinations of each.

The first is *biologic*. The forces called up in this position are genes, prenatal hormones that organize the brain for later gender and erotic behavior, postnatal hormones at critical periods in development, disease processes (e.g., temporal lobe tumor). The second is *behavioristic* (learning theory): positive and negative reinforcements of gender behavior, from infancy on, shape gender identity fortuitously, with the strength of these reinforcements and their timing being crucial. The third is the *developmental/psychodynamic:* the desires and dangers the infant/child experiences in its relationships with mother and father (the oedipal situation) create conflicts, the responses to which gradually congeal into identity.

My version of gender development finds all three factors crucial and perhaps equally important. ("Perhaps" summarizes my awareness that the three factors are as yet unquantifiable.) Starting before birth is the biologic. Animal experiments invariably show and human "natural experiments" invariably confirm that mammalian tissue (except for the testes and certain Wolffian structures) in its resting state is protofemale and becomes male only when androgens are present: the right kind, in the right amount, and at the right time in development. This occurs regardless of chromosomes (XX in females and XY in males). So, if androgens are appropriately present in fetal life, an anatomic male develops, and if they are absent, a female. In addition, the brain, in the presence of these androgens, is androgenized, that is, organized in a male direction, which, in postnatal development, will produce the behavior, including reproductive, typical of males of that species. In human "natural experiments" (e.g., certain prenatal enzymatic disorders of androgen physiology), we find subjects who, from childhood on, behave as we would expect members of the opposite sex and, as adults, wish to be reassigned as members of the opposite sex, choosing their erotic objects from those of the opposite sex (these findings are reviewed in Money and Ehrhardt, 1972).

The second factor—conditioning as a cause of gender identity—is less intensely investigated in animals and humans. Nonetheless, observations of mother-infant interplay and, later in childhood, father-child interplay show how positive reinforcement of a behavior and thereby the attitudes underlying that behavior can be encouraged or discouraged by parents and later by siblings, peers, teachers, society at large—e.g., the media (these findings are reviewed in Green, 1987).

The third factor—developmental/psychodynamic—reveals a process ignored by the other two: the role of conflict, frustration, and pain—physical or psychic—in forcing the infant/child to defend itself. The chronic, habitual, permanent defenses thereby raised become the "structure" called identity. Since this third factor is at the center of my work, let me expand on it.

Invented by Freud, this model has been the classical description of the development of masculinity and femininity (or, as he put it, of "sexuality"). Let me review Freud's description, first for males and then for females. Given the importance of biologic factors—scarcely dreamed of, much less described, in Freud's life—the boy has two usually insuperable advantages over girls: he starts out heterosexual, since his first love object is a female, his mother; and he has a visible, highly sensual organ—his penis—to embody and signal his maleness. But despite the at first unabashed intensity of this combination—a male body that expresses his desire for his mother—he is psychologically and biologically far too immature to work out a successful system for gratifying his desires. In addition, he senses his father—large, mature, competent—as an overwhelmingly powerful rival. So he must give up hope for his mother and postpone till later years his heterosexual drives. If his mother helps him, without marked trauma and frustration, he is a good way toward resolving this dangerous conflict. And if his father serves as a measure for masculinity and also implies a promise of future heterosexual success, the boy proceeds with his gender and erotic development.

The girl, on the other hand, has, for Freud, essentially insuperable problems that can be only assuaged, not solved (this being the reason women, Freud believed, are so damaged in character structure). First, the girl starts with a homosexual, not heterosexual love object. So she must perform an act of great renunciation in order to move to a heterosexual mode, that is, desire for her father. Second, she, with (as Freud saw it) an inadequate genital—out of sight and erotically immature as well as incompetent—must spend her development chronically disappointed and envious. Her chances of negotiating these perils are poor.

My version of gender development differs from Freud's in two ways, one inconsequential, the other significant (Stoller, 1968, 1975, 1985). The inconsequential difference is that I have available the biologic and behavioristic research done since Freud's time. So I can better describe—precisely at times—how these factors work in development and—great comfort—can refer to them knowing they are not simply speculations in a philosophic discourse. The consequential factor is my noting a stage in gender development—core gender identity—that begins at birth and therefore precedes the period when Freud's description begins. In my[1] version, the first stage of gender development is spent with the infant, male and female, more or less merged physically and psychologically with mother, only gradually becoming aware of a separation. This merging is powerfully reinforced by biologic necessity, neoteny that produces an infant unable to survive birth without mother's presence. This presence is not only life-and-death necessity to the infant but also, to the extent that it approaches perfection, the ultimate happiness—bliss; absence of pain, distress, frustration, terror. There are, of course, biologic forces (e.g., neuromuscular development) that push an infant toward separating from mother's body and psyche. (In lower animals, these are more marked in males than females; I suspect that is so in humans as well.) But if something should interfere with the natural unfolding of separation—if the infant, male or female, is too close, too long, too blissfully—then the infant's sensing himself or herself as a creature separate from mother is delayed. Should that happen with a girl, whatever the price in the development of independence and competence, merging with mother's body and psyche ("identification") favors femininity. Unfortunately, the same holds for the boy: he too may become feminine if this influence is powerfully present.

Because the pull to mother is so enticing, so gratifying, a boy must create inside himself a dam against this pull that is also inside him. This barrier—this set of beliefs, desires, counterdesires, opinions about oneself and others—I have called "symbiosis anxiety" or "merging anxiety." It takes the form of fantasies (though I believe its underpinning is biologically and behavioristically reinforced) that tell the boy he does not want to be a female, to be like a female, or to be too close to females lest their femaleness and femininity pull him back to that earliest, blissful, protofeminine state. Much of that defined as masculinity by all cultures in all eras is, I believe, the manifestations of this hidden process.

Girls, on the other hand, need not create the same barrier to symbiosis. Though they must do something of the same sort in order to become separate beings, society's demands—reinforcements—do not push them to avoid femininity.

---

1. "My" connotes squatters' more than discoverers' rights, for others have, in one way or another, disagreed with Freud's description.

The resultant rules, confirmable by observations (reported elsewhere), are as follows:

1. If a boy is held too intimately, with too little frustration, with too much pleasure, and too long against his mother's body *and* psyche, he is at risk for maldeveloping his masculinity.
2. The risk increases when his father is not sufficiently present to shield the son against this mother's influence and is not present as a model for masculinity.
3. When, in the case of a girl, the mother-infant symbiosis is disrupted, the child risks becoming masculine.
4. The risk increases the more her father moves in and is intrusively present.
5. The stronger these factors, the greater the gender reversal.

Two examples test the rules: the most feminine of biologically intact males and the most masculine of biologically intact females. In the origins of both the mother-infant symbiosis is a powerful factor. When extremely feminine boys are studied in childhood, I find (Stoller, 1968, 1975, 1985) that their mothers try to maintain indefinitely a blissfully intimate symbiosis with their son, he being chosen over his mother's other children because she perceived him from birth on to be physically beautiful, cuddly, and loving. And in all these cases, father is an absent nonentity. The reverse dominates the situation with extremely masculine girls, where mother was unable (e.g., because sorely depressed) to function adequately as a mother during this daughter's infancy, the baby having been perceived by the mother as not pretty, not feminine, not cuddly. And in each case, the child's father moves into the vacuum caused by mother's inability to mother, with father being the close parent. Unfortunately (and this exemplifies the behavioristic aspects of the etiology), father and daughter join not in a heterosexual style but with father encouraging his daughter to be like him.

This theory of the development of masculinity and femininity is too general, however, to explain convincingly the origins and dynamics of the various aberrations of gender identity. To do so requires, I believe, a better knowledge than we yet have of infantile and childhood conflicts and defenses.

Nonetheless, in recent years, I think I have caught a glimpse of *a* dynamic that contributes to these perverse conditions. They may be the outcome of efforts to defend oneself against humiliation, with the gender disorder and its related erotic behavior functioning to reverse, undo, and replace the humiliation, transforming trauma to overt or hidden triumph. The memory and form of the humiliation of childhood is re-peated, in the adult aberrance, but now with a happy conclusion. Thus the pedophile is likely to have been a sexually abused child and the transvestite to have been forced into humiliating cross-dressing as a child.

PROGNOSIS

What happens to people with manifest gender disorders without or with treatment? Though dozens of papers and books have been published on this subject, I believe the prognosis, in children and adults, with or without treatment—and regardless of the kind of treatment—is guarded if one's hope is to undo the gender reversal. I shall not, in discussing this issue, review or cite the literature (having done so elsewhere; Stoller, 1985) but shall try to present, impres-sionistically, a reliable summary drawn from a generation of both pub-lished reports and absences of reports (e.g., the failure to publish follow-up studies).

Gender Disorders in Adults

Let me organize this discussion by using a differential diagnostic sys-tem that, though rough-and-ready, differentiates gender disorders. I begin with adults, since conditions present in adults may be invisible or absent in children.

Transsexualism. I divide transsexualism—the sense of belonging to the opposite sex and of wanting to change one's anatomy to fit that inner sense of sex—into primary and secondary. By "primary" I mean (1) that the condition appears at the start of identity development, (2) that it does not change (if not treated) throughout life, and (3) that these primary transsexuals have the most extreme gender reversal. Second-ary transsexualism (1) first manifests not in infancy but at any time from later childhood through to senescence, (2) with the patients having less extreme gender reversal than do primary transsexuals, and (3) usually with episodes of behavior (masculinity in a male, femininity in a female) appropriate for the patient's sex. Primary transsexualism is much rarer than secondary.

The literature reports few cases of transsexuals, children or adults, treated by nonsomatic methods. One, a teenage male, underwent be-havior modification and was reported to have become masculine after being feminine and to have changed from erotically desiring males to desiring females. But no follow-up into adult life was published. Two boys became more masculine after treatment by psychoanalysts, but no follow-ups have been published in the years since the first reports. (Failure to follow up treatment may cover treatment failure.) I know of no lasting successful change (i.e., to sex-appropriate gender behavior and sex-appropriate object choice) by means of psychoanalysis, psychoanalytically oriented psychotherapy, or other psychotherapies.

In the past, somatic therapies were tried. Same-sex hormones were used, for example, to make a feminine male feel masculine. This treatment technique failed. Reports of brain interventions have been repudiated. The principle treatment in transsexuals, primary or secondary, has been alteration of anatomy—by administering opposite-sex hormones, removing gonads to deplete same-sex hormones, producing or removing facial and body hair, using cosmetic surgery to change secondary sex characteristics, and transforming genital appearance to approximate that of the opposite sex. Proponents of these procedures report good results, and those opposed report poor results. The research methods used to measure outcome are so crude, so far from the mark of measuring what they claim, so based on superficial report that they are, to me, useless. In addition, the price paid in surgical complications and poor appearance of the altered genitals—findings universally understated in the reports—is high.

My impression, from following a few operated patients for one to two decades and from trying to decipher clouded research reports of others, is that primary transsexuals do better, on the whole, with these procedures than do secondary transsexuals, though some of the latter do as well in fitting into the world as do the former. Nonetheless, the primary transsexuals I have talked with for years express not only their relief in having gotten the treatment but their awareness that it was not enough and that they are forever condemned to not achieving the goal of truly changing their sex. From secondary transsexuals are recruited, I believe, those who revert to their original sex, who become deeply depressed, who become otherwise mentally disturbed, and who sue their physicians.

At present, I agree with those few colleagues who say that most patients wanting sex reassignment are best served by a psychotherapy that, in revealing the realities of the treatment and its outcome, teaches them to live with the gender disorder since they cannot be cured.

Transvestism (fetishistic cross-dressing). This condition, found almost exclusively in males and usually not manifested before puberty, has not been treated successfully, to judge from the literature, by any method. There are, however, a handful of optimistic reports regarding psychotherapy and behavior modification but none that describes how the patients did as the years passed. My experience is that the condition persists.

Gender-disordered homosexuality. No matter what the treatment used with homosexuals, male or female, gender-aberrant or not, the literature at present swings markedly between the optimism of proponents of a particular treatment technique (and their related pessimism for the techniques of others) and negative appraisals of these techniques. This holds whether the treatment be analysis, psychotherapy, or behavior modification. (Use of same-sex hormones has been abandoned following clear-cut failures.) The reports are so suspect as to describing precisely the nature of the treatment, the nature of the patients, controls, and follow-up that we should preserve our skepticism.

Intersexuality. By "intersexuality" I mean demonstrably genetic, anatomic, and/or physiologic defect in one or another aspect of biologic sex (e.g., chromosomes, external genitals, gonads). There are, of course, many conditions in this category, and so I shall make do now with a few generalizations. Treatment of the anatomic/physiologic defects should be based not on the defects themselves but on the gender identity present. For instance, in a person with unquestioned belief that he is a male but who has hermaphroditic genitals, the genitals should be dealt with according to his core gender identity—that is, his unswerving belief that he is a male. If the same physical condition is found in a person who feels unequivocally female, then the appropriate hormonal/surgical decisions will again depend on the state not of the anatomy but of the identity. When, however, the intersexuality is found at birth or within the first two or three years of life, the decisions can be based on the ease with which the hormonal/surgical problems can be solved, since, in general, gender identity is not finally set in the first years of life. (Should research show that the above is not true and that permanent aspects of gender identity are laid down as early as the first months of life, then decisions about anatomy will be made on this new understanding of early fixity of gender identity.)

Psychosis and gender identity. There are rare cases where desire for sex change and psychosis—not schizophrenic—coexist. When these patients have had physical sex reassignment treatment—hormones and/or surgery—the psychosis has mitigated or disappeared.

Gender Disorder in Children

As noted, the above differential diagnosis does not manifest clinically in children. What does is cross-gender behavior, primarily dressing in the clothes of the opposite sex (without erotic excitement), interest in games and stories usually only with members of the opposite sex, and styles of behavior (e.g., walking, talking) typical of members of the opposite sex. To the psychoanalyst, this would seem the ideal group at which to aim treatment, before behaviors become fixed in the forms seen in adolescents and adults. Surprisingly, however, there are only a handful of reports from psychoanalysts (some still not published) and from behaviorists attempting to straighten the twig before the tree grows bent. In none is there a follow-up by the therapists to show whether the successes were sustained. For children treated behavioristically, I know that in the paradigmatic case, representing for the researchers the best example of their treatment technique and outcome, the result has been a gender-disordered adolescent. The researchers have published no follow-ups of their series into adolescence.

Two extensive studies following gender-disordered children for ten to fifteen and more years agree that the majority of gender-disordered children, treated or not, are gender-disordered young adults (Green, 1987; Zuger, 1984). One of these projects (Green, 1987) also used controls (non-gender-disordered children); none of the controls has become aberrant gender-wise. With no proven treatment of children (but with no proof we must despair), we clearly need more research. Unless we learn differently, we probably should treat such children.

A pretty bleak picture emerges, indicating that we have few reliable data, poor research methodologies, unknown outcomes, profound disagreements among experts, strongly stated but poorly supported opinions, and powerful treatment maneuvers with sometimes inalterable consequences based on insufficient knowledge. An unedifying spectacle.

REFERENCES

Green, R. (1987). *The "Sissy Boy Syndrome" and the Development of Homosexuality*. New Haven: Yale University Press.
Money, J., and Ehrhardt, A. A. (1972). *Man and Woman, Boy and Girl*. Baltimore: Johns Hopkins University Press.
Stoller, R. J. (1968). *Sex and Gender*. Vol. 1. New York: Science House.

———— (1975). *Sex and Gender.* Vol. 2. London: International Psycho-
Analytical Library.

———— (1985). *Presentations of Gender.* New Haven: Yale University Press.

Zuger, B. (1984). "Early Effeminate Behavior in Boys." *Journal of Nervous
and Mental Disease* 172:90–97.

9

The Effects of Early Maternal Deprivation and Later Family Experience on Adolescents

JILL HODGES

BARBARA TIZARD

In 1951, Bowlby characterized maternal deprivation as "not uncommonly almost complete in institutions . . . where the child often has no one person who cares for him in a personal way and with whom he feels secure." We shall discuss a study of children whose earliest years were spent in institutions which, though they provided good physical care and opportunities for cognitive development, offered very little opportunity for the children to make close attachments to an adult.

The children were mainly illegitimate and entered residential nurseries as very young infants. By the time they were age two, an average of twenty-four different caregivers had looked after them for at least a week; by age four, the average for those children remaining in the institutions was fifty. So, on average, there was a change of major caregiver for every month of the child's life. There was an explicit policy against allowing a close attachment to develop between children and the staff who cared for them; a child who became specifically attached to one adult tended to disrupt the smooth running of the group, and because any such attachments that did develop were inevitably going to be broken, it was felt that to allow them to develop was fair neither to staff member nor to child. As Barbara Tizard's work has documented (Tizard and Tizard, 1971; Tizard and Rees, 1975; Tizard, 1977), the children's attachment behavior was very unusual. At two, they would run to be picked up when any familiar staff member came in and cry when he or she left, but they were more fearful of strangers than a home-reared comparison group. By the age of four, 70 percent of those still in institutions were said by the staff "not to care deeply about anyone."

At various ages after two and half years, most of the study children left the institutions, the majority being adopted and some "restored" to their biological parent. This move into a family represented the children's first real chance to make close, selective, mutual attachments to adults. So the study took the form of a natural experiment; it is rare for a child's life to undergo such a radical change. Usually a poor early environment continues and becomes a poor later one. To state the question in general terms, this study allows us to look at whether experiences in the early years have an effect on later functioning *despite* the change to a more adequate environment, suggesting that the early years are a "critical" or "sensitive" period; or whether the effects of early institutionalization are entirely reversible if children spend long enough in a family setting.

Families differ, however, and there were considerable differences between the adoptive and "restored" families. Adoptive parents were older, always two-parent families, predominantly middle class, and less likely to have other children. They put more time into shared activities with their child and were usually ready to accept very dependent behavior, initially, from the child placed with them. This was in sharp contrast to the parents of restored children, who expected greater independence of their young child, much more so than the parents of home-reared children let alone of adopted ones (Tizard, 1977).

So, as well as comparing children who were previously in institutional care with children who had grown up in their families, we can compare children who were restored to biological parents with children who were adopted. Although by this stage we have only a very small group of restored adolescents, the comparison is still worth making because this is an issue on which very little information is available.

DESCRIPTION OF THE STUDY

Figure 9.1 illustrates the basic structure of the study. Over time, more children moved from the institutions either into an adoptive family or to a biological parent, forming the two groups of study children. So few children were still in institutions at age sixteen, and their histories were so varied, that we cannot sensibly present systematic data on them as a group. The figure indicates the ages at which the children were studied. Some were seen in institutions at two, and all were fol-

Figure 9.1 *Illustration of changes over the course of the study in numbers and composition of groups.*

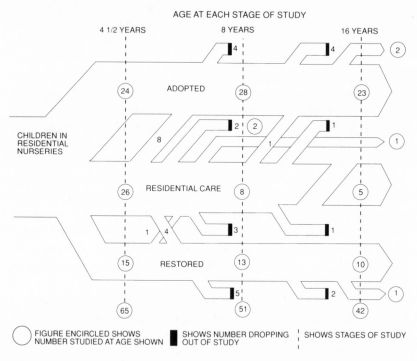

AGE AT EACH STAGE OF STUDY

lowed at four and a half, eight, and sixteen years. The findings of the study up to age eight have been described fully in Barbara Tizard's book (Tizard, 1977); here we focus mainly on the sixteen-year-old stage.

Comparison groups. We compared the study children with children who had always lived in their families. At earlier stages we used a comparison group of working-class children born into two-parent families. When we studied them as adolescents, we paired each study sixteen-year-old with a comparison adolescent matched for age, sex, position in family, one- or two-parent family, and occupational classification of the main breadwinner. At ages eight and sixteen we also used classmate comparison groups, asking the teachers to complete questionnaires on the named study child and on the same-sex classmate next in age to the child.

Attrition. Figure 9.1 also shows the *number* of children we were able to see at each age level. Inevitably, these numbers decrease over the course of a long study. Though we succeeded in tracing all the families, some had gone abroad and some refused to see us. From age four, when the full group was first seen, to age sixteen, the rate of attrition was 35 percent. The large-scale National Child Development Study (Lambert and Streather, 1980) lost a similar proportion of adopted children by the age of eleven. The question of attrition bias will be considered as the findings are reported.

Assessment. The parents and adolescents were seen in their homes. The parent was interviewed and completed the "A" scale questionnaire (developed and reported by Rutter et al. in 1970) on the adolescent's behavior. The adolescent was interviewed and filled in a questionnaire on social difficulty (Lindsay and Lindsay, 1982), and the study adolescents were tested on the WAIS (Wechsler, 1955). With the permission of the parents and the adolescents, the school was asked to complete the "B" scale (Rutter, 1967; Rutter et al., 1970) and an additional questionnaire devised for the study, which focused on relationships with teachers, other adults, and peers. Teachers also completed these measures for the same-sex classmate next in age to the adolescent, forming the school comparison group. The matched comparison group was assessed in the same way as the study adolescents, except that the WAIS was not given.

RESULTS

We shall look briefly at cognitive developments, then at behavioral adjustment, and then at the area of social and family relationships.

Figure 9.2 shows mean WAIS I.Q. scores and means for the same children on the WISC at age eight. Evidently, there has been little change for children remaining in the same setting, and the adopted children's mean scores are considerably higher.

So what was the picture before this? Again, the figure shows that at age four and a half restored children scored around the average, adopted children well above; and there was not a great deal of change between four and a half and eight. The interval between the two scores for each group at each age level shows the effect of attrition. There was no indication that the striking difference between the groups could be accounted for by the loss of high-scoring children from the restored group and low-scoring adoptees.

Why should we find this considerable I.Q. difference between the groups? Did the adopted children come from more intelligent biological parents? Were they selected for adoption because they were brighter?

Figure 9.2 *Trends in I.Q. scores for children placed before four and one-half years.*

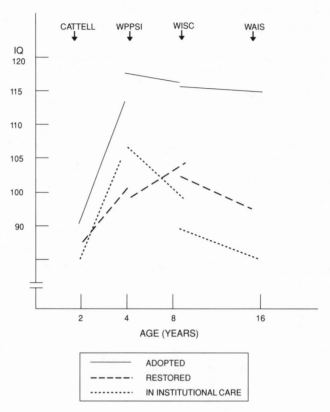

That is, did placement depend on I.Q.? Or did the different placements, adoption or restoration, *produce* the I.Q. difference?

Selective placement does not in our view account for the difference. We do not know the I.Q.s of the biological parents of the adopted children, but their occupational status was, if anything, lower than that of the parents whose children were restored. Nor was there evidence that the children were differentially placed according to how bright they were. No I.Q. assessments were made of the children for placement purposes. We tested some of the children at the age of two, but the scores were not made available to the staff. As the figure shows, the Cattell scores of those who stayed in the institutions were all but identical to those of the children who were adopted. But at age four, the mean score of the adopted group was much higher than that of the restored children. Simply leaving the institution for a family did not automatically mean a large I.Q. rise; the type of placement mattered. Adoptive parents, as already described, spent much more time and emotional energy on their child, and they were predominantly middle class. As one would expect, we found social class itself significantly related to I.Q.

The mean scores of the different groups did not alter greatly after age four and a half. This raises the question of whether adoption *after* four and a half has as dramatic an effect on I.Q. as earlier adoption. We have only nine cases to go on, adopted between four years seven months and nine years ten months of age; by sixteen, six children's I.Q. had not risen by more than a few points or had fallen; but three showed increases of 10 I.Q. points or more. So adoption *after* four and a half did not in this study lead to I.Q. increases with either the speed or the frequency apparent in the earlier-placed children.

Clearly, then, early institutional care has not resulted in intellectual deficits of the kind found in the earliest studies, where the institution was often grossly depriving. But what stands out is that different types of placement are associated with different I.Q. scores.

How far is the same pattern found if we turn from cognitive development to behavior and adjustment? When the children were eight, we found that behavior difficulties were noted at school rather than at home, with teachers reporting about half the ex-institutional children as showing restlessness, distractibility, and poor peer relations, a constellation of problems very similar in type, if not in severity, to those described in the early studies (Goldfarb, 1945). By age sixteen, fewer of the study children showed these problems, but still between a third and a half were to some degree restless and distractible, quarrelsome with peers, irritable and resentful if corrected by adults. At eight, adopted and restored children had not shown differences in their general pattern of difficulties, but we found that by age sixteen adopted adolescents were reported to show more behaviors indicating anxiety than their comparisons, whereas the restored group tended more toward antisocial types of behavior or apathy—also noted, incidentally, in Goldfarb's group in 1945. Not only did the restored adolescents show more problems at school overall than the adopted children, but most of the restored children had had considerable problems at school when they were eight. None of these had improved substantially by the time they were sixteen, in contrast to adoptees, where improvement occurred in most such cases. Any comparisons, however, must be tentative because of the small numbers of children involved.

On the Rutter "B" scale (teachers' inventory), we found that neither group of study adolescents scored significantly above their classmate comparisons. In relation to their matched comparison, however, their mean problem scores were significantly higher. That is, the study children's difficulties appeared most strongly when compared with children matched for family circumstances. Similarly, the National Child Development Study (Lambert and Streather, 1980) found that their adopted sample did relatively well as against comparison children in general, but poorly when compared to a nonadopted group in family circumstances as favorable as their own.

A score of 9 on the total score is used as the cut-off point for psychiatric screening. Figure 9.3 shows that the majority of the restored adolescents scored above this point, unlike the adoptees or any comparison group.

When the children were eight, parents had reported fewer difficulties in their children than did the teachers. According to the parents, the study children did not show significantly more difficulties than the home-reared comparison children. Parents tended to see some of the same behavior as the teachers did, but not to see it as a problem. Since some of the children's difficult behavior in school seemed to stem from a wish for adult attention, it is not surprising that teachers, dealing with a whole class of children, found their behavior more problematic than parents—especially adoptive parents, who particularly welcomed their child's wish for attention from them as part of their developing relationship.

At sixteen, on the Rutter "A" scale (a parent inventory of health problems, habits, and behavior), we again found no difference between study adolescents and their matched comparisons (table 9.1).

Table 9.1 *"A" Scale Scores*

Group	N	Mean score	sd
Adopted adolescents	22	6	4.5
Restored adolescents	10	11	8.3
Matched comparisons:			
for adopted group	21	5.4	3.3
for restored group	10	8.1	5.9
All ex-institutional	32	7.6	6.3
All comparisons	31	6.3	4.4

Figure 9.3 *Percentage of each group scoring 9 or more on "B" scale.*

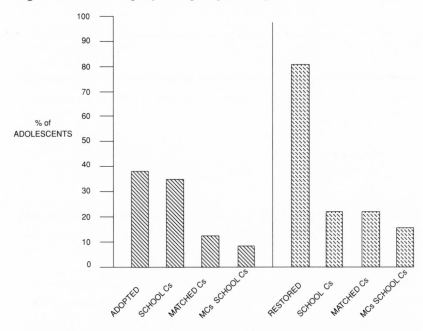

We also constructed a problem score for each adolescent based on our interview with the parent and another one based on our interview with the adolescent. Both covered a wide range of items, including family and peer relationships, which we shall examine in more detail shortly. On both problem scores (tables 9.2 and 9.3) we found that the adopted and restored groups did not differ significantly from each other, but that the total ex-institutional group had significantly higher problem scores than their matched comparisons.

Table 9.2 *Combined Problem Score (Parents' Interview) by Group*

Group	N	Mean	sd
All adopted	21	9.5	7.5
Their comparisons	21	5.7	3.2
All restored	8	11.7	9.2
Their comparisons	10	6.0	3.3
All ex-institutional	29	10.1	7.9
All comparisons	31	7.8	3.2

Table 9.3 *Combined Problem Score (Sixteen-Year-Olds' Interviews) by Group*

Group	N	Mean	sd
All adopted	19	18.2	5.8
Their comparisons	21	14.2	5.4
All restored	9	20.1	7.2
Their comparisons	10	11.1	3.3
All ex-institutional	28	18.8	6.2
All comparisons	31	13.2	5.0

So, despite the fact that the study adolescents have spent a very long time in their family settings compared to the few early years they spent in the institutions, they did show more difficulties than children who had always grown up within their families. Unlike I.Q., behavior scores were adversely affected by early institutionalization, even in the adopted group. However, as at eight years old, the restored group seemed still to be doing particularly badly. Almost all of them—seven out of nine—by age sixteen had been referred to child psychological or child psychiatric services, a significantly higher proportion than either the adopted adolescents or their own matched comparison group. Significantly more of them than their comparisons or adoptees had been in some trouble with the police.

Now let us look specifically at emotional attachments. As already described, these were children who usually had no opportunity to form a close, lasting attachment to one particular adult until they were at least two and a half. So how far were they then able to make close relationships?

This depends very much on the family environment. Figure 9.4 shows that close attachments to the mother did develop, but much more often when the child was adopted than when she or he was restored. And if an attachment had not developed by age eight, the picture was unlikely to have improved by sixteen. Similarly with attachments to the father; only one out of twenty-one adopted adolescents, but half of those who were restored, were seen as definitely *not* attached to the father or stepfather.

Equally, the parents of the restored children were less often attached to them than adoptive parents to their children. Where there were siblings, mothers of restored children generally preferred a sibling to the

Figure 9.4 *Attachment to mother at eight and sixteen years.*

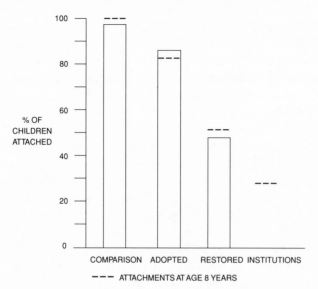

restored child. Thus, comparing the adopted and restored groups, it is evident that the children could still develop close attachments after leaving institutional care, but whether they did develop them depended very largely on the family setting.

We found other differences in family relationships. When the children were eight, we found that the adopted children showed more physical affection than comparison children, and restored children showed less than any other group. At sixteen, the adopted adolescents were no different from their matched comparisons, but the restored group still showed affection very rarely, less than any other group. Their parents, equally, found difficulty in showing affection to them. There were indications that the restored children wanted less involvement in family decisions than adoptees or comparisons and identified themselves less with their parents. Though both adopted and restored adolescents tended to have more difficulty with siblings than their comparisons, the restored group had especially great difficulty. Most restored children had reentered their families to find younger siblings already there; the difficulties to which this had apparently given rise had not been overcome by mid-adolescence.

The picture as regards family relationships was not entirely bleak for the restored group. We did find that restored as well as adopted adolescents were as likely as their comparisons to confide in a parent for support (about half would turn to a parent); about half of them, again, nominated a parent when asked who knew them best as a person, and this was not significantly different from comparisons; and we found no difference between the adopted and restored groups and comparisons in how far the parents felt that their child's views on major issues coincided with their own, or in how far they felt their child would, as an adult, resemble them in attitudes, personality, or life-style. In these respects, restored as well as adopted adolescents were seen as just as much a part of their families as other adolescents.

It remains clear, however, that attachments developed much more satisfactorily for adopted than for restored children. We have no evidence to suggest that this was because of differences in the children before they were placed (Tizard, 1977). Instead, we view the differences as a result of the very different family settings offered to the children by, on the one hand, the adoptive parents, who usually wanted the child very much and put a lot of time and energy into building up the relationship, and, on the other hand, the "restored" parents, who felt more ambivalent about the child, as well as having other children and fewer resources.

Given the differences in the adopted and restored children's attachments, it is all the more striking that we do not find differences when we turn to their other social relationships. They show very similar patterns, different in turn from the comparison group, which we believe indicate some long-term effects of their earlier institutional experiences. Before describing them, though, it should be stressed that by no means all the ex-institutional adolescents showed such patterns and equally that these patterns were generally not unique to the ex-institutional group, merely more frequent within it. That is, we are describing not a severe and inevitable syndrome of difficulties in each ex-institutional adolescent but some ways in which as a group they differed from comparison adolescents who had never lived in institutions.

That said, how did they differ? Ex-institutional adolescents seemed still to be rather more oriented than comparisons toward adult attention and approval, and this was similar to the picture we had found when they were eight. At eight, about a third of the ex-institutional group had also been described as indiscriminately "overfriendly" toward adults. By sixteen, this was much reduced, and there was no relationship between "overfriendliness" toward adults at age eight and at age sixteen. Eight-year-olds who were overfriendly to adults, however, showed a significant tendency to become sixteen-year-olds who were unselectively friendly toward peers. We had information about this on thirty-three adolescents. Ten of these had been overfriendly eight-year-olds, and five of these ten were said by parents to be friendly with any peer who was friendly toward them at age sixteen, as opposed to choosing their friends. These five out of ten compare to only one out of twenty-three children who had not been overfriendly at eight. Expectably, then, nonselectiveness toward peers was more common in ex-institutional adolescents (about one-fifth of them), though the parents did not generally see it as a problem.

We consistently found that ex-institutional adolescents were more likely than their comparisons to have difficulty with peer relationships, whether one rated this on the basis of the parents' account, the teachers' account, or that of the adolescents themselves. In adolescence, we expect to see peer relationships becoming increasingly important as children begin to move away from the earlier forms of dependence on their parents. We were therefore very much interested to find that the ex-institutional adolescents were less likely to have a definite special friend than their comparisons. Figure 9.5 shows the findings from the interview with the mothers; when the sixteen-year-olds were interviewed the same pattern emerged, but to a less marked (and statistically nonsignificant) degree.

We also found that ex-institutional adolescents were less likely than comparisons to confide in peers and turn to them for support if they felt worried or unhappy. This was not merely because fewer of them had a special friend to confide in. Even when, according to the parents or the adolescents themselves, they did have a special friend, they were less likely to turn to that friend than were the comparison adolescents. These differences tend to form a pattern—of greater orientation toward adult attention, more difficulties with peers, and fewer close peer relationships—that resembles the picture found when the study children were eight.

This raises the questions of how these effects have been perpetuated and whether they are permanent or whether, given still more time in a family setting, the ex-institutional group will come to resemble more closely people who have always lived within their families. If permanent, further questions present themselves about how far as adults they will be able to make satisfactory social and sexual relationships.

Various models are possible in considering the ex-institutional group's difficulties with peers. One is that families who took their "own" or an adopted child after a period of institutionalization might be characterized by particular patterns of child-rearing which produce the differences between their children and children who have always lived at home. The difficulty with this hypothesis is the considerable differences

Figure 9.5 *Number of adolescents said by parent to have special friend.*

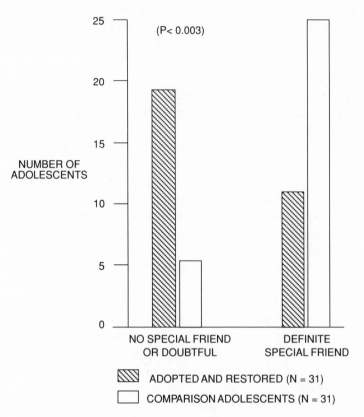

in the attitudes, feelings, circumstances, and child-rearing patterns of the adoptive and restored parents as opposed to the similarity of the ways in which both groups of adolescents differed from their comparison group. But we cannot rule out the possibility that missing the early years of their child's development affected both groups of parents in some way that produced the differences found.

Another type of model, which we find more appealing, is a transactional one. Sroufe's work (LaFrenière and Sroufe, 1985; Waters, Wippman, and Sroufe, 1979) suggests that children lacking a secure attachment in infancy are found to cope less well with peer relationships when investigated at age three and a half and five. Once a particular way of relating to peers has been set up, the child adapts to subsequent situations on that basis, and difficulties become self-perpetuating. Clarke and Clarke (1979) have emphasized the responses of others to the child.

Adoptive parents, they found, made great efforts to foster close parent-child attachments but did not put the same kind of effort into helping their children get on with peers. And, unlike the highly motivated parents, peers had no reason to make special efforts toward, or even tolerate, children who could not already relate adequately. Thus, again, the difficulties could perpetuate themselves.

Another model, not necessarily an alternative, would be of a delay in development. Anna Freud (1966) outlined a detailed "developmental line," a sequence in which adequate development of the child's relationship to parents forms a precondition for normal later relationships to peers and others outside the family. The study children's first opportunity for close attachments came later than for children who were with their parents from birth. The study children may have continued to lag somewhat behind in the broadening of their social horizons beyond the family and the increase in the emotional importance of peers relative to parents. We found some support for this in indications that children whose emotional energies were particularly focused on the parents at age eight were more likely than others to have good peer relationships later on. Close attachment to a parent at eight was related to good peer relationships at sixteen, whereas attachment at sixteen was not so related; close attachment at eight was more strongly linked than attachment at sixteen to selectivity in choosing friends; and children described as "solitary through choice" at eight, suggesting less peer involvement and possibly more involvement with adults than usual at that age, seemed to have the most satisfactory peer relationships at sixteen. Their relationships were better than those of the children said at eight to have a "small group of special friends"—a finding one might not expect on a straightforward transactional model.

In conclusion, we can summarize what seem the most important implications of the study as follows. In terms of child-placement policy, the findings support the view that the best alternative is for children to stay with their own family, provided that they are wanted there; if this is impossible, a decision should be reached swiftly to place the child for adoption rather than keeping the child in care for years because of the possibility of eventual restoration. More generally, the study provides evidence that strong and lasting attachments to adults can be made by children who have been deprived of such attachments in the first few years, but that whether such attachments are made depends importantly upon the adults concerned and how much they foster these attachments. Despite the formation of strong attachments to parents, however, certain differences in social relationships are found up to twelve years after the child has joined a family. Whether these differences are now permanent or further modifiable we do not know.

REFERENCES

Bowlby, J. (1951). *Maternal Care and Mental Health*. Geneva: World Health Organization.

Clarke, A. D. B., and Clarke, A. M. (1979). "Early Experience: Its Limited Effect upon Later Development." In H. R. Shaffer, and J. Dunn, eds., *The First Year of Life*. Chichester: Wiley.

Freud, A. (1966). *Normality and Pathology in Childhood: Assessments of Development*. London: Hogarth Press and the Institute of Psychoanalysis.

Goldfarb, W. (1945). "Effects of Psychological Deprivation in Infancy and Subsequent Stimulation." *American Journal of Psychiatry* 102:18–33.

LaFrenière, P. J., and Sroufe, L. A. (1985). "Profiles of Peer Competence in the Preschool: Interrelations between Measures, Influence of Social Ecology, and Relation to Attachment History." *Developmental Psychology* 21:56–69.

Lambert, L., and Streather, J. (1980). *Children in Changing Families*. London: National Children's Bureau.

Tizard, B. (1977). *Adoption: A Second Chance*. London: Open Books.

Tizard, B., and Rees, J. (1975). "The Effect of Early Institutional Rearing on the Behavior Problems and Affectional Relationships of 4-Year-Old Children." *Journal of Child Psychology and Psychiatry* 16:61–73.

Tizard, J., and Tizard, B. (1971). "Social Development of 2-Year-Old Children in Residential Nurseries." In H. R. Shaffer, ed., *The Origins of Human Social Relations*. London: Academic Press.

Waters, E., Wippman, J., and Sroufe, L. A. (1979). "Attainment, Positive Affect, and Competence in the Peer Group: Two Studies in Construct Validation." *Child Development* 50:821–829.

III

Biological Approaches to
Developmental Psychopathology

10

Introduction

J. GERALD YOUNG

Novel methods for examining the biological basis of developmental disorders have created a wave of optimism about prospects for new discoveries. The techniques of molecular biology and brain imaging are imposing examples, but methods rooted in the biological understanding of development can take many forms. This is exemplified in chapter 11, "Developmental Language Disorders" by Dugas and Gerard, in which they consider the impact of the biological maturation of the brain on the form of language disorders during the developmental period. They argue against the use of models of language pathology drawn from research on the aphasias acquired during the adult years. Instead, they examine the molding exerted by development on the deficits in language and speech production in childhood disorders. Subtyping of developmental language disorders according to localization models drawn from the mature brain is deceptive because of differences in neuroanatomy, neural connections, and vascular patterns; the rapidity of developmental changes in brain structure during childhood calls for sequential observations and new formulations of syndromes for the major developmental periods. The enhanced potential for compensatory restitution of function following a developmental interference is an additional characteristic to be considered during childhood.

Dugas and Gérard describe the application of brain-imaging techniques to developmental language disorders, including computed tomography, regional cerebral blood flow techniques, PET-scan methods, magnetic resonance imaging (MRI), and brain electrical activity mapping. Although there has been little application of these methods (with the exception of computed tomography) to developmental language disorders, they promise to be informative when applied to rigorously evaluated clinical groups in the future (Andreasen, 1988). Dugas and Gérard report the results of their own research on developmental language disorders, using an explicit developmental model, and suggest how the model might organize our understanding and further investigation of these disorders.

Another clinical variant of biological approaches to child psychopathology is study of the natural history of a disorder. A biological perspective on natural history emphasizes genetic and early childhood origins of psychopathology as the potentially dominant determinants of outcome, minimizing later environmental and therapeutic influences. Many illnesses fit this pattern; prominent examples are cystic fibrosis, Down syndrome, and many neurodegenerative disorders. The more complex and subtle neuropsychiatric disorders, however, appear to be environmentally responsive. At the same time, groups of these disorders share nonspecific component symptoms, and diagnostic differentiation is difficult. Disorders with strong genetic contributions are mixed with environmentally induced illnesses in clinical samples, so that the primary origin of each is obscured by the presence of the other groups. This clinical observation, coupled with data emerging from other methods (e.g., familial aggregation research or neurochemical studies), has inspired a search for discrete syndromes with a developmental integrity minimally modified by environmental influences. The broad group of disorders encompassed by such terms as attention deficit–hyperactivity disorder (ADHD), minimal brain dysfunction, conduct disorder, and related syndromes has been the center of the greatest controversy (Werry, Reeves, and Elkind, 1987; Halperin et al., 1988). Are they varying manifestations of a single disorder, homogeneous in its essentials, if our diagnostic methods were to include an identifying biological marker? Is there a subgroup, genetically determined, with a preordained natural history that can be separated from other mimicking illnesses? Schmidt and Esser, in chapter 13, have used a combined epidemiological and longitudinal research design to examine these questions.

The inherent complexities of this research are magnified by differing terminology and nosological criteria across national boundaries, a focus of continuing efforts toward international cooperation. Yet their findings are similar to those emerging at other research centers. Refinement of clinical concepts in order to develop better operational methods for symptom definition will be essential to clarifying the biology of these disorders. When improved techniques are available to determine objectively the presence or absence of specific symptoms, they will enable investigators to map the natural histories of subgroups of the major disorders (Halperin et al., 1988; Young et al., 1987).

Research on Tourette's disorder exemplifies a pathway to better understanding of childhood psychiatric disorders, suggesting the possible course of discoveries over the next decade. Tourette's disorder was considered to be rare as recently as fifteen years ago. There was little recognition of the range of symptoms or their classification in the context of other tic disorders. The genetic basis of Tourette's disorder had not yet been clarified; the major cause for hope was the beneficial effect of treatment with haloperidol. A surge of research activity by several groups since then has dramatically expanded our knowledge about Tourette's disorder, leading to its current status as a model for understanding childhood neuropsychiatric disorders (Pauls and Leckman, 1986; Shapiro et al., 1987).

Cohen and his colleagues, in chapter 12, infuse these methods with an additional scientific perspective that makes this a practical, authentic approach to the conceptualization of childhood disorders in two ways. First, they refuse to dichotomize biological and psychological viewpoints on etiology and attribute to genetics the sole clinical significance. Instead, they present the genetic contributions in a full clinical context. As an example, there is a substantial discussion of psychodynamic psychotherapy, family counseling and therapy, and educational and occupational interventions as integral components of a treatment regimen.

Second, they inquire into the psychodynamic relevance and integrity of the genetically based symptoms; this is both an engrossing topic for clinicians and a useful perspective for guiding therapy for patients (when the psychodynamic perspective is not distorted into having a primary etiological role). Most important, it is a foundation for future research examining psychodynamic aspects of psychic conflict, the biological basis of the capacity to regulate drive expression, and the effects of disinhibition (Cohen, 1980). The results of elegant genetic research should keep us open to further discoveries in other domains.

Pharmacological agents used for psychiatric conditions appear to have greater specificity for neuronal target systems than other treatments, which is a source of their leading role in biological research methods. Determination of discrete therapeutic effects in response to neurotransmitter-specific drugs is a guiding objective for research. Regrettably, most pediatric psychopharmacological studies have not applied careful research design with detailed assessment of dose levels, therapeutic effects, and side effects in the context of a placebo, crossover between drugs, and blind raters. Campbell and her colleagues have defined the essential components of optimal research design for clinical trials here and in other publications (Campbell, Green, and Deutsch, 1985). The effects of neglect of these requirements—every clinical situation carries with it reasons for not attending to good design features "in this particular case"—are concretely depicted in Campbell's chronicle of psychopharmacological research on autism over a period of two decades (chap. 14). Although research on several individual drugs has been productive, perhaps more significant than any of these findings is the research by Campbell and her colleagues that demonstrated combined haloperidol and behavior therapy to be superior to either treatment alone, indicating the central role of psychosocial interventions, even in severely disturbed children with brain dysfunction (Campbell et al., 1978). This links with the work of Cohen, Leckman, and their colleagues and echoes the perspective of Chiland in her introductory chapter: multiple dispassionate viewpoints help us grasp the causes of these perplexing illnesses and determine the best treatments.

REFERENCES

Andreasen, N. C. (1988). "Brain Imaging: Applications in Psychiatry." *Science* 239:1381–1388.
Campbell, M.; Anderson, L. T.; Meier, M.; Cohen, I. L.; Small, A. M.; Samit, C.; and Sachar, E. J. (1978). "A Comparison of Haloperidol, Behavior Therapy and Their Interaction in Autistic Children." *Journal of the American Academy of Child Psychiatry* 17, no. 4:640–655.
Campbell, M., Green, W. H., and Deutsch, S. I. (1985). *Child and Adolescent Psychopharmacology.* Beverly Hills: Sage.
Cohen, D. J. (1980). "The Pathology of the Self in Primary Childhood Autism and Gilles de la Tourette Syndrome." In B. Blinder, ed., *Psychiatric Clinics of North America.* Vol. 3. Philadelphia: W. B. Saunders.
Halperin, J. M.; Wolf, L. E.; Pascualvaca, D. M.; Newcorn, J.; Healey, J. M.; O'Brien, J. D.; Morganstein, A.; and Young, J. G. (1988). "Differential Assessment of Attention and Impulsivity in Children." *Journal of the American Academy of Child and Adolescent Psychiatry* 27:326–329.
Pauls, D. L., and Leckman, J. F. (1986). "The Inheritance of Gilles de la Tourette's Syndrome and Associated Behaviors: Evidence for Autosomal Dominant Transmission." *New England Journal of Medicine* 315:993–997.
Shapiro, A. K.; Shapiro, E.; Young, J. G.; and Feinberg, T. E. (1987). *Gilles de la Tourette Syndrome.* 2nd ed. New York: Raven Press.
Werry, J. S., Reeves, J. C., Elkind, G. S. (1987). "Attention deficit, Conduct, Oppositional, and Anxiety Disorders in Children: I. A Review of Research

on Differentiating Characteristics." *Journal of American Academy of Child and Adolescent Psychiatry* 26:133–143.

Young, J. G.; Halperin, J. M.; Leven, L. I.; Shaywitz, B. A.; and Cohen, D. J. (1987). "Developmental Neuropharmacology: Clinical and Neurochemical Perspectives on the Regulation of Attention, Learning and Movement. In L. L. Iversen, S. D. Iversen, and S. H. Snyder, eds., *Handbook of Psychopharmacology: New Directions in Behavioral Pharmacology*. New York: Plenum Press, 19:59–121.

11

Developmental Language Disorders: A Paradigm for Child Psychiatry?

MICHEL DUGAS

CHRISTOPHE GÉRARD

In order to confirm the interest that child psychiatrists should demonstrate in developmental language disorders (DLD), it seems superfluous to mention Cotard's (1868) or Sigmund Freud and Rie's (1891) works, or to quote Lacan's statement: "The unconscious is structured in the same way as language." Epidemiological studies involving three-year-old children (Stevenson and Richman, 1976), investigations bearing on children with communication disorders (Cantwell and Baker, 1984), and studies on children with reading disabilities have all shown that psychiatric disorders are frequently associated with learning disorders (Rutter and Yule, 1973). Thus, among 1,110 patients who were assessed in 1984 and 1985 at the Child and Adolescent Psychiatry Unit of Herold Hospital in Paris, and who were diagnosed according to D.S.M.-III criteria, we observed 373 cases of specific developmental disorders (33.6 percent); 167 of those cases involved developmental language disorders (15.04 percent), and 130 cases represented developmental reading disorders (11.7 percent).

A clinician who is interested in investigating DLD, taken as a specific entity that results from cognitive dysfunctioning, is faced with numerous methodological problems and with a diversity of possible answers. But the same issues arise whenever we try to analyze the pathological development of a child's behavior. We list three of these questions:

1. To what extent does the development of the disorder represent a simple deviation from the norm or a pathological deviance?

2. What is the spontaneous evolution of those deviations that have been diagnosed early?
3. What are the logical rules governing the behavioral phenomena observed in children who have a specific developmental disorder?

In order to answer these questions, one must draw from numerous disciplines: cognitive psychology, behavioral psychology, developmental psychology, psychophysiology, and neurolinguistics. In other words, one has to choose a language in which to talk about language and to systematize one's clinical approach to language disorders in terms of pathological behaviors.

But why should we entrust child psychiatry with the leadership in studying DLD? First, there are historical reasons: the neuropsychology of acquired language disorders in adults has shown, for the first time, how a mental function can have other bases than mere speculative ones. We do not, however, advocate a simple transposition of those data dealing with acquired pathology (aphasias); instead, clinical psychiatrists must think about the possible use they can make of findings from classical neuropsychology and developmental neuropsychology in the study of a population of pathological children, both for predictive purposes and in order to arrive at individualized diagnostic and therapeutic decisions.

Within the body of neuropsychological knowledge, we distinguish between retrospective and prospective data. *Retrospective data* permit us to hypothesize, for each case, which structural constraints were involved in the specific cognitive development associated with the emergence of a language disorder. The traditional procedure consisted in trying to associate the stigmata of a specific area of cerebral dysfunction with DLD. The most frequently invoked areas were, in the left cerebral hemisphere, the parieto-temporal region and the premotor area of the frontal lobe. This reasoning was based on evidence that specific language and nonlanguage patterns existed. This link between cognitive disorder and cerebral region used the map of hemispheric localizations developed on the basis of adult acquired pathology.

In this manner, Petrauskas and Rourke (1979) delineated three subtypes of dyslexia which they associated with a dysfunction in a specific brain area: the left temporal region for subtype 1, the left parieto-temporo-occipital region for subtype 2, and the left frontal lobe for subtype 3.

Rapin and Allen followed the same reasoning when they suggested, in 1983, a DLD classification that assumes the existence of a bitemporal dysfunction or lesion for auditory-verbal agnosias, a prefrontal pathology for the group they called phonological-syntactical, or when they linked their severe expressive syndrome to adult aphemias. This type of procedure and the resulting nosology seem quite fragile: they are based on an analogy with an adult model, and the hypothesized lesion is supported neither by actual localizing of neurological signs nor by imaging of the lesion. Even the notion of anomalous dominance, established by Geschwind and Galaburda (1985), goes against a simple transposition of an adult map of localizations to children.

The neuropathology of early brain lesions also differs from that of adults. The impact of pre- or perinatal injuries on the CNS is often diffuse; even when vascular mechanisms are involved, the areas of prevailing alteration do not correspond with adult vascular territories. They vary, during the intrauterine period, according to the development of the cerebral angioarchitecture (de Reuck, 1984).

Actually, neuropsychology cannot approach DLD in terms of lesions, as is the case for adults. Instead, it should try to reconstruct the process of reorganization of the cognitive systems in response to an early pathological factor, a factor that may have taken place during the embryonic life or possibly be genetically determined. One is thus interested in the dynamic reconstitution of development that is imposed by such a pathological event rather than in the nature of this event. On an individual level, our approach to this dynamic process of compensatory reconstitution is still unrefined, but modern imaging gives us some points of reference.

A cerebral lesion is seldom observed on the CT-scan of children with a specific DLD. But, in the absence of a lesion, a CT-scan or magnetic resonance imaging (MRI) may reveal a developmental hemispheric asymmetry. When the lesion is visible, a study of its type and localization allows us to date the occurrence of the causal pathological process and thus to estimate the extent to which embryonic migration has been disturbed. Before the twenty-eighth week of fetal life, hemorrhagic lesions are localized in the juxta-ependymal regions and the germinative matrix is a preferential site of such hemorrhages. Between the twenty-fourth week and the eighth month of gestation, anoxia leads to leucomalacia in the bordering subcortical and periventricular areas, between the territories where the two types of vascularization divide the brain (corticifugal and ventriculofugal vessels). As we get closer to term, the type of vascularization that develops resembles more and more that which we know in adults. The topography of ischemic vascular accidents therefore involves traditional territories.

Currently we have few precise clinical data for each stage of cerebral development. But we believe that this type of approach is very promising and should allow neurologists, psychiatrists, and cognitive psychologists to meet within the vast framework of behavioral neurobiology. We would like to illustrate such possibilities by quoting a study we conducted on a population of fourteen children suffering from a neurological hemisyndrome and a congenital macroscopic brain lesion (Gérard, 1986). For each child, historical data, CT-scan findings, and a description of the major cognitive functions allowed us to contrast (in a purely retrospective fashion) two types of possible reorganization, depending on the presumed date of the lesion in relation to intrauterine life.

In the first group of cases, we postulated the occurrence of an early left hemisphere lesion (prior to the end of the eighth month of gestation). These children displayed a developmental oral and/or written language disorder, and a disorder in sequential skills. Their difficulties were similar to those noted among children who do not have focal neurological deficits but have specific developmental disorders. In our group of subjects, types of performance that are normally attributed to the right hemisphere were adequate, sometimes even excellent. In the second group of cases, we postulated a tardive left hemisphere lesion (after the eighth month or at birth). These children's language did develop, but within the limits of the right hemisphere abilities, owing to a phenomenon of hemispheric "crowding." These patterns are in agreement with hypotheses that Geschwind (1985) developed on the basis of Goldman's work (1978) contrasting post-fetal-lesion reorganization with acquired-lesion reorganization.

Such speculations can be useful in planning for the treatment of DLD. Our hypotheses concerning the initial distribution of tasks between right and left hemispheres brings us closer to those neurocognitive learning models described by Goldberg and Costa (1981). Such models hypothesize the acquisition of "unit descriptive systems"—that is, of the necessary supports for information processing, supports that are specific to a particular activity (language, reading, arithmetic) and the development of which allows for a progression from the "profane" stage to the "professional" state. The acquisition of such systems follows a specific sequence of events: initial use of global, holistic, "right hemisphere" strategies, finally leading to mode-specific information-precoding strategies that are based on the development of coding-unit repertoires in the left hemisphere (lexical, syntactical, for example).

This process of intellectual reconstruction of the conditions of early brain development leads to a description of the structural constraints within which information-processing strategies had to develop and to elucidation of the right-left hemispheric imbalances that may have resulted from them. To some extent, this is what Bakker (1983) intended to do when he contrasted P (perceptive) and L (language) dyslexias. But there was no organic support for his theory.

In order to be complete, this type of developmental neuropsychology should be able to establish, for a given learning disorder, a logical hierarchy of behavioral events resulting from the initial pathological phenomenon: a disturbance in embryonic migration toward specific cortical regions, or a macrolesion of those same regions. The functional consequences of this early pathological event can be categorized as primary, secondary, or tertiary:

1. *Primary consequences* are directly related to the injury of the specific area, which cannot express its predetermined potentialities.
2. *Secondary consequences* represent the reorganization that follows the lesion (regulation of neuronal death, synaptic competition in the intact areas).
3. *Tertiary consequences* result from the disturbances the primary and secondary consequences impose upon the learning dynamics.

It is only within such a developmental framework that the above-mentioned regroupings of traditional cognitive performance should take place. The logic of such regrouping should be based not on simplistic localization maps derived from adult pathology but on the subtle construction of a sequence of neurobiological events derived from individual history, brain imaging, and neuropsychological and psychophysiological investigations geared to specify some of the unique information-processing characteristics of the subject (for instance, the presence of a sequential disorder or the types of different perceptual asymmetries).

Our retrospective mode of reasoning was at this point based on the delineation of a primitive lesion. We indicated, however, that most often a lesion could probably not be proven either through neurological signs or through traditional imaging. Moreover, the causal relationships between an early cerebral lesion and cognitive disorders seem very ambiguous. Thus, with regard to the fourteen cases of children suffering from a neurological hemisyndrome, we were unable to demonstrate anatomical-clinical correlations. Their semiology did not distinguish these disorders from those observed in children with a severe DLD in the absence of a macroscopic cerebral lesion. Rather than being linked by a direct cause-effect relationship, cerebral lesions and language disorders seem to share a common pathological condition: the model of anomalous dominance. This model is based upon the hypothesis of a disturbance in the developmental dynamics of the left hemisphere, which explains learning disorders (disturbance of embryonic migration), as well as a higher lesional risk for this hemisphere.

Functional brain imaging may provide a more dynamic imagery of those relationships between brain and cognitive activities than traditional imaging. It should provide snapshots, which would show both the points of impact of the primitive injury (in the form of focal hypoactivity) and the repercussions on the development of functionally related regions. In other words, we would have a chance to specify the primary and secondary functional consequences of the primitive pathological disturbance.

Duffy (1979, 1985) developed a procedure for topographical imaging known as "brain electrical activity mapping" (BEAM). Such mapping, assisted by computer representations of EEG activities and evoked potentials, gives clinicians immediate visual access to spectral and spatial-temporal information. In ten- to 12-year-old children categorized as having "pure dyslexia," Duffy and McAnnulty (1985) observed several spectral abnormalities: an increase of alpha activity in the left hemisphere, a limited variation of frequencies even during cognitive activities, and a particular spatial-temporal distribution of EEG frequencies and evoked potentials (posterior distribution, as well as anterior, left frontal, and bihemispheric).

Such imaging involves only cortical activities; yet we have mentioned that an important part of the disturbances in fetal development involves subcortical regions. Imaging techniques based on the metabolic activities of brain tissue appear to be more promising. The most productive method seems to be the positron emission tomography (PET-scan) method, which uses 18 fluoro-deoxyglucose. But the presence of technical and ethical constraints makes its application to children difficult.

The study of cerebral blood flow in children with Xenon 133 is feasible. With this technique, Lou, Henricksen, and Bruhn (1984) demonstrated in eight dysphasic children the presence of a basic and, under language stimulation, focal cerebral hypoperfusion in temporal and frontal regions, bilaterally and symmetrically. In addition to providing information on the current function of specific cortical regions in specific situations, this technique has visualized and localized, in dysphasic children, traces of the early cerebral damage in the subcortical territories that border cerebral vascularization.

One may question the significance of the relative hypofrontality noted in dysphasic children with this metabolic technique and that of the frontal cortex hypoactivity, which the BEAM technique has found in dyslexic children under specific conditions of cognitive stimulation. Could hypofrontality be the consequence of a postlesional reorganization of structures involved in cognitive activities, thus indicating the existence of what we previously called the secondary functional consequences?

Can neuropsychological knowledge contribute to a prospective approach to DLD? In other words, can we answer these three questions:

1. Which children are at risk for learning disorders, or how can one make a very early diagnosis of them?
2. How can one distinguish the deviant and pathological character of a language deficit in relation to set norms that take chronological age and level of intellectual function into account?
3. Once a diagnosis of specific DLD is made, do we have prognostic indicators regarding the evolution of the disorder and its impact on the socioeducational adjustment of the subject?

In an attempt to resolve the issue of very early diagnosis, two methods have been proposed:

1. The first method attempts to find psychophysiological markers in the subjects which would precede the occurrence of the disorder. Such markers would be either prerequisites of the learning process under study or indicators of the pathological factor responsible for the learning disorder with which they are associated. The status of DLD marker was given to the deficit in temporal information processing in children with learning disorders. The same applies to the verbal segmentation disorder of future dyslexic children. But we lack evidence of a specific marker-disorder link.

2. A second strategy utilizes, at a very early age, batteries of psycholinguistic development. Actually, validation of such batteries (which are said to be predictive) raises numerous problems. For instance, the epidemiological study of Silva, McGee, and Williams (1983) has shown that, between the ages of three and seven, those groups for which the psycholinguistic delay remains most stable are also those for whom I.Q. figures are lowest. This major hindrance is related to the fact that, in this age range, scales of intellectual function are heavily loaded on the verbal

factor. The great variation of performance observed in a so-called normal population is therefore compounded by a deficiency in measuring instruments.

At an age when one can readily assert the specifity of a developmental disorder, the predictive issue becomes obscured by the problem of defining a pathological disorder, such as developmental dysphasia or severe DLD. The definition is more often negative than positive (what it is not rather than what it is). A normative, quantitative definition of deviance is usually preferred over an empirical, qualitative one. Classifications of dysphasias have therefore been attempted in the absence of an operational and reliable model of language development. The few existing longitudinal studies on the evolution of DLD and its impact on social adjustment have thus dealt with an ill-defined pathological entity viewed as homogeneous, or they were based upon a vague and artificial nosology such as that which opposes expressive and receptive disorders (Paul, Cohen, and Caparulo, 1983).

A more promising strategy, one that is closer to the medical model, is based on the definition and differentiation of two types of signs:

1. A first group consists of signs the presence of which allows us to assert that the organization of some operational language functions is defective, language being considered as a voluntary purposeful act. Such a functional definition of deviance more readily allows one to link semiology with brain imaging data. Among those signs, or markers of deviance, we mention five major ones: (a) syntactic encoding disorder, (b) lexical production disorder, (c) verbal comprehension disorder (disregarding perceptual difficulties), (d) hypospontaneity, and (e) insufficient informational value (disregarding possible intelligibility problems).

2. A population of fifty-one children with a severe DLD (dysphasia) defined in this manner was followed throughout the course of their speech and language therapy. A study of this population allowed us to identify various signs that, when regrouped, yielded a second set of five distinct groups; these were also well differentiated on the basis of the subjects' history, their prognosis, and the therapeutic choices (Dugas, 1983; Le Heuzey, 1984). This second type of signs involved language behaviors as well as psychomotor, psychometric, and perceptual-motor performance and auditory information disorders. We therefore appear to be confronted with five entities that have internal and external validity—in other words, with five different diseases (see table 11.1)

Our paradigmatic discussion of modern approaches to developmental language disorders thus leads us to a better use of the medical model in

Table 11.1 *Analysis of Developmental Language Disorders*

		Group I	Group II	Group III	Group IV	Group V
		N = 13	N = 5	N = 18	N = 5	N = 10
Encoding	Spontaneous	agrammatical	reduced	basic language	agrammatical	normal
Language	Elicited	agrammatical	agrammatical	dyssyntactical	grammatical reduced	dyssyntactical
Speech	Speech output[a]	↓↓	↓	↓↓	↓↓	↓
	Word finding[b]	+	− −	− −	− −	− −
	Paraphasias[c]	0	+	+	+	+
Praxias[b]		−	+	+	+	+
Sentence	Recall[b]	−	− −	− −	−	−
Rhythms[b]	Auditory-motor	− −	−	− −	−	+
	Visual-motor	− −	− −	+/−	−	+ +
Decoding[b]		+	+	− −	−	− −
Phonemic discrimination[b]		+	+	− −	+/−	+

a. ↓ reduced   ↓↓ very reduced
b. + normal   +/− moderately altered   − altered   − − very altered
c. + paraphasias   0 no paraphasia

developmental psychiatry. With regard to the DLD, we hope to have shown (1) that the regrouping of what we called retrospective data leads to a physiopathology of the disorder, (2) that it is possible, on the basis of clinical data, to define a dysphasic syndrome (or severe DLD syndrome), and (3) that it is possible, on the basis of other data and for a given subject, to link this syndrome to individual disease entities, which will permit a better focus on prognostic and therapeutic indications.

REFERENCES

Baker, D. J. (1983). "Hemispheric Specialization and Specific Reading Retardation." In M. Rutter, ed., *Developmental Neuropsychiatry.* New York: Guilford Press.

Cantwell, D. P., and Baker, L. (1991). *Psychiatric and Learning Disorders in Children with Communication Disorders: Advances in Learning and Behavioral Disabilities.* Washington, D.C.: American Psychiatric Press.

Cotard, J. (1868). *Etude sur l'atrophie cérébrale: Thèse pour le doctorat en médecine.* Paris: A. Parent.

De Reuck, J. L. (1984). "Cerebral Angioarchitecture and Perinatal Brain Lesions in Premature and Full-Term Infants." *Acta Neurologica Scandinavia* 70:391–396.

Duffy, F. H., Burchfiel, J. L., and Lombroso, C. T. (1979). "Brain Electrical Activity Mapping (BEAM): A Method for Extending the Clinical Utility of EEG and Evoked Potential." *Annals of Neurology* 5:309.

Duffy, F. H., and McAnnulty, G. B. (1985). "Brain Electrical Activity Mapping (BEAM): The Search for a Physiological Signature of Dyslexia." In F. H. Duffy and N. Geschwind, eds., *Dyslexia.* Boston: Little, Brown, 105–122.

Dugas, M. (1984). *Les troubles sévères du développement du language: Journées d'enseignement et d'actualités neurologiques.* (Collège des Enseignants de Neurologie, Clermont-Ferrand 23–25, Mars 1983). Paris: Sidem, 167–178.

Freud, S., and Rie, O. (1891). "Clinical Study." In S. Freud, *Infantile Cerebral Paralysis.* Coral Gables, Fla: University of Miami Press, 1968.

Gérard, C. (1986). *Etude du développement cognitif de 14 enfants ayant une lésion cérébrale latéralisée survenue dans la période pré ou périnatale.* Paris: Thèse de Médecine.

Geschwind, N. (1985). "Biological Foundations of Reading." In F. H. Duffy and N. Geschwind, eds., *Dyslexia.* Boston: Little, Brown, 197–211.

Geschwind, N., and Galaburda, A. M. (1985). "Cerebral Lateralization: Biological Mechanism, Associations and Pathology: I. A Hypothesis and a Program for Research." *Archives of Neurology* 42:428–459.

Goldberg, E., and Costa, L. D. (1981). "Hemisphere Differences in the Acquisition and Use of Descriptive Systems." *Brain and Language* 14:144–173.

Goldman, P. S. (1978). "Neuronal Plasticity in Primate Telencephalon: Anomalolus Cross Cortico-Caudate Connections Induced by Prenatal Removal of Frontal Association Cortex." *Science* 202:768.

Le Heuzey, M. F. (1984). *Une nouvelle classification sémiologique des troubles sévères du développement de l'enfant.* Paris: Mémoire pour le C.E.S. de Psychiatrie.

Lou, M. C., Henriksen, L., and Bruhn, P. (1984). Focal Cerebral Hypoperfusion in Children with Dysphasia and/or Attention Deficit Disorders." *Archives of Neurology* 41:825–829.

Paul, R., Cohen, D. J., and Caparulo, B. K. (1983). "A Longitudinal Study of Patients with Severe Developmental Disorders of Language Learning." *Journal of the American Academy of Child Psychiatry* 6:525–534.

Petrauskas, R. J., and Rourke, B. P. (1979). "Identification of Subtypes of Retarded Readers: A Neuropsychological Multivariate Approach." *Journal of Clinical Neuropsychology* 1:17–37.

Rapin, I., and Allen, D. A. (1983). "Developmental Language Disorders: Nosologic Considerations." In U. Kirk, ed., *Neuropsychology of Language, Reading and Spelling.* New York: Academic Press, 155–184.

Rutter, M., and Yule, W. (1973). "Specific Reading Retardation." In L. Mann and D. Sabation eds., *The First Review of Special Education.* Philadelphia: Buttonwood Farms.

Silva, P. A., McGee, R., and Williams, S. M. (1983). "Developmental Language Delay from Three to Seven Years and Its Significance for Low Intelligence and Reading Difficulties at Age Seven." *Developmental Medicine and Child Neurology* 25:783–793.

Stevenson, J., and Richman, N. (1976). "The Prevalence of Language Delay in a Population of 3-Year-Old Children and Its Association with General Retardation." *Developmental Medicine and Child Neurology* 18:431–441.

12

Tourette's Syndrome: A Model Developmental Neuropsychiatric Disorder

DONALD J. COHEN

KENNETH E. TOWBIN

JAMES F. LECKMAN

Tourette's syndrome is a complex neuropsychiatric disorder first described more than a hundred years ago (Gilles de la Tourette, [1885] 1982). From Georges Gilles de la Tourette's identification of a core constellation of symptoms—incoordination (tics), echolalia, and coprolalia—TS has emerged as an exemplary developmental disorder, beginning during childhood or early adolescence and displaying an array of "involuntary" tic symptoms combined with fascinating psychiatric and psychological difficulties. Once thought to be rare, TS is now considered a relatively common disorder, affecting, in its complete form, up to one individual in every twenty-five hundred and three times this number in its partial expressions, including chronic motor tics and some forms of obsessive-compulsive disorder. As a serious disorder warranting study in its own right, TS takes on additional importance as a "model" neuropsychiatric condition—a disorder in which genetic and constitutional vulnerability interact with familial and social factors in the definition of the range and severity of ultimate clinical impairment. Over the past decade, clinical researchers have succeeded in learning more of the biological vulnerability, neurochemical correlates, and determinants of natural history, as well as developing increasingly effective multimodal clinical approaches. The concepts currently under investigation provide a framework which may be broadly useful in the study of other complex developmental disorders that arise early in life and reflect the interactions between genetic vulnerabilities and environmental provision, such as attention deficit disorder, obsessive-compulsive disorder, and multiplex developmental disorder.

CLINICAL FEATURES

During the last century, TS has been observed throughout the world and in every social and economic group. Although there are remarkable differences among patients, the overall pattern of clinical characteristics marks TS as a distinctive syndrome defined by the presence of tics. In addition to these tic symptoms, the TS diathesis may lead in either a primary or a secondary fashion, to alterations in the regulation of activity, the expression of instinctually organized behaviors and feelings, the development of self-control, and other personality characteristics. As with simple motor tics, TS is predominantly a disorder of boys, with a ratio of 3:1 to 8:1 in different clinical series. More recent work, however, has suggested that the underlying diathesis may be differently expressed in the sexes, with girls have a greater likelihood of developing obsessions and compulsions. As will be described later, when obsessions and compulsions are included as manifestations of TS symptoms, the sex ratio appears more equally balanced.

Tics

The syndrome is defined by the multiform, ever-changing array of motor and phonic tics that persist over many months and years. They are more often easier to observe than formally describe and classify. By convention, the motor and phonic tics are often further divided into simple and complex phenomena, although these distinctions can be ambiguous. Simple tics are abrupt movements, usually restricted to one or a few isolated muscle groups, resulting in nonpurposive short-lived actions. Complex tics involve many groups, may be carried out in longer sequences, and resemble ordinary motor activity except for their exaggerated intensity, repetitiveness, or incongruence with the situation. Clearly, tics can reproduce any motion or sound within the body's repertoire of voluntary behaviors (see table 12.1).

Several characteristic features, including abruptness, suppressibility, variability, and diminution during sleep, enable one to differentiate tics from other neurological movement disorders (Fahn, 1982; Fahn and Erenberg, 1988). They vary in anatomical location, duration, frequency, and intensity, across development and situation, and over time (Fahn,

Table 12.1 *Examples of Tourette's Syndrome Symptoms*

Simple motor: eyeblinks, grimacing, tongue thrusting, eye widening, jaw jerks, head jerks, nodding, head turning, shoulder jerks, arm movements, finger movements, stomach jerks, kicking or leg movements, tensing parts of the body.

Complex motor: holding funny expressions, squinting, grooming hair, cracking joints, repeatedly touching parts of the body, tapping, hopping, stomping, picking at things (self, clothes), pushing on eyes, hitting self, slamming things, copropraxia (giving the finger, etc.).

Simple phonic: sniffing, coughing, hawking, squeeking, "aaaaaaa," "tttttuh," throat clearing, "uh, uh, uh," blowing across upper lip, popping, snorting, gnashing teeth.

Complex phonic: "uh huh!" "you bet," "all right," "yeah, yeah," palilalia (repeating sentences after one's self), echolalia (repeating sentences after others), swearing, obscene language, obscene noises, racial slurs, colloquial insults.

1982). Anatomical variability refers to the changing distribution of movements over the body, usually beginning with eyes, face, and head and subsequently progressing to include arms, torso, abdomen, legs, and feet. This pattern of progression is not so universal as to constitute a rule, but it is common (Jagger et al., 1982). Variability of duration, frequency, amplitude, and intensity are especially characteristic of tics, when compared to other involuntary movements. Over days or weeks tics are stereotypical. But when comparing the course of abnormal movement disorders over years, one finds that tics are relatively unpredictable and inconsistent.

Variability with situation includes emotional climates as well as physical settings for many patients. During periods of increased arousal, anticipation, or anxiety many persons observe increases or decreases in symptoms. For some, tic severity follows emotional arousal peaking when the excitement is greatest (e.g., while opening Christmas presents); for others, the greatest intensity is observed following these peaks (e.g., in the hours or days following an oral classroom presentation).

Predictable variability or periodicity through the day, month, or year is commonly reported. Certain times of the day or seasons of the year may affect tic frequency and intensity. Developmental variability is seen in the decrease or cessation of symptoms in many patients following puberty. For others, there may be periodic exacerbations and remissions later in life. A small portion of TS patients experience continuous, severe symptoms throughout development.

Tourette reported an inconsistent finding that tics disappeared during sleep. Further investigation suggests that tics may occur in sleep, especially during REM stages, but, when compared to waking states, tic frequency is reduced (Glaze, Frost, and Jankovic, 1983).

Associated Behaviors, Cognitions, and Perceptions

Beyond the tics, the array of behavioral and psychological difficulties experienced by many TS patients have impressed clinicians from the early descriptions in the nineteenth century on. The most consistently reported behavioral features have been impulsivity, irritability, aggressivity, attentional problems, obsessions, compulsions, depression, immaturity, and self-injurious behaviors. There are several opinions about the etiology of these behaviors: they may represent expressions of the same biological vulnerability that leads to TS (as thought by Gilles de la Tourette himself) or reflect the individual's response to the tics and social tensions resulting from them (as argued by some neurologically oriented investigators; Shapiro, Shapiro, Bruun, and Sweet, 1978; Shapiro, Shapiro, Young, and Feinberg, 1988); or they may represent a combination of both vulnerability and adaptation (as suggested by the clinical studies in our group; Cohen, Bruun, and Leckman, 1988; Cohen, Detlor, Shaywitz, and Leckman, 1982).

Up to 50 percent of all children with TS seen by clinicians have a history of (for up to several years preceding the onset of tics) and current problems with concentration, impulsivity, and excessive motor activity. This combination of disruptive behavior problems may be diagnosed as attention deficit hyperactivity disorder (ADHD) in children with the greatest behavioral problems in school. Children with TS and ADHD are especially vulnerable to serious, long-term clinical impairment, giving special relevance to the combination. The ADHD of TS cannot be distinguished from that seen in other children with the "hyperactive child syndrome." The early appearance and high frequency of ADHD in TS patients suggest that ADHD is among the first manifestations of the underlying troubles in behavioral modulation and inhibition that later lead to tic symptoms (Cohen et al., 1982; Comings and Comings, 1984). Also, attentional problems may worsen at the onset of tics. On the other hand, it is possible that the frequency of ADHD among TS patients is a consequence of three facts: (1) the frequency of ADHD among children in general, (2) the likelihood that a child who has one problem may be more vulnerable to a second, and (3) the increased likelihood of a child with more serious problems or more than one problem receiving clinical attention. Therefore, the increased prevalence of ADHD among TS patients seen in clinics could be an example of Berkson's (1946) ascertainment bias (Pauls, Hurst, et al., 1986).

Although TS patients often present with uncomplicated multiple motor and phonic tics, as many as 50–60 percent experience obsessions and/or compulsions, which can be seriously disabling. Studies of older patients and those with a longer duration of illness have reported prevalences of these obsessions and/or compulsions as high as 90 percent (Nee et al., 1982). Conventionally, obsessions are defined as thoughts, images, or impulses that invade the consciousness of the sufferer, are involuntary, are seen as excessive or silly, arouse distress, and cannot be dismissed despite vigorous efforts. Similarly, compulsions describe behaviors arising in response to obsessions either as the executions of obsessive urges or to ward off obsessional thoughts. They also are perceived as being silly or excessive, cause distress, and cannot be dismissed even with great effort. Yet clinicians regularly observe symptoms in TS patients that cannot be so neatly categorized into either obsessive-compulsive (OC) or tic phenomena. Examples of these ambiguous symptoms are repetitive touching, self-injurious behaviors, needs for symmetry, needs to carry out tasks until they "feel" right, and mental urges to move in the absence of movements. The relationship of OC symptoms to TS has been conceptualized in various ways by different investigators: some view the experiences as completely separate from TS, whereas others have explained them as mental tics without behavioral expression (obsessions) or highly complex tics (compulsions).

Another way to think about these phenomena is based upon the relationship of the content and temporal occurrence to tics. Examples of tic-related experiences reported to us include repetitive thoughts preceding or following tics, ritualized movements substituted to ward off tics, magical arrangements of items to control movements, and an involuntary, consuming, elaborate, psychological scheme for balancing mental and physical intensity. Symptoms exhibited by TS patients that are apparently unrelated to tics have included the more traditional ones of washing, cleaning, checking, and counting rituals, needs for symmetry, obsessions of violent acts or images, and obligatory, unnecessary, exacting routines. Many TS patients experience some decrease in functioning as a result of OC symptoms, even surpassing the impairment caused by their tics.

Results from descriptive studies repeatedly have shown the prevalence of OC is 40–60 percent in TS probands, depending on their age and duration of illness (Pauls and Leckman, 1986; Jagger et al., 1982; Nee et al., 1980), compared to the 1.0 percent general population prevalence of OCD. Furthermore, the results of genetic family studies suggest that there is a 23 percent prevalence rate of OC among first degree relatives of TS probands (Pauls, Towbin, et al., 1986; Nee et al., 1982). Working with data from a family-genetic study of TS, investigators found that estimates of penetrance using the combination of TS, chronic multiple tics, and obsessions and compulsions as alternative expressions of the same gene gave the best fit of results and were consistent with a single-gene hypothesis with an autosomal dominant mode of transmission (Pauls and Leckman, 1986).

ETIOLOGY AND PATHOLOGY

A full pathophysiological profile of a neuropsychiatric disorder would include information on the pathways connecting genetic and constitutional factors to the development of neurochemical, hormonal, and behavioral systems; the relations between biological factors and behavioral development; the ways in which underlying mechanisms are expressed in clinical syndromes, including the range and severity of impairment, the social and familial context in which the individual develops; and how the individual with the disorder feels and functions as a full person. Thus, even if a disorder can be traced to a single, dominant gene, there are many biological and behavioral processes intervening between DNA and clinical functioning that need to be elucidated. Advances in the study of TS perhaps serve as the best available example of this approach to clinical epistemology.

Tourette himself proposed the concept that TS is a familial genetic disorder and noted that there were families in which the condition appeared to be transmitted across generations. Even now a casual review of family pedigrees suggests the transmission, over generations, of vulnerability to TS and tics. Evidence from carefully designed family-genetic studies and pedigree analysis provides more robust support for this observation. These studies have shown several important features of the genetic transmission. First, vulnerability is transmitted by either mothers or fathers to their sons and daughters. Second, the expression of the vulnerability is highly variable in form and severity. The diathesis may be completely expressed as TS, as seen in the proband case, or as chronic multiple tics or obsessive-compulsive disorder. Similarly, the diathesis may be expressed in a clinically severe disorder that has required treatment or, more often, in milder forms that would otherwise not come to clinical diagnosis (Pauls, Kruger, et al., 1984).

The most likely mode of transmission follows a single, dominant, autosomal pattern (Pauls and Leckman, 1986). In addition to a few isolated case reports on twins, a systematic study of TS among twins, conducted by our group, also strongly supports a genetic etiology (Price et al., 1985).

With the availability for study of large families with several generations of individuals with TS, investigations relying on restriction fragment length polymorphisms (RFLPs) and recombinant DNA technology have the potential, in the near future, to demonstrate the major genetic locus (or loci) of a putative TS gene. Once found, the exact sequence of nucleic acids in this gene and its gene products would be determined. Localization of the regions in the CNS affected by these products would elucidate the molecular pathobiology of TS. As a result, highly specific diagnostic tests and new specific treatments could be made available.

For any individual, however, genetic hypotheses do not completely explain the onset, specific manifestations, or severity of symptoms. The possibility that environmental, nongenetic contributions exert important modifying or precipitating effects is inescapable. These contributions include processes or events at different developmental periods— prenatal (e.g., fetal compromise), perinatal, or early in life (e.g., stress, exposure to stimulants). The interplay of genetic vulnerability and environmental factors shaping the final manifestations has implications at several levels of inquiry. A greater understanding of brain-behavior relationships, the neurophysiologic mediation of environmental stressors, and the psychological and pharmacologic treatment of patients are a few areas that could benefit from clarification of the role of nongenetic influences.

The catecholamine neurotransmitter dopamine also putatively exerts a major role in the pathophysiology of TS. A portion of the neurophysiological evidence supporting this derives from the clinical efficacy, in TS sufferers, of pharmacologic agents demonstrating powerful in vitro and in vivo inhibition of central nervous system dopaminergic neurons, such as the neuroleptic medications haloperidol, penfluridol, pimozide, and fluphenazine. The hypothesis is further supported by findings of tic inhibition by α-methyl tyrosine, a substance inhibiting dopamine synthesis, and by tetrabenazine, which inhibits the accumulation of dopamine in presynaptic storage vesicles. Furthermore, l-DOPA, and stimulants (e.g., methylphenidate, dextroamphetamine, pemoline), substances that facilitate dopaminergic transmission, increase symptoms in many TS patients. Although direct measurement of dopamine in the brain is not possible, levels of its major central nervous system metabolite, homovanillic acid (HVA), have been found to be decreased during baseline measures of cerebrospinal fluid (CSF) and following probenecid loading in TS patients. Consequently, some investigators believe that TS results from the hypersensitivity of postsynaptic dopamine receptors (Cohen, Shaywitz, Caparulo, et al., 1978; Butler et al., 1979).

Yet this conclusion must remain tentative until two unpredicted observations can be explained. Although the hypothesis would predict increased numbers of dopaminergic receptors, this has not been seen in positron emission tomography studies (Chase et al., 1984). In addition, the response to dopaminergic blocking agents is not universal. Taken as a whole, the evidence favors a role for dopaminergic dysfunction underlying some component of the syndrome, but further study will be required to explain where dopaminergic neurons act in the pathophysiology.

In addition, there may be some effects from norepinepherine (NE) and serotonin (5-HT). There is little direct support for hypotheses positing downstream effects by NE on dopamine activity directly, but there may be indirect effects via serotonergic neurons (Leckman, Cohen, Price, et al., 1986). Studies comparing CSF, plasma, and urine levels of either NE or its primary CNS metabolite, 3-methoxy-4-hyroxy phenylethylene glycol (MHPG) in normals and TS patients have not found differences.

Application of pharmacologic probes with specific activity sites, like clonidine or yohimbine, have not differentiated TS patients from normals. As better methods, such as debrisoquin loading, are used to obtain activity measures of central dopamine and other transmitters, the role of catecholamine physiology may be clarified (Riddle et al., 1986). The application of neuroimaging techniques, such as magnetic resonance and positron emission tomography, may identify influential anatomical regions and clarify physiologic relationships. These techniques may increase our understanding of the pathophysiology in TS of pathways communicating via dopamine transmitters and of the manner in which noradrenergic and serotonergic activity may modulate symptoms.

ASSESSMENT OF TIC DISORDERS

The difficulties experienced by TS patients may touch every segment of their lives. Beginning early in development, the formation of an internal sense of security in the body and the interplay between desire and action may be profoundly disturbed. Hyperactivity, inattention, and troubles in concentrating not only disrupt the child's relations with others; they impede the emergence of a stable, well-integrated sense of self as the site where needs, wishes, and actions are mediated (Cohen, 1980). Furthermore, the negative, intrusive interactions with others elicited by such behaviors can lead a child to feel that he is bad, subsequently reinforcing the very conduct that provokes rebukes by parents and others. For TS patients previously exhibiting behavioral and attentional problems, the emergence of tics and negative social reactions occurs in the context of other hostile relationships and a self-image that has already become distorted. Once the tics begin, the child will be faced with unanswerable questions reaching to the core of his sense of self: What can he control? What comes from within him and from his body but from outside of the self? What does he do that he wishes he did not do? What does he *really* want to do?

The assessment of a patient with TS requires an understanding reaching many levels. For the easiest cases, the entire clinical situation is displayed by the presence of motor and phonic tics; they may be of no more clinical consequence than other transient or simple tics of childhood. For the most complicated patients, however, virtually every sphere of functioning requires consideration. For the majority of patients, assessment must extend beyond the tics to include understanding of the ways in which the tics have affected self-esteem, socialization, and academic performance, the qualities of the individual's inner life, regulation of aggressive and sexual fantasies, and the quality of relations with others. The multifaceted familial nature of symptoms adds special meaning to the individual child's symptoms. Parents may see undesirable aspects of themselves (or their spouses or siblings) reflected literally in the behavior of their child, and the child will be led similarly in her identification.

Clinical assessment of individuals with TS thus starts with the current observable symptoms of tics and expands into a more thorough understanding of family history and interactions, development, and range of functioning. A detailed genetic pedigree of tic disorders and associated problems may elucidate not only the genetics of TS but psychodynamically important meanings of the symptoms. It it important to document early development and the emergence of behavioral and attentional problems, the kind of responses these problems elicited before the tics, the context and progression of tic symptoms, and the feelings the tics evoke in the child and family.

The diagnosis of TS is generally based on clinical observation and history; the array of symptoms with the natural history are pathognomonic. Yet careful medical and neurological assessment are useful in making sure that no other concurrent or underlying disorder is present and in documenting the range of an individual patient's problems. The physical examination of TS patients is usually unremarkable; some patients may have hypertrophic musculature as a result of their movements. Patients with self-injurious tics may have a variety of physical findings such as black-and-blue eyes, scabs, scars, corneal ulcerations, lacerations in the mouth, or broken limbs. Neurological examination usually fails to elicit localized findings. Up to half of childhood TS patients, however, have various nonlocalizing neuromaturational difficulties, including clumsiness and mixed dominance. Whether these are more prominent in patients with ADHD is not known but seems likely.

The electroencephalogram (EEG) may be abnormal in up to 40 percent of patients with TS. The abnormal findings are usually nonspecific slowing or sharp-wave activity. In children EEGs may also display deceptively rhythmic movement artifacts, which may worry nonspecialists. Families often wonder if the tic movements are seizures, particularly when a child has paroxysms, yet the EEG usually excludes this possibility. No relationship has been found between the presence of EEG abnormalities and clinical presentation. Skull X rays, computed brain tomograms (CAT-scans), and magnetic resonance images (MRI) are usually normal. As part of the differential diagnostic process, studies may be obtained to determine the presence of an endocrine, liver, or other metabolic abnormality that causes movement disorders. Screening tests (hemogram, liver function tests, endocrine studies, etc.) and an electrocardiogram are usually indicated before the initiation of medication.

Assessment will naturally focus on tics, obsessions, and compulsions (Leckman, Towbin, et al., 1988). The essential characteristics of tics—especially the situational, chronological, developmental, and anatomical variability of symptoms—add to the difficulty in assessing TS severity. Evaluating severity by simply following specific tic movements and rating their exacerbation or remission are impeded by this variability.

In order to assess tics accurately, the clinician must obtain reliable data from multiple sources because the patient may not be fully aware of the impact of the symptoms on his social and academic or occupational

Table 12.2 *Instruments for Assessment of Tourette's Syndrome*

I. Self-rated instruments
 Data bases:
  —Tourette's Syndrome Questionnaire (TSQ)
 Tourette's syndrome symptoms:
  —Tourette's Syndrome Symptom List (TSSL)
 Associated disorders:
  —Connor's Parents' Questionnaire (for ADHD)
  —Leyton Obsessional Inventory (adult version) (for OCD)
II. Clinician-rated or -assisted instruments
 Data bases:
  —Tourette's Syndrome and Other Behavioral Disorders Questionnaire
   (TSOBDQ)
 Tourette's syndrome symptoms:
  —Tourette's Syndrome Global Scale (TSGS)
  —Tourette's Syndrome Severity Scale (TSSS)
  —Tanner, Goetz, and Klawans Protocol
 Associated disorders:
  —TSOBDQ
  —Connor's Teacher's Questionnaire
  —Leyton Obsessional Inventory (child version) (for OCD)
 Global assessment:
  —Global Assessment Scale (GAS) (child or adult)

---

functioning. Subjective reports do not cover sufficiently the variety of symptoms and effects. Formal measures are often informative in addition to the observations in the consulting room, the parents' or family's reports, and whatever written or verbal reports are available from teachers, employers, or organization leaders. A list of instruments, parent- or self-rated and clinician-rated, is given in table 12.2.

Multiple information sources do create problems, however. Inaccuracy can be introduced when formal measures are made by laypersons, many of whom often have little experience with TS. Biases introduced by lay raters can be enormous and result in unintentional distortions that hinder qualitative assessment. The clinician may be frustrated in his or her efforts to arrive at a meaningful synthesis when combining ratings by multiple raters all of whom have made their observations under different conditions. Variability may yield wide fluctuations of severity as settings and raters change.

The accuracy of self- or parent-rated instruments is highly dependent on the rater's understanding and capacity for objective observation. Careful explanations about the nature of tics and the frequency of movements are critical. One caveat deserving emphasis is that, in some highly anxious families, the rating process can have undesirable effects. When parents or other relatives begin to pay constant, meticulous attention to a patient's every movement, the mounting anxiety and stress experienced by the family and the patient may lead to an increase in family distress and in the patient's symptoms.

Two self-rated scales have been developed for use in TS, and two other adjunctive scales, the Conner's Parents' Questionnaire and Leyton Obsessional Inventory, may be of value in rating associated symptoms. The Tourette's Syndrome Questionnaire (TSQ) is a self-administered historical data base focusing on basic family and personal data, previous evaluations, onset and severity of symptoms, and developmental history. It has been most commonly used in genetic or epidemiological studies but is also useful in clinical settings to screen for positive findings in the family and individual history and to open the way toward further exploration during the initial interview.

The Tourette's Syndrome Symptom List (TSSL) is a self-rating instrument that has been successfully used to assess severity throughout one week. It identifies current symptoms and asks the respondent to rate current severity of each symptom daily over one week. Standard anchor points for frequency are suggested.

The Connor's Parents' Questionnaire is an established diagnostic screening device for ADHD and associated problems. It offers common symptoms seen in childhood, loaded for ADHD, and asks parents to rate whether these occur never, a little, a lot, or always.

The Leyton Obsessional Inventory (adult version) is a commonly used, though methodologically limited, screening device for OCD (Cooper, 1970). The original inventory was developed as a card-sorting task requiring an examiner who would offer minor assistance and observe the respondent during its administration. Subsequent work has shown that it may be equally valid when conducted as a pencil-and-paper task. In the childhood version this original card-sorting technique was retained, but the probes and their wording were modified (Berg et al., 1986).

Clinician-rated scales may rely either on evaluations made following direct face-to-face observation of the patient or while viewing videotapes. Each has its advantages, but in general, the rating following interviews is the more common, cheaper, easier, and more versatile. For prospective longitudinal observations and under proper conditions, video recordings are highly desirable since they place less reliance on the memory of the observer, permit review at a subsequent time, and leave the data largely unaltered (Tanner et al., 1982).

There are two clinician-rated scales, the TS Global Scale (TSGS) and TS Severity Scale (TSSS). The TSGS assesses severity of symptoms. This assessment is based on scores from two domains: tics and social function. The tic domain examines the frequency and disruption (each with a dimensional range from 0 to 5) of each of the four categories of tics: simple and complex, motor and phonic. The social function domain assesses impairment in general behavior, school/occupational function, and motor restlessness on scales dimensionally ranging from 0 to 25. The scores on these domains are calculated so that a total score will fall between 0, or no impairment, and 100, most severe impairment (Harcherick et al., 1984).

The TSSS draws from five probes (are tics noticeable to others? do tics elicit curiosity? is patient considered odd or bizarre? do tics interfere with functioning? is patient homebound or hospitalized?) to ascertain the severity of impairment from TS. Each probe has a different range on an ordinal scale, although half-step ratings are permitted. Originally designed for assessment of severity during treatment with pimozide in a double-blind drug trial, this scale has been used to monitor severity over time (Shapiro and Shapiro, 1984).

Both the TSGS and TSSS need further development. The TSGS has two problems. For one, small deviations in category scores can result in large differences in the total score owing to the formula for calculation of the total score. Another is that the total score is weighted unevenly toward the social function domain. Neither scale permits a rating of the complexity and intensity of movements, which may be as important as their frequency or disruption. The anchor points of the TSSS are ambiguous, and raters may not understand what information is being requested.

The development of clinician-rated measures for assessment of ADHD remains a research challenge. At the present time no quick, reliable, and accurate cross-sectional scales have been generally adopted. The closest approximation is information from teachers in school reports using the Connor's Teacher's Questionnaire.

Overall functioning has been reliably assessed using the Global Assessment Scale (Endicott et al., 1976) or its analogue for children (Shaffer et al., 1983). The advantage of these measures is that a condensed, single rating is available for later comparison. The measure is simple, highly reliable, and useful for comparisons across disorders and conditions and over time.

The assessment of a patient with TS calls upon a variety of skills from one or more health providers. At one level of expertise it requires a general knowledge of the presentation of tic movements from the simplest to the most complex and the ability to appreciate the differential diagnosis and to interpret diagnostic tests for phenocopies. But it also requires, at another level, the ability to assess the degree of impairment derived from an understanding of the individual's progression along the dimensions of psychological development, work/academic performance, personal coping strategies, and intimate and peer relationships. The task is not eased by any established algorithm. The limitations of standard assessment tools and techniques force the clinician to evaluate information of diverse quality and variable accuracy. At times the clinician must participate as a health provider, educator, school liaison, social service worker, and family confidant.

THE TREATMENT OF TOURETTE'S SYNDROME

Tourette's syndrome is a disorder hovering between neurology and psychiatry. Consequently, the care of TS patients has mirrored prevailing concepts about pathogenesis of conditions in which both constitutional and experiential factors were prominent. Historically, there have been concurrent efforts to understand TS symptoms psychodynamically and TS as a disorder of the central nervous system. From the turn of the century, neurologically oriented theories emphasized the relations between TS and other movement disorders, implicating basal ganglia and other neuroanatomical systems involved in the regulation of motor activity. Cortical mechanisms and possible pathways that link the basal ganglia to higher brain areas subserving the expression of emotions have been proposed as involved in obsessions and compulsions.

The biological orientation to TS was elaborated into a neurochemical theory following the demonstration of the efficacy of haloperidol in the 1960s. During the past twenty years, neurochemical and pharmacological research has shaped the general orientation to treatment of TS patients. At present, the etiologic model that offers the most useful explanatory approach in relation to treatment and most accurately reflects clinical knowledge includes genetic determinants, environmental stressors, and psychological factors, which combine to produce the neurophysiological and behavioral characteristics of an individual patient.

This model—subsuming biological, psychological, and social components—is supported by studies in neurochemistry, neuropharmacology, and neurophysiology as elucidated by responses to pharmacologic probes and treatment agents (Ang et al., 1982; Leckman et al., 1983; Leckman et al., 1984; Riddle et al., 1986), and by studies in human genetics as suggested by results from twin and family studies (Pauls and Leckman, 1986). It integrates the clinical observations by patients and physicians of effects on the psyche, such as the meaning of symptoms to the patient and their family, the effects of chronic illness on psychological development, the effects of socially and personally distressing symptoms on psychological development, and the emotional cost of interventions employed to treat, inhibit, or camouflage symptoms (Bruun, 1988).

This overview synthesizes psychotherapeutic, family, educational, social, and pharmacologic perspectives on the treatment of TS. A composite intervention strategy follows from the premise that considering both patients' internal psychological experience and the reaction of their environment to their movements and sounds provides TS sufferers and their families with optimal care and reflects what we have learned about the disorder. Such an orientation offers the widest array of useful treatments.

Psychodynamic Psychotherapy

Whatever the etiology of TS, clinical experience suggests that some individuals with TS benefit from psychotherapy. The primary goal is not the elimination of tics or TS symptoms but treatment for the psychological conflicts that can result from this illness (and contribute to it) and any other psychological problems whether or not associated with TS. Patients may be helped to recognize what circumstances exacerbate their symptoms, to understand how they arise, and to work toward ways of diffusing or avoiding them. This therapeutic work includes the interpretation of unconscious intrapsychic conflict. There is, however, a difference between employing psychodynamic perspectives and methods and, alternatively, presuming a primary psychodynamic etiology. The model encompassing biological and psychological contributions recognizes a psychodynamic perspective and the variety of etiologic explanations.

Several psychological reactions are commonly reported in response to TS symptoms, although they are not unique to this disorder. The losses of impulse control, in thought and body, produce psychological reactions well described by Mahler and Rangell (1943), Ascher (1948), and Silver (1988). Accompanying the experience of feeling overwhelmed by thoughts and/or urges, patients frequently describe anxiety, anger, and the cognitive features (frequently seen in depression) of guilt, hopelessness, helplessness, and worthlessness. Obsessive and compulsive symptoms may arise and lead to some confusion about their origin.

The decision to employ psychodynamic treatment in TS rests on the presence of impairment in function with these findings: dysfunctional defenses employed against the experience of the disorder, lagging psychological development for a period following the appearance of TS, impairment in self-esteem arising from the reaction of family and social contacts to the symptoms of the disorder, and impairment in occupational or school role performance over and above physical disruption caused by symptoms. The complete evaluation of the TS patient demands an account of these features. In addition, the adjunctive value of psychodynamic treatment may be more strongly considered in patients who have had only marginal responses to pharmacotherapy and in patients whose families develop pathological dynamics related to the disorder.

Persons with TS have at least an equal likelihood of experiencing a coexisting psychiatric disorder as the general population, and given the demands of their chronic illness, they are probably at greater risk for depression and anxiety disorders. Psychodynamic treatment deserves special consideration for those with prominent neurotic dysfunction such as anxiety disorders, dysthymia, or depression, as well as those whose psychological defenses are seriously exaggerated or maladaptive.

Family Intervention

In persons with TS there is an interplay between symptoms and family members or peers. Although TS is not caused by pathological family or social relationships, the dynamics that develop among family members in response to symptoms form an integral part of patients' experience of their disorder. For many patients, troubled relationships within the family may be the most serious consequence of their disorder and can be the most impaired portion of their lives. This may be as true for adults with TS who live with their spouse and children as for children with TS who live with their family of origin. Cohen and coworkers (Cohen, Ort, et al., 1988) have described how the assessment of these relationships develops from an understanding of two or three components. From the patient's side there are the relationships to the family, the internal understanding of the role the person plays in the family, and family members' responses. From the parents' or spouses' perspective, there is their view of the child or spouse as a person, the meaning of their child or spouse to them, their expectations of and fantasies about them, and their understanding of the causes and consequences of the symptoms. When there are siblings at home, their view(s) of the family member and the symptoms and their responses to the potential encroachments by the impaired family member on the sibling's view of himself or herself, the family's life together, and social relationships comprise the third component.

The elucidation of the genetic basis of TS has added special importance to the assessment and treatment of families. As described earlier, TS is not only familial but genetic, and there is a range of expression of the underlying gene(s) that includes not only TS and chronic motor tics but also obsessions and compulsions. Therefore, it is likely that in the family of a TS patient there are other individuals who have problems related to these. It might be anticipated that an individual with similar problems will be more sensitive and empathic with someone who has much the same difficulties. Within families this may be especially true; a parent with tics may provide understanding and strength, convey optimism, and offer a sense of support to a child with TS. But familial transmission can also influence family dynamics in ways that do not facilitate a good adaptation to the disorder. A parent with tics may feel guilt for having transmitted the disorder; another with obsessions and compulsions may be completely unable to contend with the lack of control and impulsivity of a child with hyperactivity. During adolescence, when whatever problems faced by children are ordinarily blamed on their parents, teenagers may feel especially hostile toward a parent in whom they see problems like their own. Parents may not "remember" they had tics until reminded by their own parents. In situations such as these, the family assessment takes on broad and sensitive tasks. Clinicians need to be sure of their alliance with families, their motivation and preparation, before burdening them with this exploration and the awareness that results.

School and Occupational Intervention

When a TS patient's educational potential is not being met, offering assistance by providing the school with an understanding of the disorder and the pupil's educational needs can be a critical, far-reaching intervention.

Findings from studies of cognitive or learning impairments (Incagnoli and Kane, 1982; Golden, 1984; Hagin, 1988) suggest that TS patients may suffer from a particular cognitive weakness reflected on the coding subtest of the Wechsler Intelligence Scales for Children or impairment in motor control, which could affect performance on this subtest. Additional data (Hagin, 1988; Dykens, 1987) suggest that TS patients may also exhibit a specific weakness in mathematics. Whether ADHD is an intrinsic feature of TS has implications for the interpretation of weaknesses on the mathematics and coding subtests. It cannot be determined yet whether the identified neuropsychologic weaknesses are a product of ADHD comorbidity or attributable to TS itself. Some evidence suggests that the weakness may be specific and not solely attributable to ADHD (Dykens, 1987).

Adverse effects of pharmacologic treatment for TS may further influence education or work through impairments in memory, concentration, and motivation. Experienced clinicians have observed these impairments in patients treated with haloperidol and pimozide. Sedation, which may result from these agents and clonidine, can also affect learning. Emotional effects on academic functioning such as dysphoria (Caine and Polinsky, 1979; Bruun, 1982) and school phobia (Mikkelson, Detlor, and Cohen, 1981; Linet, 1985) have been noted in children treated with haloperidol and pimozide.

The secondary consequences of TS on school performance are far more varied. An interplay between internal and social experiences often develops. As a result, frightening or frustrating social experiences (such as being isolated from or teased by peers, being held up to public ridicule by adults, or being viewed as willfully oppositional by persons in authority) fuel inner vulnerabilities toward low self-esteem, poor frustration tolerance, lack of motivation, hopelessness, and anxiety. The cycle is completed when these feelings motivate behaviors that promote negative social experiences, most of which occur in school. Without strong advocacy, school can become an object of fear and anger. Anxiety, avoidance, or opposition are common results.

Interventions at school can improve social and educational adjustment. Hagin's survey (1988) of school modifications that worked successfully for TS patients suggests that a compassionate, positive, supportive attitude from teachers and efforts to reduce classroom stress are often useful. Tactics to reduce stress included classroom structure, one-to-one assistance, setting reasonable goals divided into small segments, sensitivity to and flexibility with time pressures, and specific assistance with instructions. Many children with TS benefit from being freed from any time constraints on their examinations. Typewriters can be an immense relief when writing is impossible because of specific symptoms (such as jabbing at the paper or scribbling over and over) or penmanship becomes hindered by severe symptoms. Hagin stresses that severely affected children can benefit from time to be alone. A moderate amount of structure is most appropriate for students with TS, although some students benefit from programs that are weighted toward the extremes. Not every child will need all of these aids, but most will need some of them. It is most helpful when teachers, like clinicians, view the child as a whole person, develop a broad view of a pupil's overall academic and social functioning, and avoid the temptation to fix upon target symptoms.

In the workplace, adults benefit from similar modifications. Many adults with TS are capable of working in any environment and require no modifications of tasks or expectations. More severely affected individuals, however, can benefit from the availability of structured tasks that can be broken into discrete pieces, flexibility with regard to time deadlines, specific assistance with instructions, and the freedom to arrange predictable opportunities to be alone, away from clients and coworkers. Some have benefited from working in noisy locations.

Experienced clinicians have observed a high degree of variability in symptoms on the job. An employer might logically assume that jobs requiring such tasks as detailed drawings, high-pressured sales pitches, technical presentations, or public performances would be beyond an employee with TS, especially one who is severely affected. Paradoxically, many are able to complete these assignments with skill. Such work may be beyond a person with TS, but since the waxing and waning of symptoms is unpredictable, it is more likely that given tasks will be impossible only at certain times. The complexity of this problem can be reduced by obtaining the collaboration of the employee with TS in making decisions about assignments. Employers, occupational medical staff, and job supervisors can broaden their understanding of TS in general and of their employee specifically by seeking explanations and recommendations from an expert. Flexibility, compassion, and productivity in the workplace can be increased with appropriate interventions for symptomatic patients.

Social Issues

Social policy issues have a crucial impact on TS patients. The public resources available to assist them are often limited. Clinicians corresponding with government agencies on behalf of TS patients need assistance in order to maximize the help given to their patients. Meyers (1988) has underscored that many agencies have had no experience with cases involving TS. She stresses that clinicians can be immensely helpful by offering more than mere diagnostic labels when asked to describe their patient's needs. Between agencies a categorical ambiguity about TS frequently exists, some viewing it as a "mental illness" and others not. The ambiguity can result in discrimination in access to education or vocational rehabilitation, employment, life and health insurance, housing, and disability reimbursement.

Findings from a study of 114 TS adults in Ohio (Stefl, 1983) suggest that, among TS sufferers, unemployment is four times the average and that unemployment is not necessarily correlated with the degree of disability. Bruun's study (1988) yielded similar statistics. Forty percent had reported suffering job discrimination. Similarly, a significant minority of patients with prominent vocal tics have difficulties obtaining and keeping adequate housing. Patients may be denied access to supervised care facilities. The needs in each case are often specific. For clinicians treating the most severely affected TS patients, interventions, such as finding shelter, public assistance, and vocational rehabilitation are the most basic, complex, and time-consuming therapeutic acts.

Pharmacologic Treatment

Pharmacologic treatments are widely used for TS. In the recent Ohio Tourette's Syndrome Association survey, 70 percent of patients reported a history of medication treatment (Stefl, 1983). Individual patients most want to know whether any relief from a medication is available and what side effects he or she may be required to endure. Clinicians wish for this information also, but, in addition, the effects of pharmacologic agents are heuristically important and can generate hypotheses about the pathophysiology of TS. Currently there is general agreement among clinicians treating TS about the efficacy and limitations of most currently available agents.

The aim of treatment, whatever the modality, is to assist the patient's progression along the optimal developmental path. This encompasses self-esteem, family and peer relationships, and academic or occupational functioning. Choosing an intervention must involve consideration of the benefits and adverse impacts upon each of these dimensions.

Once the decision to intervene has been reached, a consistent method of monitoring a patient's course becomes a part of the treatment process.

For patients with mild symptoms, supportive counseling and observation may be all that is needed. Standardized instruments, like those above, become objective tools for following the course and severity of symptoms.

Most cases that come for clinical care will be mild. For these, the conservative interventions including appropriate involvement of social agencies, education, and counseling of the patient, family, and school or employer are primary. During this time the patient should be followed closely. Occasional periods of increased symptoms may not be sufficient reason to change the treatment. If, however, over the course of weeks or months there is a trend toward deterioration or symptoms become much more severe and impairing, pharmacologic intervention is a logical step.

The basic principles governing pharmacotherapy of psychiatric disorders, as listed in table 12.3, apply equally to TS and deserve careful attention. In the United States there are currently only four established pharmacologic options based upon evidence from large trials: haloperidol, clonidine, pimozide, and fluphenazine.

Haloperidol. The most widely investigated agent for the treatment of TS is the butryophenone, haloperidol, a potent dopaminergic receptor blocking agent, with affinity for inducing blockade at the D_2 receptor site. Roughly 70 percent of patients with TS will improve moderately or more when treated with haloperidol. Haloperidol also has the desirable properties of being less sedating and less anticholinergic than many other dopaminergic blocking agents.

Although in the 1970s, clinicians would prescribe doses as high as 150 mg/day, it is now recognized that lower doses are effective, safer, and better tolerated. Beginning doses of 0.5 mg are given before sleep or upon arising. Increments of 0.5 mg steps at weekly intervals are prescribed if symptoms remain severe. Although maximum doses vary among clinicians and situations, in children without other serious diffi-

Table 12.3 *Basic Principles of Pharmacotherapy of TS*

- Start patients on the smallest doses of medication possible.
- Increase doses gradually.
- Ensure adequate duration of a drug trial.
- Use sufficient doses.
- Maintain the lowest effective dose.
- Avoid polypharmacy.
- Make changes in regimens as sequences of single steps.

culties, 4 mg/day is a typical maximum dose. In adults or among children with very serious tics and/or behavioral difficulties as much as 15 mg/day may be used. Usually medication is given in a single dose, although some clinicians prefer twice daily dosing.

Side effects are a major obstacle to successful maintenance use of haloperidol. Roughly 40–60 percent of TS patients treated with haloperidol will discontinue it because of side effects that include Parkinsonian side effects, sedation, weight gain, decreased concentration, social or school phobias, decreased memory, anergia, dysphoria, akathisia, personality changes, loss of libido, sexual dysfunction, and, especially after chronic use of high doses, tardive dyskinesia (TD) (Riddle, Hardin, et al., 1987). There is a diversity of opinion about how anti-Parkinsonian medication should be used with haloperidol. Some clinicians will begin low doses of anti-Parkinsonian medication, such as 0.5 mg/day of benztropine, with the first dose of haloperidol. Others begin anti-Parkinsonian treatments when haloperidol doses reach 2–3 mg/day. A third group prefers to wait until Parkinsonian side effects emerge before prescribing anti-Parkinsonian agents. Warning about TD and periodic or annual assessments for dyskinetic movements (using a scale such as the Abnormal Involuntary Movement Scale) are advisable. Given the frequency and gravity of side effects associated with haloperidol and the other neuroleptics, many clinicians reserve their use for individuals who have moderate to severe symptoms and substantial impairment in daily living.

Pimozide. Approved in the United States for the treatment of TS in 1984, pimozide is now in relatively common use. Neither a butyrophenone nor a phenothiazine, it is a di-phenylbutylpiperidine with potent dopaminergic blocking properties and, putatively, relative D_2-receptor selectivity. Like haloperidol, roughly 70–80 percent of TS patients will respond to pimozide (Shapiro and Shapiro, 1984; Moldofsky and Sandor, 1988). Pimozide appears to be better tolerated than haloperidol, and perhaps 60 percent of patients choose to remain on the medication.

Pimozide's side effects are similar to haloperidol, especially akathisia, extrapyramidal effects, and sedation, but may be less severe and appear in fewer patients. The identified side effects include the more unusual ones such as phobias, depression, and galactorrhea (Linet, 1985; Shapiro and Shapiro, 1984). This may also be true for the development of tardive dyskinesia (Chouinard and Steinberg, 1982). Concern about cardiotoxicity was raised by initial reports of electrocardiographic (ECG) abnormalities, U waves and inverted T waves, in early studies. Further investigations with larger numbers of patients have not justified these concerns (Moldofsky and Sandor, 1988). Nevertheless, routine ECG studies before initiating treatment periodically and especially after increases in doses are advised.

Initial doses of 1.0 mg with gradual increases to 3 mg/day are usually used. A majority of patients respond to this dose over a six-week trial. Some patients may require maintenance doses of 8 mg/day. Maximum recommended doses for children are 10 mg/day and for adults, 20 mg/day. The half-life of the drug permits single daily dosing or, to diminish sedation, divided doses may be given twice each day.

Other neuroleptics. Phenothiazine compounds can be alternatives to haloperidol and pimozide. Fluphenazine is the most investigated and effective agent in this category with reported side effects roughly identical to haloperidol. Some patients report fewer of them and tolerate them better. The recommended dose range is similar to haloperidol: up to 5 mg/day for the low dose responders and up to 12.5 mg/day for the higher dose responders. It is advised that lower initial doses, such as 1.0 mg/day, be prescribed.

Clonidine. Clonidine has a lower response rate than haloperidol or pimozide. It may be effective for perhaps 40–60 percent of TS patients (Cohen, Detlor, Young, et al., 1980). No known indications or constellations of symptoms predict response. In the opinion of some clinicians, the lower response rate is offset by fewer and milder side effects. Consequently, the balance between side effects and efficacy may favor clonidine as a first-line drug. Efforts to draw conclusions about the relative efficacy of clonidine have been hampered by small sample sizes, large placebo response rates for all medications, and comparisons between studies which show wide disparities with regard to comorbid conditions, baseline severity, average age, and assessments of symptom severity (Leckman, Walkup, and Cohen, 1988).

Low dose treatment usually begins with 0.05 mg daily and increases by 0.05 mg in three- to seven-day intervals. The daily dose is increased by increasing the dosing frequency (.05 mg twice daily, three times daily, etc.) to a maximum of four times daily. In some patients doses as high as .60 mg/day may be needed. In general, if patients respond to clonidine their compliance is greater because they experience fewer or less disturbing side effects. The most commonly observed side effects are sedation and dry mouth (xerostomia), which are usually improved by lowering the dose by 0.05 mg/day. Rarely, increased symptoms and manic episodes have been reported. Hypotension is more common at higher doses. In considering the duration of clonidine drug trials, there are reports suggesting that response may demand a long latency time—as long as twelve weeks; some clinicians believe that six-week trials are adequate.

Stimulant medications. At present there are no generally agreed upon guidelines for the combined treatment of tic disorders and ADHD (Golden, 1988). Some clinicians will initiate stimulant treatment in any patient with ADHD and observe them closely. Others will optimize environmental interventions and then use clonidine or one of the tricyclic antidepressants, imipramine or desipramine, avoiding stimulants altogether. A middle position has been to discontinue stimulants in ADHD patients who develop tics and, if educational and therapeutic interventions are optimal, employ clonidine or antidepressants. For patients without tics who present with ADHD and a positive family history for tic disorders, a cautious trial of stimulant medication is warranted.

There are diverse opinions about the treatment of ADHD in patients with TS. Some clinicians begin stimulants and discontinue them if tics increase; others prefer starting with clonidine or antidepressants. A third approach is a combination of haloperidol and stimulants (Shapiro and Shapiro, 1988; Comings and Comings, 1984). Clinicians using this regimen maintain that tics are not exacerbated by stimulants if the lowest possible effective dose is prescribed. The combination regimen has also been employed to relieve akinesia from haloperidol (Shapiro and Shapiro, 1988). Although transient increases in tics have been observed on this regimen, they are reportedly short-lived and easily managed. Carefully controlled investigations on larger populations of patients with tic plus ADHD are obviously necessary before one approach can be recommended.

Treatment of obsessions and compulsions in TS. Until many questions are answered, treatment for OC symptoms in TS patients will continue to be an exercise in extrapolation. Drug trials in OCD patients suggest that for some individuals, tricyclic antidepressants, such as chlorimipramine or imipramine, monoamine oxidase inhibitors, or newer heterocyclic antidepressants, such as fluoxetine, may be useful in ameliorating symptoms. Yet findings from trials such as these, employing cohorts ascertained for OCD, cannot be credibly generalized to TS patients. In response to recent studies, TS patients are now routinely evaluated for OC, and more data on the response of these symptoms to standard agents for tics, such as haloperidol, pimozide, and clonidine, should be available soon. Anecdotal reports of worsening tics in patients treated with tricyclics and monoamine oxidase inhibitors exist, although no systematic trials for the treatment of OC have been conducted on TS cohorts of sufficient sample size.

Patients with serious impairments resulting from obsessions and/or compulsions may be considered for drug treatment. Specific controlled trials are necessary to determine safety and efficacy of investigational agents in TS patients, but the responses of ocd patients offer hope to the most seriously disabled patients with TS and OC. The benefits and safety of drug combinations, such as tricyclic or heterocyclic antidepressants plus clonidine, pimozide, or haloperidol, warrant study. Our preliminary observations suggest that such combinations may be very beneficial to selected patients.

Maintenance and discontinuation. One possible outcome of treatment is the reestablishment of appropriate development and minimized tic and other symptoms. When development is proceeding smoothly, symptoms are in some control, and daily life is not seriously impaired, the gradual reduction and eventual discontinuation of medication should be attempted. Yet there is no formula for predicting the optimum duration of drug treatment. Generally patients who respond to a medication remain on it for several years or longer.

Gradual reductions are recommended for any of these agents. When clonidine is rapidly discontinued, rebound hypertension may follow and exacerbation of tics lasting as long as six or eight weeks has been reported (Leckman, Ort, et al., 1986). When abrupt reductions in haloperidol are attempted, withdrawal dyskinsias may be observed over a duration of two to three months (and as long as nine months) and can be confused with exacerbation of tics. Even when reductions in neuroleptics are carried out gradually, dyskinetic movements, previously masked by the neuroleptic, may surface. Movements arising during gradual reductions tend to be less intense and more variable in duration than those observed following abrupt cessation (Shapiro and Shapiro, 1988).

Some patients continue to have disturbed development with severe symptoms even while receiving medication. In persons who are minimally responsive or unresponsive to medication, nonpharmacologic interventions become even more important. For these patients, the immediate and future living environment and academic or vocational opportunities require vigorous development. Sometimes clinicians are tempted to prescribe ever-increasing doses of medication with the hope that this will yield better control, but it appears that greater benefits do not accrue. Increasing side effects and, especially when dopaminergic blocking agents are employed, risks of tardive dyskinesia outweigh any additional amelioration of symptoms. With clonidine higher doses usually result in hypotension and sedation.

CONCLUSION

A developmental perspective on TS is essential when counseling patients and planning treatment. All interventions (especially pharmacotherapy) must be seen in the context of their anticipated effect on the individual immediately and over subsequent years. Whatever the patient's age, treatment plans must be based upon his current and projected optimal development. Since there is as yet no cure for TS, the experienced clinician must try to help patients in the tasks of living and protect them from potential dangers. From this perspective, promoting the patient's development by supporting warm family and peer relationships, aiding socialization, facilitating school achievement or rewarding employment, and cultivating self-esteem carries greater developmental benefit than dedication to suppression of tics at any cost.

Although TS can be a devastating and lifelong condition, there are reasons for optimism. First, the pace of our understanding of the disorder is accelerating. It is likely that the genetic risks, mechanisms of transmission, and biological pathways leading to expression will be clarified during the next decade. Second, increased understanding offers hope for more effective treatment. Third, it is important to underscore that, dramatic portrayals notwithstanding, TS is most often a mild condition, perfectly compatible with a full, normal life; most persons with TS will achieve at least as much in life as those who have no tics. This has been amply borne out both by clinical experience over decades and by survey findings that suggest there is a large population of TS patients who never come for treatment. The diagnosis of TS need not arouse panic in parents and patients. Fourth, TS has grown from an obscure, exotic disorder to a widely recognized clinical entity. The growth in recognition means individuals with TS are more likely to find knowledgeable physicians, educators, psychologists, and others to whom they can turn for information, understanding, and care.

REFERENCES

Ang, L.; Borison, R.; Dysken, M.; and Davis, J. M. (1982). "Reduced Excretion of MHPG in Tourette's Syndrome." In A. J. Friedhoff and T. N.

Chase, eds., *Gilles de la Tourette Syndrome*. New York: Raven Press, 171–77.

Ascher, E. (1948). "Psychodynamic Considerations in Gilles de la Tourette Disease (Maladie des Tics)." *Am J. Psychiatry* 105:267–76.

Barkley, R. A. (1981). *Hyperactive Children: A Handbook for Diagnosis and Treatment*. New York: Guilford Press, 4–7.

Berg, C., Rapoport, J. L., and Flament, M. (1986). "The Leyton Obsessional Inventory—Child Version." *J. Am. Acad. Child Psychiat.* 25, no. 1:84–91.

Berkson, J. (1946). "Limitations of the Application of Fourfold Table Analysis to Hospital Data." *Biometrics* 2:47–50.

Bruun, R. D. (1982). "Dysphoric Phenomena Associated with Haloperidol Treatment of Tourette Syndrome." In A. J. Friedhoff and T. N. Chase, eds., *Gilles de la Tourette Syndrome*. New York: Raven Press, 433–36.

——— (1988). "The Natural History of Tourette's Syndrome." In D. J. Cohen, R. D. Bruun, and J. F. Leckman, eds., *Tourette's Syndrome and Tic Disorders: Clinical Understanding and Treatment*. New York: Wiley, 21–40.

Butler, I. J.; Koslow, S. H.; Seifert, W. E., Jr.,; Caprioli, R. M., and Singer, H. S. (1979). "Biogenic Amine Metabolism in Tourette Syndrome." *Ann. Neurol.* 6:37–39.

Caine, E. D., and Polinsky, R. J. (1979). "Haloperidol-Induced Dysphoria in Patients with Tourette Syndrome." *Am. J. Psychiat.* 136:1216–17.

Chase, T. N.; Foster, N. L., Fedro, P.; Brooks, R.; Mansi, L.; Kessler, R.; and DiChiro, G. (1984). "Gilles de la Tourette Syndrome: Studies with the Fluorine-18 Labeled Fluorodeoxyglucose Positron Emission Tomographic Method." *Ann. Neurol.* 15(Suppl.):175.

Chouinard, G., and Steinberg, S. (1982). "Type I Tardive Dyskinesia Induced by Anticholinergic Drugs, Dopamine Agonists and Neuroleptics." *Prog. Neuropsychopharmacol. and Biol. Psychiat.* 6:571–78.

Cohen, D. J. (1980). "The Pathology of the Self in Primary Childhood Autism and Gilles de la Tourette Syndrome." In B. Blinder, ed., *Psychiatric Clinics of North America*. Philadelphia: W. B. Saunders, 3, no. 3:383–402.

Cohen, D. J., Bruun, R. D., and Leckman, J. F., eds. (1988). *Tourette's Syndrome and Tic Disorders: Clinical Understanding and Treatment*. New York: Wiley.

Cohen, D. J.; Detlor, J.; Shaywitz, B.; and Leckman, J. F. (1982). "Interaction of Biological and Psychological Factors in the Natural History of Tourette's Syndrome: A Paradigm for Childhood Neuropsychiatric Disorders." In A. J. Friedhoff and T. N. Chase, eds., *Gilles de la Tourette Syndrome*. New York: Raven Press, 31–40.

Cohen, D. J.; Detlor, J.; Young, J. G.; and Shaywitz, B. A. (1980). "Clonidine Ameliorates Gilles de la Tourette Syndrome." *Arch. Gen. Psychiat.* 37:1350–57.

Cohen, D. J.; Ort, S. I.; Leckman, J. F.; Riddle, M. A.; and Hardin, M. H. (1988). "Family Functioning and Tourette Syndrome." In D. J. Cohen, R. D. Bruun, and J. F. Leckman, eds., *Tourette's Syndrome and Tic Disorders: Clinical Understanding and Treatment*. New York: Wiley, 177–96.

Cohen, D. J.; Shaywitz, B. A.; Caparulo, B. K.; Young, J. G.; and Bowers, M. B., Jr. (1988). "Chronic Multiple Tics of Gilles de la Tourette's Disease: CSF Acid Monoamine Metabolites after Probenecid Administration." *Arch. Gen. Psychiat.* 35, no. 2:245–50.

Cohen, D. J.; Shaywitz, B. A.; Young, J. G.; Carbonari, C. M.; Nathanson, J. A.; Lieberman, D.; Bowers, M. B., Jr.; and Maas, J. W. (1979). "Central Biogenic Amine Metabolism in Children with the Syndrome of Chronic Multiple Tics of Gilles de la Tourette: Norepinepherine, Serotonin, and Dopamine." *J. Am. Acad. Child Psychiat.* 18, no. 2:320–41.

Comings, D. E., and Comings, B. G. (1984). "Tourette's Syndrome and Attention Deficit Disorder with Hyperactivity: Are They Related? *J. Am. Acad. Child Psychiat.* 23:138–46.

Connell, P. H.; Corbett, J. A.; Horne, D. J.; and Mathews, A. M. (1967). "Drug Treatment of Adolescent Ticquers: A Double Blind Trial of Diazepam and Haloperidol." *Brit. J. Psychiat.* 113:375–81.

Cooper, J. (1976). "The Leyton Obsessional Inventory." *Psychol. Med.* (1):48–64.

Denkla, M., Bemporad, J., and Mackay, M. (1976). "Tics Following Methylphenidate Administration: A Report of 20 Cases." *JAMA* 235:1349–51.

Dykens, E., Leckman, J., and Riddle, M. (1987). "Intellectual and Adaptive Functioning of Tourette's Syndrome Children with and without ADDH." In *Scientific Proceedings of the Annual Meeting* (American Academy of Child and Adolescent Psychiatry). Vol. 3. Washington, D.C.

Endicott, J., Spitzer, R. L., Fliess, J. L., et al. (1976). "The Clinical Global Scale: A Procedure for Measuring Overall Severity of Psychiatric Disturbance." *Arch. Gen. Psychiat.* 33:766–71.

Fahn, S. (1982). "The Clinical Spectrum of Motor Tics." In A. J. Friedhoff and T. N. Chase, eds., *Gilles de la Tourette Syndrome*. New York: Raven Press, 341–44.

Fahn, S., and Erenberg, G. (1988). "Differential Diagnosis of Tic Phenomena: A Neurologic Perspective." In D. J. Cohen, R. D. Bruun, and J. F. Leckman, eds., *Tourette's Syndrome and Tic Disorders: Clinical Understanding and Treatment*. New York: Wiley, 41–55.

Ferenczi, S. (1921). "Psychoanalytic Observations on Tic." In S. Ferenczi, *Further Contributions to the Theory and Technique of Psychoanalysis*. London: Hogarth Press.

Gilles de la Tourette, G. ([1895] 1982). "Study of a Neurologic Condition Characterized by Motor Incoordination Accompanied by Echolalia and

Coprolalia. In A. J. Friedhoff and T. N. Chase, eds., *Gilles de la Tourette Syndrome,* New York: Raven Press, 1–16.

Glaze, D. G., Frost, J. D., and Jankovic, J. (1983). "Gilles de la Tourette's Syndrome: Disorder of Arousal." *Neurology* 33:586–92.

Golden, G. S. (1977). "The Effect of Central Nervous System Stimulants on Tourette Syndrome." *Ann. Neurol.* 2:69–70.

——— (1984). "Psychologic and Neuropsychologic Aspects of Tourette's Syndrome." *Neurol. Clin. N. Am.* 2:91–102.

——— (1988). "The Use of Stimulants and Tourette's Syndrome." In D. J. Cohen, R. D. Bruun, and J. F. Leckman, eds., *Tourette's Syndrome and Tic Disorders: Clinical Understanding and Treatment.* New York: Wiley, 317–29.

Gonce, M., and Barbeau, A. (1977). "Seven Cases of Gilles de la Tourette's Syndrome: Partial Relief with Clonazepam." *Can. J. Neurol. Sci.* 75:225–41.

Hagin, R. A. (1988). "School Problems Associated with Tourette's Syndrome." In D. J. Cohen, R. D. Bruun, and J. F. Leckman, eds., *Tourette's Syndrome and Tic Disorders: Clinical Understanding and Treatment.* New York: Wiley.

Harcherick, D. F., Leckman, J. F., Detlor, J., and Cohen, D. J. (1984). "A New Instrument for Clinical Studies of Tourette's Syndrome." *J. Am. Acad. Child Psychiat.* 23(2):153–60.

Incagnoli, T., and Kane, R. (1982). "Neuropsychological Functioning in Tourette Syndrome." In A. J. Friedhoff and T. N. Chase, eds. *Gilles de la Tourette Syndrome.* New York: Raven Press, 305–309.

Jagger, J.; Prusoff, B. A.; Cohen, D. J.; Kidd, K. K.; Carbonari, C. M.; and John, K. (1982). "The Epidemiology of Tourette's Syndrome." *Schiz. Bull.* 8(2):267–78.

Lebovici, S.; Rabain, J. F.; Nathan, T.; Thomas, R.; and Duboz, M. M. (1986). "A propos de la maladie de Gilles de la Tourette." *Psychiatrie de l'enfant* 29(1):5–59.

Leckman, J. F.; Cohen, D. J.; Gertner, J. M.; Ort, S. I.; and Harcherik, D. F. (1984). "Growth Hormone Response to Clonidine in Children Ages 4–17: Tourette's Syndrome vs. Children with Short Stature." *J. Am. Acad. Child Psychiat.* 23:174–81.

Leckman, J. F.; Cohen, D. J.; Price, R. A.; Riddle, M. A.; Minderaa, R. B.; Anderson, G. M.; and Pauls, D. L. (1986). "The Pathogenesis of Tourette Syndrome: A Review of Data and Hypotheses." In N. S. Shah and N. B. Shah, eds., *Movement Disorders.* New York Plenum Press, 257–72.

Leckman, J. F.; Detlor, J.; Harcherik, D. F.; Young, J. G.; and Anderson, G. M. (1983). "Acute and Chronic Clonidine Treatment in Tourette's Syndrome: A Preliminary Report on Clinical Response and Effect on Plasma and Urinary Catecholamine Metabolites, Growth Hormone and Blood Pressure." *J. Am. Acad. Child Psychiat.* 22:433–40.

Leckman, J. F.; Ort, S. I.; Cohen, D. J.; Caruso, K. A.; Anderson, G. M.; and Riddle, M. A. (1986). "Rebound Phenomena in Tourette's Syndrome after Abrupt Withdrawal of Clonidine: Behavioral Cardiovascular and Neurochemical Effects." *Arch. Gen. Psychiat.* 43:1168–76.

Leckman, J. F.; Price, R. A.; Walkup, J. T.; Ort, S. I.; Pauls, D. L.; and Cohen, D. J. (1987). "Nongenetic Factors in Gilles de la Tourette's Syndrome. *Arch. Gen. Psychiat.* 44:100.

Leckman, J. F.; Riddle, M. A., and Cohen, D. J. (1988). "Pathobiology of Tourette's Syndrome." In D. J. Cohen, R. D. Bruun, and J. F. Leckman, eds., *Tourette's Syndrome and Tic Disorders: Clinical Understanding and Treatment.* New York: Wiley, 103–08.

Leckman, J. F.; Towbin, K. E.; Ort, S. I.; and Cohen, D. J. (1988). "Clinical Assessment of Tic Disorder Severity." In D. J. Cohen, R. D. Bruun, and J. F. Leckman, eds., *Tourette's Syndrome and Tic Disorders: Clinical Understanding and Treatment.* New York: Wiley, 55–78.

Leckman, J. F., Walkup, J. T., and Cohen, D. J. (1988). "Clonidine Treatment of Tourette's Syndrome." In D. J. Cohen, R. D. Bruun, and J. F. Leckman, eds., *Tourette's Syndrome and Tic Disorders: Clinical Understanding and Treatment.* New York: Wiley, 291–302.

Linet, L. S. (1985). "Tourette Syndrome, Pimozide, and School Phobia: The Neuroleptic Separation Anxiety Syndrome." *Am. J. Psychiat.* 142(5):613–15.

Lowe, T. L.; Cohen, D. J.; Detlor, J.; Kremenitzer, M. W.; Shaywitz, B. A. (1982). "Stimulant Medications Precipitate Tourette's Syndrome." *JAMA* 247:1729–31.

Mahler, M. (1949). "A Psychoanalytic Evaluation of Tic in Psychopathology of Children." *Psychoanal. Study Child* 3–4:279–310.

Mahler, M. S., and Rangell, L. (1943). "A Psychosomatic Study of Maladie des Tics (Gilles de la Tourette's Disease)." *Psychiatric Q.* 17:519–605.

Meyers, A. S. (1988). "Social Issues of Tourette Syndrome." In D. J. Cohen, R. D. Bruun, and J. F. Leckman, eds., *Tourette's Syndrome and Tic Disorders: Clinical Understanding and Treatment.* New York: Wiley, 257–67.

Mikkelson, E. J., Detlor, J., and Cohen, D. J. (1981). "School Avoidance and Social Phobia Triggered by Haloperidol in Patients with Tourette's Disorder. *Am. J. Psychiat.* 138(12):1572–75.

Moldofsky, H., and Sandor, P. (1988). "Pimozide in the Treatment of Gilles de la Tourette." In D. J. Cohen, R. D. Bruun, and J. F. Leckman, eds., *Tourette's Syndrome and Tic Disorders: Clinical Understanding and Treatment.* New York: Wiley, 281–91.

Nee, L. E.; Caine, E. D.; Polinsky, R. J.; Eldridge, R.; and Ebert, M. H. (1980). "Gilles de la Tourette Syndrome: Clinical and Family Study of 50 Cases." *Ann. Neurol.* 7(1):41–49.

Nee, L. E., Polinsky, R. J., and Ebert, M. H. (1982). "Tourette Syndrome:

Clinical and Family Studies." In A. J. Friedhoff and T. N. Chase, eds., *Gilles de la Tourette Syndrome*. New York: Raven Press, 291–95.

Pauls, D. L.; Hurst, C. R.; Kruger, S. D.; Leckman, J. F.; Kidd, K. K.; and Cohen, D. J. (1986). "Gilles de la Tourette Syndrome and Attention Deficit Disorder with Hyperactivity." *Arch. Gen. Psych.* 43(12):1177–79.

Pauls, D. L.; Kruger, S. D.; Leckman, J. F.; Cohen, D. J.; and Kidd, K. K. (1984). "The Risk Tourette Syndrome and Chronic Multiple Tics among Relatives of Tourette's Syndrome Patients Obtained by Direct Interview." *J. Am. Acad. Child Psychiat.* 23:134–37.

Pauls, D. L., and Leckman, J. F. (1986). "The Inheritance of Gilles de la Tourette's Syndrome and Associated Behaviors: Evidence for Autosomal Dominant Transmission." *N.E. J. Med.* 315:993–97.

Pauls, D. L.; Towbin, K. E.; Leckman, J. F.; Zahner, G. E. P.; and Cohen, D. J. (1986). "Gilles de la Tourette's Syndrome and Obsessive-Compulsive Disorder." *Arch. Gen. Psychiat.* 43(12):1180–82.

Price, R. A.; Kidd, K. K.; Cohen, D. J.; Pauls, D. L.; and Leckman, J. F. (1985). "A Twin Study of Tourette's Syndrome." *Arch. Gen. Psychiat.* 42:815–20.

Riddle, M. A.; Hardin, M. T.; Towbin, K. E.; Leckman, J. F.; and Cohen, D. J. (1987). "Tardive Dyskinesia Following Haloperidol Treatment in Tourette's Syndrome." *Arch. Gen. Psychiat.* 44:98–99.

Riddle, M. A.; Shaywitz, B. A.; Leckman, J. F.; Anderson, G. M.; Shaywitz, S. E.; Hardin, M. T.; Ort, S. I.; and Cohen, D. J. (1986). "Brief Debrisoquin Administration to Assess Central Dopaminergic Function in Children." *Life Sci.* 38:1041–48.

Rosen, M., and Wesner, C. (1979). "A Behavioral Approach to Tourette's Syndrome." *J. Can. Clin. Psychol.* 41:303–12.

Shaffer, D.; Gould, M. S.; Brasic, J.; Ambrosini, P.; Fisher, P.; Bird, H.; and Aluwahalia, S. (1983). "A Children's Global Assessment Scale." *Arch. Gen. Psychiat.* 40:1228–31.

Shapiro, A. K., and Shapiro, E. (1984). "Controlled Study of Pimozide vs. Placebo in Tourette's Syndrome." *J. Am. Acad. Child Psychiat.* 23(2):161–73.

——— (1988). "Treatment of Tic Disorders with Haloperidol." In D. J. Cohen, R. D. Bruun, and J. F. Leckman, eds., *Tourette's Syndrome and Tic Disorders: Clinical Understanding and Treatment*. New York: Wiley.

Shapiro, A. K.; Shapiro, E.; Bruun, R. D.; and Sweet, R. (1978). *Gilles de la Tourette Syndrome*. New York: Raven Press.

Shapiro, A. K.; Shapiro, E.; Young, J. G.; and Feinberg, T. E. (1988). *Gilles de la Tourette Syndrome*. 2nd ed. New York: Raven Press.

Silver, A. A. (1988). "Intrapsychic Processes and Adjustment in Tourette Syndrome." In D. J. Cohen, R. D. Bruun, and J. F. Leckman, eds., *Tourette's Syndrome and Tic Disorders: Clinical Understanding and Treatment*. New York: Wiley.

Stefl, M. E. (1983). *The Ohio Tourette Study: An Investigation of the Special Service Needs of Tourette Syndrome Patients*. Cincinnati: School of Planning, University of Cincinnati.

Tanner, C. M., Goetz, C. G., and Klawans, H. L. (1982). "Cholinergic Mechanisms in Tourette's Syndrome." *Neurol.* 32:1315–17.

Towbin, K. E. (1988). "Obsessive-Compulsive Symptoms in Gilles de la Tourette Syndrome." In D. J. Cohen, R. D. Bruun, and J. F. Leckman, eds., *Tourette's Syndrome and Tic Disorders: Clinical Understanding and Treatment*. New York: Wiley, 137–51.

van Woert, M. H., Rosenbaum, D., and Enna, S. J. (1982). "Overview of Pharmacological Approaches to Therapy for Tourette's Syndrome." In A. J. Friedhoff and T. N. Chase, eds., *Gilles de la Tourette Syndrome*. New York: Raven Press, 369–75.

Wolff, E. (1988). "Psychotherapeutic Interventions with Tourette Syndrome." In D. J. Cohen, R. D. Bruun, and J. F. Leckman, eds., *Tourette's Syndrome and Tic Disorders: Clinical Understanding and Treatment*. New York: Wiley, 207–33.

Zahner, G. E. P.; Clubb, M. M.; Leckman, J. F.; and Pauls, D. L. (1988). "The Epidemiology of Tourette's Syndrome." In D. J. Cohen, R. D. Bruun, and J. F. Leckman, eds., *Tourette's Syndrome and Tic Disorders: Clinical Understanding and Treatment*. New York: Wiley, 79–90.

Zubenko, G. S.; Cohen, B. M.; Lipinski, J. F.; and Jonas, J. M. (1984). "Use of Clonidine in the Treatment of Akathisia." *Psychiat. Res.* 13:253–59.

13

A Follow-up Study of Young Adolescents with Attention Deficit Disorder

MARTIN H. SCHMIDT

GUNTHER ESSER

The problem with talking about attention deficit disorder (ADD) or hyperactivity is the confused terminology and the lack of agreement on diagnostic criteria. The term ADD is shorthand for a cluster of complaints about children's behavior; inattentiveness, distractibility, restless overactivity, impulsiveness, and affective lability are the most prominent ones. A similar cluster of psychopathological symptoms is strongly connected with the diagnosis of cerebral dysfunction, also called minimal cerebral dysfunction (MCD) or minimal brain dysfunction (MBD). Hence, both terms are sometimes considered identical. In clinical practice (in Europe, but also in the United States) the diagnosis of ADD often is one of the factors determining MBD. According to this convention, it may happen that subjects are classified as MBD cases only because of their hyperkinetic syndrome.

Last, because of its blurred definitions, the MBD concept increasingly received criticism from various quarters. In particular, the syndromic nature of MBD and the existence of a uniform psychopathology associated with it were doubted. Nevertheless, the putative syndrome enjoys great popularity among child psychiatrists. One of the points raised in criticism concerns the claim that MBD can be assessed by simply adding up arbitrary symptoms from diverse areas. Another point concerns etiological assumptions holding that the symptoms can be traced to brain injury suffered early in life. Although not always detected, such causal traumata are usually taken for granted in clinical practice.

Against this background, we conducted an epidemiological study in

Figure 13.1 *Intersections of three diagnostic levels of manifestation of* MBD.

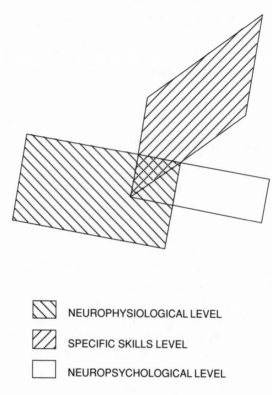

NEUROPHYSIOLOGICAL LEVEL

SPECIFIC SKILLS LEVEL

NEUROPSYCHOLOGICAL LEVEL

Mannheim, Germany, aiming to evaluate the meaning of cerebral dysfunction and its impact on ADD. We investigated a field sample of 399 eight-year-olds by a comprehensive test battery. In a follow-up study five years later, 334 of these children (90 percent) could be completely reexamined by comparable instruments. All the results below stem from this study.

Using an alternative procedure of case definition and factor-analytic data aggregation, we postulated that MBD could manifest itself at each of three diagnostic levels: neurophysiological level, neuropsychological level, and level of specific skills. In our alternative case definition procedure, subjects were classified as MBD cases if their individual score on at least one of the three diagnostic levels was more than two standard deviations below the respective mean. Further statistical analyses showed these three diagnostic dimensions to be almost completely inde-

Figure 13.2 *Distribution of psychiatric diagnoses among psychiatrically disordered children with and without minimal brain dysfunction.*

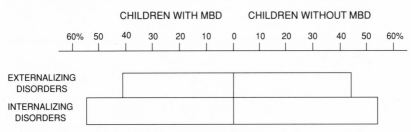

pendent of one another, which is inconsistent with the assumption of a single uniform syndrome of MBD (figure 13.1).

In a next step we investigated the intersection between MBD and psychiatric disorders. As detailed statistical analyses were not possible, owing to low frequencies of specific diagnoses, two diagnostic groups were formed representing an internalizing category of neurotic and emotional disorders and another one with externalizing disorders, including conduct disorder and ADD. Comparison of psychiatrically disordered children with and without MBD yielded symmetrical distributions with respect to these two diagnostic categories (figure 13.2). In particular, there was no accumulation of MBD cases with a diagnosis of ADD. Thus, in what follows, MBD and ADD are regarded as representing different diagnoses. Longitudinal findings on both forms of disorder are reported, starting with MBD.

STABILITY AND CHANGE OF MBD

Using a three-level case definition procedure as outlined above, 42 MBD cases could be identified in our sample of 334 thirteen-year-olds (figure 13.3). In about half of them ($N = 22$), this diagnosis was present at age eight; symptoms faded away within the five-year span for half of the children with MBD at age eight. On the other hand, there was the considerable number of 20 new cases; this means that 50 percent of MBD cases at age thirteen were "newcomers." The fact that new cases emerged contradicts the common view that MBD is caused by brain injuries suffered *early* in life and thus diagnostically loses relevance in adolescence.

Figure 13.3 *Stability and changes of minimal brain dysfunction.*

MBD AT AGE 8

		NO	YES	
MBD AT AGE 13	NO	271	21	292
	YES	20	22	42
		291	43	

STABILITY AND CHANGE OF ADD

The terms "attention deficit disorder" and "hyperactive/ hyperkinetic syndrome" are commonly used synonymously; we will follow this convention.

Usually ADD is taken as a form of disorder having a strong developmental component. Hence, it can be expected to decrease with advancing years. To address this assumption we examined stability and change of hyperkinetic disorders between ages eight and thirteen. The findings reported below are based on a nonrepresentative field sample of 356 children examined at ages eight and thirteen. Of these, 42 were classified as having ADD at age eight and only 20 at age thirteen. Thus the prevalence of ADD was cut in half within the five-year span. The results of more detailed analyses, with regard to three grades of severity, are shown in figures 13.4 and 13.5.

Figure 13.4 displays data from a retrospective point of view, proceeding from 20 thirteen-year-olds diagnosed as ADD and looking back to their psychiatric status at eight. Severity of psychiatric disorders was rated on a three-point scale, as follows: "1" stands for mildly disturbed (symptoms are present without intervention being necessary); "2" means moderately disturbed (pronounced symptoms exist, and treatment is desirable but not mandatory); "3" is severely disturbed (pronounced symptoms demand therapeutic intervention).

At age thirteen there were only 5 moderately disturbed and no severely disturbed ADD children. Thus, most of the 20 ADD cases in adolescence were of minor severity ($N = 15$ with severity 1). Seven of these were undisturbed at age eight. Thus, 7 new cases of ADD occurred at age thirteen. More than half (11) remained unchanged; this means they

Figure 13.4 *Attention deficit disorder at age thirteen: retrospective viewpoint of status at age eight.*

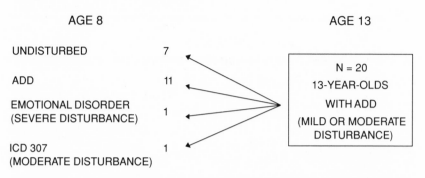

had already been diagnosed as ADD at age eight. Only two changed diagnostic labels from emotional disorder (monosymptomatic disorders such as enuresis or tics; ICD 307) at age eight to ADD at age thirteen.

These retrospective findings shed a rather favorable light on the prognosis of ADD, which does not mirror the real situation. More detailed information can be obtained from a prospective viewpoint: proceeding from ADD children at age eight and looking at what has become of them at age thirteen (figure 13.5). Cases identified as ADD at age eight amounted to 20 mild (degree of severity 1) and 22 moderate or severe (degree of severity 2 or 3) cases. Of the 20 mildly hyperkinetic eight-year-olds (severity 1; top of figure 13.5), as many as 5 (one quarter) were psychiatrically undisturbed at age thirteen; they recovered from age eight to thirteen. Another quarter remained unchanged. Half of the former mildly disturbed ADD children changed diagnoses, most of them developing neurotic disorders or emotional disturbances specific to childhood and adolescence. Only two shifted into the category "conduct disorders."

Of the 22 more severely disturbed hyperkinetic eight-year-olds (bottom of figure 13.5), only 3 were undisturbed at age thirteen. Six kept their former diagnoses, yet were slightly improved in degree of severity. A total of 13 subjects with ADD changed diagnostic classification. Contrary to the mildly disturbed ADD cases, the majority of the severely disturbed children shifted to the category "conduct disorders"; what is more, two-thirds had a severity of 2 or 3. Only 4 subjects developed emotional disorders.

Summing up these findings, we can say that the overall occurrence rate of ADD decreases with advancing years, but this is due mainly to

Figure 13.5 *Attention deficit disorder at age eight and its outcome at age thirteen, grouped according to severity.*

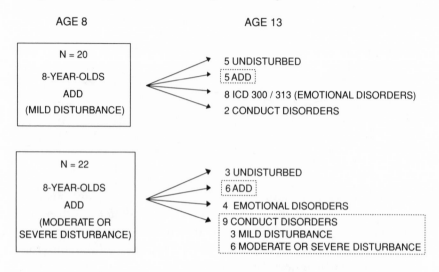

diagnostic shifts. A marked number of ADD children change their symptom pattern in the direction of social disorders. This applies, in particular, to severe forms of ADD, whereas prognosis in mild forms is rather good. This touches the problem of differentiating between ADD and conduct disorders, as already pointed out by Taylor and coworkers (see Taylor, 1985).

CORRELATION OF MBD AND ADD

As already mentioned, the demarcation of MBD and ADD is rather blurred. Some authors even regard them as identical. To determine whether this assumption finds support in the data of our study, we examined the degree of association between ADD and MBD.

Both a psychiatric disorder and MBD were found to be simultaneously present in 16 subjects at age eight. Among these 16 psychiatrically disturbed MBD children, 8 ADD cases were identified. This co-occurrence of both disturbances was significant by a narrow margin. When, however, I.Q. variation was taken into account by excluding children with I.Q.s below 85, the correlation failed to reach significance. Thus, there was no suggestion of an association between MBD and ADD, at least within an average range of intelligence. Replicating the findings with the data set of thirteen-year-olds further strengthened the conclusion drawn: there was no statistically significant correlation between ADD and MBD in adolescents. The same applies to longitudinal data analyses (MBD at age eight and ADD at age thirteen).

The findings reported so far are restricted to marked forms of ADD, those with a degree of severity of 2 or 3. In general, the results remain unchanged if the calculations are repeated while including mild forms of ADD (severity 1). The only dissimilarity is that the correlation between ADD and MBD at age eight reaches significance. This can be explained by the blurred demarcation of both diagnoses, affecting mainly the less severely disturbed ADD cases.

Summing up, it may be said that:

1. The conventional clinical concept of MBD is not confirmed by empirical tests; it is hardly tenable.
2. Using an alternative approach of case definition we failed to find an accumulation of MBD cases with a diagnosis of ADD. Hence, the terms cannot be used synonymously.
3. Declining overall occurrence rates of ADD in adolescence suggest fading symptoms with advancing age. This is true only in ADD of minor severity, however.
4. In general, our findings indicate high persistence of psychiatric disorders in ADD children. Yet there is a marked shift in symptom pattern toward more antisocial forms of behavior. In particular, this applies to severe forms of ADD. In this sense, the diagnosis of severe hyperactivity should be an indication for early intervention.

REFERENCES

Esser, G., and Schmidt, M. H. (1986). "Prognose und Verlauf kinderpsychiatrischer Storungen im Langschnitt von acht bis dreizehn Jahren." In M. H. Schmidt and S. Dromann, eds., *Der Langzeitverlauf kinder- und jugendpsychiatrischer Erkrankungen*. Enke, 79–90.
Schmidt, M. D. (1985). "Hirnfunktionsstorungen bei Achtjahrigen: Ergebnisse aus einer Feld- und Inanspruchnahmepopulation." *Psychiat. Neurol. Med. Psychol.* 37 (1985):30–38.
Schmidt, M. H.; Esser, G.; Allehoff, W.; Eisert, H. G.; Geisel, B.; Laucht, M.; Poustka, F.; and Voll, R. (1983). "Prevalence and Meaning of Cerebral Dysfunction in Eight-Year-Old Children in Mannheim." In M. H. Schmidt

and H. Remschmidt, eds., *Epidemiological Approaches in Child Psychiatry.* Stuttgart: Thieme, 2:121–137.

Taylor, E. (1985). "Syndromes of Overactivity and Attention Deficit." In M. Rutter and L. Hersov, eds., *Child and Adolescent Psychiatry: Modern Approaches.* 2nd ed. London: Blackwell, 424–443.

14

Psychopharmacological Approaches in the Treatment of Autism

MAGDA CAMPBELL

ARTHUR M. SMALL

RICHARD PERRY

The goal of treatment with autistic children is to decrease behavioral symptoms and promote development and learning. Pharmacotherapy—the use of a safe, effective drug—is viewed as a treatment modality that can make the autistic child more amenable to special education, behavior therapy, and other psychosocial treatments, and even to enhance the effect of these treatments. The autistic child requires a comprehensive, carefully planned treatment program, tailored to his individual needs: drug therapy can be a useful and, in some cases, an essential part of such treatment.

Pharmacotherapy is not viewed as a desirable intervention by some professionals. A psychoactive drug is often prescribed only when other interventions have failed or when the autistic child's behavior is intolerable. This attitude is maintained even though experience and research indicate that certain drugs can decrease maladaptive behaviors in the absence of serious side effects, when administered over a short-term period, and, in conjunction with behavior modification and/or special education, help the child acquire adaptive and self-care skills.

INDICATIONS AND DURATION OF TREATMENT

As in other clinical conditions, there is no single specific drug for the treatment of autistic children. The currently available psychoactive agents that have been shown to have therapeutic value in this population seem to be most effective in reducing certain target symptoms. Children with symptoms of hyperactivity, impulsivity, aggressiveness, stereotypies, and withdrawal, as a group, respond best to the high-potency neuroleptics, such as haloperidol. Children with alternating symptoms of hyper- and hypoactivity seem to respond equally well to this drug. In our clinical experience, exclusively hypoactive and anergic patients with little initiative are nonresponders to haloperidol and show only untoward effects at certain doses: particularly sleepiness and psychomotor retardation.

There is less knowledge about indications and effectiveness of psychoactive drugs in the treatment of autistic children who have little or no initiative and are hypoactive, anergic, apathetic, and withdrawn. L-dopa (Campbell, Small, et al., 1976), and triiodothyronine (T_3) (for review, see Campbell, 1978) seemed to reduce these "negative" symptoms and increase verbal production in a few children. Such stimulating effects were also reported in a few patients who were treated with fenfluramine (Campbell, Deutsch, et al., 1986). In a two-year-old girl, administration of trifluoperazine (20 mg/day, considered a very high dose) was associated with dramatic decrease of severe negative symptoms and improvement in general; discontinuation of the drug resulted in a rapid return of apathy, anergy, and hypoactivity (Fish, Shapiro, and Campbell, 1966).

In cases of severe self-mutilation, aggressiveness, and explosive affect, and where behavior modification and standard drugs have failed to yield reduction of these maladaptive behaviors, a trial of lithium is indicated (Campbell, Fish, et al., 1972; Gram and Rafaelsen, 1972). With more data on the efficacy and safety of naltrexone, this opiate antagonist, too, may be considered (Campbell, Overall, et al., 1989).

Clinical experience has shown that it is possible to determine within three or four weeks whether a drug is effective in reducing target symptoms, when dosage is titrated. When a therapeutically effective drug is found, it should be discontinued every four to six months in order to determine whether the child requires further pharmacotherapy and whether withdrawal phenomena will emerge upon the drug's withdrawal (Campbell, Grega, et al., 1983; Campbell, Adams, Perry, et al., 1988). Throughout the drug maintenance and for at least a month after its discontinuation, careful clinical and laboratory monitoring is required (untoward effects of drugs and their assessment have been reviewed by Campbell and Palij, 1985c; Campbell, Green, and Deutsch, 1985). It has been said that the only lasting effects of pharmacotherapy are those that are due to conjoint psychosocial interventions (Irwin,

1968). Many autistic children who participate in a comprehensive treatment program may not need a drug after a six-month maintenance.

PHARMACOTHERAPY: THE PAST TWO DECADES

The period 1966 to 1978 was characterized by investigators laying the groundwork for research in psychopharmacology involving autistic children (Fish, 1968) and conducting a series of clinical trials that were, with the exception of one (Fish, Shapiro and Campbell, 1966) pilot studies (for review, see Campbell, 1978; Campbell, Geller, and Cohen, 1977). This work represented a search for more effective and safer drugs in a population that had showed only modest improvements in response to a variety of treatments. Fish (1970) made the important observation that autistic children respond poorly to the low-potency neuroleptics (e.g., chlorpromazine) and often develop sedation at low doses without clinical improvement. With the administration of a high-potency neuroleptic, such as trifluoperazine (Fish, Shapiro, and Campbell, 1966), trifluperidol, thiothixene, and molindone, a decrease of symptoms could be obtained without accompanying sedation, which interferes with learning (for a review of these studies, see Campbell, Geller, and Cohen, 1977; Campbell, 1978).

In addition, a variety of other drugs with "stimulating" properties were also explored in an attempt to promote and stimulate language and adaptive and social behaviors in the young autistic child, who is usually functioning on a retarded level, and in whom these skills are only rudimentary, or even absent. However, these treatment interventions, which included methysergide, imipramine, d-amphetamine, triiodothyronine or T_3 (for review, see Campbell, Geller, and Cohen, 1977; Campbell, 1978), l-amphetamine, and L-dopa (Campbell, Small, et al., 1976; Ritvo, Yuwiler, Geller, Kales, et al., 1971), either yielded positive effects only in a few children, or the few positive effects were outweighed by side effects. In general, the dopamine agonists, particularly d- and l-amphetamine, yielded poor results.

The period 1978 to 1985 was characterized by the systematic and critical evaluation of the potent dopamine antagonist (also a high-potency neuroleptic) haloperidol (for review, Campbell, 1985, 1987). In addition, a study of pimozide was conducted in a large sample of autistic children (Naruse et al., 1982). There was some suggestion that a subgroup of autistic children showed evidence of excess dopaminergic activity (for review, Young et al., 1982); both haloperidol and pimozide are potent antidopaminergic agents.

Haloperidol is a butyrophenone; trifluperidol, another member of this class of drugs, was found to reduce a variety of target symptoms in pre-school-age children (Fish et al., 1969a). But because its administration to adult patients was associated with a very high rate of Parkinsonian side effects, trifluperidol was withdrawn from investigational use in the United States. Earlier studies of haloperidol (Engelhardt et al., 1973; Faretra, Dooher, and Dowling, 1970) suggested that it decreases various symptoms in autistic children; however, these studies had methodological flaws.

Subsequently, in a double-blind trial involving forty carefully diagnosed pre-school-age autistic children, it was demonstrated that haloperidol is significantly superior to placebo in reducing withdrawal and stereotypies in doses of 0.5 to 4.0 mg/day (mean, 1.65; Campbell, Anderson, et al., 1978). At these doses, the drug had no adverse effects on cognition in the laboratory, and no untoward effects were observed. The positive behavioral effects of haloperidol were replicated in another double-blind and placebo-controlled trial, conducted with ten subjects and using an ABAB design (Cohen et al., 1980). Subsequently, a study was designed to assess the effects of haloperidol on discrimination learning in the laboratory and on behavioral symptoms under several ecological conditions; drug levels in blood were also measured. Forty children, ages 2.33 to 6.92 years, completed the study. Haloperidol, at 0.5 to 3.0 mg/day (mean 1.11), was significantly superior to placebo in reducing withdrawal, stereotypies, hyperactivity, angry and labile affect, negativism, and fidgetiness (Anderson et al., 1984). In the automated laboratory, administration of haloperidol was associated with facilitation and retention of discrimination learning, but it failed to show a significant effect on stereotypies, hyperactivity, and carpet activity. In the classroom, however, maladaptive behavior significantly decreased as rated by the teachers on the Conner's Parent-Teacher Questionnaire. As in the studies discussed above, dosage was individually regulated. At therapeutic doses, no adverse effects were observed, but above therapeutic doses, excessive sedation and acute dystonic reaction were the most common side effects. Haloperidol levels were measured in blood, and at therapeutic doses, they ranged from nondetectable ($<$ .50 ng/ml) to 8.30 ng/ml; serum levels were associated with significant decreases of withdrawal and stereotypies (Poland et al., 1982).

Haloperidol remained effective in reducing behavioral symptoms when administered on a long-term basis (Perry, Campbell, Adams, et al.,

1989), and it did not adversely affect the patients' I.Q.s (Die Trill et al., 1984). But its cumulative administration over a period of up to 4.23 years was associated with the development of reversible tardive or withdrawal dyskinesias in 29.27 percent of cases, in a prospective study (Campbell, Adams, Perry, et al., 1988; Perry, Campbell, Green, et al., 1985). Long-term effects on linear growth did not seem to be significant (Campbell, unpublished data).

Pimozide, a diphenylbutyl piperidine, is thought to have fewer extrapyramidal untoward effects than haloperidol. In a multicenter study involving eighty-seven subjects ages three to sixteen years, pimozide (1 to 4 mg/day) was significantly superior to placebo; thirty-four of the children were autistic (Naruse et al., 1982).

The search for novel, more effective and safer drugs for the treatment of infantile autism has continued. In the 1980s a large multicenter study, of fenfluramine was conducted, as well as some individual studies (Campbell, 1988). Studies of naltrexone are also underway (for review, Campbell and Spencer, 1988). The rationale for exploring and studying these two drugs in this population concerned their biochemical properties: fenfluramine is an antiserotonergic agent, and naltrexone is a potent opiate antagonist.

Systematic studies have shown that about one-third of autistic children have hyperserotonemia (Ritvo, Yuwiler, Geller, Ornitz, et al., 1970; Campbell, Friedman, et al., 1975; for review, Young et al., 1982). It was hypothesized by Ritvo and his associates that behavioral and cognitive abnormalities in autistic children are associated with abnormalities of the serotonergic system, and it was hoped that by reducing serotonin levels in blood with a potent antiserotonergic agent a decrease of maladaptive behaviors would result (Geller et al., 1982; Ritvo, Freeman, Geller, and Yuwiler, 1983; Ritvo, Freeman, Yuwiler, et al., 1986). The data on eighty-one autistic subjects, thirty-three months to twenty-four years old, who received 1.5 mg/kg of fenfluramine daily, were pooled and analyzed; these outpatients represented a subsample of the eighteen centers participating in the study (Ritvo, Freeman, Yuwiler, et al., 1986). During the four-month period of this double-blind and placebo-controlled study, only 33 percent of the subjects were shown to be strong responders to fenfluramine. Behavioral improvements were not accompanied by significant increases of I.Q.s, and there was an inverse correlation between clinical response and baseline serotonin levels. Lower serotonin levels on baseline were associated with higher I.Q.s. There was a significant reduction of serotonin by fenfluramine in all subjects.

In a double-blind and placebo-controlled study of fenfluramine, employing a parallel-groups design with random assignment of subjects to treatment, the superiority of fenfluramine over placebo was not confirmed (Campbell, Adams, Small, et al., 1988). The study comprised twenty-eight children, ages 2.56 to 6.66 years. In this population, fenfluramine had a retarding effect on discrimination learning in an automated laboratory.

There is some speculation (Panksepp, 1979; Sandyk and Gillman, 1986) and supportive, though inconclusive evidence (Gillberg, Terenius and Lonnerholm, 1985; Weizman et al., 1984) that a subgroup of autistic children show abnormalities of the endogenous opioid system. Opiate antagonists yielded decreased self-mutilation in a few mentally retarded individuals (for review, Deutsch, 1986). Naltrexone, a potent oral opiate antagonist, seemed to be a promising agent in an acute dose range tolerance trial involving ten autistic children (Campbell, Overall, et al., 1989). The findings warrant further studies of naltrexone and a critical assessment of its efficacy and safety in this population.

PHARMACOTHERAPY COMBINED WITH PSYCHOSOCIAL INTERVENTION

In a carefully designed and placebo-controlled study, the efficacy of haloperidol was compared to behavior therapy, and the interaction of the two treatments was assessed; the behavior therapy focused on language acquisition. The forty children, ages 2.6–7.2 years, were assigned randomly to four treatments, employing a factorial design. The combination of haloperidol and contingent reinforcement was superior to the three other treatment conditions in facilitating language acquisition (Campbell, Anderson, et al., 1978).

Future research should focus on combining pharmacotherapy with psychosocial interventions, in order to promote cognitive and language functions in the autistic child.

REFERENCES

Anderson, L. T.; Campbell, M.; Grega, D. M.; Perry, R.; Small, A. M.; and Green, W. H. (1984). "Haloperidol in Infantile Autism: Effects on Learning and Behavioral Symptoms." *American Journal of Psychiatry* 141(10):1195–1202.

Campbell, M. (1978). "The Use of Drug Treatment in Infantile Autism and Childhood Schizophrenia: A Review." In *Psychopharmacology: A Generation of Progress,* eds. M. A. Lipton, A. DiMascio, and K. Killam. New York: Raven Press, 1451–1461.

—— (1985). "Pervasive Developmental Disorders: Autistic and Schizophrenic Disorders." In *Psychopharmacology of Childhood and Adolescence,* ed. J. M. Wiener. New York: Wiley, 113–150.

—— (1987). "Drug Treatment of Infantile Autism: The Past Decade." In *Psychopharmacology: The Third Generation of Progress,* ed. H. Y. Meltzer. New York: Raven Press, 1225–1231.

—— (1988). "Fenfluramine Treatment of Autism: Annotation." *Journal of Child Psychology and Psychiatry* 29(1):1–10.

Campbell, M.; Adams, P.; Perry, R.; Spencer, E. K.; and Overall, J. E. (1988). "Tardive and Withdrawal Dyskinesia in Autistic Children: A Prospective Study." *Psychopharmacology Bulletin* 24(2):251–255.

Campbell, M.; Adams, P.; Small, A. M.; Curren, E. L.; Overall, J. E.; Anderson, L. T.; Lynch, N.; and Perry, R. (1988). "Efficacy and Safety of Fenfluramine in Autistic Children." *Journal of the American Academy of Child and Adolescent Psychiatry* 27(4):434–439.

Campbell, M.; Anderson, L. T.; Meier, M.; Cohen, I. L.; Small, A. M.; Samit, C.; and Sachar, E. J. (1978). "A Comparison of Haloperidol, Behavior Therapy and Their Interaction in Autistic Children." *Journal of the American Academy of Child Psychiatry* 17(4):640–655.

Campbell, M.; Deutsch, S. I.; Perry, R.; Wolsky, B. B.; and Palij, M. (1986). "Short-Term Efficacy and Safety of Fenfluramine in Hospitalized Preschool-Age Autistic Children: An Open Study." *Psychopharmacology Bulletin* 22(1):141–147.

Campbell, M.; Fish, B.; Korein, J.; Shapiro, T.; Collins, P.; and Koh, C. (1972). "Lithium and Chlorpromazine: A Controlled Crossover Study of Hyperactive Severely Disturbed Young Children." *Journal of Autism and Childhood Schizophrenia* 2(3):234–263.

Campbell, M.; Friedman, E.; Green, W. H.; Collins, P. J.; Small, A. M.; and Breuer, H. (1975). "Blood Serotonin in Schizophrenic Children: A Preliminary Study." *International Pharmacopsychiatry* 10:213–221.

Campbell, M.; Geller, B.; and Cohen, I. L. (1977). "Current Status of Drug Research and Treatment with Autistic Children." *Journal of Pediatric Psychology* 2:153–161.

Campbell, M.; Green, W. H.; and Deutsch, S. I. (1985). *Childhood and Adolescent Psychopharmacology.* Beverly Hills: Sage.

Campbell, M.; Grega, D. M.; Green, W. H.; and Bennett, W. G. (1983). "Neuroleptic-Induced Dyskinesias in Children." *Clinical Neuropharmacology* 6:207–222.

Campbell, M.; Overall, J. E.; Small, A. M.; Sokol, M. S.; Spencer, E. K.; Adams, P.; Foltz, R. L.; Monti, K. M.; Perry, R.; Nobler, M.; and Roberts,

E. (1989). "Naltrexone in Autistic Children: An Acute Open Dose Range Tolerance Trial." *Journal of the American Academy of Child and Adolescent Psychiatry* 28(2):200–206.

Campbell, M., and Palij, M. (1985a). "Documentation of Demographic Data and Family History of Psychiatric Illness." *Psychopharmacology Bulletin* 21(4):719–733.

——— (1985b). "Behavioral and Cognitive Measures Used in Psychopharmacological Studies of Infantile Autism." *Psychopharmacology Bulletin* 21(4):1047–1053.

——— (1985c). "Measurement of Untoward Effects including Tardive Dyskinesia." *Psychopharmacology Bulletin* 21(4):1063–1082.

Campbell, M.; Small, A. M.; Collins, P. J.; Friedman, E.; David, R.; and Genieser, N. (1976). "Levodopa and Levoamphetamine: A Crossover Study in Young Schizophrenic Children." *Current Therapeutic Research* 19(1):70–86.

Campbell, M., and Spencer, E. K. (1988). "Psychopharmacology in Child and Adolescent Psychiatry: A Review of the Past Five Years." *Journal of the American Academy of Child and Adolescent Psychiatry* 27(3):269–279.

Cohen, I. L.; Campbell, M.; Posner, D.; Small, A. M.; Triebel, D.; and Anderson, L. T. (1980). "Behavioral Effects of Haloperidol in Young Autistic Children: An Objective Analysis Using a Within-Subjects Reversal Design." *Journal of the American Academy of Child Psychiatry* 19:665–677.

Deutsch, S. I. (1986). "Rationale for the Administration of Opiate Antagonists in Treating Infantile Autism." *American Journal of Mental Deficiency* 90(6):631–635.

Die Trill, M. L.; Wolsky, B. B.; Shell, J.; Green, W. H.; Perry, R.; and Campbell, M. (1984). "Effects of Long-Term Haloperidol Treatment on Intellectual Functioning in Autistic Children: A Pilot Study." Paper presented at the 31st Annual Meeting of the American Academy of Child Psychiatry, Toronto, Canada, October 10–14.

Engelhardt, D. M.; Polizos, P.; Waizer, J.; and Hoffman, S. P. (1973). "A Double-Blind Comparison of Fluphenazine and Haloperidol." *Journal of Autism and Childhood Schizophrenia* 3:128–137.

Faretra, G.; Dooher, L.; and Dowling, J. (1970). "Comparison of Haloperidol and Fluphenazine in Disturbed Children." *American Journal of Psychiatry* 126:1670–1673.

Fish, B. (1968). "Methodology in Child Psychopharmacology." In *Psychopharmacology: A Review of Progress, 1957–1967*, ed. D. H. Efron, J. O. Cole, J. Levine, and J. R. Wittenborn. Public Health Service Publication no. 1836. Washington, D.C.: U.S. Government Printing Office, 989–1001.

——— (1970). "Psychopharmacologic Response of Chronic Schizophrenic

Adults as Predictors of Responses in Young Schizophrenic Children." *Psychopharmacology Bulletin* 6:12–15.

Fish, B.; Campbell, M.; Shapiro, T.; and Floyd, A., Jr. (1969a). "Comparison of Trifluperidol, Trifluoperazine, and Chlorpromazine in Preschool Schizophrenic Children: The Value of Less Sedative Antipsychotic Agents." *Current Therapeutic Research* 11:589–595.

——— (1969b). "Schizophrenic Children Treated with Methysergide (Sansert)." *Diseases of the Nervous System* 30:534–540.

Fish, B.; Shapiro, T.; Campbell, M. (1966). "Long-Term Prognosis and the Response of Schizophrenic Children to Drug Therapy: A Controlled Study of Triflurperazine." *American Journal of Psychiatry* 123:32–39.

Geller, E.; Ritvo, E. R.; Freeman, B. J.; and Yuwiler, A. (1982). "Preliminary Observations on the Effects of Fenfluramine on Blood Serotonin and Symptoms in Three Autistic Boys." *New England Journal of Medicine* 307:165–169.

Gillberg, C.; Terenius, L., and Lonnerholm, G. (1985). "Endorphin Activity in Childhood Psychosis: Spinal Fluid Levels in 24 Cases." *Archives of General Psychiatry* 42:780–783.

Gram, L. F., and Rafaelsen, O. J. (1972). "Lithium Treatment of Psychotic Children: A Controlled Clinical Trial." In *Depressive States in Childhood and Adolescence,* ed. A.-L. Annell. Stockholm: Almqvist and Wiksell, 488–490.

Irwin, S. (1968). "A Rational Framework for the Development, Evaluation, and Use of Psychoactive Drugs." *American Journal of Psychiatry* 124(Suppl.):1–19.

Naruse, H.; Nagahata, M.; Nakane, Y.; Shirahashi, K.; Takesada, M.; and Yamazaki, K. (1982). "A Multicenter Double-Blind Trial of Pimozide (Orap), Haloperidol and Placebo in Children with Behavioral Disorders, Using Crossover Design." *Acta Paedopsychiatrica* 48:173–184.

Panksepp, J. (1979). "A Neurochemical Theory of Autism." *Trends in Neuroscience* 2:174–177.

Perry, R.; Campbell, M.; Adams, P.; Lynch, N.; Spencer, E. K.; Curren, E. L.; and Overall, J. E. (1989). "Long-Term Efficacy of Haloperidol in Autistic Children: Continuous Versus Discontinuous Drug Administration." *Journal of the American Academy of Child and Adolescent Psychiatry* 28(1):87–92.

Perry, R.; Campbell, M.; Green, W. H.; Small, A. M.; Die Trill, M. L.; Meiselas, K.; Golden, R. R.; and Deutsch, S. I. (1985). "Neuroleptic-Related Dyskinesias in Autistic Children: A Prospective Study." *Psychopharmacology Bulletin* 21(1):140–143.

Poland, R. E.; Campbell, M.; Rubin, R. T.; Perry, R.; and Anderson, L. (1982). "Relationship of Serum Haloperidol Levels and Clinical Response in Autistic Children." Abstracts of the 13th CINP Congress, Jerusalem, Israel, June 20–25, 2:591.

Ritvo, E. R., and Freeman, B. J. (1978). "Current Research on the Syndrome of Autism: Introduction, The National Society for Autistic Children's Definition of the Syndrome of Autism." *Journal of the American Academy of Child Psychiatry* 17:565–575.

Ritvo, E. R.; Freeman, B. J.; Geller, E.; and Yuwiler, A. (1983). "Effects of Fenfluramine on 14 Outpatients with the Syndrome of Autism." *Journal of the American Academy of Child Psychiatry* 22:549–558.

Ritvo, E. R.; Freeman, B. J.; Yuwiler, A.; Geller, E.; Schroth, P.; Yokota, A.; Mason-Brothers, A.; August, G. J.; Klykylo, W.; Leventhal, B.; Lewis, K.; Piggott, L.; Realmuto, G.; Stubbs, E. G.; and Umansky, R. (1986). "Fenfluramine Treatment of Autism: UCLA Collaborative Study of 81 Patients at Nine Medical Centers." *Psychopharmacology Bulletin* 22(1):133–140.

Ritvo, E. R.; Yuwiler, A.; Geller, E.; Kales, S. R.; Schicor, A.; and Plotkin, S. (1971). "Effects of L-Dopa in Autism." *Journal of Autism and Childhood Schizophrenia* 1(2):190–205.

Ritvo, E. R.; Yuwiler, A.; Geller, E.; Ornitz, E. M.; Saeger, K.; and Plotkin, S. (1970). "Increased Blood Serotonin and Platelets in Early Infantile Autism." *Archives of General Psychiatry* 23:566–572.

Sandyk, R., and Gillman, M. A. (1986). "Infantile Autism: A Dysfunction of the Opioids?" *Medical Hypotheses* 19:41–45.

Volkmar, F. R.; Cohen, D. J.; and Paul, R. (1986). "An Evaluation of DSM-III Criteria for Infantile Autism." *Journal of the American Academy of Child Psychiatry* 25:190–197.

Weizman, R.; Weizman, A.; Tyano, S.; Szekely, G.; Weissman, B. A.; and Sarne, Y. (1984). "Humoral-Endorphin Blood Levels in Autistic, Schizophrenic and Healthy Subjects." *Psychopharmacology* 82:368–370.

Young, J. G.; Kavanagh, M. E.; Anderson, G. M.; Shaywitz, B. A.; and Cohen, D. J. (1982). "Clinical Neurochemistry of Autism and Associated Disorders." *Journal of Autism and Developmental Disorders* 12:147–165.

IV

Appraisal of the Current Status of the Psychoanalytic Approach

15

Introduction

COLETTE CHILAND

Psychoanalysis has had considerable influence on the development of child and adolescent psychiatry throughout the world, as Hersov pointed out in chapter 5. But increasing emphasis is being given to biological and behavioral approaches in the United States, Canada, Germany, and other countries as well. In England, although psychoanalysts have been active in such institutions as the British Psychoanalytical Society, the Tavistock Clinic, and the Hampstead Clinic (now known as the Anna Freud Centre), they have not had a marked influence on child psychiatry or on culture as a whole.

Speaking of *the* psychoanalytic approach seems to imply that this is a single and exclusive approach in time and space, whereas the fact is that ideas have evolved differently and taken different shapes in different places. Nonetheless, there are certain ideas common to all psychoanalysts, corresponding to what Freud called the cornerstones of psychoanalytic theory. They include recognition of the following:

- The existence of the unconscious, not only in its descriptive and qualitative connotation but also in a systemic sense: unconscious psychic phenomena have their own specific modes of organization and action.
- The significance of dreams, symptoms, and delusions.
- The phenomenon of the transference: earlier relational experiences organize subsequent human relationships.
- Sexuality as an active force in the organization of personality and pathology from early childhood on.

Some of these ideas have become an integral part of what is known as dynamic psychology, and many psychiatrists who are not themselves psychoanalysts make use of psychoanalytic concepts. On the other hand, there remains a hard core of psychiatrists who reject out of hand anything that derives from psychoanalysis.

As Lebovici pointed out in chapter 3, psychoanalysis as a form of treatment is appropriate for carefully selected cases and must be applied only by thoroughly trained therapists. But many psychiatrists and psychologists incorporate psychoanalytic theory into their own conceptual framework.

Chapter 16, by René Diatkine, is an example of a psychoanalyst's reflection on the etiology of infantile autism. It is not a collection of symptoms but a particular form of mental functioning, a balanced system that is hard to stimulate and mobilize because it fails to respond to outside intervention. Autonomy in relation to the mother is immediate, contrary to the normal developmental progress toward autonomy.

In chapter 17, Frances Marton outlines the work currently being done at the Anna Freud Centre. Here again, we see that psychoanalysis is not merely a form of treatment but gives rise to various lines of research and therapeutic action. The author presents the case of Tom, a boy under intensive treatment, following the course of the various services he uses in the Centre and the ins and outs of his history and treatment. His case illustrates two of the themes dealt with in this book: (1) Tom is the son of an ummarried mother, and (2) his mother's rejection of his virility and her attempts to feminize him create gender-identity problems for Tom, to the point where he says, "I hate my penis. It's long, fat, and stupid!" polishes his fingernails, and engages in other forms of feminine behavior.

Chapter 18, by Lore Schacht, presents an example of the analyst's work in treatment. She summarizes the analysis of a "pseudo-backward" girl and shows how an interpretation made by the analyst allowed reconstruction of a traumatic event in which the girl and her mother were simultaneously terrified. The mother's account enabled the analyst to understand what was being worked through in the transference repetition so that she could help the child achieve a less confused body image and resume her intellectual development.

The examples of treatment presented in chapters 17 and 18 show parent-child interactions. They provide elements for understanding the child's reactions, as a simple description of behavior would not do, and for offering the child the possibility of a different form of mental functioning.

16

A Psychoanalytic Viewpoint on Etiology: Apropos of Infantile Autism

RENÉ DIATKINE

Attempting to explain the appearance and persistence of a syndrome as serious as early infantile autism is something so necessary as to require no justification, but it is far from obvious what method should be adopted. The problems start with the definition of the syndrome, according to whether the definition is taken in a limited or a wider sense. The choice is not an insignificant matter, since it depends on the clinical and theoretical system selected, and if from the outset this system lacks a precise etiology, it at least provides a method that can produce results within its own terms.

Kanner's 1943 description of early infantile autism related to a small number of cases with a distinct and precise semiology and whose pathology could be explained neither by retarded mental development nor by brain lesions. Today, the scope of the group studied under this heading depends on the initial options and practice adopted by the individual clinician.

Such incontrovertible signs as absence of contact with others, absence of language, and stereotyped gestures are considered relevant by researchers working on large-scale patient populations. Many subjects with acquired cerebral lesions or known genetic abnormalities suffer from an impairment causing severe disturbance of contact with the outside world. They can also present stereotypes and absence or seriously delayed appearance of language. Using this genetic and biological perspective, our understanding of some specific mental phenomena of some of these children is uncertain and easily criticized, while their low performance on tests is given primary significance and justifies classifying them as mentally retarded. Statistical correlations then show the high incidence of cerebral pathology in the broad group studied, whereas autistic children who show good intellectual development are a narrow group with a relatively rare abnormality for which we have as yet found no explanation.

As a child psychiatrist who has followed patients initially affected by early infantile autism and has studied their successive changes over a period of many years, I take a very different position. Indeed, early infantile autism can be considered a special form of mental functioning, which has its own laws and results at a very early stage in a homeostatic system. The fact that it permits no intervention from others means that there is a strong tendency toward repetition and little potential for development. Seen in this light, the differences in adaptation to normal situations become irrelevant, and a whole series of other clinical phenomena takes on great importance. These phenomena include:

- Early specific features of emotional expression (silent insomnia is one example among many)
- Indifference to afferent stimuli, similar to the effects of blindness or deafness
- Indifference to the presence or absence of the mother and other people
- Active withdrawal reactions toward animate creatures
- Active avoidance of being looked at
- Specific stereotypies and mannerisms, with hand and finger movements in front of the eyes followed by object manipulation, then an interest in moving inanimate objects and "traces" ("autistic shapes," as Frances Tustin calls them)

These clinical signs constitute a specific clinical syndrome that contrasts with other serious developmental disorders. A similar specificity is found in the various ways of "exit" from the initial state of early infantile autism, whatever the ensuing development. The child may recognize his parents, although for a long time the child does not seem to realize that they have any mental life of their own or that they could have anything to do with each other. When language is organized, it appears with some peculiar characteristics, the most significant of which are echolalia and the subject's use of "you" instead of "I" to designate him- or herself. Very persistent oddities in personal relationships occur in adults with even the most favorable development.

This set of what are considered relevant clinical features explains the hypothesis outlined above, according to which autism is an atypical form of mental functioning that is very effective in early life and therefore has little likelihood of being changed in response to internal contradictions. The homeostatic value of this structure can be measured if one bears in mind the intensity of the disorder resulting from any attempt to force entry into the child's mental field—perhaps by obliging him to look at someone else, by interfering with his manipulations of his fingers or his "autistic objects," or by trying to change his place or that of the objects around him. Among the factors frequently observed in unfavorable development, repeated changes of home are high on the list.

All these elements indicate that a different valorization of external factors and probably an unusual regrouping of stimuli have set up a very specific pleasure-unpleasure homeostasis, which is impossible to decipher if the observer tries to fit it into the usual grid pattern (the D.S.M. III mentions "bizarre" responses). This is not an a priori ideological standpoint; it is a view allowing therapeutic action that is fairly conclusive over the short term. If the therapist respects the child's dynamic and economic system and approaches him with great patience, her physical presence, and especially her voice, may eventually be admitted into the relatively closed system of the patient's psychological space. This extension is likely to create an initial imbalance, as happens quite often with parents who intuitively adopt a comparable approach. In both instances what occurs is that the system is destabilized, and the ensuing breach opens up the possibility of development. The child emerges from the stage of primary autism and enters a postautistic phase. This change does not always happen, however, and very subtle environmental factors sometimes play a decisive role in the differences in development.

With this approach to early infantile autism the syndrome acquires a paradigmatic value of interest to psychiatric research as a whole with regard to both adult and child patients. Our discipline has great difficulty in emancipating itself completely from the anatomical-clinical model of nineteenth-century medicine. At that time the etiological procedure was based on the general principle of "normality"—embryogenetic and maturative, functional, anatomical, and histological—as opposed to "pathology," a deviation from normality caused by a "pathogenic agent," which had to be identified. This approach has yielded remarkable results and even today continues to bring new knowledge to light. All forms of trisomy and chromosomal abnormalities are described in terms of their deviation from the topographical norms of chromosome pairs. These differences are considered in relation to the exact psychic characteristics of the children affected by them (although our understanding still shows a gap when it comes to specifying chromosomes in relation to abnormalities in mental functioning). The hypothesis of a divergence from "normal" development or "standard" mental functioning caused by a known or unknown pathogenic factor is still often used as an implicit model in pathophysiological research and psychoanalytic thinking. It is nonetheless not a foregone conclusion that it can provide the means of solving all the etiological problems of psychopathology.

Another line of thought takes into account the uncertain nature of psychic development (the concept of the norm refers to a model impossible to achieve) and the importance of epigenesis in the constitution of human mental life. What has to be done is first to describe the etiology of what is considered satisfactory development in a given civilization at a given time and then to compare it with the etiology of pathological developments. This approach necessarily includes all the functional phenomena determined by all types of pathological processes, although without systematically postulating their existence. In other words, importance is given to the events and mental experiences that contribute to the transformation of the original mental functioning. Temporary or permanent somatic disabilities necessarily have their significance in both the constitution of such events or experiences and the choice as to the mode of resolution of these critical states, but identical forms of functional organization can also be produced by other causes of dysfunction. One question has to be discussed with some caution: which elements or circumstances contribute to the stability or instability of the successive structures, and to whether or not they are reversible?

The infant's mental activity can be detected from birth, and I will not discuss here the continuity and discontinuity between this almost instantaneous activity and fetal neural functioning. Everyday experience leads to two somewhat contradictory ideas. The first is that this mental activity is fragile and easily disorganized in all children, whatever path their development takes; the second, on the contrary, underlines the tenacity of mental life, which always tends to restore an equilibrium—often vulnerable—and to reach forward. Is the balance between vulnerability and invulnerability determined by genetic factors? The idea is intuitively plausible, even if it cannot be demonstrated. It is a subjective impression that cannot yet be reliably examined in genetic research on sufficiently large-scale groups. Whatever the case may be, it quickly becomes obvious that the initial homeostasis reappears in the course of the patient's experiences and is modified by these experiences. This is how the psychic state of parents and others who handle the baby has a decisive effect on the changes in this equilibrium. If they believe firmly in the baby's future mental development, they naturally tend to establish bridges between phases of activity and to minimize the effects of

times of disorganization—on condition that the child's activity is sufficient to enable them to establish themselves as parents. Hence, the sum
of their psychic activity—initially, that of the mother—shapes the
child's development. This has been described by psychoanalysts, on the
basis of their clinical experience, as "primary maternal preoccupation"
(Winnicott), "anticipatory illusion" (Lebovici, Diatkine), "maternal
capacity for reverie" (Bion), or "fantasy interactions" (Lebovici).

Except in periods of need (for food and other physical stimuli), infants
alternately show various appeal behaviors—interaction-eliciting behaviors which are quickly differentiated—and phases of withdrawal.
Immediate responses by the mother, in turn, transform the appeal behaviors. Rather than a simple reinforcement, this is a generative interaction that creates diverse forms of exchange unrelated to nourishment
and survival, since these interactions are developed during phases of
waking tranquillity. This development, linked to nervous system maturation, culminates in the transition from preferential orientation toward
the mother to recognition (i.e., a discreetly or intensely negative reaction) in the presence of any individual other than the mother. It is a
negative reaction with no "useful" function as far as safeguarding the
baby's life is concerned, and one that can have pathogenic effects in the
event of separation. From the standpoint of psychoanalytic theory,
the examination of subsequent mental transformations takes account of
circumstances surrounding the processes through which the subject
acquires autonomy.

Different patterns characterize the psychic development of children
affected by early infantile autism, as the syndrome is described above.
Here, autonomy is immediate, which cannot be explained by maturational deficiency. Describing failure to recognize a part of the mother's
face as a fundamental disorder "of a cognitive type" belongs, of course, to
a different approach altogether. From my point of view, no new knowledge is brought to light by attributing causal value to a descriptive
element.

Given current knowledge, the following hypotheses can usefully be
stated:

1. Nonautistic children (whatever their psychopathological future)
progress from a differential reaction toward the mother to recognition of
her and, with this, to the risk of disorganization through loss of the
ability to form an image of her. This development is delicate and vulnerable to interference from various factors, which can induce a homeostasis in the form of autism.

2. Research must begin with the interactions between the infant and

the caregivers—a proposal that is often misinterpreted both by professionals and by parents of autistic children. As Kanner's initial study pointed out, early infantile autism arises neither from situations of deprivation nor from those in which the parents suffer from psychiatric disorders. In several cases I have dealt with personally, one of several children in a family was affected by autism while all the others developed satisfactorily. It was only after long therapeutic work with the child that I discovered in the course of a conversation that after his birth the mother had experienced a mild depression. Usually linked to life circumstances, and more often than not concealed from the rest of the family, this state invariably had the same consequences: the baby was attended to conscientiously but with no joy, and the mother's sadness was made even worse because of this absence of pleasure. In some cases the autistic baby was considered exceptionally quiet and docile, with the mother usually adding, "Thank goodness he wasn't as demanding as the others were, because I was too exhausted to face up to it." This probably constitutes a second stage, from which the syndrome derives its stability and the strength of its tendency to repetition.

3. It must be remembered that every human being can go through a bad period without it being pathological, and that in a therapeutic anamnesis the memory of this disagreeable state is not the first thing that comes up. It is quite probable that normal, mature people are more vulnerable to such episodes than those who are shielded by characterological or psychopathological features.

4. Lack of liveliness in a baby—which may be due to any number of organic causes—can bring on this "absence of joy" in the mother and undermine the effects of her own "capacity for reverie." If this is a temporary process, the clinical picture of early infantile autism can develop, whereas if the initial abnormality is permanent (in the case of fragile X syndrome, for example) the pathology characteristic of that disorder will predominate.

The ideas set out above have therapeutic consequences that should make it possible to evaluate their heuristic qualities. From the standpoint outlined here, treatments must not aim at ameliorating an initial defect or symptom; they must take into account the dynamic and economic efficiency of the child's (pathological) structure and take advantage of beneficial alterations in his pathological homeostasis inevitably brought about by any new approach.

17

Current Work at the Anna Freud Centre: Interacting Clinical Services during the Analysis of a Child

FRANCES MARTON

The Hampstead Child Therapy Clinic, now called the Anna Freud Centre, has an international reputation as an institute for treatment, research, and training. For nearly forty years, psychoanalytically oriented observations and psychoanalytic assessment and treatment of children and adolescents have provided opportunities to study normal and abnormal development. The presentation of a clinical case will illustrate the interaction of services we provide and the way we try to make the most of our opportunities to learn something new from each case.

Tom's analysis, on a five-times-weekly basis, was conducted under supervision, and his mother had weekly interviews with the therapist. This was one of the few cases in which both mother and child were in analytic treatment. Tom, a boy of mixed race living in a single-parent family, was initially referred to the nursery by a psychiatrist from a local child guidance clinic. Tom's mother, Miss T., an attractive and anxious woman in her late twenties, had approached the referring clinic because of difficulties in weaning her sixteen-months-old toddler from the breast. After several consultations, the psychiatrist recommended entry to our nursery, known to make special provisions for children of under-privileged or disadvantaged families. The full-day nursery program is tailored to meet individual needs and provide whatever developmental assistance may be required. This is facilitated by regular consultations with clinic staff. At weekly meetings attended by the nursery staff, the clinic pediatrician, child analysts, and student observers, each child is discussed in turn, his progress assessed and lines of action laid down.

Tom made weekly visits to the nursery with his mother for several months to prepare him for entering full-time. He separated from mother easily and appeared to be a bright boy with a dynamic personality. Within a few weeks, however, staff and observers noted that Tom, though charming and appealing, found it difficult to tolerate frustration and consistently tested limits. He was prone to aggressive outbursts and sometimes looked overwhelmingly sad. The nursery provided him with support and a benevolent, yet consistent and structured environment. For Miss T., Tom's attendance at the nursery offered new models of identification through which she could learn more effective ways of managing Tom's behavior. It also afforded her a little time to herself for the first time since Tom's birth.

Whereas for many children the nursery experience is sufficient in itself, Tom's increasing aggressive outbursts toward adults and children, his episodes of sadness and depressed affect, and the observable strain between mother and child were indications that both Tom and Miss T. needed more. When approached by Tom's teacher Miss T. said that she and Tom were at the "breaking point." To provide some support and relief, as well as to explore the idea of treatment for Tom, Miss T. had several interviews with the nursery's consultant and consequently agreed he should have a full diagnostic assessment.

Each case referred to the clinic is examined from the point of view of its developmental status as well as its pathology. During the assessment it became clear that Miss T. was familiar with Tom's alternating fury and sadness. Any frustration of his wishes by her led to rage and a physical attack. At times she felt totally tyrannized and was helpless in dealing with him. At other times she would lose her patience, become enraged, and then be plagued by guilt. She was fearful of losing control of her own aggressive impulses and expressed her belief that Tom had acquired his aggressive behavior and shouting from her when he was an infant and waking every few hours. Most nights Tom slept in mother's bed, twisting and grasping her long blond hair, to which he was intensely attached. If returned to his own bed he cried, remained unsettled, and would soon return to mother's bed and stay for the rest of the night. There were long-standing feeding problems. Tom, from the age of six months until he was weaned at nineteenth months, would feed from only one breast, and at the time of referral his attitude toward feeding remained very passive. His first experience of feeding himself occurred in the nursery, yet with mother he continued to demand her active involvement, insisting that she feed him.

We learned that the mother's childhood had been rife with difficulties. Following the death of her parents in infancy, Miss T. was brought up by relatives. She was repeatedly told she was an unwanted member of their family and was involved in sexual seductions by her uncle. In late adolescence she ran away with a younger man and had a sexual relationship with him that lasted several years and ended with a termination of pregnancy. Somewhat later, during a holiday abroad, Tom was conceived. Miss T. had decided to be a single parent, rejecting any possibility of a permanent relationship with Tom's father, a West Indian with a severe clubfoot. Little else is known about father. He has never met his son, although he knows of him, and he provides no financial support.

Tom's birth fulfilled what Miss T. described as "an urgent need." But although she wanted a baby, she was unprepared for the impact a child would have on her life. The early years were difficult. Miss T., alone with her infant, felt extremely isolated, unsupported, and depressed. Nevertheless, she enjoyed the exclusive relationship with her baby. Tom had prolonged access to mother's body through breast-feeding and sleeping and bathing together. Breast-feeding continued into toddlerhood, and toilet training was not introduced until Tom was into his third year. Until this time Tom did all his bowel movements in the bath, and mother's only way of dealing with this was not to bathe him for several days.

Miss T.'s own conflicts and wishes interfered with her mothering and her ability to respond appropriately to Tom's developmental needs. The protracted access to her body was sexually overstimulating and fostered his passive dependency. When Tom made age-appropriate moves toward independence and became more aggressive and assertive, mother's ambivalence toward him was heightened. As a result his own ambivalence increased. Subsequent to this one could observe the alternation of Tom's push toward individuation with his expression of infantile wishes, exacerbated by his anxiety.

Miss T.'s wishes for a girl child and her continued longings for the closeness she had enjoyed in Tom's infancy intensified as Tom attempted to move away from her and increasingly asserted his masculinity. She found it hard to support his masculine strivings and interests. His emulation of superhero figures disturbed and annoyed her, and she refused his requests for toy guns or swords in the hope that this would curb his active, aggressive behavior. In one interview, Miss T. said that she would rather Tom be gay than a he-man type. She was also aware of Tom's phallic wishes toward her. Although she noted his erections and his gazing at her with a "look of desire" as he fondled her hair, she did not curtail the activity. She felt guilty about her participation, perhaps because it reminded her of her own sexual seductions. Tom's emerging need/wish for a male figure with whom he could identify was experienced by his mother as rejection and exacerbated her feelings of guilt and inadequacy. She was, in turn, more rejecting of him. In short, the relationship between mother and child had developed into one that was intense, possessive, and highly ambivalent.

At the time of the diagnostic assessment, Tom's progressive development was endangered. Many areas of his development were strained, and he faced problems in consolidating his view of himself as a male. These difficulties were accentuated and compounded by his color, the absence of a father, his mother's ambivalence, and the nature of her conflicts. Since Miss T. impressed us as a woman who both needed and could use help in her own right, and because Tom's gains from treatment might otherwise be jeopardized, she was offered analytic treatment in conjunction with intensive treatment for Tom.

Anna Freud, in an introduction to a paper by Levy on simultaneous analysis, maintained that

> the tool of simultaneous analysis can be used profitably to throw light on developmental problems. . . . As a child moves forward on the developmental scale, each step demands the giving up of former positions and gains, not only from the child himself but also from the parent. It is only in the most healthy and normal cases that both sides—parent and child—wholly welcome the progressive move and enjoy the child's increasing maturity and gradually increasing libidinal and moral independence. More often it is one or the other partner who lags behind, the child being unable to free himself from fixations, or the parent clinging to attitudes of protectiveness and mothering which have become unjustified. In the worst cases, mother and child may join forces in a regressive move. (A. Freud, 1960)

In simultaneous analysis at the Anna Freud Centre the treatment is carried out separately but at the same time. The mother's treatment is not conducted on clinic premises. For scientific reasons, a third analyst acts as a coordinator, receiving weekly reports from the two therapists. The coordinator follows the material in order to study how fantasies in mother and child coexist, overlap, and influence each other. In addition, the coordinator has the opportunity to see how the interaction between mother and child is reflected in the analysis of each, how common events are experienced differently (or similarly), and how the pathologies appear to interact and influence each other (Yorke, 1983). In the case of Tom and his mother, the resulting study will be the subject of a separate report. Here I will concentrate on some of Tom's developmental struggles as they revealed themselves in his treatment and recount how these were affected by the nature of the mother-child relationship and other external impingements.

When he started treatment Tom was a slim, agile boy of three who seemed lively and intelligent. Although dressed in pastel shades, like his mother, Tom impressed the observer as a masculine little boy. Upon meeting him I was struck by the intense nature of his feelings. In addition to his sad or angry expressions, Tom appeared frightened and anxious.

During treatment several aspects of his contemporary relationship to his mother were soon reflected. He was possessive toward me and was provocative and demanding. Ungratified wishes and the maintenance of limits prompted him to walk out of sessions or to resort to physical attacks. After behaving provocatively he would run away from me and anxiously ask, "Will you get angry?" Invariably he placed himself in dangerous positions in the sessions and needed reassurance about his safety and about my intention to protect him. He frequently showed me his scrapes and bruises, sometimes saying, "I jumped and mummy didn't catch me." In one session Tom used a box as a baby carriage and instructed me to "push it fast," causing it to crash into things and the boy doll to fall out of it. Miss T., in a parent interview, commented that Tom often sensed her anger by the manner in which she pushed his stroller. Tom would tell her not to push him "that way," meaning quickly or in a jerky fashion. Sexual wishes and longings toward mother soon emerged in the transference relationship. He invited me to sleep with him on the bed and to play kissing games. In one session, he seductively told me that his penis was long and hard and pulled down his trousers. In subsequent sessions, the action of displaying his penis took on various meanings. Sometimes it was a defiant attack; sometimes an exhibitionistic act. Very early in treatment Tom's preoccupation with sexual differences was a dominant theme and involved dangerously aggressive characters of whom he was afraid. His awareness of his mother's aggression toward him increased his sense of danger and was reinforced by his own aggression and its projection. His use of projection and displacement defended against his aggressive wishes as well as his castration anxiety. With the introduction of castrating figures, Tom dealt defensively with his anxiety by denial and by identifying with the aggressor. In one session Tom told me that monsters "bit mummy" and were coming to bite off Snoopy Dog's gun. When I commented that maybe he was frightened that they might come and bite him, he assured me, "I'm not frightened—they don't bite me." In the following sessions, Tom pretended to be a monster and often arrived wearing a mask. When concerns about sexual differences were addressed, Tom said that he didn't have a willy (penis) and didn't want one. He wanted to wee from his bottom. The establishment of his sexual identity was complicated by the absence of a male model as an object for identification and by an active/passive conflict.

In the early months Tom frequently engaged in water play. Once, while he played, he asked me to make "eyes" on the blackboard, around which he drew "long hair" and a "string." Exclaiming that he didn't like the eyes looking at him, he grabbed the baby doll and repeatedly smashed it against "the lady." In another session, after holding the doll under water and telling me, "Look, the baby's gone under water!" he again hit the "lady" and agreed with me that this was because the baby was cross at the "lady" for not keeping him safe. A few days later, Tom recalled an accident in which he fell into a swimming pool. Although this happened a year and a half earlier, Tom attributed the event to the day before. As treatment progressed, the theme of falling in water was conspicuous, epitomizing situations of anxiety in which he felt uncared for or unprotected by his mother and at the mercy of her ambivalent feelings.

Important aspects of Tom's relationship with his mother were reflected in material about "hair" and through the use of the fairy tale "Rapunzel." This became clearest at a time when mother was withdrawn from Tom and was also involved in evening classes. Tom's vulnerable state and his alternating rageful attacks and passive behavior were linked to mother's unavailability. In the nursery, he chose Sally, a classmate with long blonde hair, to be his "darling." When it was time to go outside, he stood quietly sucking his thumb as she and younger children put on his coat for him and buttoned it up. At naptime, he began taking a long-haired doll to his cot, where he would undress it and stroke its hair until he fell asleep. In the sessions, he busied himself tying cars together with string, which he referred to as "hair." As he cut the string, he called some of the pieces of "hair" "sweeties" and others "monster hair," reflecting his double and opposing views of his mother.

On another occasion, he talked about the hair of a "beautiful lovely princess" and told the story of Rapunzel, emphasizing that she was locked in a room with no doors. After this, he attached a long piece of string, again called "hair," to the lock on the door. He stretched it across the room and attached the other end to the sink faucet. This material reflected the sexualized relationship between mother and child but was also understood as a wish to regain an idealized early exclusive tie with mother.

For four-year-old Tom the sexualized relationship with mother intensified his castration anxiety. The emergent longings for a father were influenced by his view of his mother as castrating and dangerous as well as by his own developmental thrust and contact with other boys. An added factor was his growing relationship with a male boarder, whom mother had taken on for income and as a caretaker for Tom when she had evening classes. "Fathers" became a predominant feature in Tom's material, and various aspects of his longings could be seen. At times, Tom wished for someone to protect him from the "unsafe" mother; at others, he felt a father would be more available as well as a better provider; and sometimes, he just wanted to have a daddy to share and support what Tom called his "boy activities." Tom got on well with the male lodger and reacted strongly when mother asked him to leave. Following this event, Tom protected all his possessions vehemently. In his play, battles were fought between and over objects; through his material Tom expressed his feeling that mother was a depriving and powerful woman who got rid of men. Tom's anger increased when a new boarder, this time female, arrived. Miss T. reported that Tom frequently ran away from her and on several occasions had locked her out of the house. This was also played out in the sessions with Tom running away and hiding from me. We began to understand this as his way of showing how cross he felt at mummy's unavailability and her sending "men"— the male boarder and daddy—away. Following this interpretation he remained in the treatment room.

As treatment progressed and the castration anxiety and defense against it were more fully worked through, Tom became more assertive of his masculinity. He made use of the therapist to reinforce and admire his physical strength and prowess and his boyish interests and activities, possibly because mother liked only the passive/girlish side. After a long holiday in the second year of treatment, Tom returned wearing a girl's clothes. His long hair made him appear even more feminine, and in the street he was often mistaken for a girl. By dressing him in this way, mother was reacting partly to Tom's increasingly phallic behavior but also to his anxiety-driven aggression and open masturbation in her presence. After returning to school and treatment, however, Tom refused to be dressed like a girl and demanded that his hair be cut.

Unfortunately, at this time certain external events occurred that led Miss T. to become increasingly depressed and rejecting of Tom. The aggressive wishes that came to the fore were conflictual, and he told me that he was not Tom but "Obicaca"—a motherless and fatherless boy from Jamaica who owned two dragons and possessed magic powers that enabled him to make things appear and disappear. He had powerful wishes that his depriving mother would be replaced by another. As we talked of his anger at and disappointment in his mother he called me "daddy." The intensity of his aggressive wishes provoked anxiety. In one session he revealed his secret plan to kill a girl in the nursery. He concealed himself under a chair and "changed" into Obicaca. I talked to Obicaca about a friend who had such strong killing thoughts/feelings that he sometimes became frightened that they would come true and that somebody would do something to him. He came out from under the chair and, with hands on hips, said, "Is your friend a boy? I know, it's Tom!" Gradually the character of Obicaca was acknowledged to represent, on the one hand, Tom's omnipotent wishes and feelings and, on the other, his feelings of worthlessness.

Masturbation was conflictual and created much anxiety, as would be expected in light of Tom's circumstances. Repeated inflammations, which necessitated circumcision when he was nearly five, intensified his anxiety about his penis. The internalization of mother's view of him as destructive and the contribution of his own conflictual aggressive feelings were reflected in his understanding of the event. Following a visit to the general practitioner, Tom stated that the infection was "his fault," and in subsequent sessions he portrayed himself as a "breaker" and "destroyer" of things. In his play, he broke off bits of toys and anxiously asked whether they still worked properly. Sometimes he would bring "girls' stories" for me to read and when he was particularly worried, he would take the role of Wonder Woman instead of He-Man. Once, when these feelings were related to masturbation anxieties, Tom told me, "I hate my penis. It's long, fat, and stupid!" The circumcision acted as a confirmation of his self-destructiveness and was also felt to be a punishment for his burgeoning sexual wishes and masculinity. Following the operation, Tom refused to look at his penis, calling it "horrible," and prohibited his mother and friends from doing so.

Several elements of Tom's pathology seemed to be brought together by his experience of the inflammation and circumcision. Any disappointment, whether in his objects or in himself, was attributed to his "damaged" masculinity and to the fact that he was a boy and was black.

Tom's difficulties in learning and his lack of "readiness" to enter primary school were evident to the nursery teachers even before these disturbing events. In his "regressed" and "anxious" state following the operation, he reacted badly to the change in school. A strong nostalgia for the nursery persisted, and in one visit there he told the teacher, "I just haven't been eating." On leaving, he asked her whether the teachers were glad he was gone and then begged her not to forget him, adding that he thought about her all the time.

At his new school, Tom refused to "look" when told to do so, and after completing some written work he would scribble over it, making it "horrible." It also became clear that Tom's battling relationship with his mother was being displaced to school and the learning situation.

Tom's treatment has continued and he has started to settle down at school. He is still vulnerable, however, and finds it difficult to maintain a positive view of himself and his masculinity. Recently, Tom's school-teacher (male) left suddenly. Tom said sadly, "He knew we loved him. Why did he leave? Didn't he like us?" In the following sessions, Tom arrived with his fingernails painted with nail polish and his pockets filled with bottles of perfume and bracelets as well as broken Matchbox cars, over which he had scribbled with felt pens in an attempt to change their color.

This case demonstrates disturbances in development where the environment and the mother's pathology interfered with normal progress. From the beginning, Miss T.'s pathology affected her ability to meet Tom's ordinary developmental needs. In his oral phase she used Tom to satisfy her own needs for closeness, but she also felt him to be a burden. Her attempts to deal with her ambivalence were evident in her inability to wean him until he was nineteen months old. Once Tom became mobile, Miss T. increasingly felt him to be hostile and rejecting toward her. The externalization of her own aggression reinforced her view of him as "a destructive creature"; consequently, she was unable to help him contain instinctual impulses through the establishment of his own inner controls. The emergence of Tom's age-appropriate phallic interests met with denigration rather than praise and admiration.

A close and sexualized relationship became established quite early in his life. Mother's periodic depressive withdrawal and rejection of Tom led to the development of a narcissistic vulnerability. The mother as a sole caretaker increased his threatened loss of object. Later on, the absence of a male figure for identification and the actual experience of circumcision at the age of four and one-half further reinforced Tom's view of himself as damaged and unlovable and led to considerable conflict in establishing his sexual identity.

The mother was, by turns, totally rejecting and overgratifying. Her bodily availability increased Tom's eagerness to be close to her and acted as a reassurance against his own aggression and fear of object loss. The mother's inability to provide protective limits became particularly threatening in the phallic phase, when mother was experienced as a potential castrator. Tom's passive wishes were then reinforced by the mother's wish that he were a girl. As Tom passed through some of these developmental phases during treatment, I was able to follow his developmental struggles and see how these fed into neurotic conflict and how the traumatic experiences around the phimosis and circumcision contributed to his disturbance. The value of simultaneous analysis in cases such as these will, I hope, be evident. The mutual interaction between the mother's pathology and the child's growing disturbance can be understood more clearly.

Detailed case material of this kind offers many opportunities for study and research. Inter alia, it exemplifies certain problems that may arise when children are reared in single-parent families. It illustrates one of the ways in which external circumstances and parental pathology can influence conflicts over gender identity. It demonstrates, too, how even the most careful preparation and working through in the treatment situation can fail to mitigate sufficiently the traumatic effects of this particular operation during a vulnerable period. All these matters caught the interest of a number of the study groups at our Centre— those concerned with developmental disturbances, with one-parent families, with the impact of physical misfortune on psychological development, and with the project for simultaneous analyses of parent and child. It also illustrates the way in which clinic services can work together—in this instance, the Educational Unit, Diagnostic Services, Parent Guidance, and treatment facilities.

REFERENCES

Brenner, N. (1984). Nursery School Annual Report, Anna Freud Centre, London. Unpublished.
Burlingham, D., Goldberger, A., and Lussier, A. (1955). "Simultaneous Analysis of Mother and Child." *Psychoanal. Study Child* 10:165–186.
Freud, A. (1960). Introduction to "Simultaneous Analysis of a Mother and Her Adolescent Daughter: The Mother's Contribution to the Loosening of the Infantile Object Tie," by Kate Levy. *Psychoanal. Study Child* 15:378–380.
Marton, F. (1984). "Developmental Struggles of a Four-Year-Old Boy in a Single-Parent Family." Presented at a Wednesday Conference, Anna Freud Centre, London. Unpublished.
Yorke, C. (1983). Annual Report on Simultaneous Analyses. Anna Freud Centre, London. Unpublished.

18

Reconstruction of a Traumatic Experience in the Analysis of a Pseudo-Backward Girl

LORE SCHACHT

When is the present?
—R. M. Rilke

In child analysis, the work of reconstruction is conducted in more than two "separate localities" (Freud, 1937), for the parents, too, have a remembering function for the child in their role as supporting egos. This can be of importance when an event in the first years of a child's life is being reconstructed, as in the case to be presented.

"It is useful to consider two terms as reciprocal: constructions are the early stages of the process of reconstruction. They are frankly tentative and must involve speculations which are put to further test as the process progresses to a convincing stage of reconstruction" (Greenacre, 1975). Using the distinction between construction and reconstruction, as Greenacre suggested, it will be established that the child analyst's construction making is dependent on whether and how the lost event is still accessible to the parents, and on their willingness and ability to hint at or communicate it. It is easy to see that this makes reconstructive efforts in child analysis immensely more complicated. In the alternating interactions with parents and the child in child analysis, confusing inferences from "traces" are easily drawn in the process of guessing and evaluating.

The immaturity of the child's personality is responsible for another treatment idiosyncrasy, particularly regarding reconstruction: it sometimes poses delicate questions of appropriate timing. The child therapist sometimes has to suspend this construction in order to wait for the maturation of the child, for her growing ability to integrate; this integration, in its turn, may be furthered by the analytic process. In other words, the time span between the formation of a construction and the beginning of the reconstructive process can be considerable, and this puts a heavy burden on the child therapist's tolerance for unclear and confused material and on his or her capacity for letting things unfold gradually.

This chapter reviews a time span of about three years. Because this creates the danger of a simplified reduction of the material, the work of reconstruction is examined step by step in order to give a clear picture (as if in slow motion) of the sequence of events and the gathering momentum. The etiological factors of this case, which is psychopathologically unusual and poses many questions, will only be touched on. The argument will follow the stages of the therapist's growing understanding and her therapeutic procedures: formulation of constructions; communication from the mother about the traumatic event corresponding to the therapist's expectations; repetition of the traumatic event in the course of the analysis; reconstruction of two aspects of the traumatic event, nine months and one and a half years after the mother's communication; and the reactions of the child.

CASE STUDY

Lisa, named by her mother after a well-known literary heroine, was referred to the analyst at age four years and three months. The following symptoms were coupled to considerable general developmental retardation: enuresis, encopresis, hyperactivity, lack of spontaneity, compulsive eating, retarded speech development, and difficulties in relating to peers and adults. The picture was completed by rather gauche body movements and a continual dribble.

During the anamnesis, the analyst gathered from the parents that the child had been wanted and that both pregnancy and birth had been uneventful. The infant refused the breast. The mother, who had been very unhappy about this, said this was because the doctors "had thrust the baby" onto her breast and then "snatched it away again." Apart from the fact that the mother had a postnatal depression that lasted about three months and that both parents wore mask and white coat when feeding the baby, the first months passed, according to the parents, without disquieting surprises.

At five months each parent independently felt that the baby appeared odd: she did not move the way they had expected and seemed to be deaf. Medical examinations carried out at the time did not show any pathology. Because of her slow body movements the child received physiotherapy, from the age of nine months, for two and three-quarter years. This began with a three-month treatment course, using the Vojta technique, after which the mother refused to cooperate.[1] The treatment demanded that she supervise her child in the performance of almost sadistic exercises that were pushed to the pain threshold and beyond. After this, the gentler and more soothing therapy of Bobat was prescribed.[2] As the mother was then still working, the parents took turns in looking after the baby. In addition, she received two years of play therapy from occupational therapy students, one of whom was described as rather clumsy and unfriendly. When Lisa was two and three-quarter years old, her sister Masha was born. After her birth, the father withdrew from the family, and the mother soon made plans to separate from him, taking the girls with her.

These details of Lisa's developmental history made the therapist curious. At first contact, the therapist was surprised by the child's appearance: she looked pitiful, like a sack of potatoes on two tiny legs. In spite of the gloomy factual material, the therapist had an impression of her openness and sensed her ability to communicate. This interest on the analyst's part contributed to Lisa's beginning to open up in the course of conversation, which laid the foundation for a good therapeutic relationship. The diagnostic hypothesis was pseudo-debility. This was reinforced by two themes arising in the initial interview: the dominant theme of low self-esteem, and curiosity and prying. The treatment was set at once a week for one year and then four times a week for two years.

The therapist was not satisfied with information from the developmental history that suggested, as an explanation of the grave symptomatology, a cumulative psychic stress at all stages of development. On reflection, the therapist remembered being struck by the bizarre

1. The Vojta therapy (V. Vojta) is a physiotherapy for babies suffering from cerebral palsy. It must be applied within the first months of life, usually by the mother herself. The intention is to avoid fixation of pathological movement patterns. In order to achieve this, the therapist (mother) forces the baby to make certain reactive movements by putting pressure on different body areas or body points after having fixed the baby's arms and back to her own body. For the baby, this physiotherapy is very painful. Quite often mothers discontinue the therapy, as they cannot tolerate making their own baby suffer and cry.

2. The Bobath therapy (B. and K. Bobath) is a mild form of physiotherapy, which does not make the baby suffer. In Lisa's case the idea apparently was to stimulate the adynamic baby.

and uncoordinated nature of Lisa's movements and play products. What struck the analyst next, at the beginning of analysis proper, was a discrepancy between Lisa's wish to draw herself and her total inability to do so; that led to the therapist's first hunch. When Lisa made the first plasticine figures of herself, her father, and her sister, she communicated, over and above a definitely symbolic expression of penis envy and castration anxiety, a grotesque distortion of her body image. Psychological testing yielded no organic cerebral cause for her striking inability to draw or form bodies, and it was suggested that there might be a psychogenic cause. At the testing session with a psychologist, Lisa behaved in such a way that the psychologist at first thought she was suffering from bad eyesight.

The analyst spoke to the mother over the phone, saying that something unusual must have happened that the parents had not told her. The mother described a traumatic scene that seemed a possible explanation for these aspects of distortion in Lisa's perception.

Eight weeks after the beginning of analysis proper, and just before the Christmas break two weeks after the last meeting with the parents, the mother called the therapist. She told the therapist how pleasant Lisa had been and particularly how differentiated her speech had become. Then she said she had to tell the therapist something that she had carried around within herself for weeks since the therapist had spoken of her guess that something must have occurred that was responsible for Lisa's confused body image. It had happened when Lisa was one and a half or two years old. Lisa's father was taking a shower, and she had awakened and called for him. The mother told her that he was in the shower, but Lisa persisted in asking for him. The mother finally got angry and said, "I will show him to you." Then she dragged Lisa to the bathroom. But the moment she pushed aside the shower curtain thinking "There he is," she was scared herself. Lisa, still half asleep, had never before seen her father wet, his hair falling over his face, without glasses, and from below. She started crying, and the mother found herself crying, too. Later, trying to comfort Lisa, she explained again and again that it was her Papa she had seen. Lisa had been confused, and it took a long time to comfort her.

Blum (1980) has commented on the process of reconstruction:

Reconstruction assists in the analytic restoration of the continuity and cohesion of the personality. But what may be as important or even more important, reconstruction is fundamental for the analyst. The analyst may not be explicitly aware of his use of reconstruction, but he will inevitably reconstruct aspects of the patient's personality disorder. . . . How could the analyst understand the case without some utilization of reconstruction? . . . Reconstruction is not only an important technical tool, but is essential for comprehensive psychoanalytic exploration.

After receiving this information, the therapist was now more certain than ever that Lisa's complex confusion, which seemed to crystallize around certain memory fragments, was connected with this traumatic event. This was probably less important for the continuing analytic procedure than for the hope that continued analysis would be meaningful—that there was meaning in the child's confusion. Of course, as in Bornstein's (1948) poignant description of her treatment of a patient with a pseudo-debility, the analyst had recurring doubts. Whenever she became convinced that she was after all dealing with a case of debility, she was tempted to give up.

The reported scene emphasized the intensity of a visual trauma, the reason for the voyeuristic themes (Greenacre), and the erotic action of seeing. Because of space limitations, the interpretive decipherment of this condensed shower scene will not be presented. Suffice it to say that like the primal scene, it yielded evidence of the possible stimulation of penis envy, traumatic realization of gender difference (Roiphe and Galenson), and castration anxiety. The reconstructive effort in the narrower sense (to be presented later) was not feasible until one year further into the analysis. It stressed another aspect of the experience, based on the assumption (Bergen, 1958) that the real trauma for Lisa might have been the experience of being exposed to her mother's fear and terror. Presumably her mother thought that she had harmed her daughter, since she was so ashamed of her failure and her action that she had to tell the therapist about it over the phone. It was certainly one reason she had forgotten the event and had tried to keep it a secret.

Two weeks after the Christmas break, Lisa appeared in analysis with a bandage on her forehead. After a week's difficult analytic work and questioning of the mother, it emerged that the girl had fallen on the stairs while carrying a bottle of apple juice and had cut her forehead, which required attention at the hospital. When Lisa was able to speak coherently to the therapist about the accident, she emphasized with regard to the hospital experience, "And Mummy did comfort me." So this time the mother was able to comfort Lisa, in contrast to the time of the shower scene. Much later, Lisa's mother reported that, while coming upstairs just before the accident happened, Lisa stared with fascination at her father standing on top of the stairs surrounded by the rest of the family. She stared and stared and then missed a step. The similarity of the girl's position to that in the shower scene was unmistakable: facing her father, looking up at him and along his legs, she saw him towering above her. This reference to a repetition of the traumatic event was reconstructed during the week after the accident and directed the analyst's attention to the mother's attitude and affect. Two aspects of the scene were probably experienced as traumatic: the sudden confrontation with the father, and the sharing of terror between Lisa and her mother. The purpose here is to present the repetition and the beginning of working through in the transference relationship.

Nine months after the fall on the stairs (session 170) Lisa began to show an interest in the clock and the division of time. This occurred after there had been talk of being able to see, of walls, and of intimacy. Lisa put the family into a car and said emphatically, "Lisa sits opposite Papa." Two sessions later, she introduced the fairy tale of Little Red Riding Hood, which she dictated to the analyst, stressing the encounter with the wolf in a confused and stammering voice. She said, "She was walking in the woods and there was . . . Red Riding Hood went to the wolf, to the grandmother, into her bed . . ." She started again, as if exhausted, and said, "Red Riding Hood went into the woods, into the wolf to the door . . ." Later she said to the analyst with regard to her going home, "I am allowed to go home alone today—I am not allowed—I am simply going!"

Two weeks later (session 179) the confusion between Red Riding Hood and wolf, Lisa and her father, was enacted in a session. Lisa, who wanted to play with plasticine, said that she and the therapist owned a bakery, which she had built with Lego blocks.

> T H E R A P I S T [following up on an idea from the earlier theoretical argument]: Oh, I shall make something, too. I shall make an animal—the animal that meets Red Riding Hood.
> L I S A: Are you making the wolf?
> T H E R A P I S T: Yes, and I am in trouble with the legs.

When the wolf was finished, Lisa (who often went to the bakery with her father) told the therapist to come into the bakery. The therapist took the wolf to the bakery and looked at the bread from outside. Lisa had locked the door in order to keep the wolf out. Then she said, "Find me a window." The therapist took a window from the Lego box and gave it to her. Lisa put the window in place, and the therapist had the wolf look at the bread through the window.

Then said Lisa, "You can tell him that he can come to the door." The therapist took the wolf to the bakery door, which Lisa opened. She gave the wolf a basket full of bread, not asking him to pay for it. It is significant that it was the wolf who had the basket this time. This contributed to the sorting out of wolf and Red Riding Hood that the analyst sought, leading to the following step. The therapist said, "O.K. I made the wolf. Now you can make Red Riding Hood." Lisa proceeded to do this at once. She chose red plasticine and commented, "It will have a beautiful dress." She carried on, becoming excited. She made the legs very long, then the arms, and commented, "Now the head." She formed the ears, the hair, the mouth, the nose, the eyes, and then—a beard!

T H E R A P I S T : But Little Red Riding Hood does not have a beard.
L I S A [startled and whispering as if scared]: It's not Red Riding Hood, it's Papa!

After a while she formed the hands very carefully.

T H E R A P I S T : If that is Papa, then he has—
L I S A : No penis.
T H E R A P I S T : Well, you may be thinking, if I do not have one, he must—
L I S A : Oh, yes, he'll get one [she made a long penis].
T H E R A P I S T : I suppose when a child suddenly sees her papa naked in the bathroom, she thinks, goodness me, what a gigantic penis he has.

Lisa noticed that the legs were of unequal length. "Must measure them," she said (she was still whispering), and she made them equally long and added feet. The therapist simply said that the hands were very noticeable.

Lisa suddenly asked, "Shall I draw Lisa?" She seized paper and pencil and, with a new found flourish, drew a circle for the head and put in points for the eyes and shadows above them. Then she added nose and mouth, ears and hair. Into the grotesquely small body, which looked like an appendage to the head, she put three points for the breasts and belly. The therapist commented on the fingers. "The hands are nice; they can touch. They can touch the whole body and find out about it." Lisa then made the feet, put a line between the legs, and commented, when she saw the therapist's questioning face, that this was pee. After that she covered the genital region with cross-hatching; she had already cross-hatched the upper part of the body. To the therapist's remark that the body is invisible when dressed, she replied: "That's the wedding dress." The drawing was a very beautiful picture, which would not be readily attributed to a child. The following day, moreover, Lisa used the therapist's title for the first time when she greeted her.

This differentiation between Lisa and her father, the differentiation of body image, led to an exploration of the body image, done mainly by contrasting the inside and outside of a house. "I want to make another house, from inside and from outside," the therapist once heard her mumble to herself (session 247). She started enthusiastically to make complicated Lego vehicles, meant for much older children, and showed a new staying power and concentration level while doing so. Finally, and for a long time, she made a moving van and then a caravan in which patient and therapist sat and traveled during the session, usually to Africa. Africa was the unknown future (she was about to start school), and the journey indicated an enhanced perception of time. In session 249 she made observations that indicated an awareness of time changes. She told the therapist about the color of the house in which she had lived at the time of the traumatic scene and which had been changed since that time. Altogether, her development was very promising.

I want now to turn to the second aspect and its working through in analysis. In several sessions Lisa had declared that we needed water for the "desert," and she had produced mugs, glasses, and finally a small bucket full of water. Inevitably she spilt some. Attempts at interpreting this as an expression of phallic effort did not lead to any results. The therapist suddenly realized in between sessions that she had experienced anxious tension when Lisa built the caravan and particularly when she started to produce water, expecting her to spill it. The therapist began to wonder whether Lisa was staging an enactment of the terror shared with her mother and decided to tell the child about it in the following session.

When Lisa arrived in good spirits (session 269) the therapist started the conversation by announcing that yesterday she had thought hard about what had been happening in the last few weeks and that she would like to tell her about this. Lisa listened. The therapist told her that she had to spill water—yesterday a whole bucket of it—in order to give them both a big fright. Did this remind her of something she had experienced some time ago, something with her mother? As Lisa listened, the therapist said that her mother had once told her about what had happened in the bathroom when Lisa was very small, how they had both been scared when they had seen Papa standing there. The therapist's casual remark that Lisa might remember this was answered promptly and firmly by "yes," but then she diverted the conversation. Some time later she declared she would fill the bucket with water. When she came back with it, she asked the therapist, "Where shall we put it today?" She found a secure place, and the bucket did not spill over this time. Later in the session she started tidying up the consulting room and finally came to the toy farm. While she was busy there, the therapist heard her whisper, "The curious giraffe." The therapist was surprised to find her reverting to the "curious giraffe"; the animal had embodied her curiosity in the beginning of analysis but since then had not played a part in it. As she had done before, she made the giraffe look over a door. And as before, she introduced something new; she brought the therapist some pine cones: "For you. I found them lying in the street." Later on she said, "I am drawing a sun. It has rays."

In the next session she drew a house with a precise representation of its interior, a house in which a wedding was taking place. Later she drew a caravan furnished in great detail with, among other things, separate entrances for grownups and children, a table for changing baby, and a table for the toys. In the caravan lived Isabelle; she was drawn carefully with ears, neck, body, breasts, legs, and trousers. Finally Lisa put the sun into the caravan: "I am drawing the sun, too. In the country where she is going, the sun is shining at night, too," she added with a happy, contented smile. The therapist remarked that Isabelle looked quite happy, but perhaps she was a little alone and would like a visitor. Lisa answered promptly: "Her parents!" She now drew another caravan, in which mother was standing on the left (Lisa probably had drawn a penis under her skirt) and Isabelle and her father were standing on the other side.

This report will end with a few remarks about the next session (272), in which Lisa brought a memory of her own for the first time, a session that poses a question as to the importance and origin of screen memories. Lisa had produced untidiness in the little doll's house, and the therapist said, "You want me to help you tidy up the house the same way that we have tidied up your memories."

Lisa rearranged the furniture, so that it suddenly showed how her family sat at the table at home and where everybody's place was. In the bedroom two beds were first stacked and then placed side by side. She asked for the little chamberpot, saying the children needed it. Then she said (and it should be emphasized that this was new), "My grandma had a little chamberpot just like that." As if in an aside she continued, "Once I upset the chamberpot."

T H E R A P I S T : Was it full?

L I S A : Yes.

T H E R A P I S T : That must have been scary, for you and for grandma, too.

L I S A : And it was on the carpet.

T H E R A P I S T : You must have been scared. The other day, when the water spilt, it was on the carpet, too, and I said how much we were both scared and how that must have been like that other time with Mummy in the bathroom.

Lisa went over to the toy farm, where the kangaroo baby was put into the pocket of the mother animal. The giraffe looked around once more, and finally the little baby doll was placed in the attic together with the mother and put to bed there: "Then no animal can get there and bite something off," Lisa said. "Then the baby is safe," the therapist remarked.

Lisa gathered all the cars and trains she could find and lined them up. She was lying on the floor happily shouting, "Stand back from the platform. The train is arriving in a few minutes." After a while she added, "The train is leaving in a few minutes."

DISCUSSION

Having emphasized the special techniques of forming a construction and timing the reconstruction in a child analysis, I will discuss the clinical material from two points of view: the immediate therapeutic result of reconstruction, and further thoughts on pseudo-debility, which arose in this case expressly from the reconstructive method. "Reconstruction is useful with patients who have had disturbances in the pre-oedipal years," Greenacre (1975) has commented.

After confronting Red Riding Hood and the wolf—the father and Lisa—and formulating the reconstruction of the bathroom encounter with her father (the shower scene was not expressly mentioned), the therapist followed with a lengthy exploration of the perceptions relating to the body's structure, to inner and outer. This was done particularly in relation to the house, its interior and exterior, and was reinforced by Lisa's wish to build Lego cars and houses. As a result of the reconstruction of the affect of terror shared with her mother, Lisa was able for the first time to make a historical connection between past and present, which brought relief and integration of space and time concepts. In the picture of the sun in the caravan, the sun as a friendly companion was probably a symbolic expression that the memory and the chronological integration of the past scene made it possible to master the affect in the repetition for the first time. It is astonishing, and probably consistent, that Lisa brought a later memory in the following sessions that resembled the traumatic scene in the affect of terror. Not quite satisfied with this, however, she finally managed a symbolic representation of the time continuum by lining up the trains. By taking over the role of stationmaster she may have given an indication of what it felt like to be the master of concepts of time.

Distinguishing between enactive and representational remembering, Loewald (1980) connects the former with acting out and with repetitions in the transference: "Perhaps it would be more correct to say that the analyst's aim is to establish links between the two forms of memorial reproduction, to allow one to be illuminated by the other in a mutual recognition that leads to higher psychic organization." When Lisa brought her first memory it was obvious that representational remembering had become possible. "In representational remembering, the mind presents something to itself as its own past experience, distinguishing past from present and himself as the experiencer from what he experienced" (Loewald, 1980).

This reconstruction enriches the many existing ideas on pseudo-debility that assume that the families of these children are hiding something of a sexual nature, with evidence of a traumatic event that has been kept secret. It can be assumed that traumatization by the event described came on top of an already pathological development.

This reconstruction resulted in further problems that I will not discuss here. It led, however, to a memory that was related to the discussion of screen memories (Freud, 1937; Greenacre, 1975). This memory of Lisa allowed the hypothetical question, is it possible that in this case the reversed direction of the analysis—first the reconstruction of the scene that had to be repressed but could not be repressed fully because of its traumatic character and then the emergence of a similar memory related in its affect—illuminated the origin of screen memories? Can we ask the question whether without analysis, this memory might have been the one memory uncovered by a later analysis, if any?

REFERENCES

Bergen, M. E. (1958). "The Effect of Severe Trauma on a Four-Year-Old Child." *Psychoanal. Study Child* 13:407–429.

Blum, H. P. (1980). "The Value of Reconstruction in Adult Psychoanalysis." *Int. J. Psycho-Anal.* 61:39–52.

Bornstein, B. (1948). "The Analysis of a Phobic Child: Some Problems of Theory and Technique in Child Analysis." *Psychoanal. Study Child* 3.

Freud, S. (1937). "Constructions in Analysis." *Standard Edition,* 23:257– 269.

Greenacre, P. (1975). "On Reconstruction." *J. Am. Psycho-Anal.* 29:27–46.

Loewald, H. W. (1980). *Perspectives on Memory: Papers on Psycho-Analysis.* New Haven: Yale University Press.

Rilke, R. M. (1922). "Wann ist Gegenwart. . . ?" Letter to Lou Andreas-Salome, 11 February 1922.

V

Cognitive Perspectives

19

Introduction

COLETTE CHILAND M.D.

Considerable emphasis is being given nowadays to cognition. This part presents an overall view of the role of cognition in child development and disorder (chap. 20) as well as an original approach, inspired both by psychoanalysis and work done by Piaget, on thought containers (chap. 21).

Psychic functioning is both global and continuous. Discontinuities, particular moments, events, or psychic phenomena, can be isolated and studied separately, and the integrated aspect of the whole can be viewed from a number of different standpoints. But, despite the title of this part, "Cognitive Perspectives," what is happening now is something quite different: there is a complete change of focus, whereby cognition is viewed not as one of many parts of a whole but as the central and explanatory phenomenon with a causal role. Concomitance becomes etiology.

This change of focus is accompanied by a shift in meaning. For a great many years particular attention was given to the development of intelligence. Jean Piaget's entire work was directed toward demonstrating, through the history of our culture and child development, the construction of the invariants of thought that make it possible to acquire scientific knowledge, to achieve true thought. In Michael Rutter's chapter, *cognition* refers not to the processes through which true thought can be attained but to any of the ideational aspects of mental phenomena, such as the set of beliefs an individual has about himself.

Curiously enough, this deals with one of the two aspects of mental life distinguished by Freud: ideas or images (*Vorstellungen*), which he opposed to affects. In his view, instinct (biologically rooted instinctual energy) could never be reached directly, but only via either ideas or affects; the central, causative element remained the instinctual cathexes.

Piaget's clear purpose was to get rid of both the energy-related aspect and the biological associations in order to examine the cognitive structures in relation to logic. The elimination of cathexes and affects, however debatable it may be as far as studying the clinical subject was concerned, did make it possible to study the epistemic subject. Piaget's system, however, did not constitute an attack on the study of depression and autism, where the affective aspects cannot be ignored, even though, on the contrary, the construction of true knowledge presupposes independence from the affects.

Although it would be legitimate to declare an interest in the cognitive aspects of the depressive or autistic experience, it is factitious to give the term *cognitive* such a wide extension as to cover the affects. Is *attention* a cognitive phenomenon, or is it a phenomenon related to energy, affect, and motivation that makes cognitive activity possible? Several implicit ideas lie behind these positions—which are not cognitive, but "cognitivist."

One of these is the rapprochement among thought processes, artificial intelligence, and computer processing. But computers are manmade and fed by electric energy unmodulated by meaning. Accurate results are obtained only if the syntax is correctly followed to the complete exclusion of semantics (see John R. Searle, *Minds, Brains, and Science*, 1984).

Another is the search for deficits, turning mental illness into a handicap: one thinks of breakdown in the machine, which it may or may not be possible to repair. No consideration is given to the idea of a person with individual endowments confronting his or her environment. This mode of thinking is an extension of the theory of cerebral localization.

There is no doubt that any disturbance of thought processes has repercussions on how comfortable individuals are with themselves and their relations with their environment. In the case of the cognitive disharmonies referred to by Bernard Gibello, it is possible that providing individuals with other means of thinking, other "thought containers," might improve their capacity for relationships, behavior, and a feeling of well-being.

But when affective disturbances are at the forefront, is there any hope of altering the cathexes through an exclusively cognitive approach? The cognitivists think so. We are skeptical. If their therapies are successful, it is because much more than cognition is involved in the treatments, which is borne out by reading their own work. Although he was a philosopher and not a clinician, Spinoza put it wisely: "A true knowledge of good and evil cannot halt any emotion by virtue of being true, but only insofar as it is considered as an emotion" (*Ethics,* pt. IV, Prop. XIV).

20

The Role of Cognition in Child Development and Disorder

MICHAEL RUTTER

The study of thought processes has always been a central feature of psychiatry in all its branches. Thus, abnormalities of thinking, as reflected in delusions and hallucinations, constituted the bread and butter of Kraepelinian nosology and Jasperian psychopathology. Equally, intrapsychic defense mechanisms have been one of the central pillars of psychoanalysis from Freud's very first writings. There is nothing new in the notion that cognition plays a crucial role in both child development and child psychiatric disorder. Yet there have been important changes in the ways in which the role of cognition has been conceptualized.

It is convenient to consider cognition under two broad headings, cognitive processing and cognitive deficits, although the two cannot be regarded as wholly separate. Cognitive processing has to be invoked in four main domains. First, the last decade or so has seen a major upsurge of interest in the development of what has been called the "self-system" (Harter, 1983), a term applied to the set of beliefs that we all develop about ourselves and about our environment. Developmentalists have become interested in the mediating role of qualities such as self-esteem, self-efficacy, and locus of control. Second, child psychologists have come to emphasize the extent to which children's cognitive capacities regulate their susceptibility to the influence of different life experiences. For example, very young infants are less affected by separations from their parents because they have yet to develop the capacity to form enduring selective attachments; conversely, older children are less vulnerable to the ill-effects of separation because they have acquired the capacity to maintain relationships over the course of a period of absence (Rutter,

1981a). Third, increasing attention has come to be paid to the importance of people's cognitive interpretation of their experiences. Thus, Kagan (1980, 1984) has argued that experiences have long-term effects only by virtue of their cognitive transduction. He suggests that infants' limited abilities to process experiences in this way is the main reason experiences in infancy so rarely lead to lasting psychological sequelae. In rather different fashion, Bowlby (1969, 1973, 1980), followed by Brown and Harris (1978), argued that parental loss in childhood creates a negative cognitive set that provides a vulnerability to respond with depression to later loss events. The suggestion is that it is not the immediate pain of the loss itself that is damaging but rather the lasting impairment to a person's sense of self-esteem or self-efficacy that may be a consequence of the loss. Fourth, cognitions have been postulated as important causal factors in the genesis and prolongation of psychiatric disorders, especially depression. Beck (1967) and others have emphasized that depression is not just a state of profoundly dysphoric mood; it is also a cognitive state characterized by a negative view of the self, of the life situation, and of the future. Moreover, it is hypothesized that this belief that one is powerless to influence the bad things happening to oneself forestalls coping actions that could bring the depressive state to an end. The negative mood is prolonged by the thought processes that accompany or form part of the abnormal mood disorder.

It is evident in all four domains that there has been a coming together of developmental and clinical perspectives (Rutter, 1986a; Rutter and Garmezy, 1983; Rutter and Sandberg, 1985; Sroufe and Rutter, 1984). There is an assumption that there are likely to be continuities, as well as discontinuities, in the span of behavioral variation from normality to psychopathology. Similarly, it is presumed that events and happenings at one phase of development are likely to have implications for those in later phases. Once more, there is nothing particularly novel in those suggestions, but the ways in which clinical and developmental perspectives have been conjoined do have some components that differ from those that have been traditional in psychiatry, psychoanalysis, and child development.

The second aspect of cognition, cognitive deficits, appears at first glance to refer to an entirely different set of mechanisms and concepts, although in reality the differences may not be as great as they appear. Such deficits have been thought to operate in both direct and indirect ways. Autism constitutes an example of hypothesized direct effects stemming from cognitive deficits (Rutter, 1983). Autistic individuals' failure to engage in normal reciprocal responsive social interchanges and their failure to make and maintain love relationships constitute the social incapacity that defines the disorder (Fein et al., 1986). It is known, however, that autism is accompanied by a variety of cognitive deficits, and it has been suggested that these may underlie the social deviance and social impairment (Rutter, 1983). Similarly, it has been argued that attentional deficits may constitute the core of both hyperkinetic disorders (Douglas, 1983) and schizophrenia (Nuechterlein and Dawson, 1984), with the specific type of attentional problem not quite the same in the two conditions (Nuechterlein, 1983). Possible indirect effects are exemplified by the relatively strong and well-documented associations between language retardation and psychiatric disorder (Howlin and Rutter, 1987) and between reading disabilities and conduct disorders (Rutter and Giller, 1983; Yule and Rutter, 1985). The mechanisms involved in these associations remain poorly understood, but it is generally presumed that in some manner the language and reading difficulties predispose to psychiatric disorder.

The evidence on these various links between cognition and development or disorder has been extensively reviewed by several writers, and I will not provide a critique of the mass of relevant empirical findings. Instead I will briefly summarize the current state of the art in order to discuss the theoretical and clinical implications that derive from the research.

COGNITIVE PROCESSING

The Self-System

Let me begin with the complex composite of ideas encompassed by the concept of the self-system (Harter, 1983). The central notion is that personality involves, among other things, a set of cognitions about ourselves, our relationships, and our interactions with the environment. We see ourselves as having a coherence of functioning that is related to our concept of ourselves as witty or incompetent, as pushed around by external forces or as firmly in control of our destinies. The counterpart to our self-image is our tendency to respond to others on the basis of their reputations or our perceptions of what sort of person they are. That we do so respond to such percepts, and not just to people's immediate behaviors, has been well demonstrated both experimentally and naturalistically with respect, for example, to gender and aggressivity. In other words, it has been shown that to an important extent we respond to people on the basis of the label "male" or "female" and not just to their tendency to behave in male or female ways. The studies of ambiguously dressed toddlers given names that are the opposite of their biological sex illustrate this tendency (Condry and Ross, 1985; Smith and Lloyd, 1978). In similar fashion it has been found that we respond negatively to people regarded as aggressive on the basis of their previous behavior, even when at the moment they are behaving in a prosocial or compliant fashion (Asher, 1983; Brunk and Hengeller, 1984; Dodge, 1980).

In the same sort of way, it has been demonstrated that our allocated social roles influence our concepts and ideas about ourselves, which in turn influence our behavior. For instance, longitudinal studies have shown that factory workers' attitudes change when they are promoted to supervisory positions or join management (see Kelvin, 1969). Children who are treated as if they have certain qualities tend to live up (or down) to their reputations (see Maccoby and Martin, 1983). There is an abundance of evidence that people vary greatly in their levels of self-esteem (Harter, 1983) or self-efficacy (Bandura, 1977), and there is a more limited body of data suggesting that these self-concepts influence how they respond to life situations. Clearly, people do respond differently to, for example, task failure. Some react by increasing their efforts to succeed, whereas others are more likely to give up trying. Thus, this contrast has been shown to differentiate secure and insecure infants (Lutkenhaus et al., 1985) and adolescent boys and girls in certain task situations. Even when no mediating self-concept has been demonstrated, there seems to be a need to impute some such intervening mechanism.

It is obvious that there is still an immense amount to learn about the self-system, but we can infer that it exists in some form. Several consequences flow from that inference. First, it has implications for views on personality and personality development. Some theorists suppose the personality comprises a collection of constitutionally determined traits or temperamental attributes such as neuroticism (Eysenck, 1953) or behavioral inhibition (Kagan, 1984; Reznick et al., 1986). That such traits exist, that they show modest stability over time, and that to a limited extent they predict people's behavior in various situations can be accepted. But the evidence on the role of cognitive concepts in the self-system argues strongly against this being the role of personality. Indeed, it seems preferable to refer to the traits as temperament in order to retain the concept of personality for the coherence of functioning that derives from how people react to their given attributes, how they think about themselves, and how they put these concepts together into some form of conceptual whole (Rutter, in preparation). The need to reject the view of personality as just a collection of traits is shown by the evidence that people's behavior is often predictable in terms of an understandable psychological coherence rather than a generalization of behavior (Rutter, 1984). Indeed, the coherence may be shown by people behaving in opposite ways in different situations, an opposite that is predictable and understandable in terms of the contrasting meaning of the situations. But thought processes have to be invoked; functioning is not explicable solely on the basis of generalized tendencies to be inhibited or outgoing, emotionally stable or unstable.

The view that personality development involves the operation of intrapsychic thought processes of which we may lack awareness is, of course, central to psychoanalytic theory. Nevertheless, it is important for psychoanalysts to recognize that the specifics of their theory do not fit the facts as demonstrated and that many of the mechanisms postulated in traditional Freudian views have not stood up to empirical test. It is right that those within psychoanalysis have drawn attention to the very wide range of psychoanalytic concepts that have had to be abandoned (such as the energy flow of libidinal energies or some of the specifics of psychosexual stages)—a range so wide that it necessarily raises the question of whether it would not be better to start anew rather than pretend that the original tenets still remain (Eagle, 1984). Psychiatry and psychology have been greatly enhanced by the immense contributions of psychoanalysis in opening our ideas to the richness of the workings of the human mind, to the crucial importance of the meanings attached to experiences, to the influence on development of early family relationships, and to the process of psychosocial development itself. But the very success of psychoanalysis lies in the extent to which many of its ideas have become so part of the currency of other theories that they are no longer distinctively psychoanalytic. Some of the differences that remain are seriously blocking progress because they serve to prevent people from seeing the need to change their ways of looking at personality development and personality functioning.

Psychosocial Experiences and Their Effects

It is not necessary to dwell on the importance of children's growing cognitive capacities for their ability to perceive and respond to different life experiences, as it is obvious and well accepted. Thus, young babies fail to show the separation anxiety and fear of strangers that are characteristic of toddlers, probably because they lack the cognitive skills to appreciate differences between people, to maintain schemata in active memory, and to remember the past (Kagan, 1984). The capacity of anticipation, which arises toward the end of the first year, is important for both pleasurable emotions (as in the peek-a-boo game; Sroufe, 1979a) and unpleasant ones (as in the anticipatory fear associated with previous experience of the inoculation needle; Izard, 1978). Cognitive factors also influence the salience of experiences (Maccoby and Martin, 1983). For example, three-year-olds are deterred from touching a forbidden object if its fragility is stressed, but they are relatively impervious to appeals to property rights. By contrast, five-year-olds are responsive to being told that the object belongs to someone else (Parke, 1974). Similarly, imagination plays little part in the fears of infants but a major role in those of older children (Rutter, 1980). Concepts of moral rights and of external control also come to influence children's reactions to external pressures (Lepper, 1982). Children who are rewarded for doing something that they want to do tend to lose spontaneous interest in the activity; conversely, if children perceive threats or punishments as excessive, they are less likely to comply than if the pressure is mild but sufficient. Punishment reduces disruptive behavior, but unduly severe punishment may actually increase it—presumably because the ill effects of the resentment so induced predominate (Rutter and Giller, 1983).

These cognitive effects on children's responsivity to particular experiences are clearly evident. What requires more discussion, however, is the role of cognitive processing in the changes brought about by psychosocial experiences and, more especially, in the maintenance or otherwise of the effects of those experiences. Two separate questions are involved here. The first is "what happens to the organism as a result of experiences, good or bad?" (Rutter, 1984). Curiously, this is a question that has received very little attention so far from either developmentalists or social researchers. Yet, surely, we have to pose the query. The answer could be that nothing happens to the organism other than the acquisition of conditioned emotions or learned skills or habits or styles of responding. But we already know that is not a sufficient answer, although undoubtedly it is part of the explanation. Thus, for example, altered neuroendocrine responses play a role in the process of adaptation to both physical and psychosocial acute stressors (see Rutter, 1981a). The suggestion put forward in recent times is that cognitive attributions and other forms of cognitive processing must be added to the list of mechanisms. The need, it must be emphasized, is to find mechanisms to account for both continuities and discontinuities in development and especially in the long-term effects of early life experiences (Rutter, 1987a).

The overall pattern of findings is complex and fascinating but not easy to account for in terms of any single process, cognitive or noncognitive. Let me take selective attachments as an example. Initially stimulated by the writings of Bowlby (1969, 1973, 1980) and Ainsworth (1969; Ainsworth et al., 1978), the concept of attachment as a crucial aspect of personal relationships and as a major mediator in the process of psychosocial development has become firmly established (Sroufe, 1979a, 1985; Bretherton and Waters, 1985; Parkes and Stevenson-Hinde, 1982; Emde and Harmon, 1982). The main findings and ideas are too well known to need any review here. But let me point out a few of the apparent paradoxes that require explanation. First, although the security of a child's relationship with one parent does not predict to the relationship with the other parent at the same time (i.e., it is a dyadic measure, not an individual attribute), it does predict peer relationships several years later (Bretherton and Waters, 1985). In part this may be a function of the demonstrated responsivity to varying social circumstances, but also it seems necessary to invoke some mechanism by which a dyadic quality leads to some characteristic in the individual that endures over time and situation to some degree. What is that quality? Second, although children's first selective attachments ordinarily develop in the first couple of years, Tizard and Hodges (1978) found that institution-reared children who were adopted as late as the ages of four, five, six, or even seven years developed close intimate ties with their adoptive parents even at that relatively late age. Changed social circumstances led to a changed pattern of attachments. Yet, in spite of that change, follow-up to sixteen years of age showed that there were persisting differences in the children's pattern of peer relationships and in their tendency to confide in others (Hodges and Tizard, chap. 9). Why? Something had endured from the experiences in infancy in spite of a radical change in the later social environment. Yet why did that show in peer relationships, and why did the secure adoptive parent-child relationship not enable the child to go on to a normal pattern of friendships? Third, although the sequelae of poor parent-child relationships can sometimes be seen in adult life or even in the next generation, it is also the case that a good marital relationship in adult life can do much to remedy the ill effects of early bad experiences (Rutter, 1987b). We have to explain both persistence and change.

The concept of an "internal working model" of relationships has become a popular contender as an explanatory variable (Bretherton and Waters, 1985). The general idea is that children derive a set of expectations about their relationship capacities and about other people's responses to their social overtures and interactions from their early parent-child attachments. In other words, to some extent, children shape their later relationships as a result of cognitive concepts derived from earlier relationships. Nevertheless, later relationships may be markedly better or worse than earlier ones, so that the working models may change. It has been suggested that later relationships, or even later thoughts, may alter the meaning of earlier experiences and, by so doing, alter their impact. Thus, Ricks (1985) suggested that it may be adaptive for someone to reconceptualize his earlier rejection by his mother as being due to his mother's depression or social circumstances rather than to dislike of him as a person. The reconceptualization thereby removes the connotation of personal failing and allows reestablishment of self-esteem. Some theorists, too, suggest that it is necessary to accept the reality of past bad experiences and to integrate them into a coherent whole (Main et al., 1985). Thus, Epstein (cited by Ricks, 1985) argues that even an unpleasant concept of the world is preferable to a chaotic and inherently contradictory one.

The ideas are important and intuitively plausible but largely untested. Because of their importance, we need to develop ways of measuring attachment relationships after infancy and of measuring children's (and adults') concepts or models of relationships. The crucial role of relationships in personality development is obvious, but it is nowhere near as obvious which processes in the organism mediate continuities and discontinuities. Internal working models provide a possibility, but numerous questions remain. How early are such models within children's cognitive capacities? How complex and differentiated are the models for different types of relationships? How important is coherence, and why? What is necessary to bring about change, and which features work against change? How can the models serve to account for contradictory and ambivalent patterns of relationships? The postulate of cognitive models seems helpful, but it is apparent that the models must include affective as well as cognitive components.

Risk, Vulnerability, and Protective Mechanisms

Numerous studies have attested to the immense variations in children's responses to stress and adversity, both in the short term and in the extent to which effects persist over time (Rutter, 1981a, 1981b, 1985).

Numerous factors determine these individual differences. Many of the factors are unconnected with cognitive mechanisms, but some involve thought processes in crucial ways. To begin with, cognitive capacities necessarily define the salience of events for children. In addition, past experiences may alter the meaning of new ones or may change the way in which happenings are appraised and understood. Thus, both previous happy separations and preventive programs designed to prepare children for hospital admission have been shown to reduce the rate of distress reactions (Rutter, 1979a). Conversely, a previous admission to a hospital during the preschool years increases the likelihood that children will develop disorder following a later admission (Douglas, 1975; Quinton and Rutter, 1976). Clearly, something was changed that altered the later reaction, but just what that something was remains obscure. It seems likely that part of the explanation may lie in the children's mental sets about hospital admission and about being separated from their families, but the suggestion has yet to be put to the critical test.

The observation, however, raises a more general issue—namely, that commonly, people's responses to stress and adversity are modified by prior experiences that either increase their vulnerability or protect them from ill effects (Rutter, 1987a, 1987c). Research has followed several approaches to the elucidation of the processes underlying resilience. First, there were attempts to identify the happenings or circumstances that seemed to increase the likelihood that people would escape unscathed. These were found to include harmonious, close, confiding relationships, a wide range of social support, successful task accomplishment, and effective coping with previous similar life hazards (Garmezy, 1985; Masten and Garmezy, 1985; Rutter, 1979b, 1985). Second, investigators focused on the personal qualities that appeared to be protective. Some of these involved temperamental features that were likely to be at least partially constitutional in origin, although others were described in terms of self-concepts. The implication was that people's cognitive sets make a difference to how they react to potentially negative life experiences. The evidence required to provide a crucial test of the postulated mediating role of cognitive sets is not yet available, but it seems likely that they do indeed play a role. What is much less certain, however, is which aspect of the self-concept is most important in this connection.

One possibility is that what matters is a high sense of self-esteem or a global feeling of one's own worth as an individual. The suggestion is that it is easier to ride the psychosocial storm if you feel good about yourself as a person. But even this apparently straightforward notion is more complicated than it appears at first sight (Harter, 1986). To begin with, a person's self-evaluation of his worth is not synonymous with his appraisal of his competence, although the two are likely to be interconnected. The extent to which poor competence leads to low self-esteem will be influenced by the value placed on that skill by the individual and by society (everyone is poor at some things, but often that does not matter because it is not a domain of personal importance or investment). Also, it will be affected by the individual's social comparison group (other handicapped people, the general population, or high achievers), by the value placed on the balance between his skills and deficits, and by the gap between his performance and his aspirations. Finally, self-esteem may be at least as much a result of being loved and wanted as being good at anything (other than personal relationships).

Self-esteem may not be the crucial dimension, however. Bandura (1977) emphasized the role of self-efficacy—the belief that one is able to control one's life and deal with life's challenges. The concept here is of a self-confidence that the individual is able to cope with whatever has to be faced. But this concept too is multifaceted. The reverse pole emphasized by Seligman (Abrahamson et al., 1978; Peterson and Seligman, 1984) under the term *learned helplessness* is similar but slightly different in its details. The central notion is that people tend to attribute bad experiences to global faults in themselves that are unalterable and lasting. The implication, as with self-efficacy, is that vulnerability resides in a tendency to assume that bad circumstances are outside one's control and that there is nothing that can be done to make things better. Conversely, protection comes from a belief that action is possible and likely to be effective.

The third hypothesized mediating factor, after self-esteem and self-efficacy, concerns social problem–solving skills (Pellegrini, 1985). The suggestion here differs in proposing that what matters is the specific knowledge on how to deal with life crises rather than a general belief in one's worth as a person or a concept of one's self as a capable individual who can take positive and effective action to overcome hazards and adversities. The factor sounds very different in its focus on specific skills, but it is clear that what is involved is not only a repertoire of responses but also an approach to social problems that recognizes a need to take action to deal with them and that reflects a self-concept that includes a belief that this is possible.

The data are not available to allow any decision on the relative importance of these three facets of self-concept, but it seems reasonable to suppose that in varying degrees all play a part. There are effects, first, on people's appraisal of life experiences, second, on their mental reaction to them in terms of the extent to which they can be controlled or modified, and, third, on their action to deal with their situation. Such an action involves planning and coping strategies that deal with the real-life situation together with the different type of coping that is involved in dealing with one's internal emotional responses to the psychosocial stress or hazard.

There are several implications for theory and practice that follow from these views on the probable importance of cognitive mediation in vulnerability and protective mechanisms. The recent evidence on protective mechanisms (Rutter, 1987d) is in keeping with cognitive-processing concepts in its emphasis on the crucial role of turning points in people's lives in which new experiences bring about changes in people's views of themselves, of their environment, and of their relationships with other people. Such experiences need not necessarily be pleasant; indeed, some positive reappraisals of self-concept come from successful coping with adversity rather than from happy events in the ordinary sense of the word. To be protective, probably the reappraisal must lead to active coping and not just passive acceptance. It is important that people feel in control of their lives and act on that belief. This belief may well be influenced by lasting personality qualities, but it may also be changed (for better or worse) by new experiences in adult life as well as childhood.

Depression

Let me turn now to a more directly clinical issue. At one time, psychiatrists supposed that major depressive disorders could not occur in childhood because children lacked both a well-developed superego and the necessary intrapsychic structures required to turn in anger against the self (Rie, 1966). There are doubts regarding the validity of the psychoanalytic ideas that constituted the basis for that view, but in any case, empirical observations have shown that, contrary to theoretical presuppositions, depressive conditions can and do occur in childhood (Rutter, Izard, and Read, 1986). Nevertheless, the same evidence has shown that major affective disorders are decidedly less frequent in early childhood than they are in adult life, with the main rise in incidence occurring during the adolescent years. This has been shown for clinical cases of depression and of mania, for suicide and attempted suicide, and for depressive feelings as reported by young people in the general population. The question that has to be posed is, why is there such a marked age trend?

Clearly, it is not that young children lack the ability to experience misery and unhappiness. Dysphoric mood occurs at all ages, and some types of expression, for example, crying, are actually more frequent in early life (Shepperd et al., 1971). But depressive disorders consist of much more than sadness. The cognitive components of depression are a major part of the clinical picture (Beck, 1967). The depressive state is characterized as much by guilt, self-blame, self-depreciation, helplessness, and hopelessness as by dysphoric mood. Emphasis has come to be placed on the cognitive triad of negative feelings about the self, the immediate life situation, and the future. Could it be that young children are protected against depression because they lack the cognitive capacities to experience these thoughts, at least with the depth or extent that is required for depression?

There is indeed a certain amount of evidence in support of that proposition. If children are to experience a feeling of unworthiness and a sense of failure, presumably they must appreciate the meaning of standards, be able to compare themselves with others, and understand the concept of failure to meet expected standards. Kagan's (1981) data suggest that these self-concepts related to guilt do not arise until about two years of age. But depressive feelings of hopelessness require more than a sense of failure; that sense must be experienced as generalized and projected into the future. Other evidence suggests that the tendency to do this does not become established until much later in childhood (Cicchetti and Schneider-Rosen, 1986; Schantz, 1983). Young children tend to view performance in specific task terms, and it is only in middle childhood that they begin to see people's characteristics as stable psychological traits and to make general comparisons between themselves and other people. At first, children tend to have rather overoptimistic views of their own competence and are less likely to respond to task failure with feelings of helplessness and an inability to do better next time. Only at about eight years of age do they usually have any generalized concept about themselves as people. As they grow older, they come to have an increasing sense of their own responsibilities and power to act; moreover, there is a growing tendency to think about the future and to project feelings into it. Young children can feel guilty about what they have already done, but they are less likely to experience anticipatory guilt.

It has to be said that our knowledge about depression-related social cognitions is limited. Nevertheless, it seems that the ability to experience shame and guilt arises during the late infancy period; at first such feelings tend to be tied strictly to the immediate time. During middle childhood there is an increasing tendency to generalize the cognition to build up a view of the self in comparison with others, and it becomes more likely that task failure will result in a general feeling of helplessness. Initially such negative cognitions tend to be confined to the present situation or to conceptually related circumstances, but in later childhood there is an increasing tendency to think about the future, to project feelings of failure into the future (to proceed from helplessness to hopelessness), and to experience anticipatory guilt and shame.

If these age trends in cognition are confirmed, could they account for the relative lack of depressive disorders in early childhood and their frequency after adolescence? The possibility warrants serious study. There are both methodological and substantive problems, however. To begin with, we have to ask whether it is that children do not experience these thoughts or that they do but they lack the conceptual language to tell us about them. Also, however, we must beware of assuming cognitive primacy in depression. Although clearly depression is not just a mood disorder, it is not just a cognitive disorder either, and we lack understanding of how the two interrelate. Moreover, there is no evidence that the few young children with major depression are at all cognitively advanced; in those cases the disorder seems to have allowed the expression of negative cognitions that would otherwise be unusual at that age. Maybe the relevance of children's cognitive limitations concerns their response to threatening life events rather than the existence of depression as such. In adult life, it seems that depressive disorders are often precipitated by negative life events that carry a long-term threat, causing people to feel helpless and hopeless with a resulting depressive revaluation of themselves. Perhaps children are less likely to respond in this way. If so, one might expect children to be just as likely as adults to show acute distress following adverse life events but for there to be a lesser tendency for it to develop into a clinical disorder in which the negative cognitions and emotions persist long after the event has passed and been dealt with.

The implication is that greater attention should be paid to the possible role of cognitive processing in children's responses to life experiences as well as the development of affective disorders. It is uncertain what answers will emerge from research into these issues, but it is evident that it would be informative to ask questions about the meaning of age trends, with cognitive features as one possible mediating mechanism.

Cognitive concepts have also played a key role in recent ideas on the genesis and perpetuation of depression. Various theorists—notably Beck (1967, 1976), Brown and Harris (1978), and Seligman (Abrahamson et al., 1978; Peterson and Seligman, 1984)—have argued that negative cognitions not only are part of depressive symptomatology but also serve to bring about depression and to prevent its recovery. It has proved difficult to test the causal hypothesis, but there is stronger evidence in support of the view that negative attributions involving feelings of helplessness serve to maintain depression (Brewin, 1985). The cognitive theories have led to the development of therapeutic interventions designed to alter the negative cognitions (so-called cognitive therapies). The evidence available so far from comparative evaluations suggests that cognitive therapy is roughly equivalent to tricyclic medication in effectiveness (Mathews, 1986) and that cognitive approaches may be particularly useful for preventing relapses (Simlons et al., 1986). Up to now these techniques have been little used with children, but there is reason to suppose that they might prove to be similarly applicable. Although the field of enquiry is still in its infancy, there are already several implications for theory and practice. First, the findings cast doubt on the soma-psyche dichotomy. Just as cognitive therapies relieve mood, so also antidepressant drugs diminish dysfunctional cognitions (Murphy et al., 1984). Environmentally induced disorders may be perpetuated by biological changes in the organism, which respond to medication; conversely, endogenous conditions may involve distorted thought processes, which then serve to interfere with recovery. An integrated psychobiological approach to psychiatric disorder is required (Rutter, 1987d). Psychotherapists cannot afford to ignore the biology of psychiatric disorder any more than biological psychiatrists can ignore its psychology (Rutter, 1987d).

Second, the efficacy of cognitive methods has implications for the content and strategies of psychological therapies. Traditional psychoanalytically oriented psychotherapies have focused on the meanings of past experiences, on intrapsychic conflicts and defenses, and on analysis of the patient-therapist relationship. Work with children has required considerable modification of the techniques used, but there has been less change in the principles employed. The implication from the cognitive approaches, as well as from many other developments in psychological therapies (Rutter, 1982), is that it is necessary to focus more strongly on the ways in which people think about themselves and their experiences and the ways in which they actually deal with their current real-life situations.

Third, the findings force us to pay attention to the need in treatment to maintain therapeutic gains. There are several examples in psychiatry of methods that are most successful in the short term but not in the long term (Rutter, 1987d). One of the key goals in treatment must be to help the patient acquire coping strategies that give the skills required to maintain adaptive functioning and to deal with the hazards and adversities that lie ahead.

Conclusions on Cognitive Processing

In my discussion of cognitive processing I have concentrated on the role of cognition in relation to socioemotional development and disorders. There is much evidence that the role is an important one, but it should be recognized that the interactions are two-way. Affective states also influence cognitive processing, as the evidence on the effects of mood on memory shows (Bower, 1981). It would be foolish to suppose that either cognition or affect is primary; development involves an integrated organization of the two (Sroufe, 1979a, 1979b). My purpose has been simply to point to some of the many ways in which cognitive processing needs to be taken into account in considering child development and disorder.

COGNITIVE DEFICITS

Finally, I need to say something about the role of cognitive deficits in the genesis of child psychiatric disorder. It seems reasonable to suppose that, if cognitive processing is so important in people's appraisal of and response to experiences, then abnormalities or limitations in the ability to undertake cognitive processing might have profound implications for the risk of psychiatric disorder. The empirical evidence suggests that this is indeed the case, although the mechanisms by which the psychiatric risk comes about remain unclear.

Consequences of Language Delay and Reading Difficulties

The issues are well illustrated by the findings on the socioemotional consequences of language delay (Howlin and Rutter, 1987). General population follow-up studies of preschool children have shown consistently that those with language delay have a much increased incidence of emotional and behavioral disturbance (Drillien and Drummond, 1983; Funfudis et al., 1979; Richman et al., 1982; Silva et al., 1983).

Psychiatric problems are more frequent in those with a global intellectual deficit in addition to specific language problems (Cantwell and Baker, 1977; Silva et al., 1983), but the psychiatric risk still applies to those who are not mentally retarded. The risk also tends to be greatest when the language deficit is severe and when it involves comprehension as well as expression, but even children with relatively mild speech defects tend to show a raised incidence of fear, anxieties, and problems making friends (Baker et al., 1980). The psychiatric problems associated with language delay tend to persist, at least into middle childhood, and indeed the presence of language delay at three years is predictive of an increase in the level of disturbance over the next five years (Stevenson et al., 1985). Such disturbance does not conform to any one clinical picture; emotional and conduct problems are both common, social difficulties are frequently present, and hyperactivity is often a feature.

Several cognitive and noncognitive mechanisms have been proposed to account for the association between language delay and psychiatric disorder. First, there may be common background factors such as low I.Q., adverse temperamental features, or family problems. Second, children with oddities of any kind tend to be more than usually prone to rejection by their peers, and children with a language disability are likely to be at a disadvantage in social interactions. Both mechanisms are likely to be important but perhaps additional processes need to be invoked to account for the persistence of socioemotional problems long after the children are fluent in spoken language. Possibly the language delay is associated with cognitive deficits that are more lasting than the inability to speak. Unfortunately, we know very little about the later cognitive functioning of children with language retardation, apart from the well-documented association with reading difficulties (Howlin and Rutter, 1987). There is a great need for a systematic study of the social and cognitive functioning in adolescence of young people who have experienced a serious delay in language acquisition but who now show a normal level of spoken language.

In the absence of such data, some clues are provided by the progression from language delay to reading retardation. It has long been known that reading difficulties are associated with a substantially increased risk of conduct disorders (Rutter and Yule, 1987; Rutter and Giller, 1983). To some extent this association may reflect a maladaptive response to educational failure (Rutter, 1985), but this does not seem to be the main explanation, if only because the behavioral disturbances are often present at, or soon after, school entry, before reading failure can be manifest (McMichael, 1979).

The prior association with language delay suggests the probable role of either temperamental attributes or attentional/cognitive problems, both of which are linked with reading disabilities and conduct disturbance. On the face of it, temperament and cognition seem rather separate concepts, but in practice they have been difficult to separate. The difficulties are best illustrated by consideration of hyperkinetic/attentional deficit syndromes.

Hyperkinetic/Attentional Deficit Syndromes

In recent years clinicians have come to accept that problems in concentration constitute the core of what used to be called hyperkinetic disorder and that now tend to be called attention deficit syndromes (ADD). The suggestion is that a physiological deficit in the ability to process information coming into the brain underlies the disturbance of behavior. The idea is an important one because, if it can be validated, it would have important implications for our concepts of causation of psychiatric disorder. Unfortunately, as Taylor (1980, 1986) has pointed out, there are problems in testing the hypothesis because inattention is used both as a behavioral description (to describe the fact that children are not paying attention to some task allocated to them) and as an explanatory variable (an abnormality in the brain functions that deal with the processing of incoming sensory input). Moreover, the latter involves many processes, not one. People need to divide as well as to concentrate their attention, and to shift as well as to maintain the focus of their interest. Children may perform badly on any of these functions because they cannot process information efficiently, because they can yet choose not to do so, or because the given task is less interesting than others that they would like to engage in. Furthermore, the behavior of *looking* attentive (staring at the teacher or the textbook) may not be accompanied by relevant cognitive processing; the child's eyes may be on the task while his mind is engaged on something entirely different. Conversely, children may appear not to be listening while still taking everything in (as well illustrated by the amount picked up by children seemingly engaged in play while the parents are talking about them to someone else).

The distinctions between these various physiological processes are difficult. Nevertheless, the empirical evidence suggests that there are important cognitive-behavioral connections. Studies on hyperactive children have shown them to be impaired on tests of cognitive performance. Furthermore, within clinic groups of children of normal I.Q.

with disturbances of conduct, poor test performance is associated with hyperactivity but not with defiant aggressive behavior (Taylor, 1986). There does seem to be a real connection between inattention and over-activity. There is also a further association between overactivity and conduct disturbance. The mechanisms involved in both sets of linkages remain uncertain. The inattention linkage is not specific in that there are also associations with low I.Q., with clumsiness, and with develop-mental delays. It is not at all self-evident that the main process involved is a deficit in cognitive processing, although this may well form part of the problem. In addition, it is not known why hyperactivity is associated with conduct disturbance. It could be that the overactive behavior is irritating to others and hence leads to maladaptive patterns of interac-tion, but attributional factors may also be important. People interpret other people's behavior according to their attribution of intention (Parke and Slaby, 1983). It seems relevant that aggressive boys are more likely to attribute hostile intentions to others. As a result they elicit, as well as initiate, more negative interactions (Dodge, 1980). Is this attributional bias a result of past experiences or does it reflect some kind of deficit in cognitive processing? A complex set of cognitive-behavioral associa-tions is involved, and treatment methods would be enhanced if the meaning of that tangle could be elucidated.

Schizophrenia

A word is necessary on attentional deficits in schizophrenia. There is a mass of evidence showing associations between the two (Nuechterlein and Dawson, 1984), and it has been suggested that a deficit in signal-noise discrimination may form part of the basis of schizophrenia. The suggestion is made plausible by the finding that similar attentional problems are found in the offspring of schizophrenics and that such deficits are predictive of psychopathology within that group. Two main issues await resolution. First, do the attentional deficits specifically pre-dict schizophrenia, or is the association with a broader range of psychi-atric problems? Second, is the deficit similar to or different in type from that associated with hyperactivity or with other psychiatric syndromes? The evidence on both points is inconclusive as yet. A specific linkage is possible, but it has still to be established. The ubiquity of cognitive-behavioral associations shows their importance, but the meanings to be attached to them depend on the determination of specific mechanisms. That remains a task for the future.

Autism

The last topic to mention concerns the role of cognitive deficits in autism. There is now a mass of evidence to show that autistic children do indeed have serious cognitive deficits that tend to follow a distinctive pattern—with impairments in sequencing, abstraction, conceptualization, and the use of meaning (Rutter, 1983). Moreover, these deficits are resistant to treatment and constitute the most important predictors of outcome. It has seemed plausible to suggest that they might underlie autistic children's social difficulties. The problem has been to know how this might operate. Hobson (1983, 1986) showed that autistic children were impaired in their ability to distinguish emotional cues and to discriminate age and gender features. The implication seemed to be that there was some type of cognitive deficit that applied to the processing of social and emotional stimuli. But what could that deficit be, and how did it relate to autistic children's other cognitive problems?

Recent research by Baron-Cohen and his colleagues (1986) suggests that the deficit may involve an inability to infer other people's intentions. Because of this, autistic children lack a theory of mind that might allow them to appreciate other people's feelings, beliefs, and mental states. They suggest that the critical feature may not be a turning away from social interactions as such but rather a specific dysfunction in conceiving mental states. This comes nearest to a directly cognitive explanation for a social phenomenon, but much further research is needed to put the hypothesis to critical tests. Of all psychiatric conditions, autism is the one in which there is the closest and probably most direct connection between cognitive deficits and social malfunction. Elucidation of the processes involved seems to be on the horizon, and if that riddle can be solved, it should throw light on aspects of development and disorder that extend beyond autism.

CONCLUSIONS

This necessarily selective overview of some of the ways in which cognition may play a role in child development and in psychiatric disorder indicates the richness of the territory. The associations between cognition and socioemotional functioning are many and various. The ways in which we appraise our life circumstances and the ways in which we react to experiences of all kinds are greatly influenced by how we think about ourselves and our environment. Research has begun to suggest some of the mechanisms that may be involved in these cognitive processes. It is clear that biases and distortions in such processing may be associated with social and emotional malfunction. These biases may derive from earlier experiences, from intrinsic temperamental styles, or from deficits in the ability to process incoming information. The further study of cognitive processing and cognitive deficits is likely to be rewarding and helpful for clinical practice.

REFERENCES

Abrahamson, L. Y., Seligman, M. E. P. and Teasdale, J. D. (1978). "Learned Helplessness in Humans: Critique and Reformulation." *Journal of Abnormal Psychology* 87:49–74.
Ainsworth, M. (1969). "Object Relations, Dependency and Attachment: A Theoretical Review of Mother-Infant Relationship." *Child Development* 40:969–1025.
Ainsworth, M.; Blehar, M. C.; Waters, E.; and Wall, S. (1978). *Patterns of Attachment*. Hillsdale, N.J.: Erlbaum.
Asher, S. R. (1983). "Social Competence and Peer Status: Recent Advances and Future Directions." *Child Development* 54:1427–1434.
Baker, L., Cantwell, D., and Mattison, R. (1980). "Behavior Problems in Children with Pure Speech Disorders and in Children with Combined Speech and Language Disorders." *Journal of Abnormal Psychology* 8:245–250.
Bandura, A. (1977). *Social Learning Theory*. Englewood Cliffs, N.J.: Prentice-Hall.
Baron-Cohen, S., Leslie, A. M., and Frith, U. (1986). "Mechanical, Behavioral and Intentional Understanding of Picture Stories in Autistic Children." *British Journal of Developmental Psychology* 4:113–125.
Beck, A. T. (1967). *Depression: Causes and Treatment*. Philadelphia: University of Pennsylvania Press.
——— (1976). "Cognitive Therapy and the Emotional Disorders." New York: International Universities Press.
Bower, G. N. (1981). "Mood and Memory." *American Psychologist* 36:129–148.
Bowlby, J. (1969). *Attachment and Loss*. Vol. 1, *Attachment*. London: Hogarth Press.
——— (1973). *Attachment and Loss*. Vol. 2, *Separation Anxiety and Anger*. London: Hogarth Press.
——— (1980). *Attachment and Loss*. Vol. 3, *Loss, Sadness and Depression*. New York: Basic Books.

Bretherton, I., and Waters, E., eds. (1985). "Growing Points of Attachment Theory and Research." *Monographs for the Study of Research in Child Development, no. 209.* 50:66.

Brewin, C. (1985). "Depression and Causal Attributions: What Is Their Relation?" *Psychological Bulletin* 98:297–309.

Brown, G. W., and Harris, T. O. (1978). *Social Origins of Depression: A Study of Psychiatric Disorders in Women.* London: Tavistock.

Brunk, M. A., and Hengeller, S. W. (1984). "Child Influences on Adult Controls: An Experimental Investigation." *Developmental Psychology* 20, no. 5 6:1074–1081.

Cantwell, D., and Baker, L. (1977). "Psychiatric Disorder in Children with Speech and Language Retardation: A Critical Review." *Archives of General Psychiatry* 34:583–591.

Cicchetti, D., and Schneider-Rosen, K. (1986). "An Organizational Approach to Childhood Depression." In M. Rutter, C. Izard, and P. Read, eds., *Depression in Young People: Developmental and Clinical Perspectives.* New York: Guilford Press, 71–134.

Condry, J. D., and Ross, D. F. (1985). "Sex and Aggression: The Influence of Gender Label on the Perception of Aggression in Children." *Child Development* 56:225–233.

Dodge, K. A. (1980). "Social Cognition and Children's Aggressive Behavior." *Child Development* 51:162–172.

Dodge, K. A., Murphy, R. R., and Buchsnaum, K. (1984). "The Assessment of Intention and Detection Skills in Children: Implications for Developmental Psychopathology." *Child Development* 55:163–173.

Douglas, J. W. B. (1975). "Early Hospital Admissions and Later Disturbances of Behavior and Learning." *Developmental Medicine and Child Neurology* 17:456–480.

Douglas, V. I. (1983). "Attentional and Cognitive Problems." In M. Rutter, ed., *Developmental Neuropsychiatry.* New York: Guilford Press, 280–329.

Drillien, C., and Drummond, M. (1983). "Achievement Motivation." In E. M. Hetherington, ed., *Socialization, Personality and Social Development.* Vol. 4, *Mussen's Handbook of Child Psychology.* 4th ed. New York: Wiley.

Eagle, M. N. (1984). *Recent Developments in Psychoanalysis: A Critical Evaluation.* New York: McGraw-Hill.

Emde, R. N., and Harmon, R. J., eds. (1982). *The Development of Attachment and Affiliative Systems.* New York: Plenum Press.

Eysenck, H. J. (1953). *The Structure of Human Personality.* New York: Wiley.

Fein, D.; Pennington, B.; Markowitz, P.; Braverman, M.; and Waterhouse, L. (1986). "Toward a Neuropsychological Model of Infantile Autism: Are the Social Deficits Primary?" *Journal of the American Academy of Child Psychiatry* 25:198–212.

Funfudis, T., Kolvin, I., and Garside, R., eds. (1979). *Speech Retarded and*

Deaf Children: Their Psychological Development. London: Academic Press.

Garmezy, N. (1985). "Stress Resistant Children: The Search for Protective Factors." In J. Stevenson, eds., *Recent Research in Developmental Psychology*. Book supplement to the *Journal of Child Psychology and Psychiatry, no. 4*. Oxford: Pergamon Press.

Harter, S. (1983). "Developmental Perspectives on the Self-System." In E. M. Hetherington, ed., *Socialization, Personality and Social Development*. Vol. 4, *Mussen's Handbook of Child Psychology*. 4th Ed. New York: Wiley.

—— (1986). "Processes Underlying the Construction, Maintenance and Enhancement of the Self-Concept in Children." In J. Suls and A. Greenwald, eds., *Psychological Perspectives on the Self*. Vol. 3. New York: Erlbaum.

Hobson, R. P. (1983). "The Autistic Child's Recognition of Age-Related Features of People, Animals and Things." *British Journal of Developmental Psychology* 1:343–352.

—— (1986). "The Autistic Child's Appraisal of Expressions of Emotion." *Journal of Child Psychology and Psychiatry* 27:321–342.

Hodges, J., and Tizard, B. (In press a). "I.Q. and Behavioral Adjustment of Ex-institutional Adolescents." *Journal of Child Psychology and Psychiatry*.

—— (In press b). "Social and Family Relationships of Ex-institutional Adolescents." *Journal of Child Psychology and Psychiatry*.

Howlin, P., and Rutter, M. (1987). "The Consequences of Language Delay for Other Aspects of Development." In W. Yule and M. Rutter, eds., *Language Development and Disorder: Clinics in Developmental Medicine* London: MacKeith/Blackwell.

Izard, C. E. (1978). "On the Ontogenesis of Emotions and Emotion-Cognitive Relationships in Infancy." In M. Lewis and L. A. Rosenblum, eds., *The Development of Affect*. New York: Plenum.

Kagan, J. (1980). "Perspectives on Continuity." In O. Brim and J. Kagan, eds., *Constancy and Change in Human Development*. Cambridge, Mass.: Harvard University Press.

—— (1981). *The Second Year: The Emergence of Self-Awareness*. Cambridge, Mass.: Harvard University Press.

—— (1984). *The Nature of the Child*. New York: Basic Books.

Kelvin, P. (1969). *The Bases of Social Behavior: An Approach in Terms of Order and Value*. London: Holt, Rinehart, and Winston.

Lepper, M. R. (1982). "Social Control Processes, Attribution of Motivation and the Internalization of Social Values." In E. T. Higgins, D. N. Ruble, and W. W. Hartup, eds., *Social Cognition and Social Behavior: Developmental Perspectives*. Cambridge: Cambridge University Press.

Lutkenhaus, P., Grossman, K. R., and Grossman, D. (1985). "Infant-Mother Attachment at Twelve Months and Style of Interaction with a Stranger at Age of Three Years." *Child Development* 56:1535–1542.

Maccoby, E. E., and Martin, J. A. (1983). "Socialization in the Context of the Family: Parent-Child Interaction." In E. M. Hetherington, ed., *Socialization, Personality and Social Development*. Vol. 4, *Mussen's Handbook of Child Psychology*. 4th ed. New York: Wiley.

Main, M., Kaplan, N., and Cassidy, J. (1985). "Security in Infancy, Childhood and Adulthood." In I. Bretherton and E. Waters, eds., op. cit., 66–104.

Masten, A. S., and Garmezy, N. (1985). "Risk, Vulnerability and Protective Factors in Developmental Psychology." In B. B. Lahey and A. E. Kazdin, eds., *Advances in Clinical Child Psychology*. Vol. 8. New York: Plenum Press.

Mathews, A. (1986). "Cognitive Processes in Anxiety and Depression: A Discussion Paper." *Journal of the Royal Society of Medicine* 79:158–161.

McMichael, P. (1979). "The Hen or the Egg? Which Comes First—Antisocial Emotional Disorders or Reading Disability?" *British Journal of Educational Psychology* 49:226–238.

Murphy, G. E.; Simmons, A. D.; Wetzel, R. D.; and Lustman, P. J. (1984). "Cognitive Theory and Pharmacotherapy: Singly and Together in the Treatment of Depression." *Archives of General Psychiatry* 41:33–41.

Nuechterlein, K. E. (1983). "Signal Detection in Vigilance Tasks and Behavioral Attributes among Offspring of Schizophrenic Mothers and among Hyperactive Children." *Journal of Abnormal Psychology* 92:4–28.

——— (1986). "Childhood Precursors of Adult Schizophrenia: Annotation." *Journal of Child Psychology and Psychiatry* 27:133–144.

Nuechterlein, K. E., and Dawson, M. E. (1984). "Information Processing and Attentional Functioning in the Developmental Cause of Schizophrenic Disorders." *Schizophrenia Bulletin* 10:160–203.

Parke, R. D. (1974). "Rules and Roles and Resistance to Deviation: Recent Advances in Punishment, Discipline, and Self-Control." In A. D. Pick, ed., *Minnesota Symposium on Child Psychology*. Vol. 8. Minneapolis: University of Minnesota Press.

Parke, R. D., and Slaby, R. G. (1983). "The Development of aggression." In E. M. Hetherington, ed., *Socialization, Personality and Social Development*. Vol. 4, *Mussen's Handbook of Child Psychiatry*. 4th ed. New York: Wiley, 547–651.

Parkes, C. M., and Stevenson-Hinde, J., eds. (1982). *The Place of Attachment in Human Behavior*. New York: Basic Books.

Pellegrini, D. (1985). "Training in Social Problem-Solving." In M. Rutter and L. Hersov, eds., *Child and Adolescent Psychiatry: Modern Approaches*. 2nd ed. Oxford: Blackwell Scientific, 839–850.

Peterson, C., and Seligman, M. E. P. (1984). "Causal Explanation as a Risk Factor for Depression: Theory and Evidence." *Psychological Review* 91:347–374.

Quinton, D., and Rutter, M. (1976). "Early Hospital Admissions and Later

Disturbance of Behavior: An Attempted Replication of Douglas's Finding." *Developmental Medicine and Child Neurology* 18:447–459.

Reznick, J. B.; Kagan, J.; Snidman, N.; Gersten, M.; Baak, K.; and Rosenberg, A. (1986). "Inhibited and Uninhibited Children: A Follow-up Study." *Child Development* 55:600–630.

Richman, N., Stevenson, J., and Graham, P. (1982). *Preschool to School: A Behavioral Study.* London: Academic Press.

Ricks, M. H. (1985). "The Social Transmission of Parental Behavior: Attachment Across Generations." In J. Bretherton and E. Water, eds., op. cit., 211–227.

Rie, H. E. (1966). "Depression in Childhood: A Survey of Some Pertinent Contributions." *Journal of the American Academy of Child Psychiatry* 5:653–685.

Rutter, M. (1979a). "Separation Experiences: A New Look at an Old Topic." *Journal of Psychiatrics* 95:147–154.

——— (1979b). "Protective Factors in Children's Responses to Stress and Disadvantage." In M. W. Kent and J. E. Rolf, eds., *Primary Prevention of Psychopathology.* Vol. 3, *Social Competence in Children.* Hanover, N.H.: University Press of New England, 49–74.

——— (1980). "Emotional Development." In M. Rutter, ed., *Scientific Foundations of Developmental Psychiatry.* London: Heinemann Medical.

——— (1981a). "Stress, Coping and Development: Some Issues and Some Questions." *Journal of Child Psychology and Psychiatry* 22:323–356.

——— (1981b). *Maternal Deprivation Reassessed.* 2nd ed. Harmondsworth: Penguin.

——— (1982). "Psychological Therapies: Issues and Prospects." *Psychological Medicine* 12:723–740.

——— (1983). "Cognitive Deficits in the Pathogenesis of Autism." *Journal of Child Psychology and Psychiatry* 24:513–531.

——— (1984). "Psychopathology and Development, II, Childhood Experiences and Personality Development." *Australian and New Zealand Journal of Psychiatry* 18:314–327.

——— (1985). "Resilience in the Face of Adversity: Protective Factors and Resistance to Psychiatric Disorder." *British Journal of Psychiatry* 147:598–611.

——— (1986a). "Child Psychiatry: The Interface between Clinical and Developmental Research." *Psychological Medicine* 10:152–160.

——— (1986b). "Meyerian Psychobiology, Personality Development and the Role of Life Experiences." *American Journal of Psychiatry* 143:1077–1087.

——— (1986c). "Child Psychiatry: Looking 30 Years Ahead." *Journal of Child Psychology and Psychiatry* 27:802–840.

——— (1987a). "Continuities and Discontinuities from Infancy." In J.

Osolsky, ed., *Handbook of Infant Development*. 2nd ed. New York: Wiley, 201–223.

—— (1987b). "Intergenerational Continuities and Discontinuities in Serious Parenting Difficulties." In D. Cicchetti and V. Carlson, eds., *Research on the Consequences of Child Maltreatment*. New York: Cambridge University Press, 96–111.

—— (1987c). "Psychosocial Resilience and Protective Mechanisms." *American Journal of Orthopsychiatry* 57:316–331.

—— (1987d). "Temperament, Personality and Personality Disorder." *British Journal of Psychiatry* 150:443–458.

Rutter, M., and Garmezy, N. (1983). "Developmental Psychology." In E. M. Hetherington, ed., *Socialization, Personality and Social Development*. Vol. 4, *Mussen's Handbook of Child Psychology*. 4th ed. New York: Wiley.

Rutter, M., and Giller, N. (1983). *Juvenile Delinquency: Trends and Perspectives*. New York: Guilford Press.

Rutter, M., Izard, C. E., and Read, P. E. eds. (1986). *Depression in Young People: Developmental and Clinical Perspectives*. New York: Guilford Press.

Rutter, M., and Standberg, S. (1985). "Epidemiology of Child Psychiatric Disorder: Methodological Issues and Some Substantive Findings." *Child Psychiatry and Human Development* 15:209–233.

Rutter, M., and Yule, W. (1987). "Specific Reading Retardation." In L. Mann and D. Sabatino, eds., *The First Review of Special Education*. Philadelphia: Buttonwood Farms.

Schantz, C. E. (1983). "Social Cognition." In J. H. Flavell and E. M. Markman, eds., *Cognitive Development*. Vol. 3, *Mussen's Handbook of Child Psychology*. 4th ed. New York: Wiley, 485–555.

Scott, D. E. (1981). "Behavior Disturbance and Failure to Learn: A Study of Cause and Effect." *Educational Research* 23:163–172.

Shepperd, M., Oppenheim, B., and Mitchell, S. (1971). *Childhood Behavior and Mental Health*. London: University of London Press.

Silva, P., McGee, R., and Williams, S. (1983). "Developmental Language Delay from 3 to 7 Years and Its Significance for Low Intelligence and Reading Difficulties at Age Seven." *Developmental Medicine and Child Neurology* 28:783–793.

Simlons, A. D.; Murphy, C. E.; Levine, J. L.; and Wetzel, R. D. (1986). "Cognitive Therapy and Pharmacotherapy for Depression: Sustained Improvement over One Year." *Archives of General Psychiatry* 43:43–48.

Smith, C., and Lloyd, B. (1978). "Maternal Behavior and Perceived Sex of Infant: Revisited." *Child Development* 40:1263–1265.

Sroufe, L. A. (1979a). "Socioemotional Development." In J. D. Osofsky, ed., *Handbook of Infant Development*. New York: Wiley.

—— (1979b). "The Coherence of Individual Development." *American Psychologist* 34:834–841.

——— (1985). "Attachment Classification from the Perspective of Infant Temperament." *Child Development* 56:1–14.

Sroufe, L. A., and Rutter, M. (1984). "The Domain of Developmental Psychopathology." *Child Development* 55:17–29.

Stevenson, L. A., Richman, N., and Graham, P. (1985). "Behavior Problems and Language Abilities at 3 Years and Behavioral Deviance at 8 Years." *Journal of Child Psychology and Psychiatry* 26:215–230.

Taylor, E. (1980). "Development of Attention." In M. Rutter, ed., *Scientific Foundations of Developmental Psychiatry.* London: Heinemann Medical, 185–197.

——— (1986). *The Overactive Child: Clinics in Developmental Medicine no. 97.* Oxford: Blackwell Scientific.

Tizard, B., and Hodges, J. (1978). "The Effect of Early Institutional Rearing on the Development of Eight-Year-Old Children." *Journal of Child Psychology and Psychiatry* 19:435–453.

Winters, K. C.; Stone, A. A.; Weintraub, S.; and Neale, J. M. (1981). "Cognitive and Attentional Deficits in Children Vulnerable to Psychopathology." *Journal of Abnormal Child Psychology* 9:435–453.

Yule, W., and Rutter, M. (1985). "Reading and Other Learning Difficulties." In M. Rutter and L. Hersov, eds., *Child and Adolescent Psychiatry: Modern Approaches.* 2nd ed. Oxford: Blackwell Scientific.

21

Thought Container Disorders, Disorders of Intelligence, Learning Disorders

BERNARD GIBELLO

Some twenty years ago, Dr. Bruno Castets pointed out to me that madness is the patient's departure from the common system of signs, which Castets understands as consisting of all the objects around us that are meaningful to us. These include not only all the words in our language but also all the everyday things in our environment—for example, the chairs and tables in a room, clothes, a theme from the Ninth Symphony, a tape measure in a sewing box, a no parking sign, the grocer's scales, a tennis racket, and so on. These are all objects that have some significance for us, that we recognize and know how to use, but that to people from another culture or time would be meaningless or would be understood or used in a way "contrary to common sense."

What is it that confers meaning? How can meaning be lost, acquire an opposite connotation, be wrongly construed, or become nonsensical? To me, these questions are crucial to understanding the pathology of thinking and intelligence, and mental pathology as a whole.

Another, equally important line of inquiry is to find out what it is in our thought processes today that gives (or does not give) meaning to what we perceive or imagine: How do we discover that things have a meaning? How do we learn to attribute meaning to things?

SOURCES OF ANSWERS

Three sources can be used to find answers as to how meaning arises and how we learn to give meaning.

Biological and Neurological Research

Among a great many other things, the disciplines of biology and neurology describe the development and organization, as well as the loss, of the symbolic value of perceptions, gestures, and words. I remember one particularly striking example. This was a patient who had been operated on for a temporal brain tumor, and who was unable after surgery to tell time on a clock or watch, despite the fact that he could see the dial and the hands and knew perfectly well that one could normally tell time by them. For this man, a very small part of the environment had lost its significance as a result of a surgical brain lesion.

Modern-day neurochemical research has contributed to the understanding of the role of neurotransmitters in modulating the affective tone of the organization of thought and action, which ranges between enthusiasm and indifference or anxiety.

Generally speaking, the human body and the innumerable chemical reactions occurring there constitute the necessary scaffolding for our psychic and mental existence.

Research by Geneticists and Cognitivist Psychologists

This research provides knowledge of a different kind. Through Baldwin, Wallon, Piaget, and those who continued their work, we learned that understanding of oneself and the environment develops gradually, and that the ability to understand and give meaning to experiences is normally acquired through a process of thought-construction activities carried out during the period between birth and the end of adolescence.

As an example of recent work done by this school, I would quote Bullinger. He shows how a reflex activity gradually comes to be seen as an inherent characteristic through what he calls a process of instrumentalization, with the establishment of both a self-image and an image of the effect of the activity.

Bullinger's work on the instrumentalization of visual function opens up new perspectives on the oddities of vision observed in autistic children (Bullinger and Robert-Tissot, 1984). He shows that in these children, everything happens as though the instrumentalization of sight occurred through preferential peripheral rather than macular vision. The preference for peripheral vision causes the subject to direct the axis of the eye to a point *beside* the object being observed, so as to project the visual image onto the peripheral retina. This unusual eye action is often

wrongly interpreted as indicating a refusal to relate to others—an interpretation that in turn gives rise to mistaken attitudes among people
around them. Being aware that autistic children instrumentalize their
vision in an unusual way makes it possible to avoid hasty misinterpreta-
tions of their behavior. It nonetheless remains unclear what causes
such a curious form of instrumentalization in these children.

Other important work has been done on differential developmental
lag in the acquisition of what seem to be very similar skills. This is a
question the Piagetians have had difficulty with for a long time, and on
which they are still divided today. Here, I shall address only the question
of this developmental lag in individuals.

To observe the development of cognitive-intellectual processes,
Piaget used the cross-sectional method, which examines characteristics of a population of children at various ages. Subsequent comparison
of the results observed at different ages can give a global view of a child's
development. But this method describes the development of a theoretical individual, whom the Piagetians call the "cognitive subject," whose
development is reconstructed from successive cross sections of samples. There is no proof that the development of individual children follows the exact path of the overall statistical pattern. Or, as the Piagetians
would say, there is no proof that the "clinical" subject will normally
follow the development of the "cognitive" subject.

On the contrary, in fact, there is a considerable body of work showing
that appreciable developmental lags are commonly observed in individuals. The question is, are these lags normal or are they not? The answer
to that is, it all depends.

I myself have demonstrated that these discrepancies are normal and
commonplace up to a point, and that they become pathological once the
lags go beyond a certain degree of magnitude. I have compared the lags
in a normal population with those of a population of psychopathic delinquent adolescents, and the difference between the two populations was
highly significant. This enabled me to demonstrate clearly the pathological cognitive disharmony syndrome, which I have since come across in
a great many pathological cases other than psychopaths: psychoses,
various developmental disharmonies, and borderline states. Shakelford
and Gilbert Voyat have found the same syndrome in autistic children and
given it the name of "cognitive heterogeneity."

The inadequacy of the standard measurement instruments at our
disposal makes it difficult to evaluate the developmental lag discrepancies accurately. Nonetheless, when it comes to pathological cases, these
are no longer barely perceptible peculiarities but, on the contrary, very

definite abnormalities that appear under appropriate clinical examination. I will give just one example, the case of a fourteen-year-old adolescent with a normal intellectual level. He was capable of abstract thinking as far as numbers, time, or logical combinations were concerned but could conceive of space only in topological terms: Euclidian rules of equality of geometrical figures made no sense to him.

As Serge Larrivée has remarked, this work can be criticized on a methodological level from several points of view. I particularly regret not yet having a more sophisticated instrument of evaluation than F. Longeot's Logical Thought Scale (EPL). It must be emphasized, however, that, despite its imperfections, this instrument makes it easy to distinguish clearly between commonplace and pathological cognitive disharmonies and that these distinctions are confirmed by clinical data.

The Psychoanalytic Perspective

This approach provides a variety of answers to the problem of meaning-related disorders, but I shall look at only a few aspects here. First of all, some of Freud's essential points:

- Only instinctually cathected situations are remembered. One perceives only things that bring to mind an instinctually cathected memory.
- Pleasant memories tend to be recalled repeatedly, and traumatic memories tend to be reexperienced.
- The psychic apparatus tries to either push aside or avoid painful experiences, or else to control them, whether symbolically, as in playing with a bobbin reel, or through denial in thought, or by transposing the distressing elements into acts, delusions, or psychosomatic lesions.

Winnicott has shown the importance of transitional phenomena, whereby the child proceeds from a megalomanic self-image to awareness of the constraints of reality through the evolution of the mother-child relationship. In short, it is by way of the transitional phenomena that, as Freud wrote in *The Interpretation of Dreams*, "thought is . . . a substitute for a hallucinatory wish."

My own experience led me to suggest a complement to classic psychoanalytic theory in order to take account of, among other things, recent observations by psychologists studying early infancy (particularly H. Papousek). They have shown the existence of intentional reality-control activities in newborn babies.

Freud called a form of thought that takes external reality into account a "secondary process" in the functioning of the psychic apparatus. I hypothesize that this form of thought, or something very like it, is present from birth in situations over which the child has direct physical control to its great satisfaction. In my view, the drive cathexis at work here is the possessive instinct, avatar of the death instinct. It gives rise to a particular psychic object, which I refer to as the "cognitive object," as distinct from the libidinal object being constituted. I postulate that the fusion of the cognitive and libidinal objects normally occurs during the first depressive phase toward the end of the first three months of life. From then onward they follow a common destiny, subject to the problems of depressive and castration anxieties.

Finally, the significance of perceptions and memories is the result of a combination of processes described by biologists and neurologists, cognitivists and psychoanalysts, and I see no clear reason why one or another of these points of view should be either privileged or unrecognized.

THOUGHT CONTAINER AND THOUGHT CONTENT

In the light of these general considerations and my own experience, I find it convenient to use the opposing terms *thought container* and *thought content* when dealing with meaning-acquisition processes in the clinical context.

By *thought container* I refer to whatever gives meaning to content. For instance, the sequence of sounds in a word of a language is a *thought content* whose linguistic meaning or absence of it depends on whether or not we understand the language the word belongs to. As another example, knowledge that organizes visual information and memories acts as containers for visual perceptions. This is borne out by observation of children who have undergone surgery at adolescence for congenital cataract: blind until then, they describe their first experience of light perception as a violent, deafening clanging of bells. In the same way, the adolescent I mentioned earlier thought of space in topological terms. This thought container did not enable him to make the distinction between a square and any other convex polyhedron: it was no use trying to teach him geometry, since he was incapable of giving geometric figures the meaning they have in Euclidian geometry.

Broadly speaking, it seems to me that thought containers should be divided into three categories:

- The Piagetian schemata of assimilation and their evolution into logical structures, by means of which objects are assimilated and "comprehended" in the etymological sense of "being taken within." These schemata are also able to adapt and to adjust to conflicts brought about by new contents.
- Unconscious fantasies, the ebb and flow of desires that are more or less disguised by a variety of defense mechanisms: devouring/vomiting, controlling/losing, dominating/enduring, exhibiting/admiring, possessing/killing. These fantasies give symbolic value to objects in the environment and also to oneself, and make it possible to put various elements of symbolic play into action.
- Language, whose signifiers surround the infant from birth, which he begins to appropriate for himself from the age of two years onward and which very soon becomes the main vehicle of thought.

These different containers confer meaning on thought contents, which would otherwise remain undetermined, senseless.

This approach helps identify thought container disorders; it casts new light on some disturbances and enables others to be identified. The disappearance of thought containers leads to acute mental confusion, where all perceptions and memories are entangled in the horror of nonsense. Less dramatically, but with more permanent consequences, a limited development of thought containers leads to the mental deficiency configuration.

Above all, however, I have identified two particular syndromes arising from the incoherent development of thought containers. On the one hand, there are different forms of pathological cognitive disharmonies, which can show heterogeneous development of the structures of reasoning, with a number of lags that emerge as markedly excessive under a Piagetian assessment; overall intellectual abilities that are normal in terms of general developmental level and I.Q.; and variable disturbances in symbolization processes, most frequently with a combination of dysphasic-dyslexic disorders, disorders of the organization of thought (particularly with regard to space, time, etc.), and dyspraxic disorders. These pathological cognitive disharmonies are not uncommon. They affect something like one in every twenty schoolchildren and have catastrophic repercussions on their educational and professional acquisition of knowledge as well as constituting a serious handicap in their social outcome.

The other syndrome relates to delays in the organization of reasoning, where an apparently normal intellectual level is accompanied by reasoning arrested at an embryonic stage of its development and a number of disturbances in symbolization. I am increasingly inclined to compare these reasoning organization delays with the regressive processes observed in the various forms of dementia.

As often happens in psychiatry, these syndromes, where alterations in thought containers are predominant, seem to be a final common pathway for a great many etiological conditions. Here, depending on the individual case, we find hereditary disorders, head injuries, and cerebral palsy, as well as psychic trauma of different kinds, intrapsychic conflicts, family conflicts, and so on.

The advantage of this perspective lies in the possibility of integrating complementary inputs and proposing therapeutic methods designed to reactivate the development of learning processes that have been arrested for whatever reason. What seem to be the most adequate interventions in the cases we have come across are those that draw on the possibility of reactivating transitional phenomena, thus enabling the construction of thought containers to be completed and concluded. But other methods, dealing with the improvement of self-image, or that proposed by Feuerstein, also look promising in certain cases.

REFERENCES

Bullinger, A., and Robert-Tissot, C. (1984). *Contribution de la psychologie du développement à la compréhension de quelques aspects de l'autisme précoce.* Paris: Commission ARAPI.
Longeot, F. (1967). *Aspects différentiels de la psychologie génétique BINOP.* Paris: No spécial.
——— (1978). *Les stades opératoires de Piaget et les facteurs de l'intelligence.* Grenoble: Presses Universitaires.

VI

Infantile Autism

22

Introduction

COLETTE CHILAND

In this part, infantile autism will be looked at from two points of view.

First, Colette Chiland will present her comments on a theme that was the subject of a round table discussion at a Paris Congress: the causes of infantile autism and the consequences of etiological hypotheses for therapy.

Whereas putting forward working hypotheses on the role of biological factors (genes, brain damage, biochemical dysfunctions) is both legitimate and valuable, it is questionable that generalizations and dogmatic stands should be established on the basis of incomplete results. No less debatable is the exclusion of working hypotheses leading to the study of interactions during the course of development; unless one is in a position to observe them, it is easy to conclude that they do not exist. In any case, whatever the etiological hypotheses may be, our therapeutic resources are still limited. No one knows how to cure autism. All that can be done is to try to improve the situation for the child and the family. It is agreed that therapy and education are necessary, but there is divergence on the concept of education: some people see behavior modification as the only valid aspect, whereas for others the problem is to restore the patient's capacity for initiative.

The second chapter in this part deals with the outcome of autistic children, and how important and difficult it is for them to become self-supporting and independent. Ryuji Kobayashi and Toyohisa Murata observe the evolution of thirty autistic Japanese children, twenty-four boys and six girls (which corresponds to the usual sex ratio for infantile autism), now aged between twenty and twenty-nine. The study takes intellectual level, adaptive level, and the evolution of symptoms into consideration. Seven of these autistic children managed to become employed, although in modest capacities, and all seven live with their parents.

Three other chapters in this book deal with infantile autism. They could have been included here, but they have been placed in other parts because they illustrate particular approaches whose importance we wanted to emphasize.

The first of these, by Magda Campbell, Arthur M. Small, and Richard Perry, "Psychopharmacological Approaches in the Treatment of Autism," will be found in part III on biological approaches. It takes stock of the efficacy of various drugs monitored in clinical trials. In the second, René Diatkine uses the example of infantile autism to illustrate the concept of etiology as seen today by a psychoanalyst. This chapter is in part IV, "Appraisal of the Current Status of the Psychoanalytic Approach." The third chapter, by Tao Kuo-Tai, relates the experience of the longest-practicing child psychiatrist in China and comes in part IX, "Transcultural Perspectives." Tao Kuo-Tai has seen cases of autism, albeit rarely, whereas other Chinese psychiatrists say they have never come across one. This could be because autism has been diagnosed as something else or possibly because there are fewer cases of autism. If the latter is so, two hypotheses can be suggested, one genetic and the other cultural. Whatever the case may be, for the time being it would not be justified to state, as some do, that autism is present in all countries and to the same extent everywhere.

23

Infantile Autism: A Discussion

COLETTE CHILAND

With a view to facilitating dialogue among clinicians and researchers from different parts of the world and various theoretical horizons, I organized a roundtable on the subject, "The Causes of Infantile Autism and the Consequences of Etiological Hypotheses for Therapy," held during the Eleventh International Congress of Child and Adolescent Psychiatry and Allied Professions. Roundtables of this kind are somewhat optimistic in that they are invariably pressed for time and spontaneous exchanges are difficult. For the exchange of ideas to culminate in mutual understanding, if such a thing is possible, participants should know each other relatively well and be aware of their work in the places in which they treat children.

The participants in this panel, which I chaired, were Donald J. Cohen (United States), René Diatkine (France), Pierre Ferrari (France), Christopher Gillberg (Sweden), Philip J. Graham (United Kingdom), Edward R. Ritvo (United States), Bertram A. Ruttenberg (United States), and J. Gerald Young (United States). The following text is not a summary of the discussions but a personal attempt to review the answers available today to the questions raised by the subject of the roundtable.

The diagnostic criteria for infantile autism, first described by Leo Kanner, will not be discussed here. It is easy to reach agreement on this point, even if there is at present some argument as to whether late onset autism should be included in the same diagnostic category. The criteria of Rutter, Ritvo, and the D.S.M.-III all concur.

POINTS OF DISCUSSION

Specific cause or multifactorial syndrome? Some authors fall back on ambiguous phraseology implying that this question is settled: autism is a sickness of the brain. This is a too simplistic statement, although autism is indeed a sickness of the brain in the sense that, to quote Ajuriaguerra, "everything goes through the brain, nothing through the halo."

When it comes to precise signs, however, no sign is present in all cases. A number of different signs of cerebral dysfunction are found with varying frequency (Coleman and Gillberg, 1985), and it is difficult to extrapolate any exact etiological role from observation of their concomitance with infantile autism. The autistic syndrome is the same, whether organic signs are present or not. Furthermore, it is hard to distinguish whether the concomitant signs are causes or consequences. For example, hyperserotonemia is observed in sensory disafferentation in subjects who are not autistic. We are faced, then, with a behavioral syndrome that is associated with a number of possible etiologies. There are as many subgroups as there are indexes—chromosomes, EEG, CT-scan, biochemical measurements, and so on.

Although most authors agree about the utility of the multifactorial model for autism, it would be interesting to know why some of them exclude interactions with the environment from the list of possible etiological factors.

Interactions with the environment. The very mention of interactions with the environment tends to produce immediate defensive reactions from parents (and a number of researchers have investigated infantile autism because they themselves have had an autistic child).

It is true that some professionals have adopted an attitude rejected by most of us, telling mothers, "It's your fault that the child is autistic." Some mothers are masochistic enough to believe this, and there are cases in which such an accusation has made them permanently incapable of looking after their autistic child. But in the current state of knowledge there is no justification for such an attitude. Professionals should remember they are dealing with parents who are in great distress and whose lives are particularly difficult.

Not just any baby becomes autistic. It can be an especially frail infant, whose fragility makes it impossible for the mother and father to carry out their parental tasks (Soule, 1978). It could be a baby who is less delicate, but in whose case particular circumstances prevent exchanges with its parents and with the environment from taking place normally. These circumstances can be external events, or they can be connected with the parents' experience at the time of the infant's birth and with what that particular child represents to them (Jeammet, 1985). The autistic organization is gradually consolidated, and once established, it is extremely difficult to change.

Philip Graham has spoken of the need for facts, evidence, but there are no clear-cut hard facts. To collect facts one first has to enter a situation in which it is possible to do so. Confining investigations to questionnaires and target interviews gives parents no opportunity to talk about their experience in connection with the birth of their autistic child. This can sometimes come up very late in a series of interviews and throw light on what has made parenting so very difficult. But in this case, we are looking at something different from the diagnostic labeling of a particular pathology in accordance with the usual nosological criteria. We know that the parents of autistic children do not have any such pathology.

This leads some authors, such as René Diatkine, for example, to the firm conviction of the importance of in-depth case studies. A certain amount of data can be obtained by studying indexes that are easier to observe, enumerate, and computerize on a large scale, but such an approach gives no access at all to these other data, which are also facts and constitute evidence.

Is there a cure? Whatever etiological hypotheses are adopted, everyone agrees that infantile autism is a severe condition with a guarded prognosis. It is difficult to counteract sweeping statements in the mass media about which treatments to use and which to avoid. The same applies to associations of parents of autistic children, where an admission that neither we nor anyone else knows how to cure infantile autism has a damaging effect: we deprive the parents of the hope they need to fight against it.

Although it is true to say that there is no known guaranteed cure, this is nonetheless a statement that must be qualified. The fact is that there do exist a few rare cases in which autistic children have had a favorable outcome, and who have even been "cured." One of these was a child treated by Anni Bergmann (1983), whose case was documented on film and videocassette material presented at the Dublin Congress and later published. This autistic child is observed as she grows into a pleasant young girl whose speech, and especially her intonation, is quite normal. She goes to secondary school, marries, and becomes the mother of two children whom she takes care of, although not without problems. The immediate reaction of many colleagues to this case is to dispute the accuracy of the initial diagnosis—which only goes to show how few professionals believe in the possibility of cure for an autistic child. Donald Cohen speaks of a "lifetime prescription of education and treatment."

Our present knowledge, then, enables us only to do our best to improve things, without knowing for certain what we might achieve.

Therapeutic directions. If there were any proof of a clear genetic etiology that could be detected in the same way as, say, trisomy 21, doing an amniocentesis and karyotype would make it possible to carry out a therapeutic abortion (except when abortion as such is objected to). This is not the case, however, and for the time being etiological hypotheses relating to hereditary endowment and chromosomal abnormalities are not used therapeutically. Similarly, where there is brain damage, there is no remedy.

Biochemical hypotheses are more promising and give rise to pharmacological treatment strategies (as discussed in chap. 14). But their effect is limited in that medication addresses only the symptoms, not the syndrome.

Whatever the case may be, the child still has to be educated, the most favorable development possible ensured, and detrimental behavior eliminated.

Education. This is where divergence concerning etiological hypotheses is compounded by a misunderstanding. Being a psychoanalyst does not mean that one considers it unnecessary to be concerned with the education of autistic children—in other words, with trying to enable them to establish human relationships or to develop their intellectual potential and their language. I recommend that colleagues from other countries visit therapeutic centers in France, where they will find not only that the children's treatment is not merely a matter of sessions of psychotherapy and interpretations but that some are not necessarily followed individually by a psychotherapist. These are *living* centers: children are provided with activities, and there are people to give them the attention they need. Education is also offered by staffs composed of academic teachers, remedial teachers and counselors.

The misunderstanding regarding education arises from divergent concepts as to what the word *education* means, which in turn reflect various ideas concerning the nature of human mental activity. To some, the individual is a set of behavior patterns. Education is as much a behavioral matter as therapy is: the aim is to induce the production of desirable behavior and the elimination of unwanted behavior. To achieve this, a system of positive and negative sanctions is applied. Others think that the individual initiates behavior from within, and their aim is not to produce a given behavior but to instill the ability to generate other forms of behavior, to function not like a robot, but like a living person.

There is such concern for individual freedom in France that the establishment of registers is restricted, which means that we have no record of the outcomes for large numbers of patients. Neither do we have, fortunately, large-scale institutions specializing in the treatment of autistic individuals; on the contrary, it is considered inadvisable to have too many autistic people in the same therapy center. All of us, however, have followed for many years autistic children whose outcomes have varied widely.

Lacking statistical comparisons, it is difficult to establish irrefutably what has been effective in treatment for any given individual. What is striking, though, is the fact that progress has often occurred when there has been an encounter with a therapist (in the wider sense of anyone involved in a child's treatment, not just a psychotherapist). That person has achieved an understanding of the child's inner world, his anxieties and distress, and has provided metaphors whereby this inner world is reorganized (Haag, 1985).

The parents. Psychoanalysts have been accused of loading guilt on parents. Colleagues from other countries have assured us that the parents they encounter have no spontaneous sense of guilt, which is very different from our experience in France. Most parents ask "What have I done (to the Lord) to deserve having a child like this?" ("the Lord" is invoked or not depending on religious attitudes). Occasionally, though not often, parents declare aggressively, "It has nothing to do with me." All parents, however, ask about the cause. Some are relieved to hear genetic hypotheses, but others are stricken with guilt at what they have transmitted through their chromosomes.

Having a mentally sick child is such a deep narcissistic wound and living with an autistic child is so distressing that the therapist's role, far from creating guilt feelings, should be to alleviate them. It is a long and difficult process.

There is general agreement about the need to give support to parents, but here again, divergences occur along lines dictated by differing conceptions of human mental activity. Some feel that strict advice should be given; others learn from experience that even the best advice is not followed if the parents are in no condition to do so. This has given rise to different ways of approaching parents and trying to help them.

ON WORKING HYPOTHESES AND DOGMATIC CONVICTIONS

It is clear that research must be pursued in every possible direction. Current information is only partial, and nothing explains the syndrome as a whole and in all its forms.

The misguided use of biological hypotheses is to be condemned. Such use is seen not only when hypotheses are converted into dogmatic convictions but also when there is an unjustifiable assumption of a *linear* biological causality, to the exclusion of any interaction among the various biological factors themselves or between these and the outside environment (which Roubertoux and Nosten criticize vehemently in chap. 7).

An interest in biological hypotheses, however, need not automatically lead to such errors. Gerald Young, for example, wrote in his paper for this round-table:

> It is known that the environment can measurably alter various indices of brain function, including enzyme activities and neurotransmitter levels. Similarly, ethological observations and tissue culture experiments have suggested the importance of critical periods, including time-locked expectancies of specific mother-child interactions, in the emergence of individual behavioral sequences. Yet is not clear whether environmental influences might bring about the profound abnormalities characteristic of autism.

We have put the psychoanalytic contribution in the framework of parent-child interactions, and not in that of a pure dogmatic psychogenesis. Freud himself did not adhere to the latter: he included in the etiological equation both life events, on the one hand, and heredity, constitution, and predisposition, on the other. Psychoanalysis has provided many of us with a theoretical framework for our efforts to understand in every case what the autistic child and his or her parents are experiencing; in a limited number of cases analytic therapy is initiated. We should not lose sight of the fact that "the child's illness belongs to the child," as Winnicott says: it is his own response, with the psychobiological resources at his disposal, to promptings from the environment. The freedom or the randomness governing the selection of one of the possible responses at the start is always more limited in the final moments. In the case of autism, a developmental potential to mobilize is sealed off (see Diatkine, chap. 16).

REFERENCES

Bergmann, A. (1983). "From Psychological Birth to Motherhood: The Treatment of an Autistic Child with Follow-up into Her Adult Life as a Mother." In E. J. Anthony and E. H. Pollock, eds., *Parental Influences in Health and Disease*. Boston: Little, Brown, 91–120.

Coleman, M., and Gillberg, C. (1985). *The Biology of the Autistic Syndromes*. new York: Praeger.

Haag, G. (1985). "Psychothérapie d'un enfant autiste." *Lieux de l'enfance,* no. 3:65–78.

Jeammet, N. (1985). "L'enfant autiste replacé dans une histoire." *Lieux de l'enfance,* no. 3:247–277.

Soule, M. (1978). "L'enfant qui venait du froid." In S. Lebovici and E. Kestemberg, *Le devenir de la psychose de l'enfant*. Paris: P.U.F., 179–212.

24

Factors Determining the Capacity of Autistic Adults to Become Independent and Self-Supporting

RYUJI KOBAYASHI

TOYOHISA MURATA

Almost forty years have passed since the first case of early infantile autism was reported in Japan in 1952, nine years after Leo Kanner (1943) proposed the syndrome. During the 1950s and 1960s, the treatment for autistic children in Japan was mainly play therapy. In the 1970s and 1980s, however, they have been given intensive education in public elementary schools, in special education programs, and in integrative programs. Autistic children's development has improved because of these intensive therapeutic approaches. Yet this must be judged in the light of many follow-up studies indicating that as adults autistic persons are not in good clinical condition.

In the city of Fukuoka, Japan, we began treating autistic children in a group therapeutic "Saturday class" setting, with volunteers under the supervision of psychiatrists (Murata, 1975). Soon after that, a special program was introduced into selected public elementary schools. Most of those who were treated in the 1970s are now in adulthood.

THE STUDY

We examined thirty autistic adults, who have been observed continually from childhood to the present time, taking into consider-

We wish to thank Professor M. Nishizono of Fukuoka University School of Medicine for his advice and critical reading of this manuscript. This study was supported in part by a grant-in-aid for scientific research for autism from the Ministry of Welfare of Fukuoka Prefecture in Japan.

ation their mental level, psychological status, and lifelong development. We examined their developmental course and developmental level, their present clinical symptoms, and their unique problems in adulthood (Kobayashi, 1985). By investigating the living and working conditions of employed autistic adults, the study attempted to ascertain what factors are most important for autistic adults to become independent and self-supporting in Japanese society.

All the subjects were at least twenty years old when we assessed their current developmental level in April 1986. Those who died during the follow-up period were excluded from the data. Of the thirty subjects, twenty-four were males and six were females with a mean age of 22.5 years (S.D. = 2.8). The youngest was twenty years old and the oldest, twenty-nine (see Table 24.1).

Current Social Outcome

The current social outcome (table 24.2) included seven who were employed (23 percent of the total), a relatively high employment ratio. One autistic person undergoing training at an occupational center was expected to obtain employment in the near future. Three were in a sheltered workshop, and nine, in special care units for the mentally handicapped. Four were in a specialized unit for autistic people, which was founded by their parents in the spring of 1986. Three were hospitalized, and three were cared for at home. Table 24.3 shows the I.Q., education, occupation, income, and residence of the seven employed autistic adults. Some were mildly or moderately mentally retarded, but achieved a good adaptive level. Although they were employed, their income was low, about 50,000—60,000 yen (or about $337) a month. This reveals their low valuation and status in society.

Table 24.1 *Subjects*

| | Age | | | | | |
Sex	20–21	22–23	24–25	26–27	28–29	Total
Male	12	8	0	3	1	24 (80%)
Female	3	0	0	1	2	6 (20%)
Total	15	8	0	4	3	30 (100%)

Table 24.2 *Current Social Outcome*

Social Outcome	Male	Female	Total
Employed	6	1	7 (23%)
Vocational training center	1	0	1 (3%)
Sheltered workshop	2	1	3 (10%)
Specialized unit for autistic people	4	0	4 (13%)
Special care unit for mentally handi-capped	7	1	8 (27%)
Hospitalization	2	1	3 (10%)
Home	2	2	4 (13%)
Total	24	6	30 (100%)

Current Developmental Level

Patients' social adaptation is not always equal to their intellectual level. Thus, we examined their developmental level in two modalities, an intellectual level and an adaptive level.

The intellectual level was assessed by Binet or Wechsler intelligence tests and was categorized as follows: good: I.Q. higher than 70; fair: I.Q. 50 to 70; poor: I.Q. less than 50.

The adaptive level was assessed in terms of the patient's adaptive level of social competence at that time and was categorized as follows:

Good: The patient was leading a normal or near-normal social life and functioning satisfactorily at work in spite of mild abnormalities in behavior or interpersonal relationships.

Fair: The patient was making social progress in spite of significant, even marked, abnormalities in behavior or interpersonal relationships.

Poor: The patient was severely handicapped and unable to lead any kind of independent existence.

Table 24.4 shows that in the intellectual area, seven cases were classified as good, five cases as fair, and nineteen cases as poor. On both an intellectual and an adaptive level, about 60 percent fell in the poor group. Table 24.5 shows the relation between the intellectual and adaptive levels. Those who were at a good intellectual level did not always

Table 24.3 *Social-Adaptive Functioning of Seven Employed Autistic Adults*

Case	Age	Sex	I.Q.	Education	Employment	Monthly Income (Yen)[a]	Residence
1. Y.H.	29	male	103	Technical high school	Japanese cake maker	5–60,000	with parents
2. Y.S.	27	female	72	Special school[b]	Japanese futon maker	5–60,000	with parents
3. H.O.	26	male	115	High school	Bus guide (part-timer)	7–80,000	with parents
4. K.T.	23	male	46	Special school	Laundry	5–60,000	with parents
5. K.S.	22	male	51	Special school	Laundry	5–60,000	with parents
6. J.K.	22	male	61	Special school	Laundry	5–60,000	with parents
7. T.M.	20	male	77	Special school	Hakata-doll maker	5–60,000	with parents

a. About 160 yen is one dollar.
b. Special school is one for the mentally disturbed.

Table 24.4 *Current Developmental Level*

Developmental Level	Intelligence	Adaptation
Good	7 (23%)	9 (30%)
Fair	5 (17%)	2 (7%)
Poor	18 (60%)	19 (63%)
Total	30 (100%)	30 (100%)

reach a good adaptive level, and some not at a good intellectual level could achieve a good adaptive level. This discrepancy reveals the difficulty predicting the development of autistic people.

Current Clinical Symptoms

The subjects' clinical symptoms were examined in relation to intellectual levels. The results are shown in table 24.6. Hyperkinesis decreased with higher intellectual levels, but akinesis became a difficult problem in its place. Lack of spontaneity is one of the most serious problems in autistic adults. In this group, seven had epileptic seizures, all grand mal in type (most of the seven exhibited severe mental retardation). The age of onset of the epilepsy was ten to twenty years of age.

There were various neurotic symptoms in these patients—polyuria, obsessive ideas and phobic reactions. Tics were not present. There were some psychotic symptoms, such as engaging in monologues, inappropriate laughter, fantastic ideas, oddness and delusions, ideas of refer-

Table 24.5 *Correlation between Intelligence and Adaptation*

Intelligence	Adaptation			
	Good	Fair	Poor	Total
Good	5	2	0	7
Fair	4	0	1	5
Poor	0	0	18	18
Total	9	2	19	30

Table 24.6 *Intellectual Level and Current Clinical Symptoms*

Symptoms	Intellectual level (I.Q.)				
	Normal N = 7	Mild MRª N = 8	Moderate MR N = 2	Severe MR N = 13	Total N = 30
Epilepsy	0	1	1	5	7 (23%)
Panic	0	4	0	9	13 (43)
Self-injurious behavior	1	4	1	10	16 (53)
Aggressive behavior	0	3	0	5	8 (27)
Lack of spontaneity	0	2	0	10	12 (40)
Minimal facial expression	4	8	2	12	26 (87)
Open masturbation	0	2	0	10	12 (40)
Interest in heterosexual relationship	3	2	1	1	7 (23)
Sameness	1	4	1	12	18 (60)
Hyperkinesis	0	0	0	3	3 (10)
Autistic features	0	8	1	12	21 (70)
Polyuria	0	1	0	1	2 (7)
Obsessive behavior	2	5	2	12	21 (70)
Obsessive ideas	5	2	1	2	10 (33)
Phobic	1	1	1	3	6 (20)
Tic	0	0	0	0	0 (0)
Monologue	0	4	1	6	11 (37)
Inappropriate laughter	0	3	1	4	8 (27)
Fantastic ideas	1	4	1	1	7 (23)
Oddness	1	1	0	0	2 (7)
Delusion	1	0	1	0	2 (7)
Hallucination	0	0	0	0	0 (0)

a. MR = mental retardation

ence or hypochondriacal delusions. They responded well to drug treatment.

Psychosexual development was very poor. The subjects had little interest in sex, either with the opposite sex or the same, and they were indifferent to changes in their body. Many openly masturbated. Because of their difficulty in relating to others, they were incapable of sexual involvement.

The most persistent, unresponsive clinical symptoms were obsessive tendencies, poor emotional expression, and autistic features. These symptoms, combined with the inability to experience emotional rapport with others, were basic problems unique to the autistic patient.

To summarize, there were several changes in clinical symptoms in adulthood. First, a decrease in hyperkinesis was evident, and a lack of spontaneity followed as a result. This was mainly related to brain maturation. In addition, epileptic seizures occurred in about 20 percent of the adults, consistent with other reports. Second, various neurotic and psychotic symptoms were present. In particular, the subjects were confronted with the growing pains and frustrations of adolescence, and they commonly responded with neurotic or psychotic defense mechanisms. These symptoms were strongly associated with psychosocial factors. Third, some symptoms were persistent and unresponsive. Obsessive symptoms, minimal facial expression, and autistic features were characteristic; closely related to autism, they had continued throughout life. Clinical symptoms underwent changes in relation to the experiences of the patient in his or her lifelong development.

AUTISTIC PERSONS AND ADOLESCENT CRISES

When we discuss the social independence of autistic persons, the most important issue is how the subjects may overcome adolescent crises. The first crisis comes during the "gang" age. During the preadolescent period, one develops friendships with schoolmates, but autistic persons cannot easily socialize because of their difficulty in relating to others. This is a result of their inability to recognize social cues and their lack of social awareness. The second crisis has to do with body image changes. Autistic individuals have disturbances of body schema, so that they cannot easily accept changes in their body. They cope through the defense mechanism of rejection or denial.

The third crisis has to do with the acquisition of self-awareness or a feeling of identity. Autistic adolescents have difficulty in differentiating between themselves and others, so they cannot gain ego fulfillment by identifying through modeling. Instead, they imitate life-styles rigidly and faithfully. Too dependent on the sources of their ego ideal, they utilize a strong ego ideal as a vehicle toward their social identity. They have a basic amenability to parent and teacher authority, enhancing their tendency to live a dogmatic life-style, which in turn builds their social identity.

The fourth and last crisis is one of the most important: their psychological separation from the mother and eventual individuation (the second individuation; Blos, 1962). In Japan it is common for fathers to be occupied with work and mothers to care for their children, and this applies to families of autistic children. Even in adolescence they continue to be too close emotionally to their mothers, hindering them from reaching social individuation. Autistic adolescents, like their normal counterparts, have a desire to be independent of their parents. Taking this into consideration, we should help them on the road to independence or semi-independence at least.

FACTORS IN AUTISTIC ADULTS BECOMING INDEPENDENT

We have discussed the development of autistic individuals cross-sectionally and longitudinally. Now we will examine what factors are important in order for them to be independent by considering the employed autistic adults in our study.

Case 1

At the time of our study, J. K., a male, was twenty-two. He had been the full-term product of an uneventful pregnancy and delivery. His physical development was good in infancy and he did not resist separation from breast-feeding, which disappointed his mother. Also he did not cling to her when she put him on her back—a characteristic that upset her because her maternal needs were not satisfied. At one year of age, he started uttering a few words like "Papa" and "Mama," but had stopped doing so a few months later. He was sensitive to noise, so he could not sleep in the daytime. Because he was hyperkinetic, it was dangerous to leave him alone.

At three, after being referred to a university hospital, he was diagnosed as suffering from early infantile autism. He was taken to Tokyo for special care because there were no special-care services for autistic patients in Fukuoka at that time. At age five, he began to utter phrases from television commercials, and at six, he entered a normal class in a public elementary school. When he was nine years old, his family returned to Fukuoka. His teacher there was strict about punctuality, and he criticized the patient for being late for school. The boy and his mother both became sensitive, irritable, unable to sleep at night, and neurotic and unstable. At thirteen, the patient was admitted to our hospital.

His parents had been taught the importance of physical affection while bringing him up, and they had so influenced him that he overwhelmed others with his affection. His habit of kissing others did not disappear when he reached adolescence. Our nursing staff could not accept his need to kiss them, and their rejection caused panic behavior on his part. Haloperidol calmed his temper tantrums, he gained weight, and his obsession with kissing weakened. At sixteen, he was accepted into a special school for the mentally disturbed, where he took part in a vocational training program for high school-aged adolescents. At this stage of development he disliked his mother's touching him, and she grew lonely. Soon after, however, she had her second baby, an experience that encouraged her and made her more self-confident as a mother. As a result, she became more stable emotionally.

The patient, in turn, wanted to act his age, and not play as a child would. At nineteen, he was employed at a laundry, where his job was to classify the laundry according to the shop it came from. He made no errors, and his employer valued him highly. When he received his first wages, he gave his father some money for his use and his mother ten thousand yen for living expenses. His being self-supporting, it can be assumed, added to his self-esteem. His hobby was traveling on trains by himself, and whenever he took a trip, he brought souvenirs back for his family and his coworkers.

His mother's having a new baby had led him to become psychologically separated from her in mid-adolescence. Getting a job and succeeding at it made it possible for him to be self-confident and self-supporting. He attained a good adaptive level, beyond expectation.

Case 2

The second case is that of T. H., a twenty-nine-year-old man. He too was the full-term product of an uneventful pregnancy and delivery. When he was three, his hyperkinesis, restlessness, and gaze aversion caused him to be referred to a mental hospital. Although he was suspected of having a childhood schizophrenic disorder, he received little treatment at that time. He entered an elementary school, but did not play with his schoolmates and was always isolated. He gradually calmed down naturally and passed his time by playing with and manipulating mechanical gadgets.

After graduating from technical high school, he entered the Self-Defense Forces of Japan, having obtained excellent results on the Morse code signals test in his entrance examination. He did not get along with others there and saved most of his salary. As a result he accumulated three million yen (or $17,000) in four years. After he left the Self-Defense Forces, he got a job as a dishwasher in a restaurant. There he worked as hard and as steadily as ever, saving one million yen in a year and a half. But, at the age of twenty-four, during a busy Christmas season, he could not take a holiday and became overtired, restless, and psychotic. He mumbled to himself, and his smile became forced. He would return home very late and stopped praying at the family Buddhist altar and visiting the family grave. He became obsessed with using the toilet countless times a day. His parents then took him to a mental hospital where he stayed for four months and recovered quickly.

After several interviews with him, the reason for his psychotic breakdown became clear. At his workplace, he said, there had been a lazy fellow worker, who was often truant. The patient had been asked to work in his place on his holiday. He could not refuse and suffered fatigue as a result. The patient's charge that his fellow worker was lazy was a direct trigger for his maladjustment, but his history, since childhood, of compulsive behavior with the need to maintain "sameness" was seen to play a large part in his action. It became clear during his treatment that, when he became anxious that his obsessive behavior pattern might be interrupted, he was forced to say something to other workers in defense of that pattern.

This patient functioned at a good intellectual level and was similarly adapted. He was, however, overly zealous with things or details to the extent that he later suffered several consequences.

CONCLUSIONS

These cases and others suggest the factors that are important to keep in mind if autistics are to be self-supporting in adulthood.

1. They might have a strong desire to work, so they should be given the chance to do so. Because of their learning disabilities and their difficulty socializing, they often live in situations affording only low self-esteem. Thus, their working in adulthood assumes great importance. When planning their vocations, therapists should arrange work for them according to their mental and behavioral characteristics. Obsessiveness is one such trait, so they should be pointed toward work in which obsessiveness is a positive quality.

2. Overadaptation can cause maladjustment. As illustrated in the

second case above, autistic persons cannot work with flexibility, and they become compulsive about routine. This obsessive tendency should be recognized in order to better understand and accommodate autistic patients in the work realm. If this can be done, psychotic breakdown can probably be prevented.

3. Because of their clumsiness it takes great patience on the part of autistic persons to acquire skilled techniques on the job.

4. Their inability to communicate, as well as their awkwardness with interpersonal relationships, should be taken into account in job selection. They should be offered simple physical work, since they are handicapped in communicating verbally. Close contact with others should be avoided.

5. The autistic person, like others, needs relaxation time (Shopler and Mesibov, 1983). Thus, cultivating a simple hobby or pastime is of great importance. Collecting things or repetitive writing can be continued into and throughout adulthood. Knowing how to play and what to enjoy are very important for their mental state.

These are the factors that make it possible for autistic adults to be independent. They need special help and planning as they cope with the developmental issues of adolescence and adulthood, and the transition between these stages.

REFERENCES

Blos, P. (1962). *On Adolescence: A Psychodynamic Interpretation*. New York: Free Press.

DeMeyer, M.; Baraton, S.; DeMeyer, W. E.; Norton, J. A.; Allen, J.; and Steele, R. (1973). "Prognosis in Autism: A Follow-up Study." *J. Autism Child. Schizophr.* 3:199–246.

Kanner, L. (1943). "Autistic Disturbances of Emotional Contact." *Nervous Child* 2:217–250.

Kobayasi, R. (1985). "A Clinical Study on the Mental Development and the Clinical Course of Autistic Children." *Psychiat. Neurol. Jpn.* 87:546–582. (In Japanese)

Lotter, V. (1978). "Follow-up Studies." In M. Rutter and E. Schopler, eds., *Autism: A Reappraisal of Concepts and Treatment*. New York: Plenum Press.

Mittler, P., Gilles, S., and Jukes, E. (1966). "Prognosis in Psychotic Children: Report of a Follow-up Study." *J. Ment. Def. Res.* 10:73–83.

Murata, T.; Sarady, Y.; Inoue, T.; Toya, H.; Tanaka, N.; Masahiro, F.; Okuma, H.; and Nawa, A. (1975). "A Group Therapy for Autistic Children

Organized by Volunteer Activities." *Jap. J. Child Psychiat.* 16:152–163. (In Japanese)

Rumsey, J. M., and Rapoport, J. L. (1985). "Autistic Children as Adults: Psychiatric, Social and Behavioral Outcomes." *J. Am. Acad. Child Psychiat.* 24:465–473.

Rutter, M., Greenfield, D., and Lockyer, L. (1967). "A Five-to-Fifteen-Year Follow-up Study of Infantile Psychosis; II, Social and Behavioral Outcome." *Brit. J. Psychiat.* 113:1183–1199.

Shopler, E., and Mesibov, G. B., eds. (1983). *Autism in Adolescents and Adults.* New York: Plenum Press.

Sumi, T. (1952). "A Case Report of Early Infantile Autism." *Psychiat. Neurol. Jpn.* 54:566. (In Japanese)

Wakabayashi, S., and Mizuno, M. (1975). "On the Prognosis of Infantile Autism." *Jap. J. Child Psychiat.* 16:177–196. (In Japanese)

VII

From Infant to Adolescent

25

Introduction

COLETTE CHILAND

Infancy and adolescence have been the subject of intense clinical activity and research in recent years. This has been reflected in the great number of works published and in the establishment of the World Association for Infant Psychiatry and Allied Disciplines and the International Society for Adolescent Psychiatry. Books have also been published as the outcome of the congresses held by these associations. Obviously, then, we cannot cover here the entire range of the research done in these fields.

The investigations carried out by Arnold Sameroff and his colleagues (reported in chap. 26) are of particular importance both from the theoretical standpoint and from that of therapy and prevention. Environmental risk factors outweigh inadequacies of infant competencies. The overriding risk remains poverty, which entails multiple risk factors—and the accumulation of various factors has a significant effect by virtue of their *number* rather than their nature.

This was also found to be the case in our own earlier studies involving not babies but six-year-old children. Learning failure in reading during the first year of school was statistically overwhelmingly linked to family sociocultural levels.

A therapeutic system for the treatment of psychotic infants is proposed by Eleanor Galenson in chapter 27. Throughout this book we keep coming back to the leitmotiv: "The earlier the better." We also insist on the necessity of considering the infant in the context of the family, taking into account the effects on the parents of having a sick child and in turn the repercussions the illness and the parents' difficulties have on the child.

It would take a book in itself to deal adequately with the new problems involved in adolescent mental health. There is a noticeable increase in eating disorders: why should this be so? And how should one go about treating these disturbances, which affect girls in particular? Both suicide and drug-addiction behavior are on the increase. Chapter 28 deals exclusively with psychotic states as François Ladame approaches them in his psychoanalytic capacity. It is crucial to establish a psychotherapeutic relationship with the adolescent if the ever-threatening danger of the condition's becoming chronic is to be successfully avoided.

26

Social-Environmental Risk and Early Competence

ARNOLD J. SAMEROFF

RONALD SEIFER

MELVIN ZAX

RALPH BAROCAS

STANLEY GREENSPAN

Research on the role of environmental factors in the etiology of mental disorder has been reduced in recent times by the action of a combination of scientific and political forces. The scientific forces are represented by the biologically oriented psychiatric community that has produced major successes in the treatment of serious mental illness by means of psychoactive drugs, and by proposals that such biological approaches can be extended to the explanation of etiology as well as treatment. The political forces are represented by conservative approaches to intervention in families and society that have reduced or eliminated funding for research in these areas. In the view of biological psychiatry, mental illness can be reduced to deviations in the biochemical functioning of the individual. In the view of conservative politics, mental illness can be reduced to motivational deficits within the individual. From both these perspectives, the role of experience, such as that provided by the family or the culture, is restricted to the moderation of more fundamental deviant processes.

In this chapter the role of experience will be explored not as a modera-

Research reported in this chapter was supported by grants from the United States National Institute of Mental Health and the W. T. Grant Foundation.

tor of biological organization but as a fundamental contributor to the individual's adaptive capacity. To the extent that experience is well organized and in synchrony with biological functioning, a healthy outcome will be produced. To the extent that experience is disorganized, stressful, and devoid of social supports, mental illness may be the outcome. Although individual functioning is biologically based, mental illness is a behavioral outcome. To explain behavioral outcomes, an understanding of behavioral development is required. Because there have been few demonstrations of biological determination of mental disorder, despite many hypotheses, it may be useful to examine the role of biological factors in the production of mental retardation where there is a much larger body of data involving large longitudinal studies with thousands of participants (Sameroff, 1985).

The complexity of the relationships among germs, context, and disorder is illustrated by the study of cytomegalovirus (Eisenberg, 1982). Congenital cytomegalovirus infections are found in about 1 percent of the babies born in the United States, with the highest rates in infants of low-SES (socioeconomic status) teenage mothers (Hanshaw, 1981). Of those infected, less than 5 percent are symptomatic. As a group, infants with subclinical infections had lower I.Q. scores than noninfected comparison infants, and about 10 to 20 percent of the infected group had later central nervous system deficits. These differences, however, were found only between infected *lower* SES children and their peers. When similar comparisons were made between groups of infected and noninfected *middle-class* children, no I.Q. differences were found (Hanshaw et al., 1976). For such disorders, at least two factors and probably more are involved in producing clinical symptoms. Since the combination of these factors varies in each individual, the probability that a disorder will result will vary.

When one turns directly to the study of developmental disabilities, especially mental retardation, the necessity for the consideration of nonbiological factors becomes even more apparent. Epidemiological surveys in Sweden have found a prevalence of severe mental retardation in childhood of about 3:1000, compatible with rates of severe mental retardation in the United States. On the other hand, the prevalence of mild mental retardation in Sweden is about 4:1000, eight or ten times lower than rates recorded in the United States. Susser et al. (1985) point out that these rates are related to the reduction in Sweden of cultural-familial retardation and provide evidence of the powerful impact social environment has on mental performance.

Another indication of the role of environment in mild mental retardation is the percentage of such children with detectable clinical abnormalities. In Sweden 40 percent of mildly retarded children had identifiable conditions (Hagberg et al., 1981), whereas the comparable proportion in the United States is only 10 percent. In the Collaborative Perinatal Project of the National Institute of Neurological Diseases and Stroke, the proportion of cases with mild mental retardation and detectable abnormalities was 14 percent for white children and 6 percent for blacks (Broman, 1979). Similarly, in an English study that compared rates of mild mental retardation in schools with high or low social standing, it was found that the rate for children with organic conditions was twice as high in the schools with low social standing, but the rate for mildly retarded children without clinical abnormalities was fifteen times as high (Stein and Susser, 1963).

Sameroff and Chandler (1975) proposed a "continuum of caretaking casualty" to describe the range of developmental disorders that could be attributed to the socioeconomic and familial factors that tend to overshadow the effects of early perinatal difficulties in producing emotional and intellectual problems in children. But caretaking casualty is the outcome of a number of interacting factors in the life of any particular child. To identify these factors, efforts must be directed at differentiating the effects of the many elements of experience.

The association between mental illness and poverty is well known. Hollingshead and Redlich (1958), for example, found that the prevalence rate for schizophrenia was eight times as high in the lowest socioeconomic status as in the highest. Although there are theories that explain this association by the downward drift of psychiatrically disturbed people into lower social classes, reviews of the evidence do not support this hypothesis (Kohn, 1973). On the other hand, it is also difficult to believe that poor financial and educational resources alone are the cause of mental illness.

The question we investigated was whether early emotional and social problems are associated with lower SES alone or with the accumulation of detrimental social and psychological factors that individually are found in all social class groupings. We set out to examine the relation between broad risk factors such as social class and more focused risk factors having to do with psychological, familial, and interactional variables within the family unit.

Child behavior has been typically studied using causal models in which single variables are hypothesized to uniquely determine outcomes. But a series of studies in a variety of domains have found that it is the *number* of risk factors rather than their *nature* that is the best

determinant of outcome. Studies of biological (Dawber, 1980) and behavioral (Rutter et al., 1976) disorders found that the more risk factors,
the worse the outcome, independent of the particular nature of the
variables.

In a previous report we found the intellectual functioning of a sample
of four-year-old children was highly related to a cumulative environmental risk index (Sameroff et al., 1987). The children with few risk
variables were scoring 30 points higher than children with many risk
variables. In the analyses reported here we examined whether there
would be the same relationship between the children's social-emotional
competence and the cumulative risk score.

We assumed a set of ten environmental variables that are correlates,
but not equivalents of SES. We tested a sample of four-year-old children
to see whether poor social-emotional functioning was related to the
compounding of environmental risk factors found in low-SES groups.
These variables included cognitive characteristics, attitudes, beliefs,
and values of the mother as well as stressors and supports for the family.
In addition to the variables usually associated with poverty (e.g., poor
occupational skills and lower educational achievement), we added measures of family mental health in order to assess a broader range of factors
in the child's psychological environment that might impact on later
competencies (Werner and Smith, 1982).

This report is based on data from the Rochester Longitudinal Study
(RLS), an investigation of the development of a group of children from
the prenatal period through early childhood living in a heterogeneous
set of family circumstances. Approximately half of the families originally
were selected because of maternal emotional problems. The other half
were selected to match on a number of demographic variables including
SES, race, age of mother, education of mother, and family size. (A full
report of the selection and recruitment of the families and the development of the children through two and a half years of age can be found in
Sameroff, Seifer, and Zax, 1982.)

At the four-year assessment the sample consisted of 215 families that
had been followed since the mother was pregnant with the study child.
All five of Hollingshead's (1957) SES groupings were represented. There
were 131 white families, 79 black families, and 5 Puerto Rican families.
Family size ranged from one to ten children. The mothers' ages ranged
from 15 to 40 with a mean of 24.4 at the time of the children's birth. Most
of the women were married when their child was born, but thirty-seven
were single (i.e., had never married) and seventeen were separated or
divorced at some point during the course of the study. Mothers' educa-

Table 26.1 *Variables Used for Calculating Cumulative Risk Scores for Families of Four-Year-Old Children*

Risk Variable	Low Risk	High Risk
Mental health	0–1 contact	2 or more contacts
Anxiety	75% least	25% most
Parental perspectives	75% highest	25% lowest
Interaction	75% most	25% least
Education	High school	High school not completed
Occupation	Skilled	Unskilled
Minority status	White	Nonwhite
Family support	Father present	Father absent
Life events	75% fewest	25% most
Family size	1–3 children	4 or more children

tion ranged from completion of third grade to advanced degrees. Finally, 122 of the children were boys and 93 were girls.

A set of ten risk factors was identified among the variables assessed during the four years of the RLS. Each measure was chosen based on two criteria: (1) there was a significant basis in the literature validating the variable's potential negative impact on developmental outcomes, and (2) the variable was highly reliable or there were a sufficient number of assessments of that variable during the RLS to assure reliability. These ten risk variables are listed in table 26.1.

The *mental health* rating was based on data from a local psychiatric registry and structured psychiatric interviews during the mother's pregnancy and when the child was two and a half years old. "High risk" was defined as a mother who was diagnosed as emotionally disturbed at least twice in her life. *Anxiety* was a subclinical measure of maternal mental health based on the sum of three anxiety measures. The high-risk group contained the most anxious 25 percent of the sample. The *parental perspectives* score was derived from a combination of measures that reflected rigidity or flexibility in the attitudes, beliefs, and values that a mother had in regard to her child's development. The high-risk group contained the 25 percent of the mothers with the most rigid, concrete, and authoritarian child-rearing beliefs and values. *Interaction* was a score derived from home observations of the mother and a child at four and twelve months of age. "High risk" was defined as the 25 percent of the sample that had the lowest proportion of time spent spontaneously smiling, vocalizing, and touching the infant (Sameroff et al., 1982).

Education, occupation, and *minority status* variables were obtained at the time the mother was interviewed. Although an occupation in itself is not necessarily a risk variable, to the extent that it reflects the financial resources of the family it can be considered as one. *Family support* can be conceptualized to include all the formal and informal contacts the mother has with other members of society, but for the purposes of this report the variable was simplified to indicate whether or not there was a father present in the home. Stressful *life events* were scored from several sources including social and medical histories of the families obtained when the child was two and a half and four years of age and included events such as loss of job, deaths, or physical illness of family members. The 25 percent of families with the most stressful life events were placed in the high-risk category. The last variable, *family size,* reflects the amount of competition among children for the social and physical resources of the family.

Children were tested when they were four years old. Social-emotional competence was assessed with the Rochester Adaptive Behavior Inventory (RABI), a behaviorally specific maternal interview that produces ten factor scores and a global rating of adaptive behavior (Seifer et al., 1981). The scales include items on externalizing symptoms, such as acting-out behaviors, and internalizing symptoms, such as timidity and fearfulness, in a variety of settings.

A multiple-risk score was created by summing the risks found in each family. The scores ranged from 0 to 8. The largest resulting group contained thirty-six families and the smallest, ten families.

The relation between the multiple-risk classification and the RABI global rating score is summarized graphically in figure 26.1. As the number of risk factors increases, performance decreases: the more risk factors, the worse the adaptive behavior of the child.

The data supported the view that behavioral competence scores for preschool children are multidetermined by variables in the social context, but the possibility exists that poverty may still be an overriding variable. To test for this possibility, the sample was split to determine if the same effect for multiple-risk factors would be found within different social status groups. Three SES groups were formed based on the Hollingshead (1957) scale—a high-SES white group, a low-SES white group, and a low-SES nonwhite group. There were not enough high-SES nonwhite families in our sample to compose another comparison group. Each of the SES groups was divided into families with low risk scores (0–1), families with medium risk scores (2–3) and families with high risk scores (4 or more). As can be seen in figure 26.2, the same negative

Figure 26.1. *Means of four-year-old children's* RABI *global rating for each cumulative risk score. Cumulative risk scores are totals of high-risk factors present in each child's family.*

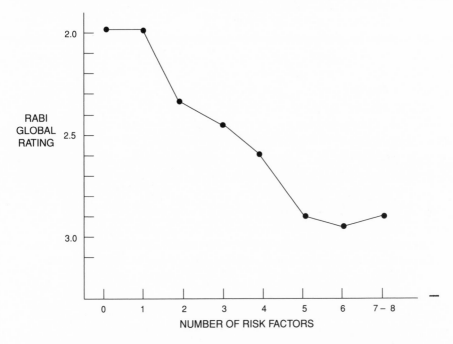

effects of multiple risks on child competence are found within different SES groups as in the total sample: the more risks, the worse the outcome.

To test the relative contribution of environmental variables and early behavioral variables of the child on the child's later performance, we created another cumulative risk score based on thirteen infant behavioral items. These were based on scores from the Research Obstetrical Scale (Sameroff et al, 1982), the Brazelton Neonatal Behavioral Assessment Scales (Brazelton, 1973), the Bayley Scales of Infant Development, and our home observations of infant behavior at four and twelve months of age.

The thirteen items were the Research Obstetrical Scale Total Score; the Brazelton cluster scores for interactive behaviors, motor behaviors, state control, and stress; the Bayley Mental Development Index at four and twelve months and the Psychomotor Development Index at four and twelve months; and home observation variables of level of activity and crying at four and twelve months of age.

The relationship between the cumulative infant risk score and the

Figure 26.2. *Means of four-year-old children's* RABI *global rating scores with high-*SES *white, low-*SES *white, and low-*SES *nonwhite groups in three cumulative risk categories: low (0 to 1 risk factors), medium (2–3 risk factors), and high (4 or more risk factors).*

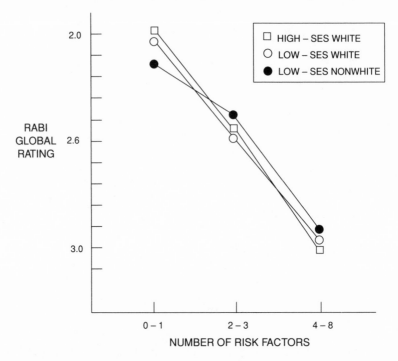

RABI global rating can be seen in figure 26.3. There is no relationship between infant low-, medium-, and high-risk scores and the outcome measure. The contrast can be seen with the environmental risk score that does have a significant relation to outcome. In a regression analysis predicting social-emotional competence scores, the infant variables only added an additional, nonsignificant, 1 percent of variance to the 20 percent of variance explained by the environmental factors.

The current study was an attempt to elaborate environmental risk factors by reducing global measures like socioeconomic status to component social and behavioral variables. We were able to identify a set of risk factors that were predominantly found in lower SES groups, but affected child outcomes in all social classes. Moreover, no single variable was determinant of outcome. Only in families with multiple risk factors was the child's intellectual competence placed in jeopardy. In the high-risk group only 2 percent had superior RABI global ratings, whereas 36

Figure 26.3. *Means of* RABI *global rating for infant and environmental risk factors in three cumulative risk categories: low (0 to 1 risk factors), medium (2–3 risk factors), and high (4 or more risk factors).*

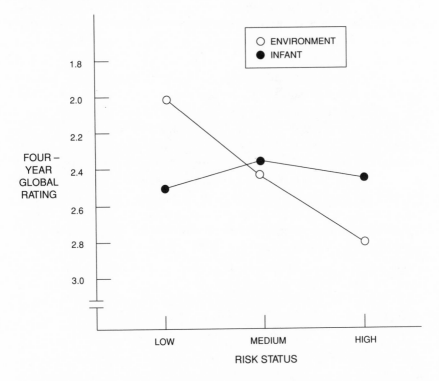

percent were rated in the poorest category. The situation was reversed in the low-risk group—26 percent were rated superior and only 5 percent were rated as poor.

The multiple pressures of environmental context in terms of amount of stress from the environment, the family's resources for coping with that stress, the number of children that must share those resources, and the parents' flexibility in understanding and dealing with their children—all play a role in the fostering or hindering of child intellectual and social competencies. We have attempted to identify some of the specific aspects of social status that have an impact on families in an effort to improve the value of environmental risk measures for predicting children's behavior. It is clear from our comparison of the relative effects of infant behavioral variables and environmental variables that prevention, intervention, and treatment may more fruitfully be devoted to changing the social and family situation of the child than to changing the child himself.

How best to change the social and family context of development requires a further understanding of how these contexts are organized. Sameroff (1985) has hypothesized an organization of behavioral experience encoded in an "environtype" analogous to the "genotype" that encodes biological experience. The environtype is composed of cultural and family codes that in normative situations transmit the values and mores of the cultural context to the developing child through regulations of experience. Social controls and social supports are institutionalized in the form of legal and educational systems. Within the family, interactions are regulated by belief systems and the capacity of the parents to integrate their own values and needs into effective child-rearing behavior. It is the disorganization of this regulatory system that produces behavioral problems in development, just as disorganization of the biological regulatory system produces biological problems. Our ability to influence development will be ultimately limited by our ability to understand these systems of regulation. Where the environment is well organized, the effects of biological trauma, such as birth complications, are reduced by good care giving. Where the environment is disorganized and characterized by multiple family and social risk factors, even children with the healthiest beginnings will have major emotional and cognitive problems during early childhood.

REFERENCES

Brazelton, T. B. (1973). *Neonatal Behavioral Assessment Scale*. London: Heinemann.
Broman, S. H. (1979). "Perinatal Anoxia and Cognitive Development in Early Childhood." In T. M. Field, ed., *Infants Born at Risk*. New York: Spectrum.
Dawber, T. R. (1980). *The Framingham Study: The Epidemiology of Atherosclerotic Disease*. Cambridge, Mass.: Harvard University Press.
Eisenberg, L. (1982). "Overview." In D. L. Parron and L. Eisenberg, eds., *Infants at Risk for Developmental Dysfunction: Health and Behavior, a Research Agenda*. Interim Report no. 4, Institute of Medicine. Washington, D.C.: National Academy Press.
Gollin, E. S. (1981). "Development and Plasticity." In E. S. Gollin, ed., *Developmental Plasticity*. New York: Academic Press.
Hagberg, B.; Hagberg, G.; Lewerth, A. and Lindberg, U. (1981). "Mild

Mental Retardation in Swedish School Children. II. Etiologic and Pathogenetic Aspects." *Acta Paediatrica Scandinavica* 70:445–452.

Hanshaw, J. (1981). "Cytomegalovirus Infections." *Pediatrics in Review* 2(8):245–251.

Hanshaw, J.; Scheiner, A.; Moxley, A.; Gaev, L.; Abel, V.; and Scheiner, B. (1976). "School Failure and Deafness after 'Silent' Congenital Cytomegalovirus Infection." *New England Journal of Medicine* 295:468–470.

Hollingshead, A. B. (1957). "Two-Factor Index of Social Position." New Haven, Conn.: Yale University, Sociology Department, mimeograph (available from the author).

Hollingshead, A. B., and Redlich, F. C. (1958). *Social Class and Mental Illness: A Community Study.* New York: Wiley.

Kohn, M. L. (1973). "Social Class and Schizophrenia: A Critical Review and Reformulation." *Schizophrenia Bulletin,* no. 7:60–79.

Rutter, M.; Tizard, J.; Yule, W.; Graham, P.; and Whitmore, K. (1976). "Research Report: Isle of Wight Studies, 1964–1974." *Psychological Medicine* 6:313–332.

Sameroff, A. J. (1985). "Primary Prevention and Psychological Disorders: A Contradiction in Terms 1." Paper presented at the annual meeting of the American Psychological Association, Los Angeles.

Sameroff, A. J., and Chandler, M. J. (1975). "Reproductive Risk and the Continuum of Caretaking Casualty." In F. D. Horowitz, S. Hetherington, S. Scarr-Salapatek, and G. Siegel, eds., *Review of Child Development Research.* Vol. 4. Chicago: University of Chicago, 187–244.

Sameroff, A. J.; Seifer, R.; Barocas, R.; Zax, M.; and Greenspan, S. (1987). "IQ Scores of 4-Year-Old Children: Social-Environmental Risk Factors." *Pediatrics* 79(3):343–350.

Sameroff, A. J., Seifer, R., and Elias, P. K. (1982). "Sociocultural Variability in Infant Temperament Ratings." *Child Development* 53:164–173.

Sameroff, A. J., Seifer, R., and Zax, M. (1982). "Early Development of Children at Risk for Emotional Disorder." *Monographs of the Society for Research in Child Development* 47(7, Serial no. 199).

Scott, K. G., and Carran, D. T. (In press). "Prevention of Mental Retardation." *American Psychologist.*

Seifer, R., Sameroff, A. J., and Jones, F. (1981). "Adaptive Behavior in Young Children of Emotionally Disturbed Women." *Journal of Applied Developmental Psychology* 1:251–276.

Stein, Z. A., and Susser, M. (1963). "The Social Distribution of Mental Retardation." *American Journal of Mental Deficiency* 67:811–821.

Susser, M.; Hauser, W. A.; Kiely, J. L.; Paneth, N.; and Stein, Z. (1985). "Quantitative Estimates of Prenatal and Perinatal Risk Factors for Perinatal Mortality, Cerebral Palsy, Mental Retardation and Epilepsy." In J. M. Freeman, ed., *Prenatal and Perinatal Factors Associated with Brain*

Disorders. Washington, D.C.: National Institutes of Health Publication no. 85-1149.

Werner, E. E., and Smith, R. S. (1982). *Vulnerable but Invincible: A Longitudinal Study of Resilient Children and Youth*. New York: McGraw-Hill.

27

A Psychoanalytic Approach to Psychotic Disturbances in Very Young Children

ELEANOR GALENSON

Two major themes dominate the literature of childhood psychosis: (1) the question of whether psychosis that occurs in children below three or four years of age—early onset psychosis—is the same psychological entity as psychosis with onset in later childhood and adolescence, and (2) the question of etiology. Current opinion favors the view that early onset psychosis is a pathological process that is different from the later form (Rutter, 1972; DeMeyer et al., 1973; Szurek and Berlin, 1973).

Furthermore, in this otherwise contradictory body of literature, the ratio of boys to girls in early onset psychosis is consistently about four boys to one girl, with a gradual increase in incidence of psychosis in girls as they get older.

Genetic data and studies implicating brain dysfunction as well as disorders of perceptual and sensorimotor integration are inconclusive and contradictory, and there remains the problem of whether the aberrant parameters are primary or secondary to the disease process itself (Wing and Wing, 1971; DeMeyer et al., 1973; Mykelbust et al., 1972; Ornitz and Ritvo, 1976; Call, 1983). Evidence for primary central nervous system abnormality in childhood schizophrenia is the report of excessive prenatal at-risk factors (e.g., Bender and Faretta, 1973), but the presence of neurological "soft" or "hard" signs (DeMeyer et al., 1973, and others) has not been confirmed by others (e.g., Bomberg et al., 1973). Some workers found abnormal EEG patterns in psychotic children (DeMeyer et al., 1973), whereas others did not (Treffert, 1970).

In regard to environmental rather than constitutional etiological factors, there is general agreement that in those children who become schizophrenic later in childhood, parent-child relationships do show typical disturbances. But these same constellations occur in families with nonpsychotic children as well.

In regard to early onset psychosis, psychoanalytically oriented studies that utilize intensive and reconstructive evaluations report a profoundly conflictual parent-child relationship (Mahler, 1968; Mahler, Pine, and Bergman, 1975; Ruttenberg et al., 1983; Bettelheim, 1967), but none of these workers excludes the possibility that certain predisposing factors may render the child more vulnerable.

Several normal developmental studies suggest there is a reciprocal interdependence between genetic and environmental factors, with certain critical factors at particularly critical periods of life playing a decisive role (Emde and Sorce, 1983; Sander, 1983; Stern, 1971, 1983; Massie, 1977; Massie and Campbell, 1983; Ruttenberg et al., 1983).

PSYCHOANALYTICALLY ORIENTED TREATMENT

The Theoretical and Conceptual Basis

Evidence from infant research and the less than encouraging therapeutic results in older children with serious psychological disturbances point to the advisability of very early diagnosis and intervention, no matter what nosological or etiological factors may be implicated. Mahler proposed that childhood psychosis begins during the first year of life, in connection with the infant's failure to experience regular and predictable gratification of his affect hunger. Within a remarkably short time, the normal infant becomes able to localize some sensations within his body boundaries, and by the end of the first year, the baby is investigating his own body as well as his mother's and making comparisons. This awareness of his body has major implications for his successful passage through the separation-individuation process and his eventual development of social relations and an autonomous ego. The average mother facilitates this process almost entirely unconsciously, by her emotional investment of her infant's body, his varied states, his emotional responsiveness.

Our treatment methods of these young children were based upon (and guided) our data concerning normative mother-child interactions as they were accumulated during an eleven-year direct-observational research study (Galenson, 1971, 1979; Galenson and Roiphe, 1976a, 1976b; Roiphe, 1968, 1973; Roiphe and Galenson, 1972, 1973a, 1975), as well as those landmarks established by Mahler and her colleagues

(Mahler, 1963, 1968; Mahler and Furer, 1972; Mahler and Gosliner, 1955; Mahler, Pine, and Bergman, 1975) in their separation-individuation research.

By the time even the youngest of the psychotic children to be described was referred to us, a mutually destructive interaction between mother and child had already been established, and the rest of the family was seriously affected by the presence of the psychotic child. We assumed that the parents of these seriously disturbed children were disturbed themselves to some degree, so that our treatment design required flexibility in order to adapt to the needs of each family. Furthermore, we were prepared to find deviations in all areas of development in the children, even in the five psychotic children who were not yet two years old at the time of their initial referral.

Developmental disturbances during this early period are rarely brought to the attention of the psychiatrist, particularly since emotional disturbances during the first and second years are frequently manifested as disordered physiological functioning and somatic problems. The pediatrician, however, is rarely in a position to appreciate the nature of the infant's psychopathology, since the stressful atmosphere of the pediatric examining room does not provide an opportunity for the detection of such early deviations as an unusual lack of vocalization, an inert baby, or one with unusually intense stranger or separation anxiety.

By the second year of life, however, behavioral disturbances indicating developmental deviations are often gross enough to alarm parents and pediatricians alike. The second year is crucial in regard to the infant's capacity to begin to function separately from the mother in regard to psychosexual advance, through the anal, urethral and early genital phases, and the emergence of such ego capacities as the symbolic function in its many aspects. This very rapid pace of development increases the infant's vulnerability to disturbances in development.

The mutual influences of psychosexual, object relations, and ego development have been of particular interest in our treatment of disturbed infants and their parents. The landmarks indicating progressive development in these three areas have been reported in the data from our own research and in Mahler's studies. We have reported on the emergence of anal, urinary, and genital behavior indicating psychological schematization, as well as various aspects of symbolic functioning during the second year of life. Certain behaviors appeared directly connected with oral, anal, and genital zonal experiences, whereas some were more distantly connected with and influenced by these zonal experiences. Thus, direct anal zone behavior included exploration of the anal area and the stool and signals of the child's awareness of defecation by his tugging at his soiled diaper, hiding during defecation, resisting soiled diaper changes, and naming the stool itself. Anal derivative behavior, in contrast, included interest in the toilet and toilet area, and in the toileting and diapering of others, crouching in enclosures, hiding or collecting and piling objects, and using toys that have a structural resemblance to the anal function (Galenson, 1971). Similar sequences have been identified in connection with the urinary and genital zones, as well as in our seventy research subjects.

Although libidinal development has been delineated fairly clearly, the situation in regard to the normal development of aggression has been difficult to outline. Anna Freud (1972) pointed to the fusion of aggression with libido during infancy, an interrelationship that leads to the "borrowing of various tools for aggressive discharge"—the teeth for biting, excrement for dirtying and polluting, the penis for aggressive display.

Treatment Method

The therapeutic nursery was housed in a large room furnished with toys, chairs, and tables appropriate for infants and toddlers and comfortable seats for the mothers. A bathroom and kitchen communicating directly with the main room were important adjunctive therapeutic areas.

Each therapeutic group consisted of eight children, mostly below three years of age, along with their mothers. They attended three two-hour sessions each week for at least two years, and many continued treatment for three years or longer. The mothers participated in a mothers' group at one end of the room twice a week for one hour. At other times, the mothers were drawn into the therapeutic work with their child and on occasion were asked to leave the nursery briefly if the child was thought to be ready for a brief separation experience. Fathers were rarely able to participate. A particular staff member was assigned to each family, and the parents were seen by this staff member in an individual session at least once a week as well.

Our treatment design, although flexible, was based upon these principles: (1) the parents, particularly the mothers, were already an integral part of the pathological situation, no matter what the etiology, and therefore required treatment themselves, along with their children; (2) maternal identification with the therapist and his or her therapeutic attitudes could be accomplished most effectively through nonverbal channels, particularly in relation to the early developmental phase of the children; (3) since therapeutic work at this relatively primitive level of largely nonverbal communication with the infant strains the resources of even the most experienced staff, constant support and refueling of the staff was necessary to prevent burnout; and (4) planning for long-term treatment was essential, if the therapeutic gains were to be consolidated. When children were ready for it, some began individual treatment in our Outpatient Child Psychiatry Clinic while they attended a modified school situation until ready for regular school classes.

Clinical Aspects

Twenty-nine children were seen in all over a six-year period; eighteen were boys and eleven girls. At the time of initial referral, nine were under two years of age, eight were between two and two and a half years, eleven were between two and a half and three and a half years, and one was five and a half years old.

The psychotic group. Of the nineteen children who remained in treatment beyond one year, ten were diagnosed as psychotic and all these were boys. Their diagnosis could be established rather easily at the initial interview—even in the youngest, who was fifteen and a half months old—on the basis of their characteristic visual aversion and their deviant social interactions, indicating various degrees of decathexis of the human environment. The initial parental complaint in nearly all instances was deviant speech development. Three boys under two years of age were excessively quiet and showed visual avoidance, head banging, and preference for inanimate objects.

Every mother in this group showed serious deviance in her relationship with her psychotic child by the time the family was referred to us. In several instances, it could be established that the mother had indeed avoided certain close contacts with her child, dating from the child's earliest months, although this information came from other sources, such as home movies, rather than from the mother herself. Furthermore, there was a history of serious maternal depression during the first year of several of our psychotic infants.

Some of the deviant infants had not been able to establish even a partially gratifying symbiotic relationship with the mother, whereas others had achieved this but had failed to move beyond it. This distortion of the separation-individuation process had given rise to a proliferation of defensive reactions, including the use of extensive denial, displacement, condensation, and perceptual dedifferentiation in which the inanimate was animated and the human dehumanized. Their ego development, including use of the symbolic function; reality testing; time, place, and person orientation; secondary process thinking; and visual, auditory, and tactile perception were all seriously compromised.

The progression of drive development in these deviant children was also disordered in that phasic primacy, with an orderly sequential progression from one instinctual phase to another, did not take place. Intense hostile aggressive impulses tended to be discharged through somatic routes on the child's own body or might find random expression toward the outside world rather than in focused aggressive acts directed at others or in phase-appropriate motor or other types of activity.

In short, the disturbance of early childhood psychosis appeared to involve failure in adequate differentiation of self from object and inadequate drive differentiation, with a predominance of aggressive impulses, which were then body bound or indiscriminately discharged. All ten psychotic children showed many behaviors that expressed drive impulses from all levels of psychosexual development simultaneously, such as excessive sucking, indiscriminate defecation and urination, and excessive genital handling.

In regard to object relations, their sexuality was autoerotic and there was no evidence of object-related fantasy life (Nagera, 1964) at an age when such fantasy has normally emerged. Self-object differentiation was delayed and not only in its libidinal but in its aggressive expression as well, and neither aggression nor affection was object-directed. Bodily pain was hardly noticed or reacted to, and the mother had not yet emerged as a special person for these children, indicating a disturbance in the progressive emergence of mental representation of both self and others.

Although none of the children was testable according to standard testing requirements, it was possible, by our utilizing many brief sessions, to obtain a baseline of performance. Secondary process development was markedly delayed in all, but there was beginning structuralization in some sectors of the seven older children: (1) a kind of categorization activity, such as piling inanimate objects according to some shared attribute (all crayons, all books, etc.); (2) a definition of objects by their use (e.g., running a car along a table, opening a book); and (3) early representational play with dolls before words were available.

Motoric development was intact in all but the three youngest boys, but there was often a lack of vigor and periods of deterioration in both gross and fine coordination.

In regard to perception, all the psychotic children avoided visual eye-to-eye encounter and tended to screen out the human voice to such a degree that almost all had been suspected of deafness. As the children improved in their human relatedness, visual and auditory perception improved also, and these sensory modalities were now utilized in the service of increasing self-object differentiation. Then the child began to make contact with the mother for the first time through the distance receptors of visual or auditory contact, rather than the more primitive tactile kinesthetic modes.

In regard to the development of the symbolic function, several children had developed what appeared to be transitional objects; however, these were not used for self-comforting but to achieve complete autistic withdrawal; and had become the sole object of their libidinal attachment, rather than a partial substitute for the mother. Some had become attached to a piece of string, a telephone book, a favorite recording, or television, the so-called psychotic fetish, which appeared to serve for screening out the animate world. They were clutched in desperation rather than being used either "playfully" or creatively. There was little if any derivative behavior noted in normal infants during their second year. We regard this derivative behavior, or play, as a fundamental foundation for the developing symbolic function and therefore a necessary precursor of language development. The autistic children showed no interest in picture books and exhibited little if any creative language; some were entirely echolalic. (In most, there had been a history of excessive quietness during their early months of life, with little babbling thereafter, and the few words that did emerge during the second year had disappeared after a short while.)

Treatment of the psychotic group. Our approach was modeled after that of Mahler's (1968), utilizing the mother as part of the therapeutic team. We, however, worked within the setting of a group where each psychotic child had his own therapist but could join with the other children whenever he was ready for such contact. We fondled, held, rocked, and fed the child, using the tactile, kinesthetic, and oral routes primarily, along with some verbal interpretation. The mother was similarly fed and catered to and gently and gradually involved in interaction with her child. Ours was a relatively structured environment—predictable, too—which was essential for treatment of these children, since they tend to disorganize under the impact of any intense or unpredictable stimuli. An illustration of a successful treatment follows.

Although the early history in the case to be described was scanty, the affective climate for potential disruption in the mother-child pair was established well before the baby's birth. The child was conceived in the setting of a pathological relationship between the parents; the father wanted a child and the mother acceded. Hence the child was a specific gift for the father and a priori an object viewed at the very least with ambivalence by the mother.

During his first two months B. was breast-fed and was carried in a body-sling by his mother for many hours at a time as she went about her housework. Both nursing and this prolonged and intense body contact were abruptly terminated when he was eight months old. About this, the mother stated simply, "He turned me off; I turned him off." Thenceforth his bottles were propped and he was left in his crib for hours on end. The mother became pregnant again when B. was five months old, a baby for herself this time. B. responded to his mother's further withdrawal into her new pregnancy by head banging and shrieking for prolonged periods as he lay in his crib, and then he began to show precocious development in the motor area. At seven and a half months, he sat without support, and at eight months he began walking without having crawled first. At eight and a half months, B. was suddenly removed from the parental bedroom and was hit by his father for his screeching on many occasions. He became mute and his head banging increased in duration and intensity. The birth of his sister when he was thirteen months old, his father's subsequent two-week absence from home, and four days spent at his grandparents' home (and with no preparation for any of these events) precipitated such a severe regression in B. that he was brought for treatment to our therapeutic nursery at his pediatrician's insistence.

At fifteen months, B. was a devastated child with severe disturbance in almost all areas of his development. The head banging, lack of speech development, avoidance of the mother and other human contact, screeching, fleeting eye contact, indifference to beatings and other pain, rejection of solid foods, and a serious sleep disturbance all attested to the seriousness of the regression.

Shortly after treatment was initiated, the head banging ceased, but at the end of one year of treatment, B. (now aged twenty-six months) remained poorly related and essentially mute. At home, the eating and sleeping disturbances continued unabated; his play in the nursery was diffuse and impoverished, and his sole attachment was to a red fire engine that produced a whirring noise when it was rolled.

On his first psychological test, B. at age twenty-four months achieved a score of 80, corresponding to the lowest end of the normal range.

During his second year of treatment, as a new therapist slowly began to develop a therapeutic relationship with B., his mother's depression deepened because of circumstances in her own life. Her attendance at the nursery dropped precipitously, but contact was maintained through a series of lengthy telephone calls, and finally a home visit was made in which a new type of therapeutic contract was drawn up. B.'s father agreed to bring B. to our nursery sessions himself and to work directly with the therapist and the child. The mother similarly agreed to assume a more active role and was to be drawn into the work whenever an appropriate opportunity presented itself. Thus both parents became an integral part of the therapeutic work with B. for the first time in what was to be a crucial turning point for treatment.

The family's attendance at the nursery improved dramatically. The therapist's prior work over many months, providing B. with a stable person for attachment, now began to take hold, and the constrictions that had marked his previous behavior began to dissipate. Anal and urethral concerns, developmental themes appropriate to the second year of life, along with their derivative play behaviors, emerged at age thirty-two months. B.'s play behavior slowly became more focused and was increasingly characterized by a marked increase in object-directed aggression. Simultaneously B. became attached to his first transitional object. This flowering expression of aggression and libidinal behavior was accompanied by the development of semisymbolic doll play that coalesced around themes of eating, sleeping, and bathing. At age thirty-four months, B. began to use three-word sentences and could utilize this new capacity to verbalize his feelings toward his parents and his therapist.

In retrospect, it was apparent that the initial period of treatment between fifteen and twenty-five months of age had permitted B. to express toward the outside world some of the rage he had formerly turned against himself. As the aggression emerged, at first diffusely and then in a focused object-related manner, his impaired ego functions began to improve, culminating in the beginning of communicative speech and the advent of symbolic play. With the beginning collaboration of his parents, however, his improvement in all areas was startling. These gains were confirmed by the findings on the psychological testing done at the end of his second year of treatment when he was three years old: he obtained an I.Q. score in the high average range, an increase of 30 points within the year. Although some evidence of his former pathology remained, the overall clinical picture resembled that of a neurotic rather than a psychotic illness.

When B. was thirty-seven months old, the family moved from our area, and he was treated thereafter by a particularly empathic speech therapist who continued to provide him with a special one-to-one relationship.

The family returned for follow-up when B. was almost four years old. He was attached to his speech therapist and had utilized the normal nursery, which he now attended quite appropriately. He was well related, and he clearly remembered and responded to important people appropriately and to playthings in the nursery. The harsh barklike quality that had characterized his speech had faded, and he now spoke fluently, albeit with some mild stammering and stuttering. The quality of the mother-child interaction was strikingly improved in that the mother appeared to derive great pleasure from her newly acquired ability to recognize and respond to B.'s needs. The brief psychological testing during the follow-up visit showed that B. had maintained the gains achieved during the previous year. There had been major strides in his symbolic play and language, and the traces of his former ego deviance were minimal.

This was a highly successful outcome, in contrast to several other children whose improvement was slow and far less dramatic. It demonstrated that this illness can be dramatically modified, particularly if treatment begins early enough and if the parents are involved in the treatment process.

Treatment results. Our data derived from the entire psychotic group indicate that the prognosis is enormously enhanced if the child is below three years of age on admission and if the mother is included from the very start, not only as part of our therapeutic team approach but also in individual treatment. With her participation, although it was a long struggle, the outlook was far more favorable. The nursery setting was appropriate for the treatment of psychotic children, provided that each child was assigned to an individual therapist as well as participating in the group and that there were no more than three psychotic children in the total group of eight children at any one time.

DISCUSSION

The vital importance of the early coenesthetic experience during the first six months of life has long been stressed by Spitz (1945), Mahler (1963, 1968), and others as providing the basis for the establishment of a core sense of self. This probably must be available during a certain critical period if normal development is to proceed at all.

Beginning at about five or six months, the visual-motor apparatus gradually takes over, providing the principal modality for self-object differentiation. Apparently this can occur only when this core body-self has been integrated. Without this, sequential psychosexual organization, progressive self-object differentiation, and adequate ego development, particularly in regard to the symbolic function, do not take place.

We are increasingly impressed by the need to maintain a sufficient maternal libidinal investment rather than the excessively strong libidinal and aggressive tie by which some mothers bind themselves to their children in a crippling, disharmonious union.

Several mothers of our psychotic children, for reasons of their own pathology or the pathology within their children, were unable to engage them in a strong enough libidinal tie, whereas others encouraged an overly close symbiotic tie from which the child could not emerge. This interfered with the normal emergence of oral, anal, and genital phase dominance and drive modulation. Inadequate self-object differentiation and delay in ego functioning, particularly in regard to the development of secondary process thinking and the autonomous functioning of visual perception, completed the psychopathological picture.

REFERENCES

Bender, L., and Faretta, G. (1973). "The Relationship between Childhood Schizophrenia and Adult Schizophrenia." In *Genetic Factors in Schizophrenia,* ed. A. Kaplan and H. Morton. Springfield, Ill.: Charles C. Thomas.

Bettleheim, B. (1967). *The Empty Fortress.* New York: Free Press.

Bomberg, D., Szurek, S., and Etemad, J. (1973). "A Statistical Study of a Group of Psychotic Children." In *Clinical Studies in Childhood Psychoses,* ed. S. Szurek and I. Berlin. New York: Brunner/Mazel.

Call, J. D. (1983). "Toward a Nosology of Psychiatric Disorders in Infancy." In *Frontiers of Infant Psychiatry,* ed. J. D. Call, E. Galenson, and R. L. Tyson. New York: Basic Books, 117–28.

DeMeyer, M.; Norton, J.; Allen, J.; Steel, R.; and Brown, S. (1973). "Prognosis in Autism." *J. Autism Child. Schiz.* 3(3):199.

Emde, R. N., and Sorce, J. F. (1983). "The Rewards of Infancy: Emotional Availability and Maternal Referencing." In *Frontiers of Infant Psychiatry,* ed. J. D. Call, E. Galenson, and R. L. Tyson. New York: Basic Books, 17–30.

Frank, G. (1965). "The Role of the Family in the Development of Psychopathology." *Psychol. Bull.* 64:191.

Franknoi, J., and Ruttenberg, B. (1971). "Formulation of the Dynamic Factors Underlying Infantile Autism." *J. Amer. Acad. Child Psychiat.* 10:713.

Freud, A. (1972). "Comments on Aggression." *Internat. J. Psycho-Anal.*
    53(Pt. 2):163–71.
Furer, M. (1964). "The Development of a Preschool Symbiotic Psychotic Boy."
    Psychoanal. Study Child 29:448–69.
Galenson, E. (1971). "A Consideration of the Nature of Thought in Childhood
    Play." In *Separation-Individuation: Essays in Honor of Margaret S.
    Mahler*, ed. J. B. McDevitt and C. F. Settlage. New York: International
    Universities Press, 41–59.
——— (1976). "The Preodipal Development of the Boy." *J. Amer. Psychoanal.*
    29:805.
——— (1979). "Development of Sexual Identity: Discoveries and
    Implications." In T. B. Karasu and C. W. Socarides, eds., *On sexuality:
    Psychoanalytic Observations*. New York: International Universities Press,
    1–17.
Galenson, E., and Roiphe, H. (1976a). "Impact of Early Sexual Discovery on
    Mood, Defensive Organization and Symbolization." *Psychoanal. Study
    Child* 26:195–216.
——— (1976b). "Some Suggested Revisions concerning Early Female
    Development." In *Female Psychology,* ed. H. P. Blum. *J. Am. Psychoanal.
    Assn.* (suppl.), no. 5:24:29–57.
Mahler, M. S. (1963). "Thoughts about Development and Individuation."
    Psychoanal. Study of Child 18:307–342.
——— (1968). *On Human Symbiosis and the Vicissitudes of Individuation.*
    New York: International Universities Press.
Mahler, M. S., and Furer, M. (1972). "Child Psychosis: A Theoretical
    Statement of Its Implications." *J. Autism Child. Schiz.* 2(3):213.
Mahler, M. S., and Gosliner, B. J. (1955). "On Symbiotic Child Psychosis:
    Genetic, Dynamic, and Restitutive Aspects." *Psychoanal. Study Child*
    10:195–212.
Mahler, M. S., Pine, F., and Bergman, A. (1975). *The Psychological Birth of
    the Human Infant*. New York: Basic Books.
Massie, H. (1977). "Patterns of Mother-Infant Behavior and Subsequent
    Childhood Psychosis." *Child Psychiat. and Human Dev.* 7:211–230.
Massie, H., and Campbell, B. K. (1983). "The Massie-Campbell Scale of
    Mother-Infant Attachment Indicators during Stress (AIDS Scale)." In
    Frontiers in Infant Psychiatry, ed. J. C. Call, E. Galenson, and R. L.
    Tyson. New York: Basic Books, 394–412.
Mykelburst, H., Killen, J., and Bannochie, M. (1972). "Emotional
    Characteristics of Learning Disability." *J. Autism Child. Schiz.* 2(2):151.
Nagera, H. (1964). "On Arrest in Development, Fixation and Regression."
    Psychoanal. Study Child 19:222–239.
Ornitz, E., and Ritvo, S. (1976). "The Syndrome of Autism." *Amer. J.
    Psychiat.* 135:1371–74.
Pollin, W.; Stabenau, J.; Mosher, L.; and Tupin, J. (1966). "Life History

Differences in Identical Twins Discordant for Schizophrenia." *Am. J. Orthopsychiat.* 36:492.

Rimland, B. (1964). *Infantile Autism.* New York: Appleton-Century-Crofts.

Roiphe, H. (1968). "On an Early Genital Phase." *Psychoanal. Study Child* 23:348–65.

——— (1973). "Some Thoughts on Childhood Psychosis, Self and Object." *Psychoanal. Study Child* 28:131–45.

Roiphe, H., and Galenson, E. (1972). "Early Genital Activity and the Castration Complex." *Psychoanal. Q.* 41:334–47.

——— (1973a). "The Infantile Fetish." *Psychoanal. Study Child* 28:147–66.

——— (1973b). "Object Loss and Early Sexual Development." *Psychoanal. Q.* 42(1):73–90.

——— (1975). "Some Observations on the Transitional Object and Infantile Fetish." *Psychoanal. Q.* 44:206–31.

Ruttenberg, B.; Kalish, B. I.; Fiese, B. H.; and D'Orazio, A. (1983). "Early Infant Assessment Using the Behavior Rating Instrument for Autistic and Atypical Children (BRIAAC)." In *Frontiers of Infant Psychiatry,* ed. J. D. Call, E. Galenson, and R. L. Tyson. New York: Basic Books, 413–24.

Rutter, M. (1967). "Psychotic Disorders in Early Childhood." *Brit. J. Psychiat.* 110:133.

——— (1972). "Childhood Schizophrenia Reconsidered." *J. Autism Child. Schiz.* 2(4):315.

Sander, L. W. (1983). "Polarity, Paradox and the Organizing Process in Development." In *Frontiers of Infant Psychiatry,* ed. J. D. Call, E. Galenson, and R. L. Tyson. New York: Basic Books, 333–46.

Spitz, R. A. (1945). "Diacritic and Coanesthetic Organization: The Psychiatric Significance of a Functional Division of the Nervous System into a Sensory and Emotive Part." *Psychoanal. Rev.* 32:146–62.

Stern, D. (1971). "A Microanalysis of Mother-Infant Interaction." *J. Amer. Acad. Child Psychiat.* 10:501.

——— (1973). "Mother and Infant at Play: The Dyadic Interaction Involving Facial, Vocal and Gaze Behaviors." In *The Origins of Behavior,* ed. M. Lewis and L. Rosenblum. Vol. 1. New York: Wiley.

——— (1983). "Early Transmission of Affect: Some Research Issues." In *Frontiers of Infant Psychiatry,* ed. J. D. Call, E. Galenson, and R. L. Tyson. New York: Basic Books, 117–28.

Szurek, S., and Berlin, I. (1973). *Clinical Studies in Childhood Psychosis.* New York: Brunner/Mazel.

Treffert, D. A. (1970). "Epidemiology of Infantile Autism." *Arch. Gen. Psychiat.* (Chicago) 22:431.

Wing, L., and Wing, J. (1971). "Multiple Impairments in Early Childhood Autism." *J. Autism Child. Schiz.* 1(3):311.

28

Psychotic States in Adolescents

FRANÇOIS LADAME

With the exception of the childhood psychoses, which are a very special group, the symptomatic psychoses emerge only from adolescence on. The psychotic disorders can be transient or chronic; they can be an isolated incident in the patient's history or be followed by further decompensations later on. In the worst event, they will, over the years, increasingly come to resemble the classic descriptions of schizophrenia. This observation can be a rallying point for all those who practice adolescent psychiatry, whatever their individual theoretical standpoints. It does, however, leave completely open the question of the origin of the connection between psychotic states accompanied by delusions, hallucinations, or mental confusion, on the one hand, and the evolution of the adolescent personality, on the other.

The first part of this chapter deals with the clinical aspect. Five psychotic patients are presented, differing in their manifestations, their degree of severity, and their evolution; they were observed among adolescents in the Geneva Adolescent Psychiatry Unit. The periods of follow-up from these acute decompensations vary from a few months to several years. The second part of the chapter describes how psychoanalytic theory can help make sense out of the elements that constantly recur in the onset of these symptomatic psychoses and give them a certain coherence beyond their clinical and prognostic diversity.

I should like to thank my coworkers for the observations on patients whom I did not treat personally.

First Observation: Elisabeth

An emergency consultation was requested by the family because of Elisabeth's delusions of persecution. Aged sixteen, she felt spied upon at school. She was convinced that a new teacher had been taken on as a psychologist and that her friend J. was in the pay of the teachers to watch her and report everything back to the psychologist. At home, she thought a neighbor was doing the same thing, and outside in the street or on the bus, she felt she was being observed and would return home to hide as quickly as she could.

A combination of circumstances was associated with the psychotic decompensation. Some weeks earlier she had fallen in love with an actor whom she met at a dance hall she went to frequently, but he quickly made it clear that he was not the man for her. During the same period her sister-in-law gave birth to her first child. Following a performance in which the young man of her choice played the major role, Elisabeth fell into a catatonic state and was eventually taken home by her classmates and teacher. From then on, delusions set in, although they were apparently quickly suppressed by a few milligrams of neuroleptics prescribed by a doctor friend of the family—without his actually seeing the patient.

Elisabeth seemed to be in a fit state to go on holiday with her family to Haiti, and there she had her first sexual experience, with a black. She later said, "I made love to get closer to my father." The following morning a neighbor suffered an acute attack of malaria, which she confused with an epileptic seizure—the grand mal—in the same way as some Nivaquine pills, prescribed as a preventive measure, and Nozinan capsules, taken along for no particular reason, were confused in her mind. The girl returned to Europe in a dreadful state, and the delusions flared up again—outside the same theater where the same inaccessible actor was still playing in the cast.

The story seemed almost too perfect—in the reconstructed form presented above, at least. Yet the key was in fact provided by the patient herself during the second session with her therapist. She asked, "Can I show you something?" and without waiting for an answer, she lowered her pants and her briefs to show the string of a tampon. Her face lit up, she adjusted her clothes immediately, and, probably relieved to have been able to denounce the corpus delicti—her adult woman's body—in such unambiguous terms, she lay down on the couch.

After that Elisabeth came for treatment regularly four times a week.

The clinical symptoms disappeared and a start was made on the essential work, focused on the disruptive effect of puberty, the renewal of instinctual activity (eroticism and destructiveness together), and the search for an object. But we shall come back to this later.

Second Observation: Michel

This seventeen-year-old was also seen as an emergency, at the request of his parents, for a state of panic that had been going on for two weeks or so. He stopped work supposedly because of pain in the knee and hardly dared to go out of the house. He had not been feeling well for almost three months, but had considerably deteriorated within the previous two weeks. Clinically, the main problem was anxious bewilderment, with intense suffering and distracted clutching to the object, but there was also intermittent discordance. Michel had the impression of being gradually invaded by insanity. He could no longer control where he looked, so that he was unable to stop his eyes resting either on specific parts of other people's anatomy (e.g., breasts, penis, buttocks), which he would look at without seeing, or on an area around the other person, in whose body there seemed to be "black holes."

The history in this case is another that many therapists will have come across. It took place in two stages, starting three years earlier when he was seduced by a homosexual football coach. He had a sexual relationship with this man for six months, which he never spoke about and which he eventually decided to break off. After that he never thought any more about it.

Then came the second phase, which began three months before his beginning treatment, when a friend of his made references to Michel's homosexuality "in front of everybody." The young man could not bear to face this past experience he was so abruptly confronted with, and psychotic decompensation ensued. His condition became worse; he shut himself up in his room, refused to eat, and convinced himself that "everybody would be talking about it."

Michel's parents later revealed that a few weeks before the consultation their son had come home in tears with a broken nose. They found out that he had gone to the house of the said friend with the intention of beating him up and had come face to face with an Arab who had given him a violent head-butt. When Michel told them what had happened three years earlier, they insisted that he should forget it all and not speak about it again.

This case seems to illustrate a number of points. It shows the difference between repression and suppression, which is a distinction fundamental to the subject in hand. Here, repression—a banishment into the unconscious, where continued silent psychic activity sends out offshoots enabling it to feed through to the conscious mind—was not put into operation. Michel never thought any more about it and then found himself abruptly confronted with an experience he had neither elaborated nor even repressed, but had simply short-circuited. This had disastrous disorganizing consequences when he was forced into a traumatic confrontation with "another self," which he had tried to blank out permanently.

Although one has to remain within the bounds of supposition, this is probably a case of acute psychotic decompensation in an adolescent functioning on a borderline level, halfway between neurosis and psychosis. What was observed in both Michel and his mother was the disappearance of the psychotic symptomatology after two weeks of frequent closely spaced interviews. After this symptomatic sedation, it was impossible to continue any further treatment. Viewed in conjunction with the "silent" evolution over the two years that elapsed after this episode, the overall picture seems to support this hypothesis. As soon as Michel was able to go back to work, which was about a month after the initial consultation, everything was back to normal as far as the family was concerned. On the surface, nothing seemed to contradict this assumption eighteen months later.

I shall come back later to certain characteristics of Michel's psychic functioning that make me query the permanence of such a rapid cure, and also to the justifiable doubts concerning his integration of a self-image as a sexual adult male.

Third Observation: Sophie

A colleague was called to Sophie's home by her parents, who were at the end of their tether after four days of events that had been dramatic for the whole family. The fifteen-year-old girl presented a rapidly and steadily deteriorating catatonic syndrome, refusing to eat or drink and unable to sleep. She would wander through the apartment in a state of bewilderment or else stay in her room, where she took out all her belongings, examining them one by one. She was convinced that she had a serious infectious illness (she wanted to throw out everything she touched) and that she had a disgusting odor. She would say, "My vagina's open," and

"My body's emptying itself"—and it was indeed doing so, with men-struation, diarrhea, nose-running, and skin eruptions occurring simul-taneously.

That was nearly five years ago, when the treatment was begun that continues at this time. What is particularly interesting about this obser-vation is precisely the length of time it covers, with all the vicissitudes of both the patient's personal evolution and the therapeutic approach in-cluded.

The acute psychotic profile emerged after her first physical separation from her mother, who had left the previous week on holiday with her own sister. Sophie "did some experiments" (with her body), "so as to be like everyone else," but "I'm only fifteen" and "I wasn't ready for it." "My biggest fault is being alive" (alive outside of the mother, of course). After an unsuccessful attempt to treat the patient at home, we finally hospi-talized her in a psychiatric clinic, where she spent four months. There, she was treated with trifluoperazine and packs, but constant regular contact was maintained with her original therapist.

Sophie was then admitted to a day therapy center for adolescents, after which an unsuccessful attempt to go back to school was followed by a decision to start an apprenticeship. We suggested psychotherapy three days a week, still with the same therapist, while another colleague saw the parents.

Sophie had a relapse after a year. It occurred shortly after she began her apprenticeship, at a point when she was living more and more outside the family with her boyfriend and making a great effort to go on with her psychotherapy, whose content was becoming increasingly su-perficial. The patient again had to be admitted to the psychiatric hospi-tal, with exactly the same clinical picture as before: catatonic syndrome, bewilderment, olfactory hallucinations, sensations of bodily deforma-tion, and impressions of disintegration of both herself and people she approached. Recovery was much faster this time, however, and hospital-ization was required for only two months.

For some time she was again able to cathect her psychotherapy, which enabled her to start elaborating the difficulties linked from the beginning of adolescence with the appearance of the sexual body ("be-fore, I never used to think about it; I was never aware of others or myself; *it just happened all of a sudden*"), her present massive peer cathexis, her inability to handle the slightest conflict with her parents, and her mirror relationship with her mother. She dropped her apprenticeship, but took up regular part-time work.

Another decompensation occurred toward the end of the second year of treatment, the day she was to leave on holiday abroad with her parents while her boyfriend remained in Geneva. The symptoms were again identical, but treatment at home proved successful this time. The parents effectively carried out their containing role, and neuroleptics were administered in lower doses than before. The wound inflicted by the relapse was enormous for Sophie, however. Shortly afterward she refused to go on with her psychotherapy, and all efforts to persuade her to change her mind were useless. The therapist responsible for the consultations with the parents took over the whole case for a year, seeing Sophie about twice a month, with the idea of preparing the ground for resumption of her individual treatment.

After we had known Sophie and her parents for more than three years, she had to be admitted to the psychiatric clinic once again—her third hospitalization. Several factors probably contributed to this relapse: the patient never came back to see the doctor under whose direction the project for renewing her psychotherapy was shaping well; her older brother left the family home; a neighbor hanged herself; her mother became less and less tolerant of the relationship with her boyfriend; and, last but not least, before becoming catatonic Sophie suddenly became aware of a tremendous violence toward her mother ("I thought she was going to hit me," the mother said).

On Sophie's leaving the hospital five weeks later, she herself made contact with the psychotherapist whose name she had been given and who she knew was available. She expressed the desire "to learn to live in a better way" and to separate herself from her mother. A year and a half later, she was still attending her three weekly sessions regularly. Within this stable and meaningful framework—and only here—she was gradually becoming able to show all her regressive needs: a cannibalistic avidity, intense rage, a need for almost total control, but also the unremitting temptation to be the ideal divine child who could answer *all* her therapist's needs.

The most delicate point in that phase of the situation was associated with Sophie's absolute determination to have a breast reduction. Although there was actually some real hypertrophy involved, the significance of the breast operation was nonetheless to produce a magical disappearance of the insanity she had been going through for three of the previous four years, to return to the prepubertal situation where she felt as though she were both a boy and a girl, and to attack the insufficiently generous maternal breast. Fortunately, the therapeutic framework was strong enough for this violent destructive urge, whose purportedly esthetic motivation faded into a very secondary concern, to be contained and subsequently elaborated.

Some months into this second phase of psychotherapy the therapist was absent for the first time; Sophie was convinced he was dead. She thought she was pregnant and flooded her room and bathroom with water and urine, but remained capable of voluntarily requesting admission to the hospital, where she stayed for only a few days.

For the first time, the holiday separation was prepared for and accepted—alongside many other changes—with no new disorganization. Sexual identity remained vague, confusion of aggressive and erotic instincts persisted, and sexuality was still assimilated to either insanity or prostitution, but it nevertheless looked as though the work of subject-object differentiation was now well under way—the obligatory prelude to the remolding of identity. Sophie was able to analyze the meaning of her delusional ideas, which she always remembered in precise detail. The recurrent pattern of hospitalization appeared to have been broken, and for the first time there seemed to be a real possibility of progress, in the sense of a genuine process of change.

Fourth Observation: Simon

This adolescent, who was nearly fifteen, was subject to hallucinations and delusions. Somebody was "muttering": "Muttering," he explained, "is a mental conditioning to force someone to do something, and that person has to do it. . . . Certain people [almost everybody] mutter to make my life unpleasant; they mutter different things, like 'You're going to lose your hair.' That makes the roots hurt and some hair falls out after a while. . . . 'You're going to purse your lips as if you were going to start making love to someone.'"

Love, sex, the body. Here, too, everything—including violence—is given from the outset. Simon's hallucinations and delusions began many months before our first meeting; his parents had decided to bring him to us because of the serious risks arising from his acts of violence and a recent inability to keep his thinking from being affected by the psychotic flare-ups. This was a boy who had been strong and confident until puberty: what could have pushed him into insanity? As one might imagine, it was a "disaster"—his first party. Here he experienced total and brutally sudden immersion into the world of postinfantile sexuality, which the well-protected child had thus far been able to disavow. Now he was brought face to face with an unbearable twofold reality: instinctual demands and the separation of the sexes. Simon found himself completely at a loss before a new and uncontrollable situation and probably fell back on "the best solution possible" to ward off panic and heal the narcissistic breach. He said that at the party, he seduced all the girls, they all fell into his arms; that's how his "playboy" reputation started. Everybody was talking about him, and that was when the voices began to bother him at home and then at school. He could have been world-famous as a great Casanova, he said, if he didn't have this awful smell because of his burnt hair.

The similarities between this and the previous cases are quite striking, but Simon set a particular therapeutic problem, related to the length of time between the appearance of his hallucinatory and delusional symptomatology and our first contact with him. It was still possible to discern the conflict inherent in the constitution of symptoms, whether of a neurotic or psychotic type. But the image of the new, pathological self that had been built up after the rupture and that revolved around gigantism was already relatively well entrenched, with every risk of becoming a closed system. As Pao (1989) underlines, the essential thing in this subacute phase of psychosis is to prevent the pathological self-concept from becoming encysted.

Simon agreed to see us again because he was suffering horribly. "The fact that . . . the delusions and the hallucinations that occur are of a most distressing character and are bound up with the generation of anxiety . . . is without doubt a sign that the whole process of remodelling is carried through against forces which oppose it violently" (Freud, 1924). The vitality of the conflict made it possible to set up a therapeutic alliance, albeit an initially precarious one, but for a very long time a desperate inability to tolerate suffering was predominant. Any attempt on our part to pinpoint a source of distress in his existence was followed by a radical change of course and a series of defensive maneuvers whose common feature was omnipotence.

Simon, who attended sessions three times a week, at last agreed to lie down on the couch. His parents had a weekly session with another colleague. His treatment course, over almost three years, was punctuated by many critical points when medication was required, although he was not hospitalized and was able to maintain school attendance. The patient finally became capable of genuinely getting in touch with his catastrophic depressions, but he was then totally vulnerable, as though he were snatched up into the spiral of the original horrors, which he was utterly helpless to stop.

Fifth Observation: Jim

This fifth and last observation is presented because it illustrates the most redoubtable possible course of a psychotic state in adolescence, which is the perverse solution. It is to be feared because it simultaneously indicates both a "cure" and the closing off of the maturational process with a generally irreversible alteration of reality testing.

We were asked to see Jim, who was eighteen, by the psychiatric hospital where he had been admitted several weeks earlier for an acute psychotic decompensation with panic anxiety, self-mutilation (punching himself in the face and eyes), feelings of derealization, dissociation, persecutory experiences, and mental automatism. Signs of the imminent catastrophe had begun a year earlier; there had been a sharp drop in school performance (he had until then been a brilliant student), use of hashish (immoderate quantities), and a number of misdemeanors. The adolescent then left the family home and took a room alone. His mood, which tended toward depression, took a manic swing; he dyed his hair, started associating with marginal groups, and was increasingly absent from school. A new depressive phase brought greater difficulties at school and severance of contacts with his friends. Jim's anxiety intensified to a crisis point. He became confused and self-mutilating and was hospitalized.

The patient's avidity and his attempts to find an anchor point in his struggle against being invaded by madness seemed promising signs for the future. From the outset, there were concerns about the eventual possibility of a "perverse" rearrangement and also about his delusional body image. He felt himself to be both a man and a woman. His first homosexual relationship took place when he was twelve, and heterosexual relationships followed from the age of sixteen, but he appeared to be unhappy about his bisexuality. After a period of evaluation we recommended intensive psychotherapy, which the patient accepted.

Jim stopped coming for treatment after a very short time, but he returned to see his therapist after an absence of several months. He talked about his problems at work (he had given up his studies after his stay in the hospital and begun a vocational training course), where he evidently had a feeling of devaluation and at the same time an enormous contempt for the people he had to work with, who were "so inferior" to him, as he said. He also spoke about his bisexuality, which he claimed was no longer a source of conflict.

A series of disturbing events followed one another in an increasingly uncontrollable spiral: Jim was dismissed from work because of his repeated absences and aggressive behavior. He shaved part and then all of his head and dressed in a more and more eccentric, feminine manner. Finally, he decided—with the blessings of both his parents!—to have his nose operated on, explaining that he wanted to get back the nose he had when he was eleven (when supposedly it had been "broken"). If he did this, he would be "good-looking" again and could become a model. The confusion between the inner world and external reality was total, with the illusion of being able to put one in order by acting on the other.

The patient came back "to show himself" for the last time. He looked absolutely awful: his nose was three times its usual size, with hair hanging in his nostrils and hematomas under the eyes. He had managed the unlikely exploit of finding in another town a surgeon with the same name as his psychotherapist who agreed to go ahead with the "aesthetic" surgery—in other words, to make his body undergo the transformations demanded by the superego. Here we were helplessly witnessing the concretization of the "perverse" alliance between an omnipotent narcissism and destructiveness, at the expense of the desirable liaison between narcissistic libido and eroticism. This type of evolution is unfortunately often interpreted as the "cure" of a symptomatic psychosis—as was confirmed by the long experience of Eglé and Moses Laufer in London (personal communication).

THE PSYCHOANALYTIC UNDERSTANDING
OF PSYCHOTIC STATES IN ADOLESCENTS

Any clinical observation is subject to a variety of interpretations, since individual reactions to it are partly determined by the reader's own practice and experience, as well as by the theoretical concepts these are based on. A psychiatrist, for example, who has opted for a medically oriented outlook will tend to focus on the idea of a point of rupture after which the subject's history implicitly makes no more sense. Particular attention will be paid to signs that, when grouped together in a more or less specific fashion, are considered indicative of a precise syndrome. The resulting diagnosis will determine therapeutic measures designed ideally to ensure a return to the former state of health. The suitability of such a model in psychiatry has been the subject of lengthy debate and remains to be convincingly demonstrated. Many psychiatrists therefore move away from what they learned in their basic training, and some turn toward a psychoanalytic approach. Even so, this does not necessarily entail a univocal reading of the case, since there are many psychoanalytic schools of though throughout the world. Some consider that the study of psychotic adolescents demonstrates flagrant maldevelopment or clearly distinguishable ego failure. Others, who adhere exclusively to the idea of previous childhood neurosis, view psychosis in adolescents essentially as an afterevent and minimize its generative aspect.

Many theorists of adolescence particularly favor the concept of a second individuation and separation. It can certainly help in understanding the appearance of psychotic decompensations in the five adolescents whose case histories are given above, where emphasis would fall on a failure in the separation process. This interpretation, however, gives insufficient weight to the specificity of the onset of these psychotic episodes after puberty, because failure of "the second individuation process" (Blos, 1967) inevitably refers us back to failure in the first. In a way, we get little further than if we use the idea of previous childhood neurosis and an adolescent afterevent. Although in no way underestimating the determining role of the infantile Oedipus complex and the pregenital stages of development, which are reorganized and unified toward the end of the oedipal phase, I suggest an interpretation of these clinical cases that is more centered on the interrelation between the evolution of personality structure in adolescence and the outbreak of a psychotic state. In other words, I would insist more strongly on adolescence as an "origin" rather than a recapitulation.

In his 1938 *Outline of Psychoanalysis*, Freud gives us the result of his final reflections on psychosis: "we learn from clinical experience . . . that the precipitating cause of the outbreak of a psychosis is either that reality has become intolerably painful or that the instincts have become extraordinarily intensified—both of which, in view of the rival claims made on the ego by the id and the external world, must lead to the same result." Let us take as a starting point the idea that in adolescence specifically, these two "precipitating causes" are not mutually exclusive, but operate in conjunction. The "intolerably painful" reality is the difference between the sexes and between generations, or in other words the reality of the body. "The instincts have become extraordinarily intensified" describes a particular characteristic of adolescence. The "results" on the ego are quite catastrophic in the case of the psychotic adolescent. Furthermore, the catastrophe is twofold, for the excessive instinctual force, which cannot be integrated, threatens to destroy the ego's structure and interrupt the process of symbolic inscription, while genitality forces the adolescent to abandon the image of the ideal pregenital body. The fact of puberty is apprehended first of all via *perception* of the new body and after that through its *representation.* Insofar as development of the relationship with reality is determined by the relationship to one's body, disavowal of this perceived "reality" (the body) is inevitably going to destroy reality testing.

Each of these observations is worth an in-depth discussion that could itself be the subject of a separate study. The two cases of adolescents whose therapy continued for several years should benefit from the material elucidating the significance of psychotic "mechanisms."

To go back to Elisabeth, the first young girl: what was her stumbling block? She fell in love and was rejected; her sister-in-law gave birth to a child. In all likelihood, these two people represented a displacement of the parental couple, from which she found herself excluded: a further rejection, or passively experienced separation. Nonetheless, at the same time she had also begun to go out dancing at night and to seek out points of reference in the world outside of the family. After this, she had her first experience of sexual relations, *whose incestuous significance was not repressed at all.*

In psychoanalytic terms, which are the unexceptional elements, those common to adolescence in general, and which are those that can be considered pathological? Instinctual intensification and the search for an object are features of adolescence itself and involve the body image. In Elisabeth's case, however, confusion set in: confusion between epilepsy and orgasm, between the incestuous object and the new object. The search for the new object turned into the *conquest* of the incestuous object. The parental relationship (or its representation, to be more exact) is what is attacked and destroyed here. This is where the trap of psychopathology opened up, because by conquering one of the two objects in the parental dyad, she barred the way that would have enabled her to situate herself outside of the dyad and thereby occupy the position of subject. A "normal" evolution of that kind would have represented a "gain" on the narcissistic and object level, as opposed to a "loss," or in other words acceptance of the position of excluded third party. In Elisabeth's case, this conquest imprisoned her in space and time, and she was brought face to face with the regressive threat of finding herself in the position of being the object of the object, with all the terrifying anxieties of absorption, reengulfment, and disintegration of the self-image. Recovery in the form of a "perverse" solution consists, among other things, of finding an accommodation between the two figures of the pathological object relations through very close splitting. As for normal-neurotic adolescence, it is the successful assumption of a position of desiring/desired subject, by way of the resolution (and not just a temporary shelving) of the Oedipal complex. In other words, it rests upon the possibility of keeping alive the image of the *relation* of the parental couple after exclusion from it. This is the real innovation—the revolution, even—of adolescence.

Elisabeth presented a delusion of persecution that was in itself of little significance, and this is probably inevitable when there is a successful defense through expulsion into reality. Things began to make sense to us when the patient clearly designated her *body* as the persecutor/conqueror. This body—or its image—is the site par excellence of the conjunction of object, instincts, and narcissism; and object libido and narcissistic libido remain absolutely indissociable, since self-apprehension comes about through the representation of a relation to the cathected object.

Simon's case further clarifies these concepts. The "catastrophe" occurred on the occasion of his first adolescent party. The breakdown, which could also be described as a narcissistic hemorrhage or destabilization of the ego, was precipitated both by being thwarted in reality and by extreme overexcitation. Failure to secure the object (i.e., the girls who refused him) swept away the foundations of the ego and opened the narcissistic breach (the psychotic patient desperately needs an object). A similar effect was produced by instinctual demonism, the "madness" of the id. The repeated sexual excitement was unbearable because the image of an active or even omnipotent self, capable of dominating any situation, gave way completely to the terrifying image of a passive self who could be engulfed by the devouring excitement or who was in danger of falling under total outside control. The fact of not situating himself as a nonobject of the object in the oedipal scene brought about a radical dissociation of the dialectic couple—the psychotic "rupture." Then the reversal from passive to active—vital if one is to ward off panic—was carried out in an archaic mode: the lost power was converted into omnipotent idealization and Simon's megalomanic delusion took over.

Being swallowed up by the desire for the object is essentially at the heart of the threat prefigured by the sexual instinct. This explains Simon's reverie (if it can still be called that), which seems to be compulsive: "I looked at a James Bond poster—it's Octopussy. I saw a woman with eight heads, then fired a revolver at a man who doubled up and fell into the poster and tore it." One of the central conflicts in the psychosis was probably linked to the simultaneous need to be close to the object (because of an inability to "lose" it) and at the same time get as far away from it as possible (to ward off the threat of absorption). The poster was "torn" by the closeness to it, which leads off toward this psychical Bermuda triangle where both object and subject disappear without trace. On the other hand, distance and "loss" can lead to exactly the same result, so that the psychotic subject's position is wholly untenable without complicated and costly maneuvers to maintain the right distance and control, which in turn sustain permanent frustration and intensified aggressivity.

So far I have deliberately emphasized the increase of the sexual instinct, which is a characteristic common to psychosis in adolescence and to adolescence in general, while underlining the radical differences in the range of intensity in the two cases. Sexuality—the sexual body and incest—is only half the picture, however, the other half being represented by aggressivity and parricide. Simon was brought to us not because of the rupture that followed the outbreak of the sexual instinct but because of his violence. He had almost throttled one of his teachers and hurled an ashtray at his father's head—and his therapist felt a certain, though short-lived, apprehension of a similar fate during the first few consultations.

Nonetheless, the problem raised by the aggressive instinct in the psychotic adolescent does seem to be of the same order as the sexual instinct: an excess that is not integrable or not representable by a mechanism of symbolization, with a permanent threat of the precarious point of balance being broken. But doesn't the reference to the "madness" of the id in psychosis and "instinctual demonism" evoke rather the world of "wild" instincts? Something that falls short of the process of establishing, breaking and renewing liaisons, which are the first "knots," where fusion is not yet indicative of anaclisis, but of confusion?

Michel's is another case illustrative of this confusion. This young man of seventeen was traumatically confronted with homosexual antecedents that he had repressed for more than three years. To be sure, his sexuality was disruptive, but it was so mixed up with aggressivity (being beaten up, getting his nose broken) in a "wild" confusion of instincts of similarly unclear origin that it cannot be considered the only factor involved. Michel could no longer distinguish whether the source of this massive, overwhelming excitation came from within or from outside. Although with only partial success, he attempted to set it outside, with regard both to the traumatic break-in of which he felt himself the victim and to the bodies, reduced to their sexual attributes, that haunted him. Everything would strike him with panic, the excess as much as the void: the "vision" of breasts and penises (where perception took the place of representation) just as much as their nonrepresentation (the "black holes"). He told his therapist about an incident that happened at the home of the friend who touched off the scandal (the effect of exposure): as he did so, he played with a dagger and was tempted to take it away with him, but put it down. Still talking, he seized a pencil, which he began to play with and which he did take away. He was barred from access to the virile penis which he wanted to possess. It was a penis-weapon, too dangerous for him because of the confusion between eroticism and destructiveness (or even the precedence of the latter over the former) and probably too dangerous for his mother as well. The pencil, yes, the dagger, no: he can still be the same boy as before, with his child's penis, but he cannot become a man with an adult sexual organ. Michel recovered very quickly from his symptomatic psychosis. But he terminated his treatment immediately afterward, and we think that the source of the psychotic state in fact eluded cure and that he is paying a heavy price for his "recovery": the abdication of his position as a desiring subject and the acceptance of a fixed regressive position.

Regression is one of the many concepts that can form a bridge between adolescence and psychosis, but in a metapsychological framework it has to be considered in its structural, dynamic, and economic dimensions together. Seen in this light, psychotic regression takes on a very different profile from normal adolescent regression. Far from being solely a general regression to an archaic developmental stage, it is mainly a ruse to conceal a whole construction and provide a means of controlling frustration and pain. When Michel was clinically psychotic and "regressed," he clearly showed his desperate need for the object, but he also took every liberty with it, submitting it to unending "manipulations," from elimination to partialization. By a "fixed" regressive position, I mean something that would be closer to extinction of the conflict and massive anticathexis.

Sophie's psychotic regression is plain to see, with percepts, instead of representations, and catatonia. The course of her treatment, however, also made it possible to realize all the complex constructions of her delusional ideas in relation to her sexuality and body image—that "rejected piece of reality" that "constantly forces itself on the mind" (Freud, 1924). This young girl's multiple symptomatic decompensations were invariably linked to factors associated with actual incidents, which could be grouped under the general heading of "separation." Separation was a traumatic event in that it left the patient stranded; we could say she had an identity breakdown, or stalled identification, if it is accepted that the self-image is subordinate to the image of a relationship to the cathected object. If the real-life object tends to be confused with its representation, the loss of the one is equivalent to the loss of the other and then to the loss of self. Subject and object, container and contents, are mixed up together and threatened with being submerged and losing all trace of their mutual inscription. To talk of separation anxiety in such a context as this seems both weak and insufficiently specific, because here we are dealing with a "panic" in the face of which the psychotic economy can be seen as a desperate effort to hold on to a "vital minimum" of representations in spite of everything. In Sophie's delusion, she saw her menstruation as the elimination of a "rotten" part of her body. When she became more realistic, she started looking for a surgeon for a breast reduction. After that the postponement of her decision provided an opportunity in the treatment to elaborate the equivalents of meaning: elimination of genitality, triumph on the oedipal *and* narcissistic fronts, destructiveness.

A concluding remark is needed concerning what I called this *perverse* "solution," because it constitutes a risk inherent in the abatement of any acute psychosis in adolescence. The resolution of the Oedipus complex, the adjustment of the relation to reality and the personal body image, are all interdependent. If the image of the sexual body is not integrated, the Oedipus complex remains added on. The oedipal triumph does not set off guilt feelings and castration anxiety: instead, it triggers off panic fear of being reengulfed. One of the possible solutions to combat this panic is to attain total mastery over the desired object, whereupon destructiveness replaces eroticism as the mainstay of narcissism and the object that can be mastered becomes "fetishized," an anemic narcissistic property.

With Sophie, it was possible to avoid this outcome—one hopes for good. In Simon's case, the perverse "temptation" was extremely strong during the first stage of his treatment: when the panic threatened he would adopt a martial demeanor and go around dressed in leather from head to foot, ready to set off "faggot-hunting." The image of an object to be violently, sadistically *possessed,* a cowed, subdued object devoid of any desire of its own, confronted the antithetical image of an object endowed with the irresistible attraction of complete and absolute power. As long as the splitting does not go into operation in too radical a way, the conflict can be kept alive, as is the case in acute psychotic states. I have underlined our failure with Jim sufficiently for further comment to be superfluous. This adolescent came out of the delusional neoreality of his symptomatic psychotic period, but he managed to make a "piece of reality" coincide with his neoidentity. In this way he "froze" his identity conflict, although without this entailing a solution to the breakdown in identification.

This chapter was not intended as a discussion of the therapeutic problems posed by psychotic states in adolescence, but my position on the subject will nonetheless have been made clear through these observations and their theoretical interpretation. Psychoanalytic treatment is often feasible and should in any case not be discarded out of hand on the basis of the clinical picture alone, however alarming it may be. Great perseverance may be necessary, sometimes over a period of years, as in the case of Sophie, before the right framework can be put into place. We should make every possible effort in this direction, even with the knowledge that we can not eliminate either the risk of treatment being prematurely terminated or the possibility of failure.

REFERENCES

Blos, P. (1967). "The Second Individuation Process of Adolescence." *Psychoanalytic Study of the Child* 22:162–186.
Freud, S. (1924). "The Loss of Reality in Neurosis and Psychosis." *Standard Edition* 19:186.
——— (1938). *An Outline of Psychoanalysis. Standard Edition,* 23:201.
Giovacchini, P. L. (1986). "Remarques sur la technique et le traitement de la psychose de l'adolescent." In *Psychanalyse, adolescence et psychose.* Collective publication. Paris: Payot, 85–95.
Pao, P. N. (1989). *Schizophrenic Disorders: Theory and Treatment from a Psychodynamic Point of View.* New York: International Universities Press.

VIII

Families in Quest of Parents:
Divorce and Death

29

Introduction

COLETTE CHILAND

Systemic family theory was developed at the moment when Western culture saw the family begin to shrink and break up. The extended family shriveled into a nuclear family consisting of the father, mother, and children, and the number of siblings became fewer. There has been a considerable increase in the rate of divorce and the frequency of single-parent families consisting of one parent (usually the mother) and a child or children. Divorces are often followed by remarriage, after which children divide their time between two separate families.

The only way to see beyond the screen of preconceived ideas and find out how children experience parental divorce and adapt to its vicissitudes is by observing the actual facts. In *Surviving the Breakup: How Children and Parents Cope with Divorce* (1980), Judith Wallerstein and Joan Kelly's unique research on this subject provides information on the first five year after divorce. A second volume covers the first ten postdivorce years.

Chapters 30 and 31 of this section do not have the advantages of research that has both a longitudinal structure and intensive case studies, such as that of Wallerstein and Kelly. They are cross-sectional studies yielding statistical and periodic data. Both pieces of research compare adolescents from intact families with adolescents from families broken either by divorce or by the death of one or (rarely) both parents.

Jean-François Saucier and Anne-Marie Ambert try, in addition, to determine whether the age at which parental loss occurs is significant. The period of greatest vulnerability is different in girls and boys: it runs from six to nine years of age for girls, and for boys, between ten and twelve and after thirteen in the case of parental death, and thirteen and over in the case of divorce.

The authors propose the hypothesis that because of their earlier maturity, girls become aware of the depth of the family drama more quickly than boys do. In addition, the father and mother have different roles with regard to boys and girls. Although this is not specified by the authors, it is more often the father who is lost (by death) or distanced (by divorce). Perhaps the presence of the father who loves the daughter as a girl (a role my own research has shown to be essential to girls) is more important during the period from six to nine years of age, whereas the presence of a father who offers a model for identification and a solid resistance to attacks could be essential in preadolescence and adolescence in boys.

The age at which children are faced with the death of a parent or divorce is not taken into account as a significant factor by Hillevi Aro and Païvi Rantanen, who specify that most cases concern the loss of the father. Their sample showed that adolescent boys were more affected by the death of a parent, whereas girls were hit harder by divorce. In both cases, symptoms of distress were greater than they were in adolescents from united families.

These facts dramatize the need to provide help for families broken up by death or divorce, and in chapter 32 Liliane Spector-Dunsky presents a preventive intervention model based on systemic theory, which she illustrates with a few brief descriptions.

30

Age at Parental Divorce or Death and Biopsychosocial Disadvantage at Adolescence

JEAN-FRANÇOIS SAUCIER

ANNE-MARIE AMBERT

Because of the significant increase in the frequency of divorce in many Western countries, clinicians are becoming concerned about the effect of parental separation on children's physical and mental health.

Landis (1960), like many other authors, considers age at the moment of separation as one of the most important factors involved. Kalter and Rembar (1981), in a paper concerned with the age factor, summarize the literature in isolating two important hypotheses that are shared by most authors. The first, *the cumulative effect of stress*, specifies that the younger the child is at the time of divorce, the more he or she will suffer from the trauma in the short, middle, and long terms. Among authors often quoted as sharing this hypothesis are Hetherington (1972) and Gardner (1977). The second hypothesis, related to the *critical developmental stage*, specifies that one precise moment in the development of the child would be more likely to cause severe and long-term effects. Up to very recently, the vast majority of authors sharing that hypothesis— among others Neubauer (1960), McDermott (1970), and Westman (1972)—influenced by psychoanalytic theory, placed this critical moment at the oedipal stage, between three and six years of age. The dominance of the oedipal hypothesis is illustrated by Kalter and Rembar (1981) who, when they divided their sample of 144 subjects into subgroups, decided on the three following groupings: preoedipal subgroup (one to two and one-half years of age), oedipal subgroup (three to five and one-half years of age), and postoedipal (six to seventeen and one-half years of age). Note that the last subgroup puts together very different developmental periods, such as latency age, preadolescence, and adolescence, with a total span of eleven and one-half years, compared to a short span of two and one-half years for each of the first two subgroups.

When Wallerstein (1985) was conducting the second stage of her longitudinal research—eighteen months after parental separation—she was inclined to support the hypothesis of the cumulative effect of stress, since at that point she found that the youngest children in her sample were the most distressed. But, when she investigated the third stage—five years after parental separation—she was surprised to see that the youngest children were in much better psychological shape than the others. Moreover, she observed that children who were around the age of ten at divorce were the ones who were the most distressed. To our knowledge, Wallerstein is the first author who mentions a critical stage other than the preoedipal or oedipal period.

Most of the studies mentioned above, however, are limited in their generalizability, either because they had only a clinical sample or because their sample was too small to allow complex statistical analyses. Finally, in most of these studies, an important subsample of broken families was lacking—namely, those broken by the death of one of the parents. The study we conducted was designed to address both shortcomings.

THE STUDY

Sample

First, a probability sample of 4,539 respondents aged ten to twenty years was drawn who were truly representative of the population of 112,000 teenagers attending all French-speaking high schools and community colleges, public as well as private, on the island of Montreal in 1976–77. Second, from this sample, subsamples were drawn: (1) 276 adolescents (165 girls, 111 boys) whose parents were divorced or separated, and (2) 181 adolescents (88 girls, 93 boys) who had lost one parent through death. At the time of the survey, the mean duration of the family breakup varied between five and five and one-half years (see table 30.1 for a detailed description of subgroups of the sample).

Method

In this chapter we analyze the relationship between age at divorce (five years of age or less, six to nine years, ten to twelve years, thirteen years

Table 30.1 *Subject Sample for Study on Age at Divorce or at Death of a Parent*

	0–5 Years	6–9 Years	10–12 Years	13+ Years	Total
Parents' divorce: girls	31	34	52	48	165
Parents' divorce: boys	15	18	40	38	111
Parents' death: girls	12	25	21	30	88
Parents' death: boys	19	15	28	31	93

Total: 457

and more) and a series of indicators of disadvantage, such as biological (height of respondents, etc.), psychological (perception of vulnerability to illness, attitude of responsibility concerning one's own health, etc.), and behavioral (selection of friends, exaggerated use of alcohol, etc.). An analysis of covariance is employed, controlling for duration of divorce and for the following background variables: social class (measured by father's occupation), mother's outside work, number of children in the family, and respondent's age and birth rank (see table 30.2 for an example of the method used).

Results

First, many important variables indicating disadvantage (such as higher frequency of nervousness, a lower academic performance, a lower level of academic aspiration, a higher use of tobacco; see table 30.3) were found among children of divorced or widowed families more often than among children of intact families, but an analysis did not reveal significant differences in relation to age at parental separation. This means that, for this series of variables, children of broken families are disadvantaged whatever their age at the moment of divorce or of a parent's death (see Saucier and Ambert, 1986).

Table 30.2 *Age at Divorce or at Death of a Parent and Height of Children (in Inches)*

	0–5 Years	6–9 Years	10–12 Years	13+ Years	P
Parents' divorce: girls	62.23	62.68	62.87	64.03	.524
Parents' divorce: boys	64.26	65.94	65.17	68.84	.017
Parents' death: girls	63.35	63.47	63.28	63.46	.995
Parents' death: boys	69.28	65.76	65.64	65.26	.207

On the other hand, other important variables did show statistically significant differences according to age. We have already seen in table 30.2 that boys from divorced families were ultimately significantly shorter if parental separation occurred when they were five years old or younger; the same did not hold for girls, however. Another important variable that showed significant differences in relation to age was perception of one's own vulnerability to illness (see table 30.4). Boys from divorced families perceived themselves as being most vulnerable to adult illnesses (see Goshman and Saucier, 1982) if they were five years

Table 30.3 *Disadvantages Found More often in Broken than in Intact Families*

1—Frequency of manifestations of nervousness
2—Frequency of consultations or therapy for nervousness
3—Academic performance in mathematics and in French
4—Level of academic aspirations
5—Daily use of tobacco

Note: The table presents variables with significant differences when comparing subjects from broken families with subjects from intact families but with no significant differences among subjects from broken families according to age at divorce or at the death of a parent.

Table 30.4 *Age at Divorce or at Death of a Parent and Self-Perception of Vulnerability to Adult Illness*

	0–5 Years	6–9 Years	10–12 Years	13+ Years	P
Parents' divorce: girls	3.53	3.25	3.44	3.48	.865
Parents' divorce: boys	3.76	2.87	2.91	3.15	.058
Parents' death: girls	3.39	3.00	3.41	3.28	.458
Parents' death: boys	2.93	3.63	3.29	2.64	.036

1: Not vulnerable at all   7: Very vulnerable

old or younger when their parents divorced, whereas boys from widowed families perceived themselves as most vulnerable if one of their parents died when they were six, seven, eight, or nine years old. No difference was found for girls. Self-esteem, measured by one's perception of being appreciated by one's family, teachers, and peers, was found to be significantly lower (see table 30.5) among girls who were between six and nine years of age when their parents divorced. No difference was found among boys. And our last variable concerned the exaggerated use of alcohol—that is, use that led to temporary amnesia, accidents, or fights (see tables 30.6 and 30.7). We found these three behaviors significantly more often among boys who had lost a parent by death when they were between ten and twelve and among girls whose parents divorced when they were younger than thirteen.

All the indicators of disadvantage that differed according to age level at a level of statistical significance equal to or lower than the .10 level of probability were combined and then weighted by giving a score of 4 for the age when the disadvantage was the highest and 1 for the age when the disadvantage was the lowest. The results are given in table 30.8 (italicized numbers indicate the highest global level of distress). Indicators of disadvantage, in addition to those already mentioned, included choice of friends according to the level of their use of tobacco, alcohol, and drugs; attitude of responsibility toward one's own health (hygiene

Table 30.5 *Age at Divorce or at Death of a Parent
and Self-Perception of Degree of Appreciation by Others*

	0–5 Years	6–9 Years	10–12 Years	13+ Years	P
Parents' divorce: girls	13.87	14.54	11.22	11.08	.036
Parents' divorce: boys	13.48	11.59	12.61	14.09	.345
Parents' death: girls	16.31	14.46	11.87	10.46	.085
Parents' death: boys	12.94	12.29	12.99	10.57	.277

4: Very much appreciated   28: Not appreciated at all

habits, care of teeth, amount of sleep); security habits (use of seat belt, use of helmet when on motorcycle); and attitudes toward prevention of future problems.

Table 30.8 reveals that for girls from *divorced families*, it is the six-to-nine-year period that is the most vulnerable, whereas for boys it is the thirteen-plus period. On the other hand, for girls from *widowed families*, it is again the six-to-nine-year period that is most vulnerable, whereas for boys it is both the ten-to-twelve-year and the thirteen-plus periods that are the most vulnerable.

Table 30.6 *Age at Death of a Parent and Tendency
toward Alcoholism, among Boys*

Drinking-Related Episodes	0–5 Years	6–9 Years	10–12 Years	13+ Years	P
Amnesia following drinking	4.99	4.13	2.99	4.10	.029
Accidents following drinking	7.99	7.37	6.97	7.02	.007
Fights following drinking	3.99	3.79	2.77	3.28	.005

1: Very frequent

Table 30.7 *Age at Parents' Divorce and Tendency toward Alcoholism, among Girls*

Drinking-Related Episodes	0–5 Years	6–9 Years	10–12 Years	13+ Years	P
Amnesia following drinking	4.23	4.36	4.01	4.84	.122
Accidents following drinking	7.02	7.75	6.83	7.97	.066
Fights following drinking	2.49	2.49	3.24	3.96	.034

1: Very frequent

DISCUSSION

The results of our study do not support the hypothesis of the cumulative effect of stress, because the youngest age period was not shown to be the most vulnerable in any of the four groups. The hypothesis of a critical developmental stage is partly supported in a sizable

Table 30.8 *Cumulative Disadvantage: Relation to Age at Parental Divorce or Death*

	0–5 Years	6–9 Years	10–12 Years	13+ Years
Parents' divorce: girls	26	32	22	20
Parents' divorce: boys	19	17	20	28
Parents' death: girls	18	22	16	14
Parents' death: boys	14	20	23	23

4: Age when disadvantage was highest
1: Age when disadvantage was lowest
Note: Summed weighing of variables indicating disadvantage that differed according to age at family breakup statistically significant at .05 level and almost significant at .06–.10 level

number of indicators of disadvantage, on the condition that one does separate analyses for boys and girls. In effect, girls are shown to be more stressed, whatever the cause of the family breakup, when the separation occurs between the ages of six and nine years. The vulnerable age period is later for boys, occurring at the thirteen-plus period for boys from divorced families and at both that period and at the ten-to-twelve-year period for boys from widowed families. In no case is the oedipal age period the most vulnerable one.

How can we explain such significant differences between girls and boys, particularly among children of divorce? A brief review of the literature concerning differences in development between girls and boys suggests that most authors believe that girls develop faster, both cognitively and affectively, from birth to the middle of adolescence. According to Bentzen (1963), girls are globally more advanced than boys by one year at the age of six, by one and a half years at the age of nine, and by two years at the age of twelve or thirteen. Following these data we propose the hypothesis that girls are more vulnerable to family breakup during the latency period because they are then fully aware of the family tragedy. This occurs earlier than in boys, who at that age period seem to be protected by their relative unawareness of the problem. It is only later that boys gain the capacity to become fully aware of the situation, and then they react with more distress.

REFERENCES

Bentzen, F. (1963). Sex Ratios in Learning and Behavior Disorders." *Am. J. Orthopsychiat.* 92–98.

Gardner, R. (1977). "Children of Divorce: Some Legal and Psychological Considerations." *J. Clin. Child Psychol.* 6:3–6.

Goshman, D. S., and Saucier, J. F. (1982). "Perceived Vulnerability in Children and Adolescents." *Health Educ. Q.*, nos. 2–3:46–59.

Hetherington, E. M. (1972). "Effects of Parental Absence on Personality Development of Adolescent Daughters." *Developm. Psychol.* 7:313–326.

Kalter, N., and Rembar, J. (1981). "The Significance of a Child's Age at the Time of Parental Divorce." *Am. J. Orthopsychiat.* 51(1):85–100.

Landis, J. (1960). "The Trauma of Children When Parents Divorce." *Marr. Fam. Living* 22:7–13.

McDermott, J. (1970). "Divorce and Its Psychiatric Sequelae in Children." *Arch. Gen. Psychiat.* 23:421–427.

Neubauer, P. (1960). "The One-Parent Child and His Oedipal Development." *Psychoanal. Study Child* 15:286–309.

Saucier, J. F., and Ambert, A. M. (1986). "Adolescents' Perception of Self and of Immediate Environment by Parental Marital Status: A Controlled Study." *Can. J. Psychiat.* 31:505–512.

Wallerstein, J. (1985). "Separation and Divorce: Treatment Issues for Children and Families." Montreal Children's Hospital, May 24.

Westman, J. (1972). "Effect of Divorce on a Child's Personality Development." *Med. Aspects Hum. Sexual.* 6:38–55.

31

Parental Loss and Adolescent Development

HILLEVI M. ARO

PAÏVI KRISTINA RANTANEN

Among mental health professionals, there has long been interest in the impact of parental loss on child development and later disturbance (e.g., Bowlby, 1951). Parental loss as a vulnerability factor for adult psychiatric disorder, especially depression, has been demonstrated (Brown and Harris, 1978), though there is some controversy in the literature (Tennant et al., 1980). Rutter (1985) concludes that the negative impact of parental loss in childhood has been established and that the focus has turned both to distinguishing the different effects of different types of parental loss and to study what kind of mechanisms are involved in the process.

Parental loss by death and that by divorce are different. Loss by death is final, whereas many children continue to see the divorced parent more or less frequently. Divorce is often associated with parental discord both before and after the divorce. The negative consequences of divorce on children may be largely due to the discord and not to the divorce as such (e.g., Chess et al., 1983). Both death and divorce may lead to a chain of experiences that may be stressful and also to changes in life circumstances long after, but these may be different in kind. Furthermore, divorce and death carry different psychological meanings for children.

Adolescence is believed to be a period during which the intrapsychic conflicts of early childhood are reactivated and finally resolved, and thus this phase in life is considered of special importance for adult mental health (e.g., Blos, 1979). The possible impact of parental loss on adolescent development may arise from different factors: the impact of earlier trauma on development, the absence of the parent during adolescence, consequences of loss for the other parent, and the family's present circumstances. All these may be fundamentally different in loss by death or by divorce.

We studied whether sixteen-year-old schoolchildren who had experienced parental death or parent divorce differed in psychological well-being and behavior from adolescents in intact families. We assumed that adolescents in both groups with parental loss would have more distress symptoms, poorer school performance, lower self-esteem, and less positive self-images than adolescents in intact families. We further assumed that dating and alcohol drinking would be more common among adolescents with parental loss. Our measures were planned not to show disturbance in the clinical sense but to reflect development in general.

METHOD

The study population included all ninth-grade pupils of secondary schools in the spring of 1983 in Tampere, an industrial and university town with 165,000 inhabitants in southern Finland. There were 2,269 pupils, most of whom were born in 1967. Of these pupils, 2,194 (97 percent) completed questionnaires in May 1983. The questionnaires were administered in classrooms in a group situation led by a research worker. The mean age of the pupils was 15.9 years (S.D. 0.3 years).

Ninety percent of the pupils, or 2,046, had participated in a similar survey seventeen months earlier, and they were included in this study. Those adolescents who had experienced parental death ($n = 11$) or divorce ($n = 46$) during the previous seventeen months were excluded from the study, as we were examining longer term consequences. Information about parental loss, as well as other data of the study, was based on self-report.

The scoring of distress symptoms included seventeen somatic and psychic complaints frequently used in different symptom checklists (see table 31.1). The scale has been used in a nationwide Finnish study of juvenile health habits (Rimpelä et al., 1982) and also in a study of an adult population (Aro, 1981). The respondents answered the question, have any of the following symptoms bothered you, and how often during the past school term? (The term had lasted for about four months.) The

Table 31.1 *Items in the Scoring of Distress Symptoms*

Abdominal pains
Loss of appetite
Headache
Lack of energy or depression
Sleeping difficulties
Nausea or vomiting
Anxiety or nervousness
Dizziness
Tremor of hands
Nightmares
Diarrhea or irregular bowel function
Fatigue or feebleness
Excessive perspiration without physical effort
Heartburn or acid troubles
Irritability or fits of anger
Breathlessness
Palpitations

symptom score was determined by summing up the following ratings of separate items: 0 = never, 1 = sometimes, 2 = quite often, and 3 = often or continuously. Girls were also asked whether some of these symptoms occurred only during menstruation; if this was the case, such symptoms were excluded from individual scores in order to obtain better comparability between the sexes. The reliability of the score, measured by five-month test-retrest correlations, was $r = .66$ among girls and $r = .69$ among boys.

A semantic differential scale of self-image developed by Rauste-von Wright (1975) among Finnish adolescents was used as a measure of self-image. The test consisted of twenty-one binary items representing various personality characteristics. In the current study, as well as in the original study, the factor analysis yielded seven factors interpreted as intelligence versus mediocrity; attractiveness versus unattractiveness; leadership versus submissiveness; matter-of-factness versus emotionality; presence of mind versus impulsiveness; relaxedness versus anxiety; and energy versus lack of energy. The self-esteem scale was a modified version of a self-esteem scale developed for Finnish students (Helenius and Lyttinen, 1974). It consisted of seven assertions with a 5-point scale indicating how well the assertion describes the person (table 31.2). The theoretical range in each self-image factor was from 5

Table 31.2 *Items in the Self-Esteem Scale*

1. "I believe in myself and in my possibilities.[a]
2. "I wish I were different from what I am."
3. "I suffer from feelings of inferiority."
4. "I think I have many good qualities."[a]
5. "I feel I lack self-confidence."
6. "I am capable of doing the same as others."[a]
7. "I am often dissatisfied with myself."

a. Inverted items

to 15 and in the self-esteem scale from 5 to 35. Self-reported means of school marks were used as a measure of school performance. Adolescents who reported that they had dated, for however short a period, were included in the group with dating experiences. Those who reported that they had been intoxicated by alcohol monthly or more frequently during the term were included in the heavy drinking group. We further asked whether the adolescent had broken the law with consequences during the past twelve months.

The data were analyzed comparing adolescents in the two groups of parental loss (divorce and death) with adolescents in intact families using two-tailed student's t-test and chi square statistics. Girls and boys were analyzed separately.

RESULTS

The group included seventy adolescents who had lost a parent by death, 394 adolescents who lived in divorced families, and 1,465 adolescents who lived in intact two-parent families. In most cases parental death meant death of the father, but 13 had lost their mother and 3 had lost both parents.

Figure 31.1 shows the means of distress symptoms in adolescents in the different groups. Compared with children in intact families, children in divorced families reported more distress symptoms, especially girls (girls $t = 4.8$, $p < .001$; boys $t = 2.3$, $p < .05$). No significant differences in symptoms were found between those living after divorce in a single-parent family and those living in a step family. Boys who had lost a parent by death had the highest scores in distress symptoms ($t = 4.8$, $p < .001$), whereas girls who had lost a parent by death did not differ from

Figure 31.1. *Means (±95 percent confidence interval) of distress symptoms among girls and boys by parental loss.*

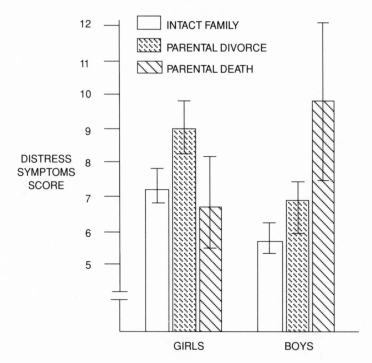

girls in intact families. Boys suffering parental death had high distress symptom scores independent of the sex of the dead parent. Girls had slightly higher scores if their mother had died, but the number of those who had lost their mother was too small to draw any conclusions. The results were similar when physical and psychic symptoms of the score were analyzed separately.

Table 31.3 shows the means of school performance, self-esteem, and self-image factors in the three groups. Adolescents in divorced families and boys in families with parental death had lower school performance than adolescents in intact families. Girls from divorced families reported lower self-esteem than the others. The self-esteem of boys with parental death was also lower than that of other boys, though this difference did not reach statistical significance. Differences in items of reported self-image were not great. Girls in divorced families rated themselves less intelligent and slightly more impulsive than girls in intact families. Compared with boys in intact families, boys with parental death scored

Table 31.3 *Means of School Performance, Self-Esteem, and Self-Image Factors among Girls and Boys*

	Girls			Boys		
	Intact Family (n = 693–706)	Parental Divorce (n = 202–206)	Parental Death (n = 33–36)	Intact Family (n = 729–742)	Parental Divorce (n = 176–182)	Parental Death (n = 33–34)
School performance	7.9	7.5[a]	7.8	7.5	7.1[a]	7.0[b]
Self-esteem (→ low)	17.5	18.6[b]	17.8	15.0	15.2	16.5
Self-image (→ high)						
intelligence	9.3	8.6[a]	9.2	10.2	9.7[c]	9.8
energy	10.2	9.9	10.3	11.0	10.9	10.4
leadership	9.8	10.0	10.1	9.6	9.7	9.8
attractiveness	9.1	9.2	9.4	9.7	9.9	9.4
presence of mind	9.2	8.5[b]	8.5	10.3	10.0	9.9
relaxedness	9.1	9.1	9.2	9.6	9.8	9.1
matter-of-factness	6.7	6.3[c]	6.7	8.7	8.4	7.6[b]

a. $p < .001$
b. $p < .01$
c. $p < .05$

themselves more emotional in the emotionality versus matter-of-factness factor.

Compared with boys in intact families, breaking the law with consequences was twice as common in boys with parental divorce (12 percent versus 6 percent, $X^2 = 6.9$, $p < 0.01$) and over three times as common among boys with parental death (22 percent versus 6 percent; $x^2 = 8.7$, $p < 0.01$). Among girls breaking the law was very rare (1.2 percent).

Table 31.4 shows the frequencies of dating and heavy drinking in the three groups. More than half of all the adolescents had had dating experiences by this age, but it was more common among groups with parental loss. Heavy drinking was twice as common among adolescents in divorced families as in intact families.

DISCUSSION

With the exception of girls who had experienced parental death, children who had lost a parent earlier in life showed more distress in adolescence than children in intact families. The most distressed groups seemed to be boys with parental death and girls in divorced families. The results are consistent with the earlier finding that the impact of parental loss on girls and on boys is probably different (e.g., Hetherington, 1981; Black, 1978), which indicates a need to study different parental losses separately (Harris and Brown, 1985).

Though boys in general had lower scores than girls in distress symptoms, boys with parental death had the highest scores. Several studies have suggested greater vulnerability of boys for family stress, at least before puberty (e.g., Rutter, 1970, 1985). Unexpectedly, girls with parental death did not differ from girls in intact families. No impact of even acute parental loss on symptoms among girls was found in our study (Aro, 1986). Any explanations for this remain highly speculative. There is some suggestion that children may be more likely to be adversely affected by the death or illness of the same-sex parent (Rutter and Quinton, 1984). In our study the majority of children with parental death had lost their father. On the other hand, no clear differences by the sex of the lost parent was demonstrated in our study, but the number of children whose mother had died was very small. Furthermore, one could suggest that girls worked through their grief at the time of the loss but boys did not, as in the Finnish culture it may be more permissible for girls than for boys to cry and show their feelings openly. Another explanation might be that the girls' grief was repressed and remained unre-

Table 31.4 *Frequencies of Dating Experiences and Heavy Drinking among Sixteen-Year-Old Girls and Boys by Parental Loss Status*

	Girls						Boys					
	Intact Family		Parental Divorce		Parental Death		Intact Family		Parental Divorce		Parental Death	
	(n)	%	(n)	%	(n)	%	(n)	%	(n)	%	(n)	%
Dating experiences												
No	(308)	44	(50)	24	(13)	36	(372)	50	(62)	34	(12)	35
Yes	(398)	56	(157)	76	(23)	64	(377)	50	(123)	66	(22)	65
			***	ns					***	ns		
Heavy drinking												
No	(597)	85	(148)	72	(29)	81	(612)	81	(114)	61	(23)	68
Yes	(109)	15	(59)	29	(7)	19	(147)	19	(73)	39	(11)	32
			***	ns					***	ns		

***p < .001
ns: not significant

solved in adolescence, making them prone to depression in adult life. Harris and Brown (1985) suggest that parental loss in childhood is associated with adult depression in women but not in men. We must also remember that our measures were limited in scope, and it is possible that girls react in a different way. Furthermore, we do not know whether it is beneficial to development for distress to be experienced in adolescence under these circumstances. Distress symptoms may reflect developmental stress that supports personal growth, or they may be signals of excessive stress, indicating that healthy development is at risk.

Both girls and boys in divorced families showed more distress than children in intact families, but unlike the case of parental death, girls in divorced families showed more distress than boys. It has been suggested that the impact of parental divorce may be delayed and stressful for girls in adolescence and that it is mainly associated with difficulties in developing sexual relationships (Hetherington, 1972). Pubertal development in girls is often an ambivalent process and accompanied by distress (e.g., Aro and Taipale, 1986). Wallerstein and Kelly (1980) reported that adolescent girls in divorced families, especially, showed heightened anxiety about their emerging sexuality. In our study, dating was more common among both girls and boys in divorced families, but we did not have the data to analyze it in more detail.

The role of social support in buffering against stress may be important (e.g., Hetherington, 1981). It has been shown that a good relationship with one parent serves to protect a child in families with discord (Rutter, 1979). Also, a beneficial school climate may support children living under conditions of psychosocial disadvantage (Rutter et al., 1979). Probably, adolescents with parental loss would benefit from support by extrafamilial adults in their development to adulthood.

All data in this study were based on self-report, and therefore it shares many of the problems of all questionnaire studies. But because the questionnaires were completed in classrooms, the situation was controlled and motivated, and less vulnerable to the bias that may be introduced by lower response rates to mailed questionnaires. Our data on loss and adolescent development nevertheless had limitations. For instance, age at the time of loss may be of importance, as well as the possible accumulation of stressors. More detailed information about the process and the circumstances surrounding the loss would be needed in order to understand the mediating mechanisms involved.

In conclusion, the adolescent process is affected by earlier parental loss, but differently according to whether the loss occurred by death or divorce and differently among girls and boys. In further analyses we intend to study the role of family relationships and social support in mediating the impact of parental loss.

REFERENCES

Aro, H. (1986). "Life Stress and Psychosomatic Symptoms among Finnish 14–16 Year Old Adolescents." *Social Psychiatry* 22:171–176.

Aro, H., and Taipale, V. (1986). "The Impact of Timing of Puberty on Psychosomatic Symptoms among 14–16 Year Old Finnish Girls." *Child Development* 58:261–268.

Aro, S. (1981). "Stress, Morbidity and Health-Related Behavior: A Five-Year Follow-up Study among Metal Industry Employees." *Scandinavian Journal of Social Medicine* (Suppl.) 25.

Black, D. (1978). "The Bereaved Child." *Journal of Child Psychology and Psychiatry* 19:287–292.

Blos, P. (1979). *The Adolescent Passage: Developmental Issues.* New York: International Universities Press.

Bowlby, J. (1951). *Mental Care and Mental Health.* Geneva: World Health Organization.

Brown, G. W., and Harris, T. (1978). *Social Origins of Depression: A Study of Psychiatric Disorders in Women.* London: Tavistock.

Chess, S.; Thomas, A.; Mittleman, M.; Korn, S.; and Cohen, J. (1983). "Early Parental Attitudes, Divorce and Separation, and Young Adult Outcome: Findings of a Longitudinal Study." *Journal of the American Academy of Child Psychiatry* 22:47–51.

Harris, T., and Brown, G. (1985). "Interpreting Data in Aetiological Studies of Affective Disorder: Some Pitfalls and Ambiguities." *British Journal of Psychiatry* 147:5–15.

Helenius, A., and Lyttinen, S. (1974). *Students and Their Studying in Tampere University: A Project of Preventive Mental Health.* Tampere: Students' Health Association and the Department of Psychology of Tampere. (In Finnish)

Hetherington, E. M. (1972). "Effects of Father Absence on Personality Development in Adolescent Daughters." *Developmental Psychology* 7:313–326.

——— (1981). "Children and Divorce." In *Parent-Child Interaction: Theory, Research and Prospects,* ed. R. W. Henderson. New York: Academic Press, 33–58.

Rauste-von Wright, M. (1975). *The Image of Man among Finnish Girls and Boys.* Report no. 41. Turku: University of Turku, Department of Psychology.

Rimpelä, M., Rimpelä, A., and Pasanen, M. (1982). "Perceived Symptoms among 12–18 Year Old Finns." *Journal of Social Medicine* 19:219–233. (In Finnish, English summary)

Rutter, M. (1970). "Sex Differences in Children's Responses to Family Stress." In *The Child in His Family,* ed. E. J. Anthony and C. Koupernik. New York: Wiley, 165–196.

———— (1979). "Protective Factors in Children's Responses to Stress and Disadvantage." In *Primary Prevention of Psychopathology.* Vol. 3, *Social Competence in Children,* ed. M. W. Kent and J. E. Rolf. Hanover: University Press of New England, 49–74.

———— (1985). "Resilience in the Face of Adversity: Protective Factors and Resilience to Psychiatric Disorder." *British Journal of Psychiatry* 147:598–611.

Rutter, M.; Maughan, B.; Mortimore, P.; and Ouston, J. (1979). *Fifteen Thousand Hours: Secondary Schools and Their Effects on Children.* London: Open Books.

Rutter, M., and Quinton, D. (1984). "Long-Term Follow-up of Women Institutionalized in Childhood: Factors Promoting Good Functioning in Adult Life." *British Journal of Developmental Psychology* 18:225–234.

Tennant, C., Bebbington, P., and Hurry, J. (1980). "Parental Death in Childhood and Risk of Adult Depressive Disorder: A Review." *Psychological Medicine* 10:289–299.

Wallerstein, J., and Kelly, J. (1980). *Surviving the Breakup. How Children and Parents Cope with Divorce.* New York: Basic Books.

32

Divorce as a Source of Pain and Source of Growth: A Postseparation Intervention Model

LILIANE SPECTOR-DUNSKY

The proliferation of divorce over recent decades should long since have made it one of the central interests of mental health professionals and a cause for concern, if not alarm, to administrators in this field. Yet we have only recently begun to obtain research findings, and they turn out to contradict certain persistent attitudes and perceptions with regard to the phenomenon.

A great many authors concur in their view of divorce as a crisis within the family, affecting each member. The phases of this crisis and the reactions generated by it have been clearly identified and described, with regard both to children and, in greater depth, to adults, (Bohannon, 1970; Weiss, 1975; Kessler and Deutsch, 1977). The mother has usually been the particular focus of attention, although the father has also lately become a subject of interest. The actual separation is only one phase of a process that begins before and continues beyond it. Finally, there seems to be a fairly generalized prevalence of remarriage.

Opinions are more sharply divided when it comes to the effects of divorce, particularly as far as children are concerned (Yudkin and Holme, 1963; Bowlby and Parkes, 1970; Rutter, 1971, 1974); Hetherington, Cox, and Cox, 1977; Wallerstein and Kelly, 1980). A number of significant variables related to this subject have been identified, but the matter of consequences, whether short or long term, has yet to be resolved. There is an important point that should be emphasized here. It will be difficult for research findings to settle the question unless the researcher's own theoretical stance is clarified and it is recognized that, however unconsciously it may be, his or her mental bias is going to determine the way the inquiry is structured (Leahey, 1984).

Although a great deal has been written about divorce with regard to the process of separation and its effects, there is very little literature concerning actual intervention, and especially intervention directed at the residual family as a system rather than toward its members as individuals. That is the aim of this chapter, which presents a preventive postseparation multifamily intervention, constructed by the author over the last seven years in the context of her clinical work with the Montreal Institute of Community and Family Psychiatry (Institut de Psychiatrie Communautaire et Familiale). It should be emphasized straight away that the terms *separation* and *divorce* are used here synonymously.

THE THEORETICAL CONTEXT

Although the model is still in the process of construction, it should be situated in the framework of the affinities (the mental bias and theoretical filiations mentioned above) that shape it.

1. The family's functioning and evolution are viewed from the angle of the general systems theory (von Bertalanffy, 1978). The family is a natural, organic system and is subject to the rules governing this type of system. These same rules determine what relationships the system establishes with neighboring systems, which it influences and by whose influences it is affected.

2. Divorce is perceived as a crisis (Wiseman, 1975; Hetherington, Cox, and Cox, 1978) whose repercussions have an impact on two fronts: on the new system being incubated and on the individuals who compose it. On the personal level we find the appearance of diminished functioning (reactions of melancholy, depression, and anger); on the systemic level there are difficulties in reorganizing daily life and establishing an adequate rhythm and quality with regard to contacts with the external parent, the extended family, and the social entourage. The stress involved in this crisis can make the adult less responsive to the needs of the children.

3. The crisis, however, is not solely a source of pain but also leads to growth (Johnson, 1977; Kessler, 1975). This is not to say that separation is a good thing, nor in any way to deny the painful shock, the distressed confusion, the hurt and turmoil, suffered by those who go through it. Although there is a profusion of scientific, clinical, and personal evidence to show the suffering caused by the crisis, there are as yet only a few brave voices who dare to point out its positive aspects and inherent challenges. Both individuals and systems possess inner resources that

are not always fully recognized and used to advantage. The upheaval, then, offers an opportunity for growth and maturity for each member of the residual family and the new system it constitutes. Rather than being restricted to reestablishing the equilibrium, the intervention should aim at guiding efforts toward finding innovative solutions that will enable the protagonists to transcend the crisis by standing up to it and to leave the past behind them. This is a dimension of the "crisis" phenomenon that is beginning to draw interest from researchers in areas other than divorce.

4. Once the family is destroyed, the predivorce unit has to be restructured into two separate ecologies: the mother/child(ren) ecology, on the one hand, and that of the father/child(ren), on the other. These constitute two distinct psychological topographies in which the children are overlapping features (Ahrons, 1980). The former partners once again become independent of each other while nonetheless remaining the joint parents of the children they have had together. The children have to learn to fit into these systems, each of which is governed by its own rules. As for the parents, they have to learn to respect the frontiers of each system and at the same time assume the new responsibility of easing the children's movement between them.

To recapitulate: the family is perceived in its dimension as an organic *system;* divorce is viewed as a *crisis* that strikes the system; among the effects of the crisis we retain the liberating aspect, which is a source of *growth;* and this rejuvenating energy can be mobilized to serve the *restructuring* of the residual systems and the individuals who compose it.

5. This brings us to a useful intervention that first of all makes it possible to accelerate the process of adaptation and then forestalls the appearance of secondary problems arising from divorce.

The model presented here draws its inspiration directly from the work of Hetherington et al. (1977) and Wallerstein and Kelly (1980), who deal with a cluster of conditions likely to intensify or minimize these problems.

CLIENTELE

The clientele consists of families in various stages of the separation process (the group is to be made as heterogeneous as possible so as to enable the participants to see for themselves that the course of events follows an evolutionary pattern). The families come either on their own initiative or on the recommendation of a professional who has usually been consulted because of a child or children's difficulties. In the former case, the family is given an evaluation that includes discussion of the appropriateness of their participation and the way it should be carried out. In the latter case, the evaluation is often completed by the professional before referral.

Two criteria are used to decide whether or not to accept the family: the absence of severe pathology, and the presence of difficulties directly linked to the separation. We emphasize the usefulness of including an asymptomatic family in the group if the case arises, as an example of "survival" and success and an encouragement to the other participants.

As it stands at present, the model is particularly attractive to mothers, although the growing frequency of shared custody is likely to lead to greater participation by fathers as well.

FORMAT

Guardian parents and children meet together at weekly sessions of about seventy-five minutes each, over a period of six months (November to May). The approach is designed to be as flexible as possible, since it allows and provides for:

- General assembly sessions including both adults and children
- Simultaneous sessions of the different generations
- Sessions at which the fathers are invited to join their children
- Where necessary, individual family therapy sessions
- Individual therapy, where the individual is referred to the child psychiatry service or whatever other means are appropriate

The groups are conducted by a therapist and cotherapist, assisted by a trainee. At the end of the course each family is evaluated individually to determine whether its further participation in the next series would be useful.

AIMS OF THE INTERVENTION

The objective is to remobilize the natural forces of the system and the individuals with a view to restructuring the family. This restructuring must also provide favorable ground for the further individual development of each member of the family.

The model distinguishes four key elements: acceptance of reality;

restatement of the situation; recognition of the double loyalty experienced by the children; and the mental well-being of the guardian parent. I will discuss the first three factors briefly and deal at greater length with the fourth, where the concept of autonomy becomes the central issue.

Acceptance of Reality

Painful and distressing though it may be, the reality of the situation has to be accepted by the adults and by the children: the fact is that the couple no longer live together. When the very last possibility of reconciliation has been exhausted, it is essential to identify and resolutely reject every single fantasy, however vague, of all living together again.

If often happens that the attachment of one of the partners (or both) constitutes a serious obstacle to acceptance of this reality (Kitson, 1982; Spanier and Thompson, 1984). In children, the desire to see their parents reunited lasts for a long time after the separation (Gardner, 1976).

Restatement of the Situation

There are numerous clinical examples of parents who are horror-struck at the idea that their children "no longer have a father (mother)" and children who are shattered by the prospect of not seeing one or the other of the parents any more. If one admits that a change at the level of perception modifies the associated affects (Goldsmith, 1982), the restatement of "We are no longer a family" in terms of "We are a different kind of family" is an encouraging indication of a constructive change.

This change becomes apparent through the creation of two new systems, as mentioned above, each with its own frontiers and style of functioning. "Dad's home" and "Mom's home" are two distinct and independent spaces and constitute a duality to which most children manage to adjust—another little-recognized proof of adaptability. It is the parents who often seem to have more difficulty in accepting the situation and respecting the independence of each space: "Dad always asks who comes to see Mom."

Recognition of the Double Loyalty

Many researchers and clinicians (Gardner, 1976; Wallerstein and Kelly, 1980) underline the existence of the child's feeling of simultaneous loyalty toward both parents. Fidelity to the other parent is often perceived as a threat, eliciting demands for exclusive loyalty: "How can you still love your father after what he's done to us?" The need to make a painful and unfair choice is eliminated when children are allowed to assume their double loyalty without being burdened by guilt about it.

The intervention therefore encourages easy access to the external parent by every possible means, such as telephone calls, brief visits, or longer stays. There are two reasons for this: first, because ease of access is one of the variables identified by the above-mentioned authors as important in children's adjustment to the separation, and second, because this helps to keep them out of situations of emotional blackmail, haggling, and quarrels over money.

The Mental Well-being of the Guardian Parent

The model uses one of the important variables identified in the work of Hetherington (1979) and Wallerstein and Kelly (1980): the satisfactory functioning of the guardian parent. Within the framework of ongoing research carried out as an extension to the present model, I put forward the hypothesis that there is an association between the autonomy of the guardian parent and successful restructuring.

The concept of autonomy is a complex one. Several authors refer to it (Berman and Turk, 1981; McCubbin and Patterson, 1983), but they do not offer any definition with a set of specific behaviors that would serve to illustrate it. Without going into details as to the methodology of the research, the intervention has pointed up three elements in particular.

Control. Divorce is often experienced as a situation of powerlessness: the individual, managed, directed, and organized by external forces, is incapable of taking things in hand. The intervention encourages the parent to retrieve control over his or her life and that of the children, and to envisage greater command over circumstances prejudicial to family life.

The case of G.: After a stormy separation, G., with provisional custody of the marriage's two sons aged nine and eleven, immigrated alone to Canada, where she had no family or friends other than those of her ex-husband. Here she found herself without a profession and with no means of financial support. With a view to ensuring her future, she began to study to become a librarian, which involved obtaining a study grant and attending part-time courses so as to be at home when the children returned from school. Her program constantly threatened to collapse under the attacks of her former spouse, which included his accusing her of being a bad mother, inciting the boys to unruliness, withholding alimony or spending certain amounts without consulting her or obtaining her consent, and so on. This was further aggravated by the never-ending disputes between the two boys and their hostile behavior toward their mother, whose authority they persistently put to the test.

At the end of her tether, G. was ready to admit defeat, hand over the children to their father, and give up her studies. But, encouraged by support from the group and the therapists who, among other things, urged her not to make any decisions of such importance while her energies were so badly depleted, she gradually managed to regain control of herself and the children and to become friends with a neighbor. Her renewed energy even led to her being offered a part-time job, which she was able to carry out while she finished her studies.

Feeling of competence. The experience of divorce has an impact on the all-important question of self-confidence and confidence in others (Bowlby, 1973), and one of the most frequent repercussions is that it affects one's feeling of competence as a parent. The task of the intervention is to reassure parents that they have not failed in their parental role and that their children still trust them.

The case of J.: The daughter J. was eleven years old, big for her age, and reserved though attentive to the group. Her mother complained of her that "she never talks to me about anything important, what she thinks about or anything. . . . She only comes to me when she needs money. . . . I don't even know if she still loves me." At one of the sessions, with the support of the group and encouraged to look one another straight in the eyes, the mother and daughter told each other about their respective fears and desires. The dialogue ended with a mutual commitment to set aside one evening a week when J. would talk about her day while her mother would do nothing but listen to her. This engendered a remarkable understanding between them, leading to a mutual trust that enabled J. even to ask her mother for advice outright!

Social interactions. Separation deals a heavy blow to one's self-image as a lovable person. The mother in particular will tend to huddle up and isolate herself from any social contact, and a feeling of being completely useless is very common. During the sessions parents are encouraged to examine their own personal needs. Greater accessibility to the outside world, maintaining former links of friendship, and building up a new social network are all explored and efforts in these directions are overtly encouraged. Whatever form it takes (group activities, classes, sports), every attempt, every move, toward reconstructing a satisfying social life (Weiss, 1975; Brown, 1976) is given support. Therapists also encourage the parent to re-create a personal social life apart from joint family activities.

The case of M: After being divorced for seven years, M.'s life revolved exclusively around her work and her ten-year-old daughter. One or two initial failures had led her to decide that she was no longer attractive, and "had no need of a man." When the group discussed heterosexual relationships (successes and failures, hopes and fears), M. would state that "none of that interests me any more." The group eventually caused her to revise her attitude through the idea that she richly deserved a holiday for herself. Although she clung to her original position at first, M. finally announced her decision to spend the Christmas holidays in the sun in the Caribbean, where she met a divorced man whom she continued to see subsequently.

THERAPEUTIC APPROACH

In line with its objective of releasing inherent resources diminished or simply camouflaged by the crisis, the model makes use of a wide range of intervention techniques taken from family therapy, psychodrama, and Multiple Family Therapy (MFT; Laqueur, 1973). This requires unfailing qualities of flexibility and adaptability to innovation on the part of the therapists.

Group members are expected to take active part—*active* being the key word—in the process of adapting to the new situation. Through their close attentiveness to the group, therapists deliberately engineer situations that "force" its members to find for themselves solutions to their difficulties. They use the following approaches:

- Increasing and improving interactions and intrafamilial communication. The group offers an intragenerational support system (children among each other, mothers among mothers) that enables them to feel stronger and more assured, and this makes it easier for them to run the risk of attempting significant exchanges within their own familial system. For example, ten-year-old D., the second of four children, was often sad and silent. The whole family was badly affected by his sulking and sullenness, his disputes with his older brother, and his constant provocation of the two younger children. His behavior was driving his mother to distraction. Matters reached a head when one day, sitting facing his mother and with the therapist standing behind him, D. dared to say out loud what it was that tormented him: he was frightened that his mother no longer loved him as much as she used to, and that she was just waiting for the moment she could send him to live with his father. The mother, a woman of a warm, open nature, told him with tears in her eyes that she had never imagined his distress; she assured him of her love and made an effort to devote more time to him. The change, first of all in D. and then, significantly, within the whole network of family relationships, was quite remarkable.

- Overcoming specific difficulties identified by the family or by the therapists, when these are a hindrance to the family's functioning smoothly. Such problems include quarreling siblings, lack of discipline, social isolation, conflict about visits to the external parent, and so on.
- Informing the group of results of recent research on divorce when these can help the understanding and acceptance of disturbing behavior. L., the mother of two boys aged three and four, was greatly alarmed by the signs of regression, fitful moods, and temperamental behavior of her younger child, and she was at a loss as to how to handle the situation. The therapist's explanations showed her how her son's reactions fitted into the pattern of behaviors commonly found in children of his age affected by divorce. This put L.'s fears to rest and enabled her to respond more effectively to her son's needs.

CONCLUSIONS

Although our model is still in the process of construction, the clinical experience has already led to a number of empirical conclusions regarding its benefits, which can be grouped under three headings.

1. *Optimization of resources.* Given the scarcity of resources available for helping families individually, it is an advantage that the model offers a formula that is both economical and quality-oriented.

2. *Group synergy.* The frequent criticism that the therapist's efforts are dispersed in group work derives from the view that the therapist is the prime agent in recovery. We find that this objection becomes less valid insofar as the therapist's efforts mobilize the energies of the group. Our groups have all been through comparable experiences, and group synergy seems to be particularly effective in triggering individual solutions to shared problems. The participants' underlying resources are an integral part of the model, and bringing them to light and using them to advantage play a key role in optimizing professional and social resources.

3. *A therapeutic and preventive tool.* The intervention's therapeutic action takes place at the level of the temporary disorganization resulting from separation. The model nonetheless does contain a preventive dimension that in our view is certainly of equal importance: it encourages the decision to restructure the family within a clearly defined systemic framework. Because the pitfalls commonly associated with separation are identified, participants can seek to avoid them, which gives them a chance to get through the crisis in a constructive way.

REFERENCES

Ahrons, C. R. (1980). "Divorce: A Crisis of Family Transition and Change." *Family Relations* 29:533–540.

Berman, W. H., and Turk, D. C. (1981). "Adaptation to Divorce: Problems and Coping Strategies." *J. Marriage and the Family* 43:179–189.

Bertalanffy, L. von. (1978). "General Systems Theory." In *General Systems Theory and Human Communication,* ed. B. D. Ruben and J. Y. Kim. Rochelle Park, N.J.: Hayden.

Bohannon, P. (1970). "The Six Stations of Divorce." In *Divorce and After,* ed. P. Bohannon. New York: Doubleday.

Bowlby, J. (1973). "Self-reliance and Some Conditions that Promote It." In *Support, Innovation and Autonomy,* ed. R. Gosling. London: Tavistock.

Bowlby, J., and Parkes, C. M. (1970). "Separation and Loss within the Family." In *The Child in His Family,* ed. E. J. Anthony and C. M. Koupernick. New York: Wiley-Interscience.

Brown, E. (1976). "Divorce Counseling." In *Treating Relationships,* ed. D. H. Olson. Lake Hills, Iowa: Graphic.

Figley, C. R., and McCubbin, H. I., eds. (1983). *Stress and the Family*. Vol. 2, *Coping with Catastrophe*, New York: Brunner/Mazel.

Gardner, R. A. (1976). *Psychotherapy with Children of Divorce*. New York: Jason Aronson.

Goldsmith, J. (1982). "The Post-Divorce Family System." In *Normal Family Processes*, ed. F. Walsh. New York: Guilford Press.

Hetherington, E. M. (1979). "Divorce: A Child's Perspective." *Am. Psych.* 34, no. 10:851–858.

Hetherington, E. M., Cox, M., and Cox, R. (1977). "Beyond Father Absence: Conceptualization on Effects of Divorce." In *Contemporary Readings in Child Psychology*, ed. E. M. Hetherington and R. Parker. New York: McGraw-Hill.

––––––– (1978). "The Aftermath of Divorce." In *Mother/Child, Father/Child Relationships*, ed. J. H. Stevens and M. Mathews. Washington, D.C.: National Association for the Education of Young Children.

Johnson, S. (1977). *First Person Singular: Living the Good Life Alone*. Philadelphia: Lippincott.

Kessler, K., and Deutsch, M. (1977). "Divorce Therapy: An In-Depth Survey of Therapists' Views." *Family Process* 16:413–444.

Kessler, S. (1975). *The American Way of Divorce: Prescription for Change*. Chicago: Nelson-Hall.

Kitson, G. C. (1982). "Attachment to the Spouse in Divorce: A Scale and Its Application." *J. Marriage and the Family* 44, no. 2:379–393.

Laqueur, H. P. (1973). "Multiple Family Therapy: Questions and Answers." In *Techniques of Family Psychotherapy*, ed. D. A. Block. New York: Grune and Stratton.

Leahey, M. (1984). "Findings from Research on Divorce: Implications for Professionals' Skill Development." *Am. J. Orthopsychiat.* 54, no. 2:298–317.

McCubbin, H. I., Joy, C. B., Cauble, A. E., Comeau, J. K., Patterson, J. M., and Needle, R. H. (1980). "Family Stress and Coping: A Decade Review." *J. Marriage and the Family* 42:855–781.

McCubbin, H. I., and Patterson, J. M. (1983). "Family Transitions: Adaptation to Stress." In *Stress and the Family*. Vol. 1, *Coping with Normative Transitions*, ed. H. I. McCubbin and C. R. Figley. New York: Brunner/Mazel.

Rutter, M. (1971). "Parent/Child Separation: Psychological Effects on the Children." *J. Child Psychol. Psychiat.* 12:223–260.

––––––– (1974). *The Quality of Mothering: Maternal Deprivation Reassessed*. Harmondsworth: Penguin.

Spanier, G. B., and Thompson, S. (1984). *The Aftermath of Separation and Divorce*. Beverly Hills: Sage.

Sprenkle, D. H., and Cyrus, C. L. (1983). "Abandonment: The Stress of Sudden Divorce." In *Stress and the Family*. Vol. 2, *Coping with*

Catastrophe, ed. C. R. Figley and H. I. McCubbin. New York: Brunner/Mazel.

Wallerstein, J., and Kelly, J. (1980). *Surviving the Breakup: How Children and Parents Cope with Divorce.* New York: Basic Books.

Weiss, R. S. (1975). *Marital Separation.* New York: Basic Books.

Wiseman, R. S. (1975). "Crisis Theory and the Process of Divorce." *Social Casework* 56:205–212.

Yudkin, S., and Holme, A. (1963). *Working Mothers and Their Children.* London: Michael Joseph.

IX

Transcultural Perspectives on Development

33

Introduction

J. GERALD YOUNG

Each society ensures both an orderly future for itself and the means for adaptation by individuals. It does so through the evolution of customs guiding enculturation of children by their families. The purpose of instruction in these customs is to give children a set of common practices known to promote a balance between individual aims and social integrity. The results are inevitably imperfect. Erik Erikson observed that "a society cannot afford to be arbitrary and anarchic." As each culture needs

> to create people who will function effectively as the bulk of the people, as energetic leaders, or as useful deviants, even the most "savage" culture must strive for what we vaguely call a "strong ego" in its majority or at least in its dominant minority—i.e., an individual core firm and flexible enough to reconcile the necessary contradictions in any human organization, to integrate individual differences, and above all to emerge from a long and unavoidably fearful infancy with a sense of identity and an idea of integrity. (Erikson, 1963, pp. 185–86).

Of course, each society is burdened by shortcomings in its social codes, which sometimes oblige a more strenuous assertion of the rules, in order to avoid a dissolution catalyzed by discontented individuals. The art of government and its form rest upon the structures it employs to determine when individual views accurately and impartially portray a need for change and when they are a self-indulgent threat to the common good.

This appraisal reveals how vigilant each society must be over the development of its children and how it prescribes a hierarchy of values to govern their enculturation and education. It implies that society will codify methods to determine when children have become pathologically deviant and develop means to aid them or isolate them. This is done systematically and rapidly in some cultures, leading to untempered homogeneity. At the other extreme, enculturation can be neglected entirely for large groups of children, as has occurred with homeless children in the United States. It is vital for theoretical and clinical purposes that child psychiatrists examine and compare the conventions that societies employ to nourish the development of children, identify deviance and pathology, and select appropriate therapies.

McClure, in chapter 34, surveys cultural guidelines for the development of children in contemporary China. He describes the administrative cleavage of child and family mental health activities (the responsibility of "social organization, the educational system, family and marriage law, and medical and paramedical services") from the professional tasks of child psychiatrists ("the treatment of severe psychiatric conditions"). From one perspective this arrangement embodies the laudable seriousness attached by China to nurturing the development of its children. These activities are to be integrated into governmental activities as a primary objective, utilizing several related agencies. From another perspective, this organization fails to utilize professional knowledge and scientific facts drawn from psychoanalysis, genetics, neurobiology, and pathophysiology that can promote understanding of normal and abnormal development, guiding all types of interventions.

Distinctive features of the Chinese approach to child development and mental health are instructive. Recent reports from China suggest less delinquency, drug abuse, anorexia nervosa, and adolescent suicide. This is a paramount challenge to transcultural inquiry, and its public health significance warrants rapid comparative epidemiological research in China and selected Western nations. The burgeoning substance abuse, homelessness, school-age pregnancy, and antisocial disorders occurring in the United States, for example, not only are a public health menace and the cause of many personal tragedies but may reflect a fundamental deterioration of the American social fabric. Democracy balances between invigorating, liberty-preserving individualism and anarchy. It is notable that these problems occur in a country uncommon among industrialized Western nations in its lack of an infant care leave policy for parents during the first six months of an infant's life and its inadequate policies, regulation, and supervision for day-care centers (Young and Zigler, 1986). This can be contrasted with the commonsense emphasis of the Chinese government on prevention of mental illness as a logical counterforce to the problems associated with having only 120 child psychiatry inpatient beds for a country with 380 million children, as reported by McClure. To what degree can child psychiatrists successfully cope with conduct disorders, substance abuse, and adolescent suicide in those Western countries that have lost many basic forms of sociocultural nurturance for children?

The cost of these advantages of Chinese social structure is, however, evocatively evident in Chiland's graphic description in chapter 35 of the details of daily life for most Chinese families. Their limited resources dramatically narrow their choices when compared to opportunities for Western families. When coupled with political-cultural restrictions conventional in current Chinese society, the horizons for individual Chinese children are not so bright and broad. But what of the perspective of the millions of children for which a society has responsibility? As Chiland pointedly asks, "Are Westerners happier?" An affirmative answer is more elusive on a scale of millions. Freedom brings its own scars, for resources are not distributed equally, and a single culture assuring predictably acceptable and rewarded behavior is lacking. Alternatives are possible, and identifying the blurred boundary of the unacceptably idiosyncratic is difficult, promoting frustrating debates as to whether a group of behaviors is, for example, symptomatic of an antisocial disorder or part of a developmental passage. Chiland eloquently points out the tensions between the mandatory birth control that seems so unacceptably intrusive to Westerners and the associated possibility of a much lower rate of child abuse. Many such uncertainties are evident. What are we to think of the child-rearing philosophies of such radically different cultures? To what extent are they mutually exclusive choices?

If dissimilar child-rearing practices between China and Western nations provide a crucible for delineating sociocultural influences on development and psychopathology, perhaps a pragmatic approach for research would be to initially set aside broad conceptual controversies that require decades to examine. To what degree do fundamentally different cultures agree on the prevalence and symptom components of a "specific" neuropsychiatric syndrome that is behaviorally defined and not unambiguously coded by obvious physical signs (e.g., classical neurological signs or facial deformities) or laboratory tests? Tao reporting on infantile autism in China in chapter 36 offers an optimistic preliminary answer; he suggests the capacity of societies to integrate scientific methods and data from other countries in relation to relatively uncontroversial clinical topics. This might appear trivial until we recall recent decades of disagreement concerning the diagnosis of autism in Western countries. Cultural differences might aggravate the dissension about criteria for the diagnosis of autism, but Tao indicates that application of criteria used in the West was readily accomplished.

An unanswered question remains at this stage of Tao's research. He continues to emphasize the rarity of autism, in spite of the dramatic increase in prevalence found in his survey when compared to earlier Chinese research. Are there other cultural influences affecting diagnostic assessments that account for the existence of a lower prevalence than in samples from Western countries, or is there an actual difference that will be a focus for fundamental etiologic research?

The work of Yamazaki and his colleagues, reported in chapter 37, exemplifies the type of research that will gradually decipher more complex riddles, particularly concerning the means through which culture contributes to the sculpting of less severe psychopathology during development. In this instance, they probe the consequences of changing social codes attributable to urbanization, fluctuating economic forces in a period of rapid economic growth, a reduced birthrate, and unsettled family structure in the context of a surviving "traditional Japanese village consciousness." These internal factors operate alongside the influence of Western (particularly American) culture on conventional Japanese social forms. They select a set of pathological behaviors for scrutiny: school refusal, bullying, and the interactions of victim and bullying victimizer. These symptoms are instructive because they occur in all countries and are responsive to shifts in social norms. This recalls earlier analysis of a primary cultural source of neurotic behavior, the requirement for each society to generate cultural forms to balance the individual's self-interest with the need for overall social harmony and group survival.

Evidence for breakdown in the social framework, whether it is adolescent drug abuse in the United States, student riots in France, or an eruption of bullying and school refusal in Japanese middle schools, leads to a search for the roots of the new malignancy. The next phase of this research will require judicious planning to explicate the relation of this unique occurrence of social change and the subsequent appearance of specific psychopathology. If a successful research design could be formulated, in spite of the complexity of the influences at work, it might encompass transcultural perspectives on developmental psychopathology (Murphy, 1985).

Differences in the physical care, educational opportunities, and psychological development of children across the Australian continent reveal that national variations in child rearing are not the sole result of differing social structures but reflect such basic phenomena as the geographic characteristics of a child's setting. Connell, in chapter 38, gives an evocative account of children in the Australian outback, isolated pioneers whose austere living conditions leave sharp imprints on their development, both advantageous and disadvantageous. Advances in technology now bring increasing relief to parents in the outback struggling to overcome the disadvantages, particularly interferences in social and language development. These technical enhancements of service include use of the postal service, radio, traveling professional teams in all-terrain vehicles, airplanes, and even direct telecast using a new communications satellite. They are applied to the evaluation and treatment of both physical illnesses and mental disorders, as well as to general education and special education services.

Connell's chapter depicts the rich, practical imagination of Australians coping with the singular challenge of ministering to a relatively small population spread across a vast landmass. Cross-national, collaborative research and planning could pinpoint which methods would be best applied in other countries with similar geographic challenges.

Another type of collaborative research across national boundaries is reported in chapter 39 by Jegede of Nigeria and Cederblad of Sweden. They achieve a true transcultural perspective in their survey of mental health problems in Nigerian children by applying the same evaluation instruments used by Cederblad in earlier studies on samples in the Sudan. The findings are noteworthy: the symptom frequencies in the Ibadan region are closely similar to those found earlier in the two Khartoum studies, and comparable to prevalence rates in previous epidemiological surveys in industrialized Western countries (Earls, 1985). These studies also verify that this type of research can be conducted with accuracy and success in developing countries in which these surveys have not previously been accomplished. The applications of data derived from such research would be quite significant: they would provide an indication of the substantial unmet mental health needs of children and adolescents across the world; they would supply a comparative basis for understanding apparent shifts in the prevalence rate of a symptom, such as school refusal in Japan; they would help identify special needs (e.g., the higher rates reported for some symptoms in the eleven-to-thirteen-year-old children in this Nigerian sample agree with the special vulnerability to problems during the middle school period described in the Japanese study and with descriptions of shifts in psychic structure during preadolescence discussed over several decades by psychoanalysts); they would suggest the likelihood that, in spite of distinct sociocultural features of a country such as China (as reported by McClure), the symptom prevalence rates for children are likely to be similar, just as the prevalence of autism in China is moving closer (in Tao's research) to that described in other surveys (Achenbach and Edelbrock, 1980; Nurcombe and Cawte, 1967; Werner and Smith, 1979).

Many questions arise following the success of this study in Ibadan. Other investigators will inquire about aspects of the research design and methods, including the instruments employed, the reliability of various components of the research, the validity of various categories selected, the need for informants beyond the mother, and many other considerations that make research such as this so perplexing. Yet questions such as these lead to increasingly elegant epidemiological methods. Jegede and Cederblad have confirmed the wisdom and feasibility of a comprehensive epidemiological survey of child and adolescent psychiatric disorders across several countries in distinctly different parts of the world. Transcultural research is advancing from theory, observations, and case studies to an integrated scientific enterprise that will be the basis for better-informed child advocacy across the world.

REFERENCES

Achenbach, T., and Edelbrock, C. (1980). "Behavioral Problems and Competencies Reported by Parents of Normal and Disturbed Children Aged 4 through 16. *Monogr. Soc. Research Child Devel.* 44, no. 185.
Earls, F. (1985). "Epidemiology of Psychiatric Disorders in Children and Adolescents." In *Psychiatry,* ed. R. Michels. Vol. 3. Philadelphia: J. B. Lippincott, chap. 12.
Erikson, E. H. (1963). *Childhood and Society.* New York: Norton.
Murphy, J. M. (1985). "Cross-Cultural Psychiatry." In *Psychiatry,* ed. R. Michels. Vol. 3. Philadelphia: J. B. Lippincott, chap. 2.
Nurcombe, B., and Cawte, J. E. (1967). "Patterns of Behavior Disorder amongst the Children of an Aboriginal Population." *Aust. N.Z. J. Psychiat.* 1:119–133.
Werner, E. E., and Smith, R. S. (1979). "An Epidemiologic Perspective on Some Antecedents and Consequences of Childhood Mental Health Problems and Learning Disabilities: A Report from the Kauai Longitudinal Study." *J. Am. Acad. Child Psychiat.* 18:292–306.
Young, K. T., and Zigler, E. (1986). "Infant and Toddler Day Care: Regulations and Policy Implications." *Am. J. Orthopsychiat.* 56:43–55.

34

Developments in Child and Family Mental Health Care in China

GUY MICHAEL MCCLURE

An appreciation of China's current philosophical and political stance is essential for understanding its approach to child and family mental health (Brown, 1981). Underlying the organization of society and its approach to mental health is a philosophy in which Marxist-Leninist thought is superimposed on deeply entrenched traditional values. During the Cultural Revolution, communist dogma sought to suppress these traditional values and prevent the influx of Western liberal and materialist concepts. Over the past decade, however, there has been an attempt to integrate these three philosophical positions.

Communism emphasizes strict allegiance and conformity to a one-party state, hierarchical social organization, and a society in which the needs of the individual are subordinate to the common good. This system was superimposed on the ancient Daoist philosophy based on concepts such as moderation, equilibrium, and balance between yin and yang. These concepts persist, as do superstition and a faith in traditional methods such as those employed in traditional Chinese medicine. In addition, the Confucian values of family loyalty, respect for elders, and social conformity still exist in modified form in the new communist state. A single-party system has been common to both ancient and modern Chinese society. More recently, there has been a gradual influx of Western liberal and materialist concepts that encourage individual effort, competition, and innovation. This modest liberalization has led to criticism by young intellectuals who are frustrated by what they see as excessive bureaucratic control. It is within this framework that child and family mental health policy has been developed.

355

CHINA'S SOCIAL ORGANIZATION

Society is strictly organized by the Communist party and controlled by party cadres. There is a hierarchical structure wherein direction and supervision passes from the Communist party to each province or city and then down through the system until it eventually impinges upon the individual family. Similarly, problems requiring assistance may be referred upward until the appropriate level of expertise is reached. In rural settings the organization is usually based on the commune and in urban centers on the neighborhood. Such a hierarchical system inhibits individuality but enhances discipline and social order.

There is an expectation to conform to what are considered desirable attitudes and behavior. Help (and pressure to conform) may be available from the extended family with considerable respect and authority still vested in grandparents. Alternatively, if problems cannot be dealt with by the family, they may be discussed in small groups of cadres and comrades in the workplace or near the individual's home. Problems are frequently dealt with by group discussions, often in terms of communist doctrine in small groups (*Xiaozu*) in which both personal and public issues are discussed (Sidel and Sidel, 1982).

Family and marital difficulties and problems with badly behaved children are often dealt with by a neighborhood committee, which includes unpaid retired workers who are respected and will have known many of those concerned all their lives. Retired workers also act as neighborhood watchdogs ("Granny Police") who may report naughty children or delinquents to their parents or the neighborhood committee. A system such as this would be considered intrusive in the West, but the assistance and supervision offered maintain a high level of public order without the need for an armed police force. More recently, however, student protest is posing a problem for the authorities, indicating an underlying unrest among urban youth.

China's Marriage Law of 1981 is concerned with the responsibilities and rights of spouses, parents, children, siblings, and grandparents (*Beijing Review*, 1981a; Hare-Mustin, 1982). Equality between spouses and the right to personal independence are stressed. After marriage, the woman may become a member of the man's family or the man a member of the woman's family, according to their wishes. Women may keep their own name, and children may adopt the name of either parent. Parents have a legal duty to rear and educate their children and to discipline and protect minors. If their children cause damage, the parents are held responsible and must pay compensation. Similar rights and responsibilities apply to illegitimate children, fostered and adopted children, and stepchildren.

Both husband and wife are required by the state to practice family planning, and there is currently the well-publicized attempt to limit population growth by encouraging the one-child family. The minimum age for marriage has been raised to twenty-two for men and twenty for women, and even later marriage is encouraged. Parents must wait their turn to have children, and they are rewarded for making a one-child pledge by being given extended maternity leave, subsidized medical care, and nursery care. Parents who try to thwart the system are put under considerable pressure to abort subsequent children; if they insist on having a second child, they are likely to forfeit allowances, preferential accommodation, and promotion at work. In practice, there is wide variation in the extent to which this policy is applied, with stricter application in cities than in the countryside (Croll et al., 1985).

Under the Marriage Law, divorce is theoretically easier and may be granted when both spouses desire it. When only one party wants a divorce, the work unit or neighborhood will try to bring about a reconciliation through mediation. Mediators are senior members of the community who ask both parties in a marital dispute to consider their responsibilities to the extended family and to the children as well as their own individual wishes. All efforts are made to protect the children in such cases. A husband may not apply for a divorce when the wife is pregnant or within one year after the birth of the child. When divorce occurs, custody and child support are carefully considered, with the best interests of the child prevailing.

In practice, divorce is still extremely rare as are other overt marital and family problems. There are few illegitimate children, single-parent families, or adopted or fostered children, and family violence is considered rare. Problems associated with intercultural or interracial marriages are uncommon, as partners usually share the same ethnic and cultural values (Baker, 1979; Croll, 1983).

CHINA'S EDUCATIONAL SYSTEM

Education of Parents

Education, both political and practical, is a cornerstone of Chinese society; the aim is to provide education and reeducation throughout life (R. Sidel, 1982). Counseling of prospective parents may take place before or after marriage, usually with the focus on contraception, though other aspects of parenthood may also be discussed (*Chinese Medical Journal,* 1984a). Envisioned is a complete network of schools for newlyweds and parents to give instruction in mothering and child care and the education of children (*Chinese Medical Journal,* 1985). After the birth of a child, the mother is given two to six months of maternity leave. During this period she receives assistance including education and support from the extended family, the community, and paramedics. Following this period only about 10 percent of children are cared for by their mother during the daytime, since she normally resumes work (R. Sidel, 1982).

Preschool Education

About 60 percent of urban children attend preschool facilities, though nationwide only 10 to 15 percent of children attend nurseries or kindergartens (*China Economic Yearbook,* 1981, p. 206; *Beijing Review,* 1981b). The remainder are cared for by a relative, friend, or neighbor. Children up to eighteen months may be placed in a nursing room attached to the mother's workplace, with the mother visiting during the day. Education starts at this level, and children are expected to cooperate in following a simple timetable (including communal potty training!) to foster group orientation and comradeship (R. Sidel, 1982).

Nurseries are for children from eighteen months to four years and kindergartens from four to seven years. They are located either close to the workplace or in the local community. In the nursery and kindergarten the children are supervised by "Aunties" who are selected on the basis of their personal qualities and competence in handling small children rather than their academic qualifications.

Although the content and manner of teaching have changed with the new political climate, both nursery and kindergarten programs are still tightly scheduled, structured, and controlled (Kessen, 1975). In the nursery emphasis is placed on social conformity. Education focuses on the self-management of personal hygiene, language development, cooperative play, and moral and political development through singing and dancing. In the kindergarten emphasis is placed upon language skills, arithmetic, and politics through cooperative activities, singing, dancing, and drawing. In their work and play, children are taught the "five loves": love of the motherland, the people, science, physical labor, and collective property ("science" replaced "the leader"). During the

1970s, initiative, competition, and individual artistic activity were also encouraged (R. Sidel, 1982).

Primary School Education

Ninety-four percent of children attend primary school, the exceptions tending to be children in remote rural areas. During the 1970s there was a renewed emphasis on study and competition in order to raise standards of numeracy and literacy (M. Sidel, 1982). Students once again are required to take examinations, and primary and middle school education has been lengthened. Although most children belong to the Young Pioneers, the junior wing of the Communist party, political study and manual labor are considered less important. In practice there is wide variation in the quality of primary school education, though efforts are being made to recruit more able teachers for rural areas.

Secondary Education

In middle school, competition is tough both to get into the Youth League (the Communist party youth wing) and to pass exams. Entrance to senior middle schools, colleges, and universities is strictly based on national entrance examinations. Teenagers are under intense pressure from their families to be admitted into higher education schools, for they are seen as the route to advancement. The many who fail suffer a loss of self-esteem, inferior job prospects, and possibly a period of unemployment after school (Hooper, 1985). The nurturance of early years is changing into fierce competition for older students in the new Chinese Society, with a consequent increase in stress.

Special boarding schools, known as work-study schools, accommodate delinquent and antisocial adolescents (Ye Gong-shao, 1985). There are about 120 such schools, each with several hundred pupils (Hooper, 1985). Antisocial behavior includes theft, violence, truancy, and sexual activity (which is not permitted before marriage). The regimes are designed to "reform" the individual ideologically, morally, and behaviorally, though it is not known to what extent this is accomplished. Adolescents who are reformed may return to normal school. The Chinese press has expressed concern about the level of antisocial behavior in adolescents, though it still appears to be at lower levels than in the West.

FACILITIES FOR CHILD MENTAL HEALTH

Because facilities are scarce, most children with psychiatric conditions are not seen by a child psychiatrist. They are more likely to receive general medical or pediatric services (Tang Ze-yuan, 1984). Health services are organized on three tiers in both urban and rural settings. In rural areas, primary health care is delivered by medical stations or clinics manned by paramedical country doctors (previously known as "barefoot doctors"). At a higher level, the commune provides a small rural hospital, and at a higher level still, the county is responsible for larger general hospitals and specialized psychiatric facilities. In the cities, primary health care is provided in health stations run by Red Cross workers and situated in the neighborhood or workplace. At the next level are district hospitals and, finally, municipal hospitals, including specialized psychiatric hospitals, which provide a child psychiatry service.

Rural child health care is relatively underdeveloped, and as two-thirds of Chinese children live in the countryside, particular emphasis has been placed on the establishment of an effective rural preschool child health care system (Xue Qinbing et al., 1982). In the 1980s, there were over 2,800 maternal and child care centers, of which over 1,800 were situated in rural areas (*Chinese Medical Journal,* 1984b, 1984c).

Pediatric facilities for child and family mental health care include well-baby clinics, pediatric outpatient clinics, and pediatric wards. At all times, the emphasis is on early detection and prevention of problems (Sidel and Sidel, 1982). These services concentrate on physical treatment and prevention, but they also provide help for psychiatrically disturbed children. There is a growing awareness of the psychosocial problems of children and adolescents, with medical colleges starting to give lectures in this area to students, parents, teachers, and child health workers (Ye Gong-shao, 1985). Psychosocial problems are managed in a simple commonsense manner, with an emphasis on socially acceptable conduct and relationships. More severe conditions are treated by pediatricians or pediatric neurologists with an interest in child psychiatry. China has twenty-four children's hospitals and eighteen institutes for child health care with a total of 31,000 pediatricians and 92,000 hospital beds. If conditions are beyond the professional competence of these pediatricians, referrals are made to specialized psychiatry or child psychiatry units.

There are only a few centers with specialized child psychiatric facilities; they are located in Beijing, Shanghai, Nanjing, Guangzhou, Harbin, and Chongking (McClure, 1987). Adolescents are more likely to be seen by adult psychiatrists or by forensic psychiatrists if they are delinquent. Because child psychiatric facilities are very limited, most children obtain treatment locally from nonspecialist professionals. Those who attend the specialist outpatient units are offered treatment by a multidisciplinary team. Current policy seeks to develop an integrated extramural psychiatric service focusing on prevention, treatment, relapse prevention, and rehabilitation (Shen Yu-cun and Zhang Wei-xi, 1982), though this is limited in child psychiatry owing to scarce resources. There are only about 120 child psychiatric inpatient beds for a population of 380 million children. Most of those admitted have some form of psychosis, and no purely behavioral disorders are treated in inpatient units.

DIAGNOSIS AND TREATMENT OF PSYCHIATRIC DISORDERS IN CHILDREN

Diagnosis and treatment are based on a mixture of traditional Chinese medicine and Western psychiatry, with the latter increasingly becoming more important. Modern Chinese psychiatrists recognize that some traditional concepts are superstitious or inadequate, though others are still used in practice. Traditionally, disorder is defined in terms of imbalance and disharmony, with treatment aimed at restoring harmonious bodily and mental functioning. This is based on long practical experience, though it is without rigorous scientific validation. Treatment methods include herbal remedies, herbal baths, and acupuncture (Xu Sheng-han 1982). Additionally, Qigong and Taijiquan, which involve controlled breathing, relaxation, and meditation, are considered beneficial for the prevention and treatment of mental disorders.

Chinese psychiatrists also recognize Western systems of classification. Disorders treated in child psychiatric facilities include childhood schizophrenia, disintegrative psychosis, periodic psychosis, manic depressive psychosis, severe obsessive-compulsive illness, epilepsy, and minimal brain dysfunction. Infantile autism has only recently been reported (Tao Kuao-tai, 1982); formerly it may have been misclassified as mental retardation or childhood schizophrenia. Many disorders recognized in the West are not regarded as specifically psychiatric disorders in China. Reaction to illness, psychosomatic complaints, developmental delay, encopresis, and enuresis are managed by the primary health network and pediatric services. Conduct disorders, emotional disorders, school nonattendance problems, and family relationship and personality problems are dealt with by the wider society, including the educational and social systems. Similarly, mental handicap is not considered specifically relevant to child psychiatrists unless there is evidence of additional mental illness. Adolescent problems, such as substance abuse, parasuicide, suicide, delinquency, anorexia nervosa, and identity confusion appear to be less common than in the West (McClure, 1988).

Western treatment is often combined with Chinese traditional medicine. Western treatment methods include the use of psychotropic medication, and ECT is very occasionally used with children. Western psychoanalytic theories are not considered useful or appropriate for China's culture, though there is a psychotherapeutic aspect to counseling and "heart-to-heart" talks. Rather than the acquisition of insight, however, the aim is to encourage responsible attitudes and behavior. There is no formal family therapy, though professionals are very aware of the importance of the family, including the extended family, and encourage relatives to understand and help a disturbed child. In addition, senior members of the community may mediate in family relationship problems. Behavioral principles are used in both schools and child psychiatric units, with desirable behavior being rewarded through red flag charts. Most emphasis, however, is placed on the group milieu to promote desirable behavior.

CONCLUSION

The political climate in China has changed significantly over the past decade, influencing the social environment of children and families and leading to changes in the mental health care system. Although greater opportunities exist, there have been difficulties in reconciling traditional Chinese culture, communism, and Western values. Encouragement of individual effort and competition is increasing opportunities for the more able children and their families. But in vulnerable individuals, this may be stressful, particularly as the new values conflict with communist dogma. Primary school children are still relatively sheltered from this stress, and there appears to be less conduct disorder and emotional disorder in young children. The very young and the old are likely to accept the constraints of a single-party system. Adolescents, however, are increasingly aware of the pressure upon them to succeed and may be frustrated by personal and environmental limitations. Although disturbed adolescents have aroused concern, there still appears to be less substance abuse, self-destructive behavior and delinquency than in the West. Reliable comparative data are required to determine whether these apparent differences are real. It will also be interesting to observe whether the recent student unrest in China has an effect on social order and delinquency among adolescents. There may well be substantial changes in future political thinking, in terms of either further liberalization or greater controls as a reaction to criticism, and this is likely to affect mental health care.

Nevertheless, China, despite its scarce resources, has developed a comprehensive policy of child and family mental health care based on social, educational, and primary health care systems. The emphasis is on mental health promotion and prevention of disturbance by early intervention. The family and community are strengthened by stressing communal responsibility and the need for acceptable behavior. China is currently learning from Western child psychiatry practitioners in an attempt to develop its own specialist facilities. Service planners in the Western developed nations and those in developing countries should similarly consider what they may learn from China's system of community child and family mental health care.

REFERENCES

Baker, H. D. R. (1979). *Chinese Family and Kinship*. London: Macmillan.
Beijing Review (1981a). "China's Marriage Law." March 16, pp. 24–27.
———— (1981b). "Care for 380 Million Children." April 6, p. 5.
Brown, L. B. (1981). *Psychology in Contemporary China*. London: Pergamon Press.
Chinese Medical Journal (1984a). "Women and Child Care Health Network in China." July, p. 472.
———— (1984b). "Article by Health Minister for World Health Day." June, p. 458.
———— (1984c). "Chinese Medical Statistics." November, p. 860.
———— (1985). "Pregnant Women's School." January, p. 74.
Croll, E. (1983). *Chinese Women since Mao*. London: Zed.
Croll, E., Davin, D., and Kane, P., eds. (1985). *China's One-Child Family Policy*. London: Macmillan.
Hare-Mustin, R. T. (1982). "China's Marriage Law: A Model for Family Responsibilities and Relationships." *Family Process* 21:477–481.
Hooper, B. (1985). "Youth in China." Harmondsworth: Penguin.
Kessen, W., ed. (1975). *Childhood in China*. New Haven: Yale University Press.

McClure, G. M. G. (1987). "Child and Family Psychiatry in China." *Journal of the American Academy of Child Psychiatry* 26:806–810.

———— (1988). "Adolescent Mental Health in China." *Journal of Adolescence* 2:1–10.

Shen Yu-cun and Zhang Wei-xi. (1982). "Psychiatric Service in the People's Republic of China." *Chinese Medical Journal* 95, no. 6:443–448.

Sidel, M. (1982). "Education: 'Red' versus 'Expert.'" In *The Health of China*, ed. R. Sidel and V. Sidel. London: Zed.

Sidel, R. (1982). *Women and Child Care in China*. Rev. Ed. Harmondsworth: Penguin.

Sidel, R., and Sidel, V. (1982). *The Health of China*. London: Zed.

Tang Ze-yuan (1984). "Pediatrics: The Development of Health Care in Children." In *Modern Chinese Medicine*, ed. Wu-Heguang. Vol. 2. Shanghai: M.T. P. Press.

Tao Kuao-tai (1982). "Diagnosis and Classification of Infantile Autism." *Chinese Journal of Neurology and Psychiatry* 15, no. 2:104.

Xiehe Liu (1981). "Psychiatry in Traditional Chinese Medicine." *British Journal of Psychiatry* 138:429–433.

Xu Sheng-han (1982). "Traditional Chinese Medicine in Mental Illnesses." *Chinese Medical Journal* 95 no. 5:325–328.

Xue Qin-bing et al. (1982). "Rural Preschool Child Health Care Organization, Content and Methods." *Chinese Medical Journal* 95, no. 8:551–556.

Ye Gong-shao (1985). "The Health and Needs of Children and Adolescents in China." *Chinese Medical Journal* 98, no. 2:79–82.

35

Three Chinese Journeys: In the Steps of a Child Psychiatrist

COLETTE CHILAND

My first contact with China occurred when I stopped off in Hong Kong in September 1978 on my way back from the International Congress of Child Psychiatry in Melbourne. To be sure, Hong Kong is not mainland China despite the fact that the population is 98 percent Chinese. In contrast to the asepsis, the social customs, and the limits of the Australian way of life I had just encountered (streets deserted as early as 5 P.M. and the ensuing dullness; on Sundays one has a hard time finding a restaurant open), Hong Kong revealed itself as a fascinating universe with its swarming mass of colorful individuals bustling about until late in the night, its dirty picturesque markets, the sampans in Aberdeen, and the crowded sheds of refugees.

Hong Kong was also my gateway to China on my first trip there in December 1978. China had just opened its doors to tourism. All groups of tourists were labeled "delegations," just as the International Study Group (ISG) of the International Association for Child and Adolescent Psychiatry and Allied Professions (IACAPAP) in 1984 had to accept the title of "delegation." On my first trip there was something more ritualistic in the Chinese welcome than on my two subsequent journeys in April 1983 and November 1984. We had taken the Canton train, and once having crossed the border, we were welcomed with a cup of tea and a political speech. On this first journey we were assigned French interpreters, with a new team of three interpreters on each stopover (Canton, Shanghai, Peking). Our skilled interpreters spoke excellent, accentless, academic French and were eager to learn more slang from us.

My other two journeys took place entirely in English, when I was with the "delegation" of the American Academy of Child Psychiatry and the International Study Group of the IACAPAP. This was a source of difficulty for me, particularly as regards proper names: Chinese nouns pronounced the English way are practically impossible to assimilate. English-speaking friends are apparently unable to fathom such traps for us French as swallowed syllables, varieties of accents, idiomatic expressions. By the time we had sorted out linguistic difficulties in order to enter into a discussion, someone else had taken the floor.

In 1978, a pleasure trip necessarily included an initial contact with Chinese life: visits were provided to factories, agricultural communes, hospitals, nursery and primary schools, families in their home surroundings (which was no longer on the program on subsequent trips). Aside from that, visits were organized to architectural sites inherited from landlords and capitalists, such as temples, the Forbidden City, and the Shanghai Museum, which had just reopened (only a few museum pieces were presented, accompanied by a number of political comments). The guides were the best I ever had, particularly in the Forbidden City. Visitors were encouraged to devote time to shopping (even more so on my second and third trips).

On this first visit I came to appreciate the hard-working, patient Chinese who, after having gone through centuries of extreme poverty, had emerged, thanks to the Liberation, suffered the hard tribulations of the Hundred Flowers, the Great Leap Forward, and the Cultural Revolution. These Chinese, so often assumed to be impassive, were brought to tears in 1978 at the evocation of the Cultural Revolution. One could not tell whether it was out of belief or the effect of propaganda (in 1977, day and night on Shanghai streets, the wrongdoings of the Gang of Four were denounced via multiple loudspeakers) that they attributed all their sufferings to the Gang of Four (what did they think about Mao whose picture was still well in view?). They were no doubt sincere when, with tears in their eyes, they spoke of the recovered rights to talk about love, heartache, and couples who had been separated, with each member assigned a different place to work in the countryside, most often dramatically distant from the spouse and the rest of the family.

Confronted with Chinese poverty one gained full insight into the term *consumer society.* Many goods were still rationed; I found out that eggs were counted by the kilo, not by the dozen, and that the mean ration for rice was 25 kilos (which appeared an enormous amount to a Frenchwoman like me who does not eat more than 40gr at a time). The ration for cotton material was 5 meters per year. Under such conditions one does not change clothes each year because shorter or longer skirts are brought into fashion.

Salaries were in 1978 what they still were in 1986: from 30 to 100 yuans and more (survivors from the ancien regime had retained some privileges, with monthly salaries up to 200–300 yuans—an exceptional situation). The exchange rate was 1 yuan to 3 French francs in 1978 and 1 yuan to 3.55 francs in 1986.

I was given the opportunity on my first trip to visit a family in Peking: the man was an engineer and the woman a primary school teacher. They lived in two tiny rooms heated by a stove fed with coaldust briquettes (something like French coal nuts), which maintained an indoor temperature no higher than 10° C when the temperature outside was below 0° C. There was no kitchen, just a wooden lean-to shared by three families in the courtyard (on my inquiring where they prepared the elaborate Chinese food, they replied, "We buy some dishes at the caterer's for celebrations". Nor was there a bathroom, or even a tap in the apartment. Just ten books or so rested on a shelf in this intellectuals' home (was it for want of room? or maybe it was because keeping too many books at home, especially foreign books, made one suspect in the eyes of the Cultural Revolution). The concrete floor must have been impossible to keep clean.

In 1978, foreigners had no trouble being allowed to watch acupuncture operations, but visiting a psychiatric hospital was almost impossible. I did visit psychiatric hospitals, though, on my second and third trips and thus had the opportunity to realize how stereotyped these visits were and how difficult to get information beyond that level.

Let us say that, in my view, my second trip was meant to prepare for the third. How naive the idea was to appear: I was well aware of what I should avoid (from my point of view and that of friends in the delegation), yet I was unable to do so. For instance, simultaneous translation sentence by sentence, which is the standard procedure, to me appeared tedious; above all it confines the speaker to a written text. I suggested that texts be written and sent in advance for translation and duplication, something we might have done ourselves. I had no guarantee, however, they could have been distributed. Clearly, such a procedure would have allowed for meetings specifically devoted to discussions among participants.

Why more direct exchanges are not favored is not clear. The same question produces varying responses according to place and respondent. What may be recognized, though, is the paramount importance of both hierarchy and bureaucracy: no one is allowed to take any initiative unless it is duly authorized. Progress, however, may be observed over the years; for instance, in 1977 in Shanghai, English-speaking Chinese and foreign practitioners were not allowed to communicate directly but could do so only through an interpreter who, before speaking, had to refer the matter to a representative of the Communist party; from 1978 on, direct conversations in English were possible and are even more so today.

Not only are the number of places one can visit and the number of people one can meet extremely limited as compared to China's vast territory and population, but all responses in conversations are loaded with an uncertainty factor. For one thing, responses usually vary. This may be due to the fact that realities vary, but it may also reflect the interlocutor's information, or what he thinks he may say or how he feels. Some do not consider themselves in danger when talking with a foreigner, but others remain cautious in all their contacts (for instance, they are not willing to receive a parcel from a foreigner directly at their home or professional address; a third party serves as their mailbox). All this seems to be directly related to the sufferings endured during the Cultural Revolution. No family was spared, whether intellectual or not: some simply suffered greater hardships than others. On listening to accounts (teachers beaten to death by their students, for example), one recognizes reports by Isaac Stern in the movie *From Mozart to Mao* and cannot help evoking the brilliant "Maoist" Parisian intellectuals justifying a reality that in fact they knew nothing about.

Child psychiatry develops only when infantile death rates slow down: clearly, children's mental health can be taken into account only insofar as children survive. The development of child psychiatry is, furthermore, directly related to an increase both in the relative number of children attending school and the period of schooling; in a population of children required to perform more complex learning, some appear to experience difficulty.

China has succeeded remarkably in reducing infantile death rates and providing its some 300 million children with schooling. Nonetheless, as compared to the ever-growing development of child psychiatry in Western culture, child psychiatry in China has lagged far behind. One may wonder why, and whether this state of affairs is a good thing or not.

The People's Republic, at its inception, benefited from Soviet technicians. (This was the time when my fellow students, at the French University, would systematically cross out the term *psychosomatic* and substitute *cortico-viscéral* on their course notes; one simply had to be Pavlovian—(and Mitchourinian and Lyssenkist.) Before the Liberation, some psychiatrists were trained abroad, notably in the United States. In Shanghai, traces of the Aurore University run by Jesuits are still present. French-speaking colleagues are more numerous; they have renewed contact with France (e.g., exchanges between Medical College no. 2 and University René Descartes—to which I happen to belong).

The Cultural Revolution, though, cut off the Chinese from what was going on outside China, and particular repression was directed at psychiatry. The mentally ill were defined as selfish beings who required political rehabilitation. In 1978, "acupuncture and political rehabilitation" were the only responses we could get to our questions on psychiatric treatments. In 1983 and 1984 the same questions were given the following responses: drugs; acupuncture (said to be particularly effective in the case of hallucinations); electroshock, without anesthetic or curare, is still in use; occupational and play therapy. Psychotherapy is also mentioned, but the term implies something rather different from what *we* call psychotherapy. Specifically, the point is to furnish both explanations (a schizophrenic patient is told that he is suffering from schizophrenia and the symptoms of his illness are explained) and advice (a moral tinge is perceptible); one of the key words I heard in 1983 was *persuasion*.

Hospital medical staffs are composed of physicians and nurses. Those with the title of "physician" have received training of varying duration: short training (three years) or long training (five to eight years). Male and female nurses are given three years of training. Both physicians and nurses have prior high school training of varying duration. (In the course of the Cultural Revolution, universities and even schools for some time were closed more often than not.) Psychiatric social workers are the exception and were trained prior to the Liberation. There are practically no clinical psychologists, nor are there rehabilitation counselors, speech therapists, and so on.

Standard mental tests are used (e.g., Wechsler, Rorschach), which are administered by nurses and physicians. The medical staff wears white coats and often caps. Beds are lined up close together in rooms with no decoration or personal objects. When we inquired about such bareness, the response was: "Administrative rule; this is a hospital."

The patient reaches the local hospital only if, in the course of the preliminary stages, the illness has failed to be "constrained"—namely, in the work unit (*danwei*), school, or community, which are the local district possibilities. More than an individual's suffering, agitation or effects on the environment are the indication for hospitalization. As regards drugs, large doses are prescribed.

In 1983 and 1984 we asked that a "schizophrenic" adolescent's file (a diagnosis of high frequency) be read and translated. It was quite an interesting experience. All descriptions of the symptoms were devoid of any developmental and relational perspective. "What happened in the course of childhood? What can be said of the relationships within the family?" Such were our questions to which it was replied: "High cultural level of the parents. They are good parents." As a matter of fact, we failed to get our point across.

The French newspaper *Le monde* had published in September 1984 a paper by Claude Lorin, "Freud, Buddha of psychoanalysis," mentioning a Chinese translation of *The Interpretation of Dreams*. Accompanied by Chinese colleagues we looked for it in bookstores in vain. Students told us they knew of a single copy available for consultation at their library, but that none was on sale.

Research work conducted, for instance, at the Nanjing Child Mental Health Research Center (Professor Tao) or at the Mental Health Institute, Beijing Medical College (Mrs. Shen), favors genetic studies of minimal brain dysfunction. Such a choice may be interpreted in various ways. The return to the biological component is a way of dealing with psychiatry as it was when the Cultural Revolution interrupted its development; in so doing the psychiatrist recovers his or her identity as a physician. We are not underrating the importance of biological psychiatry, but to innovate in this domain and not just reproduce what has been done elsewhere would require considerable means.

In addition to measures of urinary metabolites and electroencephalograms, we were interested in the fact that in China, as in Western countries, childhood hyperactivity varies inversely with parental cultural level and tolerance of the environment.

We never had the opportunity to witness ongoing work with a patient and his or her family either in consultation or in the course of hospitalization. None of the units visited was equipped with video. All we were able to observe was that consultation rooms are in no way amenable to one-to-one dialogues as we envisage them (with only partial partitions and sometimes no door at all). This was not a matter of the Chinese getting by as best they could, as was the case in the early days of Georges Heuyer's Service. To the contrary, the Chinese do not have the same sense of privacy that we have. Thus, toilets (I do not mean in psychiatric hospitals, but in public buildings) are not partitioned, or stalls are doorless, or doors are not equipped with a latch; moreover, when there is indeed a door, Chinese women (sexes being separated, I cannot speak for male Chinese) do not shut it.

But more profound than this trivial detail, the individual's life in China is not his own as is the case in the West. Without being specialists on China (which is unfortunate; ISG delegations should always include a specialist on the local culture who knows the language), we all know enough about the Chinese family, ancestor worship, and respect for parents to realize the ancient, deeply rooted sources of the emphasis placed on the group (family, work unit, homeland). In contrast, the development of Western psychiatry (should we say "development" or "hypertrophy"?) is strongly related to individualization and individualism, the rights that are recognized for the individual and those claimed by the individual.

To face up to the issues stemming from mental disease, how did the Chinese manage during the time when psychiatry was subjected to suffocation, and how do they manage currently with the limited means available? In fact, no true evaluation can be put forward without our having the opportunity to acquire a clear picture of what is going on at the root, in the family, as well as in the immediate environment.

Some troubles are probably misinterpreted; autism, for instance, is reported as either extremely infrequent or never having existed. Is this really the case, and, if so, would genetic or cultural factors be responsible for this situation? The very close links between family and infant have been put forward: the baby sleeps in its parents' bed until the age of three or four (the contraceptive virtue of this practice was not mentioned, however). Could autism have been misinterpreted in China as it was formerly in the West, where the autistic child was diagnosed as mentally retarded or deaf?

Western child psychiatrists are primarily concerned with, among other things, the prevention of adult mental illness through detection of warning signals in the child. This may be viewed as related to a developmental viewpoint, which, as mentioned above, has not been taken into account by Chinese psychiatry, notwithstanding the fact that prevention appears to be one of the main concerns of China; as an example, in the booklet that was given to me on leaving, entitled "A Brief Introduction on China's Medical and Health Services," psychiatry and prevention in the field of mental health are not even mentioned.

On the other hand, educational concern is overtly present. It may be that we visited the most efficient schools (nursery, primary, secondary schools) for "ordinary" children (1978, 1983, 1984) and deaf and dumb children (1983) or one of the best institutes of social welfare (Welfare Institute for Children in Shanghai) for children—most of whom are abandoned and physically or mentally handicapped (1984). But at least in these schools every one of us was struck by the teachers' dedication. We were permitted to see them in action, devoting communicative vitality, enthusiasm, and expressive behavior to their task. In one of the schools we visited, classes were large (up to sixty students sometimes); lectures lasted less than a hour (indeed forty minutes). The many teachers provided but a limited number of periods each (e.g., twenty periods of forty minutes each, less than fourteen hours of teaching), but they stayed much longer in the school, engaged in various tasks like preparation or coordination. In those classes with many students, however, children were all actively participating.

What are the results of this training? A specialist on China, Fox Butterfield, has reported a high proportion of school failures along with illiteracy (*China*, 1982). On my inquiring on reading and school failure, widely varying responses were given. It was generally asserted that "no teacher will drop a pupil who falls behind the others." But achievement at the end of primary schooling (from seven to twelve years of age) was variously assessed: "Yes, the child knows the three thousand characters required for newspaper reading." "No, he does not know them yet."

Two features of Chinese training—collective and selective— appeared to be distinctive. There is a tendency to send children to boarding schools, including nursery-aged children, two to six years old (out of the 399 children in a school 99 were boarders; another school reported 413 children who were boarders). One argument in favor of the boarding system was that of the importance of the parents' work, which attested to a greater interest in providing the child with boarding schools than in organizing parents' work so as to promote home child care. The adult is first a worker and only second a parent; the child is viewed as a member of a community extending far beyond the family. To our surprise, we heard people say, "We make every effort to train the members of our staff so that they love the children more than their parents do."

Schools are highly selective. Some have high standards, though others do not. Considerable pressure is brought to bear on the child, who has to get good grades to remain in the school where he has been admitted. Thus, in a primary school in Peking, in order to prepare for an entrance examination for a desirable secondary school, children of eleven or twelve years of age go to school Monday to Saturday and on

Sunday mornings. In a Youth Center in Peking in 1983 I saw children come to school voluntarily (and after selection) to attend lectures in electronics or in English (they spoke good English).

Admission to a university is the privilege of a minority. The proportion currently reported is 3 percent. Whereas childhood depression is hardly mentioned in China, one hears of adolescent suicides in relation to failure to be admitted to a university.

According to the same unformulated though to my mind active principle that the individual does not belong to himself, the student may express his preferences, but when he is assigned to a school and told what studies to undertake, he has no choice but to bow to the decisions. The same will happen later on as to his place of work, which may well be a long distance from his home and will be permanent. Such relocations may separate newlyweds who will then see each other just a few days a year. Such a situation appears to favor birth control in a society where premarital intercourse is condemned on moral grounds and where sexuality is reluctantly debated. (After some three hours of discussion, students ventured to ask us questions—moving ones, to be sure.)

From 1982, on, what had been so far a recommendation was turned into a law: only one child in a family, except when the first child is abnormal or handicapped (for other than hereditary reasons). To adopt a child is not allowed if a couple already has a child. Ethnic minorities are not subject to this law, but one is not free to marry someone from one of those minorities in order to have a larger family. People may divorce, but it must be noted that divorce is very seldom granted and pressure is brought to bear on those desiring one.

The West has been much preoccupied with the issue of child abuse. Many colleagues in our delegations (1983, 1984) asked questions about this, to which the Chinese consistently replied, "We have an only child. We cherish him as our treasure. How could we maltreat our child?" Indeed, children in the street appear to be well treated, and fathers hold their children in a very tender manner. Although discipline in the school surprises Western visitors, children nonetheless seem to be controlled by injunctions rather than violent corporal punishments. For example, games and dances in a nursery school, with the visitors invited to participate, would in France have generated into a scarcely controllable state of excitement. But on a mere call from the teacher, the children obediently and quietly gathered around her on the spot. On the other hand, in contrast to the situations just described, parents—in violation of the law—have been known to abandon their child in a hospital waiting room or railway station upon being given an unfavorable diagnosis of the child's health. And in 1983 a glimpse of possible child abuse was offered to us in the form of a common folklore theme: the stepmother.

Now, if we turn toward the West, toward our own country, we may ask the question: "What are we doing with our own resources?" They, indeed, are much more abundant than those in China, even if we take into account the fact that the cost of living is higher in Western countries.

The Chinese eat, they are clothed, they have a roof over their heads, and they may even own some property. But almost no one has a car. During the morning and afternoon rush hour, thousands of bicycles crowd the streets. A bicycle costs a minimum of 100 yuans, over a month's average salary. But are Westerners happier? The same question arose when viewing the West against the background of the African bush. The question is all the more acute in relation to China, whose long cultural past and high level of intellectual sophistication compare favorably with ours.

It has been some time now since a number of child psychiatrists moved to separate developmental problems from the realm of psychiatric disorders. They insisted that the school assume fully its educational role, thus renewing staff enthusiasm, as well as trust in teachers on the part of parents and the public. What we saw in the Chinese schools we visited invites us to rethink what is going on in our own schools.

36

Infantile Autism in China

TAO KUO-TAI

A definition developed by the U.S. National Society for Autistic Children in 1977, and subsequently approved by the American Psychiatric Association, mentioned that autism is found throughout the world in families of all racial, ethnic, and social backgrounds. Some investigators, however, considered this assertion somewhat overstated. Although they thought that infantile autism can be found in various racial, ethnic, and social groups, the question remained whether or not it exists with the same frequency in every such group (Sanua, 1984).

The prevalence of autism in China is an interesting issue. Some Western visitors have been told by their Chinese colleagues that China has no infantile autism. But certain investigators found a number of cases in Hong Kong, most in upper-class Chinese families, and thought it surprising that there were no reports of Chinese autistic children.

Initial studies conducted by the author in the Nanjing Child Mental Health Research Center in mainland China have shown that infantile autism definitely exists there. These first studies covered four cases and were reported in the *Journal of Chinese Neuropsychiatry* (Tao, 1982). Since then, I have collected eleven more cases for a total of fifteen.

The purpose of this chapter is to examine the characteristics of these fifteen cases of infantile autism, to discuss the problem of early recognition and diagnosis, and to look into the causes of autism's rarity in China in relation to China's social and cultural background.

SUMMARY OF THE FIFTEEN CASES

Until recently, there were no available statistics for an estimate of the prevalence of autism in China. From November 1955 to July 1981, 1,190 children with psychiatric disorders were admitted to the residential unit of Nanjing Neuropsychiatric Institute. Of those cases, 5 (0.42 percent) were diagnosed as infantile autism. But, during the two years after the Nanjing Child Mental Health Research Center was established in 1984, 170 childhood psychiatric cases were admitted to the residential unit. Of those cases, 8 (4.7 percent) were diagnosed as infantile autism. During this time, 2 other cases were diagnosed at the outpatient clinic of the center.

All studies have reported an excess of boys over girls, and this current sample was no exception. Although the reported ratios of boys to girls vary from sample to sample, they tend to range between 2:1 and 4:1 (Bender, 1947; Eisenberg and Kanner, 1956; Lotter, 1966; Treffert, 1970). In this sample, however, the ratio of boys to girls was 6.5:1, an even greater excess of boys over girls affected than in other reports.

Family Characteristics

Our investigation of family background included parents' educational level, occupation, and personality characteristics, and family structure, relationships, and psychiatric history. The study was designed to make comparisons among fifteen cases of infantile autism, fifteen cases of simple mental retardation (mild and moderate), and thirty normal children of the same age range who were picked at random as controls.

Of the comparisons between parents of autistic children and parents of normal children, only the differences in mothers' educational level, occupation, and personality characteristics were statistically significant. More mothers of autistic children had a college education or higher. ($X^2 = 24.237$, $P < 0.01$) and a cadre or professional-level occupation ($X^2 = 8.083$, $P < 0.05$). In China, fathers' educational level and professional position are usually near to or higher than those of their spouses. Kanner (1949) found that most of the parents of autistic children were of higher socioeconomic status. In our study, strict diagnostic criteria were used, and our findings replicated those of Kanner and of Cantwell, Rutter, and Baker (1976) on the subject of socioeconomic status of parents. Our comparison of the parents of autistic children to the parents of normal controls did not show significant differences in infant and child-rearing practices as expressed by the child being cared for by the parents, by a foster mother, or in a nursery or kindergarten. But more mothers of autistic children had introverted personality characteristics than did mothers of normal control children, and the difference was statistically significant ($X^2 = 9.848$, $P < 0.01$).

For these comparisons between parents of mentally retarded children and parents of normal children, there were no statistically significant differences in any aspect of family background.

(It should be noted that owing to the small number of autistic children in our sample, this analysis can be only tentative.)

When we compared maternal age for our autistic, mentally retarded, and normal control groups, we found no significant differences among the ages of mothers. Our finding that twelve of the fifteen cases of infantile autism were firstborns was in accordance with the tendency of autistic children to be the firstborn reported by Despert (1951) and Kolvin et al. (1971).

Infantile autism did not seem to be associated with a higher incidence of prenatal and perinatal complications. However, we did find a greater incidence of these complications for our mentally retarded group than for our autistic ($X^2 = 6.65$, $P < 0.01$) or normal control group ($X^2 = 18.409$, $P < 0.01$).

Clinical Features

The data obtained from the parents' reports indicated a very high frequency of certain clinical features that are essential for the diagnosis of infantile autism.

Onset of illness. Kanner (1943) initially reported that the basic attribute of aloneness was present from the very beginning of life. One case of ours began on the fourth day after birth following a febrile convulsion; in another case, the parents said that the aloneness started very early. Onset for the other thirteen cases was one before fourteen months, two between fifteen and twenty months, three between twenty-one and thirty months, five between thirty-one and forty months, and two after forty months of age.

Disturbances of relating. Unlike normal toddlers, all the autistic children in our sample showed an absence of the social smile, showed no concern over the departure of their parents, and did not run to greet their parents when they returned after an absence. Nearly 100 percent of our cases showed a disinterest in playing games with others and marked preference for being alone. They tended not to distinguish between parents and strangers when they needed comforting. Avoidance of eye-to-eye gaze is considered to be an important diagnostic criterion. Only 57 percent of the children in our sample avoided eye contact as compared to 75 percent reported by Ornitz, Guthrie, and Farley (1978).

In our autistic sample, seven cases (46 percent) showed a strong emotional attachment to certain inanimate objects, such as a brick, a plastic bag, a calendar, a chopstick, or a watermelon. One five-year-old girl embraced a red brick weighing 2.5 kg all the time.

An intense desire to maintain sameness in the environment, with a tendency to panic in reaction to change, was shown by six cases (40 percent) in the autistic sample. Two boys felt compelled to defecate into the same chamberpot and would pass feces into their pants when it was occupied rather than use a different unoccupied pot nearby.

Disturbances of speech and language. Language in one case did not develop from early childhood; ten cases showed delayed and four cases good or even better than average language development. After the onset of illness, speech diminished even to muteness. Echolalia or repetitive and stereotyped language appeared in eight cases (53 percent), and the misuse of personal pronouns appeared in one case (6.6 percent). Though maintaining a part of language, these cases lost the communicative value of words.

Disturbances of perception. Inattention was common in the autistic children of our sample. This could be secondary to their failure to sustain attention toward visual stimuli. Hyporeactivity to auditory stimuli was apparent in the disregard of both verbal commands and loud sounds. Even painful stimuli were often ignored.

Along with altered awareness of sensation there was often a tendency to induce sounds or sensory input with hand writhing or flapping, head banging, and biting on a piece of wood or paper. One boy frequently whirled himself as if seeking vestibular and proprioceptive input.

Disturbances of movement. Inattention, marked hyperactivity, and impulsiveness were shown by seven autistic children. The most striking disturbed patterns of movement were strange, stereotypic, repetitive behaviors. Some of these movements involved the whole body, such as whirling, rocking, and head banging, but most were restricted to the arms, hands, or feet.

Three children engaged in repetitive anal digging followed by finger sucking, and one girl played with her feces. Inappropriate laughter and self-satisfaction were seen in four cases. About half of the fifteen children were timid and fearful and often experienced night terrors during sleep.

Disturbances of intellectual functions. Before illness, five cases were of low intellectual level, five were average, and five were above average.

After onset of illness, their intellectual level declined to mental retardation. One exception was a boy of nine who, though generally retarded, had a high ability to calculate.

Associated conditions. With the onset of illness, most of the children in our sample showed a decline in physical growth as well as intellectual level. Epileptic fits developed in one case during early infancy. In our sample, the age range was between three and eight, except for one boy who was twelve. More epileptic seizures would be expected to occur when these children grow older. Two cases had CT head scans, one showing slight cerebral atrophy and one showing no abnormality. Because of poor cooperation, only five cases had EEG examinations, two showing mild dysrhythmia, two showing focal seizure patterns, and one appearing normal. We anticipate an increase in EEG abnormalities as these children grow older.

Follow-Up Studies

Follow-up studies were conducted by mailing questionnaires to parents of thirteen autistic children who were discharged from the psychiatric residential treatment unit. Two other evaluations utilizing the questionnaires were done at the outpatient clinic. The questionnaires asked parents about their childrens' present illness, any behavioral changes since hospitalization, and the degree of improvement. The questionnaires also asked parents about their attitude toward and way of caring for their autistic children, and their opinions.

The following is based on the eleven questionnaires returned out of fifteen. Of the four not returned, two of the subjects had been discharged from the hospital less than three months before, and two had been discharged five and thirty years and their home addresses may have changed. The results are presented in groups based on the time between discharge and the time the questionnaire was administered.

Four cases (ages four to seven) had been discharged less than one year. In one of these cases, useful language increased and the ability to ask questions developed. Another case improved in the ability to relate to and look people in the eye. For both, hyperactivity and impulsive behavior diminished, but inattention and difficulties in learning continued. Their parents accept them and give them training and education with patience. The other two cases showed no change in their unusual behaviors and were essentially the same as at the time of discharge. One developed seizures in early infancy, and these were not well controlled, even with any of the anticonvulsive drugs tried. The parents of these children looked after them quite well and showed a strong desire for further treatment.

Five cases (ages six to thirteen) had been discharged from one to five years. Two showed slight improvement in social relationships, but the oddities of behavior of these five cases did not change fundamentally. One case had occasional speech, but the other four lost their communicative language. All remained severely mentally handicapped and totally unable to lead independent lives. Their parents have many cares and have given up any medical treatment. One boy was under the care of a social welfare institute, one boy was sent away to the countryside, and one girl died of severe malnutrition at the age of ten.

Two cases (ages thirteen and thirty) had been discharged more than six years. The boy of thirteen, emotionally remote and echolalic, functioned below the level of a two-and-a-half-year-old. His parents were saddened by his failure, and he was sent away to the countryside. The other boy grew to be an adult who could carry out simple orders and do simple physical labor despite his difficulties with social relationships, language comprehension, impulsive behavior, and severe mental retardation. At twenty, he developed seizures that increased in frequency until his death at thirty.

Infantile autism remained a severe condition from which only two out of eleven became better rather markedly. These boys developed some useful speech by the age of five and never developed seizures. They came from harmonious middle-class homes, in line with studies by Lotter (1966) that have suggested that autistic children from harmonious middle-class homes do better than those from disrupted or socially disadvantaged families.

The other nine cases had severe language impairment and had not gained or recovered useful language by age five. They all had severe overall behavioral disturbances in early childhood, severe mental handicaps, and seizures. All these factors have some prognostic significance.

PROBLEMS OF EARLY RECOGNITION AND DIAGNOSIS

In China, children usually are referred to a clinic for evaluation and treatment by their parents. So the first step of professional recognition of this disorder is largely dependent on whether or not the parents consider the behavior of their children somewhat wrong and seek help from professionals.

The bizarre clinical features of autism described above should be recognizable by parents. But in fact, only a few of them showed this ability. The reasons for this may be many, but we found the following to be the most important.

1. Most parents did not have the scientific knowledge about the developmental stages of the first two years necessary to recognize as problems such things as delayed or absent social smile, anticipatory responses to being picked up, aversion to physical contact, and a preference for being alone. The abnormal behavior of autistic children was usually noticed by parents when their child did not speak at three or four years of age. Then they took their children for otolaryngological examination of their hearing. Although both parents of one autistic boy were college teachers, they looked for professional help only after their child did not speak at five years of age.

2. Knowing that there are different speeds of normal development among infants, some parents thought that their autistic child simply showed a maturational lag. Thus they waited and hoped that their child would make up the lag in the future.

3. Perhaps in line with the Chinese biological medical model, parents paid more attention to physical symptoms of illness than to behavioral symptoms. At present in China, about 90 percent of urban families and 70 percent of rural families have only one child. Physical symptoms in their children such as headache, dyspepsia, or vomiting usually worried parents a great deal, but mental symptoms received less attention. The young mothers often felt guilt or shame, trying to hide their children's behavioral problems from the outside and denying their own concerns about their infants' deviant development for as long as possible.

When the parents did seek help, the fifteen cases were examined at many hospitals by pediatricians, neurologists, and psychiatrists. They were diagnosed as mentally retarded, hyperactive, infantile dementia, childhood schizophrenia, and even sporadic encephalitis. Several factors have complicated the diagnosis of infantile autism in the early years of life.

1. There are not enough psychiatrists in China who are able to diagnose the disease. Because of the rarity of infantile autism, such children have been included among the mentally retarded or other groups.

2. Many psychiatrists are trained in adult psychiatry only, and even many pediatricians have no concept of infantile autism and lack the knowledge to make such a diagnosis. Because mentally retarded children are relatively common and most autistic children are also retarded, retardation is an easy diagnosis for them.

3. Psychiatrists and other physicians have focused primarily on the

disturbances of relating seen in autism while paying less attention to the disturbances of movement and perception. Because the disturbances of relating are not seen easily during the first two years of life in all cases, and the unusual motility patterns and disturbances of perception are not looked for, the diagnosis of autism may be missed.

4. Most professionals strictly limit the age of onset to thirty months. Owing to reasons already discussed, many parents paid less attention to behavioral changes and they could not identify precisely the time of onset—or they forgot or denied it. This means that professionals must inquire patiently into the details of the child's development. In our experience, we found children whose parents placed the age of onset at four or five years of age but who had actually manifested abnormal behaviors long before that.

The factors mentioned above may influence the age at which autism is recognized and diagnosed, but the rarity of infantile autism in China is a fact. For example, the population of Nanjing is 4.5 million and the birthrate was 10.16 percent in June 1986. There is a well-equipped child mental health center in Nanjing, and it seems likely that cases of infantile autism would be sent there for evaluation. Yet in fifteen cases of infantile autism, only two came from Nanjing. This is a problem that needs to be studied in further detail.

REFERENCES

Bender, L. (1947). "Childhood Schizophrenia: Clinical Study of One Hundred Schizophrenic Children." *American Journal of Orthopsychiatry* 17:40–56.

Cantwell, D., Rutter, M., and Baker, L. (1976). "Family Factors in Infantile Autism." Paper read at the International Symposium on Autism, St. Gallen, July 12–15.

Despert, J. L. (1951). "Some Considerations Relating to the Genesis of Autistic Behavior in Children." *American Journal of Orthopsychiatry* 21:335–350.

Eisenberg, L., and Kanner, L. (1956). "Early Infantile Autism, 1943–1955." *American Journal of Orthopsychiatry* 26:556–566.

Kanner, L. (1943). "Autistic Disturbance of Affective Contact." *Nervous Child* 2:217–250.

——— (1949). "Problems of Nosology and Psychodynamics of Early Infantile Autism." *American Journal of Orthopsychiatry* 19:416–426.

Kolvin, I., Ounsted, C., Humphrey, M., McNay, A., Richardson, L. M.,

Garside, R. F., Kidd, J. S. H., and Roth, M. (1971). "Six Studies in the Childhood Psychoses." *British Journal of Psychiatry* 118:381–419.

Lotter, V. (1966). "Epidemiology of Autistic Conditions in Young Children. I, Prevalence." *Social Psychiatry* 1:124–137.

Ornitz, E. M., Guthrie, D., and Farley, A. J. (1978). "The Early Symptoms of Childhood Autism." In G. Serban, ed., *Cognitive Defects in the Development of Mental Illness*. New York: Brunner/Mazel.

Sanua, V. D. (1984). "Is Infantile Autism a Universal Phenomenon? *International Journal of Social Psychiatry* 30:163–177.

Tao, K. (1982). "The Problems of Diagnosis and Classification of Infantile Autism." *Journal of Chinese Neuropsychiatry* 2:104.

Treffert, D. A. (1970). "Epidemiology of Infantile Autism." *Archives of General Psychiatry* 22:431–438.

37

Japanese Culture and Neurotic Manifestations in Childhood and Adolescence

KOSUKE YAMAZAKI

JOHJI INOMATA

KIYOSHI MAKITA

JOHN ALEX MACKENZIE

Neurotic manifestation is sensitively affected and influenced by the reigning times or era and the various specific cultural, social, and economic circumstances obtaining in each country. Yamazaki (1978–79), at the Ninth Congress of this body in Melbourne, dealt with a significant change in the role of the father in Japanese society and culture. In this chapter, we shall discuss neurotic manifestation in childhood and adolescence as it expresses itself at this particular historical period of time.

THE JAPANESE FAMILY ENVIRONMENT AND PROBLEMS OF CHILDREN

Here, we should like to discuss crucial, distinct changes in the family in Japan in relation to the process of adolescents becoming independent adults, the formation of their approaches to daily life, and their principal educational and disciplinary influences. Deriving from the effect of high economic growth and a resulting flow of population from the farming villages to the big cities, accompanied by a lowering of the birthrate, the average family size is less than 70 percent of what it was in the 1930s, presently averaging 3.3 persons. The tempo of that decrease has recently abated, however, with the advance of the phenomenon of the nuclear family. Owing to the price of land suddenly rising in the early 1970s and a decline in the rate of increase of family income, an increase in the number of three-generation families living together ensued. In March 1986, the National Economic Planning Agency published the *Survey on Citizens' Choices for Daily Life,* and according to it the number of parents living with a married son or daughter was greater than half of the population, amounting to 51.4 percent of all households. At present those expressing a future desire to live together with the husband's or wife's parents amounted to 36.8 percent of those living separately (in all, 17.5 percent of the whole population). The direction of this desire for living together was highest for the younger age brackets (twenty-five to thirty-four years of age; 42.8 percent).

On the other hand, according to a 1983 estimate of the Statistical Bureau of the Prime Minister's Office, the number of three-generation families living together amounted to 47.4 percent. As to the particular constellation of joint living, the number of eldest sons living with their parents amounted to 73 percent, second or younger sons, 14 percent, eldest daughters, 11 percent, and second or younger daughters, 3 percent. The order or sequence of children living with their parents expresses itself in the following descending ranks of occurrence: the eldest son, those other than the eldest son, the eldest daughter, and those other than the eldest daughter. Even though property inheritance is supposed to be equally distributed, in fact the legal system of primogeniture, continuing to derive its persistence from the enduring Japanese Ie household family system, demonstrates ongoing strength. In these joint-residence extended families, complicated problems are arising, for, in such families, several psychiatric problems are manifested, involving conflict between the daughter and her mother-in-law. Until twenty years ago, 80 percent of those visiting psychiatric facilities with complaints deriving from a conflict between daughter and mother-in-law were the daughters, and twenty percent the mother-in-law. Lately, however, the ratio has been reversed. The number of mothers-in-law affected by psychiatric conflicts with their daughters-in-law who are visiting psychiatric facilities has greatly increased, as has the number of children similarly affected by a conflict between the mother and the grandmother.

In the midst of this sort of change in the family composition, what has become the ideal image of the roles of father and mother? According to the *1984 White Paper on Youth,* a comparative study of young peoples throughout the world, examined the role of the father in eleven countries. Japan emerged third after Korea and the Philippines as to affirmation that the father has the leadership role in the family; however, in answer to the statement, "The father guides the daily life behavior of the children," Japanese youth placed seventh after the Philippines, Korea, Yugoslavia, Britain, Brazil, and Switzerland. And in response to the statements, "The father shows an attitude of confidence" and "The father has time to talk with his children," the number of young people responding "yes" for Japan was lowest among the eleven countries. The ideal father image of Japanese youth is that of a friendlike figure who, rather than directing, controlling, or restraining the child, holds the child in respect and esteem and even conforms to him. The father with rights and obligations of authority over his children has gone the way of other discarded elements of Japanese society and culture. On the other hand, as to the mother's relation to her children, she takes care of them with a seeming implicit promise not to make demands on them. The ideal mother image among the children is a parent who does not subject them to strict or exacting expectations as to behavior and manner. The mother performs 70 percent of the discipline in her family, and half of all mothers with children between eleven and fifteen years of age express some kind of distress or anguish over discipline.

Also shown is a characteristic Japanese outlook on the family by the children. According to the *1982 International Comparative Study Concerning the Family,* in response to a query as to "health and the family as a thing important to me," respondents in the various countries scored high affirmative rates ranging from 63–99 percent; however, as to "family system or ancestors being important to me," among the lower affirming countries was Japan with an affirmative response rate of only 25.9 percent.

If we look at these sorts of statistical studies about modern-day Japanese children, we find a strong consciousness of the family as the center for love, affection, and attachment; however, going hand-in-hand with a simpler nuclear household is a dilution of the father's authority and a growing overindulgence of the children, sometimes to the point where they are almost placed on a pedestal by their parents. Although on the surface Japanese society is becoming increasingly Westernized, it continues to exhibit a traditional Japanese village consciousness, which lends itself to conflicts in the family among the three generations, including the child.

We shall discuss the following cases, which are examples of neurotic manifestations deriving from conflicts between the mother and the grandmother, and the dependency relation between the father and the grandmother. Developing an effective therapy for such cases was time-consuming, given that both simultaneous and individual therapy with and among all three generations is a fundamental psychiatric practice at our hospital.

SCHOOL EDUCATION AND CHILDREN IN JAPAN

Neurotic school refusal is dramatically on the increase (Wakabayashi et al., 1983; Inomata et al., 1983). In October 1985, the Ministry of Education reported that over a one-year period, those exhibiting school refusal at the middle school level numbered 26,215 (0.46 percent, constituting an increase of 2,156) and at the elementary school level 3,977 (0.03 percent, an increase of 137 over 1983). As to school refusal among middle school students, it was four times what it was ten years ago and twice what it was five years ago. It has clearly become a severe problem.

To date many reports have dealt with the connection between school refusal and prevailing social and economic circumstances, including the phenomenon of the nuclear family. We shall also take up another problem of children in the context of school: there has been a rapid increase in school bullying in the 1980s. The National Police Agency has defined "bullying" (*Ijime* in Japanese) as attacks on an individual, physically and/or through words, involving threats or pushing, shoving, or punching, and shunning or exerting other psychological pressure over a period of time, resulting in great suffering for the victim. Those committing bullying acts fall into one of two groups: the gang leader—type group or the *Bosozoku* (a Hell's Angels–type) group. This bullying may be a distinct problem, but it is not openly expressed. It is carried out behind school buildings and behind the teacher's back. It is almost always concealed because the victim fears retaliation if he speaks up. Though several studies have dealt with the problem of bullying, no comprehensive statistics detailing the numbers of victims and victimizers have been published. Very often the first time the parents and teachers learn of its existence, its severity, and the child's increasing despair is when the child exhibits neurotic behavior or even, in fact, commits suicide.

The phenomenon of bullying, an especially serious problem in Japan, is illustrated by the following examples, derived from previously published reports:

Case 1: a second-year middle school male, age fourteen. Having very weak eyes from birth, he was regarded as a handicapped person and was severely bullied. He committed suicide in the school gymnasium.

Case 2: A second-year middle school male, age fourteen. He was bullied because he was clumsy and unskillful. He was said to be dirty and to have "germs." He was ganged up on and subjected to group bullying. He too committed suicide.

Case 3: A third-year middle school male, age fifteen. He was one of a four-member group, all of whom were bullied at school. While this group was on the train returning home from school, as a habitual form of letting off steam they "acted out" bullying as a game. While stopping at a station to buy some juice, one member was selected as the "victim" and then was, it turned out, accidentally cut by a knife.

We child psychiatrists constantly meet the bullied child but rarely have the opportunity to encounter the bullying child. Even though we know the bullied child, he rarely and only with the greatest reluctance speaks of what has happened; but, if the interview process is continued with patience, slowly but surely the structure of bullying becomes clear.

Case 4: A second-year middle school female, age fourteen. With school truancy as the primary problem at hand, she was brought to the hospital. The therapist required that in some sessions the parents not be present, and gradually she began to speak more freely about the actual state of affairs. When she was in the first year of middle school her parents bought a house in a new suburb and she entered the school in that area. During her first year, she participated in her club's activities and was able to make new friends. She passed her middle school life happily, but when she became a second-year student, after running for club president, she became a target for bullying. In the midst of a class, the child in the seat behind would poke and pinch her. When she walked in the hall the bullying students would say, "You make me sick!" After school was over she was led out to an area behind a building, where her school uniform was torn and she was kicked. When the bullying continued, she finally refused to go to school. The parents at first thought the child was succumbing to a kind of fad of school refusal, but after several interviews with a child psychiatrist, the true cause of her truancy came to light. Asked why she didn't reveal her secret to the teacher or her parents, she responded that talking with them would lead nowhere. In fact, if she spoke out freely, she said, the teacher would know who did it, and in the end, she would be subject to even worse bullying. The homeroom teacher asked the other students who bullied her, but no one would own up to the acts. The girl also reasoned that if she spoke to her mother about the situation, her mother, being an emotional person, would get into a fuss with school officials and in the end things would be even more disastrous. It would seem in this respect that she realistically assessed the situation, as unpleasant as it was.

We know that bullying has a special structure. Standing at the apex of the bullying operation is an invisible leader who is invariably an "honor student." The leader manipulates his or her "goons" and, while not laying a hand on the victim, directs the bullying with a barely concealed, mischievous laugh. In modern Japanese education, in which grades and academic achievement are all-important, it is as if bullying has become in response the sole means of recreation. Occasionally when a teacher happens upon a case of bullying and seeks to learn who did it, the bullying children admit their act but the bullied almost never open their mouths. The leader who has directed the bullying in safety, carrying as he does the trappings of an "honor student," is able to have his cake and eat it too. In many cases, the victim, as a means of avoiding further bullying, will allow himself to be coopted as a "goon" or lackey by the invisible leader. In terms of personal characteristics, the bullied child is often more emotionally susceptible to a strong inner, if not outer, reaction to physical or psychological attack, a quality that indeed the would-be bulliers might well be able to detect in advance, aiding them in the selection of their victims. In a world of varied groups and the resultant conformities that are the nature of adolescent school life, the children who become targets of bullying are those who in some degree differ from the norm, thus in the adolescent world constituting a kind of alien element. These victims-to-be can be attacked for not talking or not following the local dialect speech pattern, or for allegedly smelling sweaty, and so on, but, of course, the true origin of attacks lies elsewhere.

The children at school will consult with the school nurse, who has no connection with academic evaluation; they decline to consult with the homeroom teacher or the guidance counselor as to sufferings from bullying. Even in the rare case in which the homeroom teacher receives information about bullying, it is difficult for various reasons to arrange a coordinated faculty action against bullying. In fact, fragmented efforts often make the situation worse, for though the bulliers know the pressure to desist may be on, the incompletely carried out antibullying efforts only lead the victimizers to conduct their acts in a more concealed fashion.

One further, interesting point about this problem is that, by degrees, as intraschool violence was controlled, the number of cases of bullying shot up. There is a common psychology among those children who refuse to go to school, those who commit school violence, and those who commit bullying on the public stage that the school has come to be in modern Japanese life. All three groups demonstrate a paucity of understanding as to reasonable give-and-take, yielding and assertion. This is an understanding that might have been learned had the parents not been so inclined to quell childhood fights and conflicts with ready offers of material gifts, smothering the children's chance to learn naturally that other people have instincts, hopes, and inclinations similar to theirs. In the academic battlefield that is the modern Japanese primary and middle school, in which each student is fighting for the highest grade and every other student is the mortal enemy, the role of trust, faith, and confidence in the other is disregarded, if not unlearned.

CONCLUSION

The modern Japanese family has been assumed to be composed of the nuclear family, but recently the evidence shows an increase in the number of three-generation families living together—that is, the extended family. The ideal father and mother image of Japanese youth is that of a friend or a pal-like figure, which has led to role confusion in the Japanese family. As well, the Japanese family and society continue to exhibit a traditional village or group consciousness. This very complicated combination of factors exerts various pathogenic influences on neurotic manifestations in the child and adolescent.

We have taken up the major problem of bullying in the Japanese school and have discussed its psychological structure. Traditional Japanese village consciousness has helped to create both extensive and intensive human relations in Japanese society. It has, in some manner by the "pooling" of the generations, contributed to alienating some children from children's groups. Bullying has been one outcome of this alienation.

Neurotic manifestations in childhood and adolescence make clear the comprehensive social-psychological problems emerging in and from Japanese society and culture, and provide a clinical warning concerning things to come for all in the helping professions.

REFERENCES

Inomata, J., Motoyoshi, T., and Yamazaki, K. (1983). "Child and Adolescent Psychiatric Services and Delinquency." *Japanese Journal of Child and Adolescent Psychiatry* 24(3):210–223.

Wakabayashi, S., Ohtaka, K., Abe, T., and Kaneko, T. (1983). "Neuroses in a Child and Adolescent Psychiatric Clinic." *Japanese Journal of Child and Adolescent Psychiatry* 24(3):186–195.

Yamazaki, K. (1978–79). "Transition of the Father's Role in Japanese Family and Culture." *Research and Clinical Center for Child Development, Annual Report 1978–1979,* 43–53.

38

Methods to Help Children Overcome the Tyranny of Distance

HELEN MARGARET CONNELL

Australia is the oldest continent, and its relative isolation from other landmasses has resulted in its becoming a storehouse of primitive fauna and flora ('living fossils'). Its size can be judged by comparing it with the United States—8 million as against 9 million square kilometers; it is thirty times the size of the United Kingdom and ten times the size of Japan. The climate is predominantly hot, harsh, and dry, although monsoonal in the tropics. When first settled by whites in 1788, it probably supported a population of only 300,000 aborigines (Berndt and Berndt, 1981). Currently its population is a little over 15.5 million, giving a population density of two persons per square kilometer. In this it contrasts sharply with neighboring Asian countries. For example, the central area of Hong Kong supports nearly 200,000 persons per square kilometer. The Australian population is predominantly of British stock with Greeks and Italians well represented. The aboriginal population is currently estimated to be 160,000 (*Australian Encyclopaedia*). There has been a recent influx of Indo-Chinese refugees.

Approximately two-thirds of the population is concentrated along the coast (chiefly the eastern seaboard) where the rainfall is highest. This leaves the vast interior, which is known as the Centre or Outback, to families who live in small country towns (often these are only a group of houses) or on ranches, called properties or stations. These may be enormous, ranging from hundreds to thousands of square kilometers. The largest owned by a single individual is 7,800 square kilometers; those owned by companies may be much larger. In the latter case a manager and his family occupy the homestead.

This chapter looks at the life-style of children in Outback areas in two

Australian states, Queensland and Western Australia. Together these occupy 4,265,500 square kilometers and have a population of just under 4 million; they are slightly larger than India, which has a population of over 800 million.Because of the aggregation of people on the coast, Outback children live in the most geographically and socially isolated conditions in the world.

LIFE UNDER ISOLATED CONDITIONS

Life in the Outback can be very harsh, although modern technology has improved it. Temperatures soar well above 40° C by day, yet drop below freezing point at night. Roads (better called tracks) seem to stretch on forever; they are corrugated and pot-holed and can be hard to find in the frequent dust storms or may be obliterated by sand drifts. Hazards to travelers include (surprisingly) occasional floods produced by monsoonal rain thousands of kilometers away, straying stock, kangaroos who are devoid of road sense (an encounter with one can wreck a car), and even emus. One year a group of five people including three children died of dehydration in western Queensland when their vehicle broke down.

Communication between homesteads is difficult. Many still have no telephone, and even for those who do, lines may travel erratically from tree to tree and be most unreliable. Television is absent from remote areas, although the use of a new communications satellite is altering this. A radio network that covers the continent is of vital importance, bringing news of the outside world, social contacts outside the family, and help in cases of emergency. Typically the Outback family is tough and resourceful and the surviver of many near disasters.

Water is of prime importance. Rain brings prosperity; droughts may last for five to eight years. Households are dependent on bore water from the Great Artesian Basin, which underlies much of the Centre. Sometimes called fossil water because of the time it has been below ground, this can be hot, even boiling, and is often so saline it can be an embarrassment to those unaccustomed to drinking it.

Fathers may be absent from home for days or weeks, working on the boundaries of the station or hiring out their services if times are lean. Mothers are totally committed to the family and homestead. As one put it, "I have to be a parent, stationhand, and teacher. I never have enough time to do what I should."

Aside from the "property" children, whose families have traditions derived from generations of Outback existence, three other groups must be considered. The first is composed of children of railway and itinerant workers; they have a highly unsettled environment, moving wherever the father's work takes them. Their existence could be compared to that of the English "canal children" described by Cyril Burt (1917). The second group—children of miners—may live in extremely primitive conditions. Many live on the opal fields, using tents or caravans for long periods of time; others live in towns provided by the large mining companies. In keeping with the wealth derived from Australia's mineral boom, these towns may provide excellent physical facilities. There is not so much individual isolation, but the towns themselves are isolated and social problems within them are considerable. Aboriginal children who live in areas occupied by white families or with their own kind in reserves make up the third group. Some are very isolated indeed, being located in the far north or in deserts. Their families may revert to a traditional nomadic life-style and "go walkabout" in the bush for weeks or months at a time. Their culture dates back some 35,000–50,000 years. Its richness has only recently been appreciated, and attempts are now being made in the schoolroom to encourage traditional beliefs. This may lead to confusion: one small black girl asked me, "Was Jesus Christ born in the Dreamtime?"

THE PSYCHOLOGICAL EFFECTS OF ISOLATION

Most studies relating to children's psychological adjustment to their social environment have focused on life in overcrowded inner-city areas (Wallis and Maliphant, 1967; Rutter, 1981). Studies of children who live in geographical isolation are few and relate chiefly to cognitive development (Reschly and Jipson, 1976) rather than psychosocial factors. Haggard and Lippe's (1970) study of children from isolated farms in the mountains of Norway drew attention to the likelihood of emotional, social, and cognitive deprivation among them, as the result both of their mother's investment in farm activities, which left her so little time, and of their limited social contacts. Comparison with urban controls showed that isolated children differed significantly in cognitive style. In additional, they acted out their feelings and ideas rather than expressing them verbally, and their perceptions of the world were personal and sometimes idiosyncratic. Many had social difficulties when they went to boarding school at the age of seven years. These findings parallel descriptions of isolated children in Australia: their verbal and social development lags behind that of city children; they act rather than reason; and they are well known for their individual approach to life. Some may never be able to attend school; many do not go until secondary level. Adults raised in the Outback describe the difficulties that transition to urban life created. "Boarding school was the worst experience of my life" is a frequent comment.

A vignette will illustrate the degree of isolation in which an Australian child can be reared. A young girl's mother, father, and uncle own a "hotel," really a primitive collection of buildings, in far west Queensland, which operates a postal service for an enormous area, the mail being delivered to them by air. She is seven years old and has a sibling of two. The nearest children are over two hundred kilometers away and reachable only by appalling roads. Her father may be absent for days on the mail run. Her mother has to organize the mail, run the hotel, and deal with any problems that occur in relation to travelers who pass through (chiefly oil and mining prospectors). She has to supervise her daughter's lessons, which come by post and over the radio, as well as perform her domestic duties. She never leaves the property; provisions come every six months or so. She had not seen another woman for three months when I visited and begged me to send her any discarded books or magazines, as she had nothing to read and no means of getting material.

Another family in better circumstances, but even more isolated, felt so strongly about their son's lack of social experience that his mother, an experienced pilot, flew him to school every morning in the family plane, returned home, and then collected him in the afternoon. Prior to this, he had been traveling five hours per day for six hours of schooling.

In summary: the process of socialization, which includes learning roles, attitudes, behaviors, and perceptions from others in the environment, is seen as a series of interpersonal interactions in progressively wider circles. Usually, the first interaction is with the mother, then with the father, followed by siblings, extended family, neighborhood peers, school, and so on (Elkin, 1960). The importance of the peer group as a socializing agent as the child slowly individuates from his family is universally recognized: the influence of school and neighborhood are considerable (Rutter, 1983). For the child reared in geographical isolation many of these agents are missing. The main elements in his or her life-style can be seen as:

1. Intense interaction with family members in the absence of outside influences. This may lead to strong identification and, as adolescence is approached, intensification of the usual rebellion against parent figures,

as the youngster strives toward individuation in the absence of support from peers.

2. Parents may be so involved with survival in their harsh existence that they have little to give children in terms of stimulation and emotional support. The children may be left very much to their own devices, and many are expected to work on properties.

3. Lack of contact with peers may result in difficulty in establishing an identity—there are no figures with whom to compare oneself. At the same time, individual interests and activities may be pursued to the extent of producing eccentricity. The give-and-take inherent in group membership is missing.

4. Lack of cognitive stimulation in some areas may delay certain skills; verbal development is especially affected. General knowledge may be totally lacking. A ten-year-old boy, asked to describe the world's tallest building, drew a picture of the local water tower.

5. In contrast, motor development and survival skills may forge ahead. Lack of internal controls and verbal ability results in action rather than reasoning when faced with a problem. Many show a surprising degree of self-sufficiency. A ten-year-old girl drove a car forty kilometers to school every day with two younger members of her family in it. Outback children do have certain advantages. The Australian landscape is of striking beauty. The plains, scattered with rocks sparkling in the sun, create vistas giving an imposing impression of space. The mountain ranges worn by time expose rocks varying in color from yellow to ocher to vermilion. Even in the deserts, wildlife is surprisingly abundant. Very recently, most children had a horse (among numerous pets), and their contact with the wild far surpassed that of urban children. Haggard and von der Lippe (1970), quoting Hall (1966) and Barker (1968), draw attention to the influence space and distance have upon the behavior of human beings and how too much of either may impose restrictions on the development of the child. Air transport and radio communication have reduced considerably the "tyranny of distance"—a phrase first used in horse-and-buggy days—but social isolation still disadvantages Outback children when they have to compete with others who are the products of contemporary urban society.

HELPING ISOLATED CHILDREN

Methods developed to help these children living in geographical isolation will now be described. I will cover three areas: (1)

physical health (touched on only briefly), (2) mental health, and (3) education and psychosocial development. In the latter two, services in Queensland only are described.

Physical Health

Small, neglected graves in the bush testify to the hazards of Outback life for children before the advent of the Royal Flying Doctor Service. Fifty years ago, this organization, started by volunteers, began to cast its "mantle of safety" over four-fifths of the continent. By means of a radio network, help can be summoned immediately in the case of accident or illness. A medicine chest with numbered bottles is supplied with each transceiver, and diagnosis can be made and treatment started immediately through instructions over the air. Routine clinics are held where no school medical service could ever reach, often in outstations or even under the shade of an aircraft wing. Children can be transferred to a hospital when necessary. There is also a Flying Dental Service. In Western Australia a pediatrician who is also a pilot covers the state outside the capital five times per year and provides urgent consultations by radio.

Mental Health

Between 1978 and 1982, a survey of 986 primary school children looked at the extent of psychiatric disorder among them (Connell, Irvine, and Rodney, 1982a). Three groups of approximately 300 children each were examined: from far western Queensland (isolated), from two coastal towns (urban), and from the state's capital city, Brisbane. The remote children showed a lower rate (10 percent) of maladjustment than either the urban (15 percent) or the metropolitan (18 percent) groups, and the two major categories of childhood disturbance—conduct disorder and emotional disorder—were represented equally. This differs from a comparable study in England where conduct disorders were more common. The reasons for this are discussed elsewhere (Connell, Irvine, and Rodney, 1982b); it may reflect a lower reporting of antisocial behavior by Australian parents. In any event, half of the disturbed isolated children suffered from emotional problems, some of considerable degree, and half showed evidence of antisocial behavior. Apart from the metropolitan area and two small clinics in coastal towns, no psychiatric services were available to them. Some parents described how they had traveled a thousand or two thousand kilometers for a consultation. The survey led to new services being established.

A team composed of a child psychiatrist, a psychologist, and a pediatrician, traveling by commercial airline or chartered plane, now visits remote areas regularly, the farthest center visited being nearly two thousand kilometers away. The usual stay in each center is two to four days, and peripheral areas may be visited during this time by chartered plane or the Royal Flying Doctor Service. Clinics are held for the assessment and treatment of any children with psychological or physical problems and, most important, for discussions with professionals able to supervise cases between the team's visits. Contact is made with any schools in the area to enable teachers to discuss the management of disturbed pupils.

Two cases will illustrate the type of problems encountered. First, a family drove two hundred kilometers each way for a consultation when an eleven-year-old daughter was sexually abused by an employee in the house. There was no telephone. The mother worked in a bank prior to marriage and finds country life hard in the extreme. The mother's complaints were of the child's provocative behavior and failure to achieve in her schoolwork since the incident. Psychological assessment showed a minor learning (reading) disability that had gone unnoticed before, and it became apparent that the incident had aggravated a rift between the parents and produced an intense neurotic reaction in the mother, to which the child was in turn reacting. She had no other companions apart from a baby sibling.

In the second case, a seven-year-old boy was brought with complaints of hyperactivity, difficulty in learning to read, and bed wetting. The property was one hundred kilometers from the base hospital, the father was away on contract work for a considerable portion of his time, and the child had no playmates nearer than forty nine kilometers away. The mother also was a city girl before her marriage, and she reported that her son was bored and restless and that she often came close to maltreating him. The early history included a difficult labor and delivery when he was born and delayed language development. The clinical assessment confirmed his reading disability.

Also in response to needs uncovered by the survey, the psychiatric unit of the state's children's hospital developed a program to enable rural families to gain maximum benefit from inpatient admission. The referring agency is asked to provide as much information as possible about the disturbed child in advance and to ensure that parents or someone who knows the child well accompanies him. A two-week admission is arranged (this is about the maximum time parents can leave a property); accommodations are found for the parents, so they can participate intensively in the treatment. Aboriginal children become very distressed by city life and separation from parent figures, and allowances have to be made for this. Plans for appropriate psychiatric and neurological evaluation are made before arrival. A school on the hospital grounds provides educational assessment, starts remedial work if necessary, and offers explanations to the child and the parents as to why learning difficulties have developed. These can go a long way toward reversing the negative attitudes engendered by persistent failure.

Treatment involves a team effort by the ward staff. Obviously during a short admission an in-depth approach is not possible, but by utilizing wisely the available time, focusing on the specific problem the child is experiencing, and working both with the family and with the child, an improvement in symptoms may be apparent as early as the first week. If a drug is indicated, but its effects will not be immediately apparent, it may be necessary for the parents to leave the child and return for him later. The value of methylphenidate hydrochloride can be assessed rapidly, neuroleptics take more time, and antidepressants require the longest stay.

The essential for postdischarge supervision is continuing communication with a key figure in the child's environment. Family doctors, community health nurses, social workers, teachers, and the Flying Doctor Service have all been of great help. A detailed letter is sent, explaining treatment plans, the side effects of medication, and other details. Phone contact is made whenever possible, and it is equally important for someone to be easily available in the hospital should trouble arise.

Educational Aspects

Of the 450,000 school-age children in Queensland, 160,000 live outside the state capital, 15,000 are scattered through Outback areas, and 2,000 have no access to a traditional school (Queensland Education Department). Of the children from remote areas three groups must be considered: (1) those who can get to school, albeit with difficulty; often rural schools are small with, say, ten or twelve pupils of varying ages and a single teacher; (2) those who cannot attend school but have a settled existence, often with a schoolroom of their own and parents who have a tradition of supervising their children's education; and (3) those whose parents are itinerant workers or who adopt an unsettled life-style, moving from one mining area to another, thus making school attendance very erratic.

The Federal Schools Commission report of 1977–79 recognized that students in country areas could be disadvantaged, compared with urban dwellers, because they lacked "a variety of experiences and opportunities." Consequently funding was made available to establish a Priority Country Area Programme (PCAP) to enrich the environment of rural children with a cultural, social, and intellectual program. With a budget of over $1 million (Australian) a year, the program employs thirty full-time staff members. It still does not cover the state, but it affects the lives of some 16,000 pupils. Its activities are varied.

Enhancing country school education. Library facilities are regularly upgraded, and vocational guidance and literature related to it are supplied. Excursions are arranged using four minibuses stationed at strategic centers; field studies are encouraged by the provision of a caravan and complete camping outfits. Itinerant teachers, remedial teachers, and speech therapists travel from school to school in four-wheel-drive vehicles or chartered planes. Two trucks converted into mobile workshops (one fitted for metalwork, the other for carpentry) visit schools for several days at a time to give pupils instruction. An itinerant music teacher pilots his own plane and visits schools regularly. There is also a flying artist. Closed-circuit television presenting magazine-style topics is available to most schools. The name ROCTAPUS—Really Outstanding Color Television about Practically Unlimited Subjects—gives an indication of how widely the program ranges.

Helping children unable to go to school. The aim of PCAP is to augment lessons sent by mail (discussed below). Itinerant teachers visit properties and arrange for groups of four to five children to meet at the home of one of them for minischools. A mobile classroom (caravan) serves the same purpose—to allow children to experience the social concomitants of a classroom. During home visits emphasis is placed on teaching parents to teach and improving their attitudes toward education. During busy seasons there is a great temptation to hurry children through their lessons so that they can work on the property. Illiterate parents pose a special problem.

The Correspondence School is a large organization employing nearly a hundred teachers and subdivided into preschool, primary, and secondary school sections. Lessons (both written and on audiotape) go out by mail and are returned for correction. Recognizing the need for students to identify positively with their teacher as a basis for learning, efforts are directed toward conveying the identity of the person who sends the lessons. Families are encouraged to attend a yearly camp on the coast. This gives children an opportunity to meet and take home a mental image of the teacher, as well as a taste of what life is like in a traditional classroom.

The School of the Air offers another approach. It is run in conjunction with the Flying Doctor Service, using its two-way radio network for a limited time each day (for full details, see Ashton, 1971). Its aim is to augment the correspondence lessons and foster verbal and social skills. Lack of classroom experience leaves many children with no sense of competition; trying to get their turn on the radio is an excellent way to remedy this. Learning to play a musical instrument over the air is quite possible, and there are Cubs, Brownies, Guides, and Scouts of the air. One year a Christmas party was held for four hundred students scattered over some nine thousand square kilometers. Santa Claus asked about presents and then listened to children singing, exchanging riddles, and playing musical instruments. Every day, before lessons start, a *galah,* or "parrot" session is held when the children talk to each other. Sitting in on a session is fascinating: little voices are heard through the static, and the children's individual characteristics come through clearly.

In 1985, Australia's domestic communication satellite, AUSSAT, was placed in orbit, and a transponder leased for educational purposes. Eight grade six pupils were used as guinea pigs for a major-distance education program. It was expensive, for each was supplied with a satellite antenna dish, a computer, a printer, and a color monitor. This allowed one-way video and two-way audio communication. Since messages travel 72,000 kilometers and take 0.27 seconds to travel between teacher and pupil, this must surely be the largest classroom in the world. Voice communication is far superior to the H.F. radio the children are accustomed to, and moreover they can *see* the teacher. The satellite network carries computer data; thus, teacher can illustrate verbal instructions, using the computer to draw colored graphics on the children's screens. These can be stored and kept for revision on a floppy disk. Children can use their own graphics for the teacher; even writing workshops are possible. The satellite is also being used for educational films, which have always played an important part in Outback education. These are transmitted at off-peak times—for example, the early hours of the morning. Teachers at receiving centers leave videocassette recorders programmed to switch on automatically and record the transmission for use the next day. This is a far cry from the weeks, sometimes months, a film used to take to make a circuit.

The satellite is also used for teacher training and by colleges of advanced education, universities, and professional continuing education courses and seminars. A program for training family doctors has found that X rays and ultrasound pictures travel well; in fact, diagnosing the cause of an illness in a child is possible.

The problems of children with learning disabilities are intensified if they live in remote areas. The Queensland Isolated Children's Special Education Unit caters to them. Initially, the child and parent/supervisor visit a center for assessment, and a program is tailored to the child's individual needs. Postal and radio supervision follows. A team of itinerant teachers visits homes regularly and gives explanations and support to parents as well as teaching the child for a few days at a time. Liaison among all the services described above is very important; in fact, the education of Outback children is seen as a team effort throughout.

The motto of the School of the Air is "Parted but united," and this would seem appropriate for all services designed to help children in Outback Australia. There is no desire to detract from their life-style (which, it is recognized, has definite advantages) by adding the petty restrictions of urban life. Rather, the aim is to improve their social relationships and enrich their environment so that distance is no longer the controlling tyrant it once was.

REFERENCES

Ashton, J. (1971). *The School of the Air*. Sydney: Rigby.
Barker, R. (1968). *Ecological Psychology: Concepts and Methods for Studying the Environment of Human Behavior*. Stanford: Stanford University Press.
Berndt, R. M., and Berndt, C. H. (1981). *The World of the First Australians*. Rev. ed. Sydney: Landsdowne Press, 26.
Burt, C. (1917). "The Distribution and Relations of Educational Abilities." London County Council.
Connell, H. M., Irvine, L., and Rodney, J. (1982a). "The Prevalence of Psychiatric Disorder in Rural Schoolchildren." *Aust. & N.Z. J. Psychiat.* 16:43–46.
——— (1982b). "Psychiatric Disorder in Queensland Primary Schoolchildren." *Aust. Paediatr. J.* 18:177–180.
Elkin, F. (1960). *The Child and Society: The Process of Socialization*. New York: Random House.
Haggard, E. A., and von der Lippe, A. (1970). "Isolated Families in the Mountains of Norway." In E. J. Anthony and C. Koupernick, eds., *The Child in His Family*. Vol. 1. International Yearbook for Child Psychiatry and Allied Disciplines, 465–488. New York: Wiley.

Hall, E. T. (1966). *The Hidden Dimension*. New York: Doubleday.

Page, M. (1982). *A Pictorial History of the Royal Flying Doctor Service*. Sydney: Rigby.

Reschly, D. J., and Jipson, F. J. (1976). "Ethnicity, Geographic Locale, Age, Sex, and Urban-Rural Residence as Variables in the Prevalence of Mild Retardation." *Am. J. Mental Defic.* 81:154–161.

Rutter, M. (1972). "The City and the Child." *Am. J. Orthopsychiat.* 51, no. 4:610–25.

——— (1981). "The City and the Child." *Am. J. Orthopsychiat.* 51:610–625.

——— (1983). "School Effects on Pupils' Progress: Research Findings and Policy Implications." *Child Devel.* 54:1–29.

Rutter, M., and Quinton, D. (1976). "Psychiatric Disorder: Ecological factors and Concepts of Causation." In *Ecological Factors in Human Development*, ed. H. McGurk. Amsterdam: Elsevier–North Holland.

Rutter, M., Tizard, J., Yule, W., Graham, P., and Whitmore, K. (1976). "The Isle of Wight Studies, 1964–74." *Psychol. Med.* 6:313–332.

Wallis, C. P., and Maliphant, R. (1967). "Delinquent Areas in the County of London: Ecological Factors." *Brit. J. Criminol.* 7:250–284.

39

Mental Health Problems
of Nigerian Children

R. OLUKAYODE JEGEDE

MARIANNE CEDERBLAD

There are few epidemiological studies on behavioral disturbances in children from developing countries. Cederblad (1968) studied 197 children, three to fifteen years old, living in three adjacent villages on the outskirts of Khartoum, Sudan. She found that only 8 percent of the children showed disturbed adjustment. Báasher and Ibrahim (1976), studying another village outside Khartoum, found that thirteen percent of the 270 children investigated suffered from severe behavioral symptoms. In 1980 Rahim and Cederblad (1984) studied 245 children five to fifteen years old in the first-mentioned area, now an integrated suburb of Khartoum. The mental health of the children was still good, only thirteen percent of the sample having severe behavioral symptoms. In a study from the city of Salvador, Brazil, Almeida-Filho (1984) examined a representative sample of 828 children five to fourteen years old and found that 23 percent had varying degrees of psychological symptoms. No epidemiological study of child mental health has been carried out in Africa south of the Sahara.

THE STUDY

We conducted our study with two aims in mind: (1) to compare three areas in a part of Nigeria representing urban and rural ways of family life, and (2) to study the effects of acculturation by comparing families differentially affected by Westernized styles of living. (Only some of the results on behavioral disturbances in the three areas are described here.)

Subjects

The study was conducted in three areas. Idikan is a low-income area in the center of Ibadan, a city of 3 million inhabitants, two hundred kilometers inland from Lagos, Nigeria. It is an underprivileged area with poor, overcrowded houses, narrow streets, and inadequate water supplies and sewerage systems. Most women work outside the home. The majority of parents are petty traders or unskilled workers. We selected at random 152 children (84 boys and 68 girls) from this area.

The second area was Bodiga, socioeconomically a more privileged part of the city of Ibadan. It is inhabited by civil servants, teachers, and academically trained professionals. The houses are well built and equipped, and spaciously dispersed in gardens along broad streets. Water, sewage, and garbage collection function adequately. Many women hold skilled jobs. The sample from this area included 168 children (84 boys and 84 girls).

Lagun, the third area, is a large jungle village situated thirty kilometers outside the city of Ibadan. It comprises approximately three thousand people, mostly farmers cultivating cassawa, jams, bananas, and vegetables. Some parents work and live in Ibadan, returning only occasionally to their home village. Their children are therefore primarily raised by grandmothers or other relatives. There are no modern facilities in the village. The houses consist of large huts made of local material. Randomly chosen from this area were 120 children (55 boys and 65 girls) (table 39.1). No families chosen for the study refused to participate.

Method

The mothers were interviewed by three people, one psychologist and two nurses. All were trained in psychiatric epidemiological methods and had previous experience in research work. They were given special training in the use of the questionnaire for this study. The same questionnaire has been used in previous studies in the Sudan (Cederblad, 1968; Rahim and Cederblad, 1984). It consists of a manual of thirty-two operationally defined behavioral disturbances. The mother was first asked whether a certain behavior was present or not. The severity of

Table 39.1 *Subjects*

	I Idikan	II Bodiga	III Lagun	Total
All	152	168	120	440
Boys	84	84	55	223
Girls	68	84	65	217
6 years old (54–89 months)	47	38	17	102
9 years old (90–125 months)	50	59	46	155
12 years old (126–161 months)	41	48	29	118
15 years old (162–203 months)	14	23	28	65

existing disturbances was then decided by the interviewer after further questioning.

A large amount of background data was also collected regarding the somatic and developmental status of the child, educational and socio-economic facts about the family, psychiatric conditions of the parents, life events, the parents' social support system, and so on. Weight, height, midarm circumference, hearing, and vision were measured. The children's intelligence was assessed using Raven's Progressive Matrices and Goodenough's Draw-a-man test. Some of the children were assessed by one of us (O.J.) in order to check the validity of the interview data.

On the basis of the interviews, the two of us (first independently and then conjointly) placed each child in one of four clinical groups: 0 = no behavioral disturbances, 1 = slight behavioral disturbances, 2 = moderate behavioral disturbances (coping with symptoms), and 3 = severe behavioral disturbances (the child was suffering from his condition or family/peers/school were suffering from the child's condition).

Our statistical methods entailed testing differences between means using the Student t-test and a one-way analysis of variance. Other comparisons between groups were tested using the Chi^2 method.

Results
The frequency of severe behavioral disturbances in the group as a whole was 16 percent (table 39.2). There were no differences between the

Table 39.2 *Severe Behavioral Disturbances in Three Areas of Nigeria (in percent)*

	All	I Idikan	II Bodiga	III Lagun	Stat. sign. Chi²	Boys	Girls	Stat. sign. Chi²
All	16	22	14	11	*	16	16	—
5–7 years	14	19	13	0	—	21	8	°
8–10 years	14	26	10	7	*	16	13	—
11–13 years	20	22	19	21	—	15	26	—
14–16 years	15	14	17	14	—	14	19	—
Stat. sign Chi²	—	—	—	—		—	°	
Preschool children								
5–7 years	14	19	13	0	—	21	8	°
Schoolchildren								
8–16 years	17	23	15	13	—	15	18	—
Stat. sign. Chi²								
5–7/8–16	—	—	—	—		—	°	
Boys		24	14	7	*			
Girls		19	14	14	—			

° = p < 0.10
* = p < 0.05

Table 39.3 *Single Behavioral Disturbances according to Age and Sex (in percent)*

	Boys 5–7 Years	Girls 5–7 Years	Boys 8–16 Years	Girls 8–16 Years	Stat. sign Sex[a]	Stat. sign Age[b]
Sleeping difficulties	0	0	1	0	—	—
Feeding difficulties	2	2	2	2	—	—
Enuresis nocturna	12	27	10	9	—	**
Enuresis diurna	0	2	0	0	—	—
Encopresis	0	0	1	0	—	—
Headaches	21	12	26	26	—	*
Twitching	2	0	0	1	—	—
Nail biting	5	13	7	12	*	—
Thumb sucking	2	8	3	6	°	°
Stuttering	10	3	2	2	—	°
Other speech difficulties	7	3	1	2	—	—
Aggressiveness	21	10	13	17	—	—
Inhibited aggressiveness	5	3	1	0	—	*
Anxiety	7	3	1	6	—	—
Depression	2	0	2	3	—	—
Phobias	5	10	4	10	*	—

					a. Sex	b. Age
Compulsion	0	0	0	1	—	—
Fear of darkness	29	38	17	27	**	**
Lying	24	22	24	24	—	—
Stealing	2	0	3	3	—	—
Truancy	0	0	2	1	—	—
Vagrancy	0	0	2	1	—	—
Hyperactivity	10	10	12	8	—	—
Hypoactivity	0	0	2	1	—	—
Sibling rivalry	52	31	39	26	**	**
Tingling sensation	0	0	1	1	—	—
Paralysis	0	2	0	0	—	—
Weakness of the body	0	3	1	3	°	—
Lost sight	0	2	0	2	°	—
Lost hearing	0	2	0	1	—	—
Choking sensation	0	0	1	1	—	—
Eating rubbish	0	0	0	0	—	—

Conversion hysteria { Tingling sensation … Choking sensation }

° = p < 0.10
* = p < 0.05
** = p < 0.01

a. Stat. differences according to sex (all ages)
b. Stat. differences according to age (both sexes)

Table 39.4 *Single Behavioral Disturbances (in percent)*

	I Idikan	II Bodiga	III Lagun	Stat. sign Chi²
Sleeping difficulties	1	0	1	—
Feeding difficulties	1	1	4	—
Enuresis nocturna	11	11	16	—
Enuresis diurna	0	1	0	—
Encopresis	0	1	1	—
Headaches	16	36	15	***
Twitching	0	1	2	—
Nail biting	7	16	2	***
Thumb sucking	3	9	2	**
Stuttering	3	5	1	—
Other speech difficulties	1	2	3	—
Aggressiveness	19	14	11	—
Inhibited aggressiveness	4	0	1	*
Anxiety	5	2	5	—
Depression	2	1	3	—
Phobias	10	6	4	—

Compulsion	1	0	0	—
Fear of darkness	22	33	15	**
Lying	22	23	28	—
Stealing	3	1	5	—
Truancy	2	1	1	—
Vagrancy	2	0	0	°
Hyperactivity	10	16	2	***
Hypoactivity	1	1	1	—
Sibling rivalry	36	35	33	—
Tingling sensation	0	1	1	—
Paralysis	0	1	0	—
Weakness of the body	1	2	2	—
Lost sight	1	1	1	—
Lost hearing	1	1	0	—
Choking sensation	2	1	0	—
Eating rubbish	0	0	0	—

Conversion hysteria: Tingling sensation, Paralysis, Weakness of the body; Lost sight, Lost hearing, Choking sensation

°   = p < 0.10
*   = p < 0.05
** = p < 0.01
*** = p < 0.001

frequencies for boys and girls, or between the different age groups. The children of Idikan had higher frequencies of disturbances, 22 percent, than the children of Bodiga, 14 percent, and those living at Lagun, 11 percent ($p < 0.05$). The differences between the areas were most noticeable in the age group eight to ten years ($p < 0.05$). The area differences were most pronounced for the boys ($p < 0.05$).

Table 39.3 shows the frequencies of single behavioral disturbances according to sex and age. The most common behavioral disturbances were sibling rivalry, fear of darkness, lying, headaches, aggressiveness, and, for the preschool children, enuresis nocturna. Though enuresis nocturna, fear of darkness, and inhibited aggressiveness decreased with age, headaches increased. There were few sex differences. Nail biting, phobias, and fear of darkness were more preponderant in girls, and sibling rivalry was more common in boys.

The distribution of single behavioral disturbances in the three study areas is shown in table 39.4. The pattern was similar, but children in Bodiga had higher frequencies of headaches and fear of darkness. Parents in that area more often reported that their children were hyperactive, bit their nails, or sucked their thumbs. Sleeping and feeding difficulties, anxiety, and antisocial symptoms like stealing, truancy, and vagrancy were rare. Fear of darkness and hyperactivity were less common in Lagun. Signs of conversion hysteria were uncommon in all areas.

DISCUSSION

The reliability of the findings is influenced by several factors. The questionnaire mostly deals with concrete, easily described behaviors. Behavior problems have different meanings, depending on the social context and expectations. Hyperactivity, for example, becomes a problem when a child is expected to sit still in school for several hours each day, whereas it may be unnoticed in the traditional farming life. Anxiety and depressiveness would, on the other hand, be considered discomforting in all social settings. In order to check whether the mothers in these areas also considered a behavioral disturbance problematic, we always asked the informant whether they experienced a recorded behavior as a problem and whether they had tried to treat the symptom in any way. The three interviewers were trained on the questionnaire until an acceptable degree of interrater reliability was obtained.

The frequency of "problem" children was similar to that found in the Sudanese studies (Cederblad, 1968; Rahim and Cederblad, 1984); all showed higher frequencies in the urban than in the rural samples. The low-income urban sample, however, displayed a higher percentage of disturbed children than the low-income urban sample in Sudan. This is probably due to the fact that the Nigerian area is more densely populated, whereas the Sudanese suburb, to a large extent, preserved the original form of an overgrown village.

Similar urban-rural differences have also been found in earlier European studies (Rutter et al., 1975; Kastrup, 1977; Lavik, 1976). Although most of these have found that boys more frequently have problems than girls, we found such a difference only in the preschool children. But the general frequency of disturbed children is strikingly similar to those found in European studies (Cederblad and Höök, 1986; Rutter et al., 1975; Richman et al., 1975). Thus, children seem to fare equally well behaviorally and emotionally across very different socioeconomic conditions in developed and developing countries. This, of course, is not true of the somatic health of children, which improves dramatically as health care, nutrition, sanitation, and general economic situations improve. There seem to be compensatory mechanisms in the social support systems of the children of the African research areas, which compensate for the economic, nutritional, and health hazards that haunt these children (compared to the European groups; Rahim and Cederblad, 1986). Or are there detrimental psychosocial side effects to the economic and societal development of the more affluent industrial countries? These mechanisms will be further explored in coming reports.

The pattern of single behavioral disturbances was similar to that in the Sudanese urban study. In all the African groups, sleeping difficulties and anxiety were very rare compared to European studies. That is probably due to the secure emotional situation of the child in the closely knit kinship group. Antisocial symptoms were also rare compared to European studies, indicating an intact, strong social control.

REFERENCES

Almeida-Filho, N. de. (1984). Family Variables and Child Mental Disorders in a Third World Urban Area (Bahia, Brazil)." *Soc. Psychiat.* 19:23–30.
Báasher, T. A., and Ibrahim, H. H. (1976). "Childhood Psychiatric Disorders in the Sudan." *Afr. J. Psychiat.* 1:67–78.

Cederblad, M. (1968). "A Child Psychiatric Study on Sudanese Arab Children. *Acta Psychiat. Scand.,* Suppl. 200.

Cederblad, M., and Höök, B. (1986). "Epidemiologisk studie i Östergötland." *Läkartidningen* 83:953–59. In Swedish.

Kastrup, (1977). M. "Urban-Rural Differences in 6-Year-Olds." In P. J. Graham, ed., *Epidemiological Approaches in Child Psychiatry.* London: Academic Press.

Lavik, N. J. (1976). *Ungdoms mentale helse.* Oslo: Universitetsforlaget. In Norwegian.

Rahim, S. I. A., and Cederblad, M. (1984). "Effects of Rapid Urbanization on Child Behaviour and Health in a Part of Khartoum, Sudan." *J. Child Psychol. Psychiat.* 25:629–41.

Rahim, S. I. A., and Cederblad, M. (1986). "Effects of Rapid Urbanization on Child Behaviour and Health in a part of Khartoum, Sudan. III, Psychosocial Influences on the Behaviour." *Soc. Sci. Med.* 22:723–730.

Richman, N., Stevenson, J. E., and Graham, P. J. (1975). "Prevalence of Behaviour Problems in 3-Year-Old Children: An Epidemiological Study in a London Borough." *J. Child Psychol. Psychiat.* 16:277–87.

Rutter, M. (1982). "Part VI: Special Stress and Coping: The City and the Child." *Ann. Progress in Child Psychiat. and Child Dev.* 1982:353–70.

Rutter, M., Yule, B., Quinton, D., Rowlands, O., Yule, W., and Berger, M. (1975). "Attainment and Adjustment in Two Geographical Areas. III, Some Factors Accounting for Area Differences." *Brit. J. Psychiat.* 126:520–33.

X

The Evolution of Concepts of Therapy

40

Introduction

COLETTE CHILAND

Concepts of therapy are constantly renewed: the ongoing study of results obtained by various therapies leads to efforts to improve them, while long-standing problems are viewed in a new light and new problems are constantly arising.

Along with changing attitudes toward psychiatric patients—strongly linked with the emergence of the psychoanalytic approach—the discovery of neuroleptics and other psychotropic drugs has created an upheaval in general psychiatry. But such medications cannot be used in the same way among children as among adults. Not only can they have long-term side effects, but their efficacy is more limited: neuroleptics, for example, do not produce the same remarkable results in childhood psychoses that they do in some adult psychoses.

Whatever the case, research is being conducted on medications, as is illustrated in other chapters in this book (e.g., chaps. 12 and 14). In chapter 44 of this part, Roland Lazarovici and Blanche Meliarenne examine the use of psychotropic drugs by pediatricians and show that medication often short-circuits verbal interaction with the child, by both the clinical team and the family. An anxiolytic can bring about symptomatic changes; but it does not solve the painful, often unbearable problems posed by illnesses with a short-term fatal prognosis, nor does it provide a solution to difficult complications of living, and so on.

Children, whether they are sick or not, have to be educated. In chapter 41 Roger Misès discusses the relationship between education and psychotherapy in institutions providing care for severely disturbed children. In France, even when such institutions are headed by psychiatrists who are also psychoanalysts, and psychoanalytic theory is a guid-

417

ing reference for understanding the difficulties and course of the treatment process, the approach is multidisciplinary.

The family approach is present throughout: it is not possible to treat a child without having some contact with the parents, although how this is done and what use it is put to vary considerably. In chapter 42 Juan Sauceda proposes training for therapists treating the most deprived families; faced with such families, the psychiatric teams often feel discouraged and powerless. These are poor families with some cultural characteristics common to Latin America and others specific to Mexico (in this respect, the chapter complements the work presented in part IX, "Transcultural Perspectives on Development").

Incest is not a recent phenomenon, but the increase in cases identified is causing surprise in a number of countries. The legal aspects of the problem sometimes tend to obscure the importance of therapeutic measures. In chapter 43, Tilman H. Furniss proposes a therapeutic model combining individual therapy, group therapy, and family therapy. The results that have been obtained in a not inconsiderable number of cases (fifty-six) are encouraging.

Further types of preventive and therapeutic intervention have been examined in other chapters of this book, dealing with problems specific to developing countries (chaps. 4 and 36), the cognitive approach (21), the psychoanalytic approach (17, 18, 27, and 28), divorce (32), and the special situation of isolation studied in Australia (38). Such wide-ranging studies have enabled us to present a kaleidoscopic view of our discipline. There is often no guaranteed therapeutic approach to the problems faced by psychiatric teams, but with courage, optimism, and perseverance, they put their intelligence, enthusiasm, and dedication to work for the patients, trying to improve where they cannot cure. Dogmatism is inappropriate, given the present state of our knowledge. The multidisciplinary approach is imperative.

41

Concepts and Therapeutic Interventions in Dynamically Oriented Institutions

ROGER MISÈS

A great many innovations have appeared in the field of institutional treatment over the last few decades. They fall under three main headings:

1. The idea of assistance or of simple special education has been replaced by resolutely therapeutic orientations.
2. There is now a far greater range of institutional programs, starting with the development of day hospitals and including various forms of part-time arrangements. At the same time there has been a reinforcement of links within the community, through the family, school, and the social services.
3. Underlying theoretical models have also mushroomed. This is no doubt the most important point, and one that, from reductive theses, has led to some extremely violent ideological confrontations.

The conception presented here tries to avoid the simplification of direct opposition between organogenesis and psychogenesis and rests on the hypothesis of a multifactorial origin of mental pathology. It admits the possibility of action from every conceivable direction, from the biological to the social level, but insists on the importance of a dynamic understanding of the disease process, which determines the correct adjustment of the means of treatment. In France this standpoint is shared by a great many teams led by psychiatrists with psychoanalytic training.

The children admitted to these institutions suffer from serious disorders, many of them in the psychotic category and often associated with symptoms of mental retardation. The choice of institution—boarding school, day hospital, part-time center—depends on the child's age, the type of disorder, and the social and family context, but there are a number of general ideas that apply whatever solution is adopted.

The essential point is that the treatment should combine a basic psychotherapeutic approach with educational techniques without one predominating over the other. This ensures that educators, teachers, and remediation specialists all have full scope for each to contribute to the course of the treatment in both its educational and psychotherapeutic aspects. It avoids having one set of staff handling the organization of the child's life and giving educational help while another group of specialists carries out individual approaches that are the only ones officially considered psychotherapeutic. On the contrary, everybody who lives in the institution is totally involved in the whole process of the treatment.

In this context, experience has shown that normal educational or pedagogical exchanges can become the instruments of true psychotherapeutic activities subject to regular assessment by the whole team. The search for significant elements, examination of the dynamic factors, and the regulation of the economy of the therapeutic process are the subject of joint reflection and discussion. The psychotherapeutic dimension is introduced here not by precodified technical instruments but by the particular handling of play techniques and pedagogical and remediation methods used elsewhere with normal or less disturbed children. These results cannot be obtained by being confined to a predetermined pattern, and the most varied educational programs are used as a prop for forms of exchange that acquire different meanings for different children or at different moments. As part of a team of this kind, psychiatrists and psychologists with psychoanalytic training have an important role in the conceptualization of the pace and rhythms of the treatment and in identifying the areas where an opening is possible and others where there is a blockage. The other members of the team who are not psychoanalysts—by far the majority—also participate in locating these dynamic points, and in this way they acquire a perception of the principal modes of liaison and relationship and can intervene effectively to reinforce any movement in the right direction.

However important the psychoanalytic angle may be, it is nevertheless not exclusive. Other approaches are used, which express each individual's efforts to conceptualize his or her unique role with theoretical instruments related to their discipline. There are, of course, some difficulties involved in integrating such heterogeneous inputs, but this is true in every multidisciplinary approach. They are not insurmountable.

The institutional fabric this offers the child can thus not be reduced to a place defined by its physical limits; nor does it constitute a framework comparable to the clearly defined space of a psychoanalytic psychotherapy carried out in sessions. In fact, the arrangement derives the essential part of its caring—more specifically, psychotherapeutic—function from various interlocking parameters, which can be simplified as follows:

1. The mobility and the numerous polarizations of the overall approach make it easier to create times and spaces that present an opportunity for the elaboration of fertile junctures in the treatment. This occurs within a continuum that is flexible enough to allow children to be assured of sustained support and at the same time to have sufficient freedom to organize their attachments and interactions without interference from disorganizing intrusions. It has to be remembered that they need to find increasingly advanced means of shielding against agitation.

This approach reflects to some extent what Winnicott (1971) has theorized concerning the appearance and affirmation of the child's feeling of existence in a potential space: it is never completed, nor is it static.

2. Fitting into this general framework is the individual ability of each adult to encourage and support the child's activities, which demands an especially attentive availability and receptiveness to patients whose mode of individuation is heavily affected.

D. W. Winnicott (1971) wrote on the subject of the support to the child's ego provided by the mother as she participates in illusion and then again during the process of disillusion. This aids the understanding of what educators themselves have to mobilize to sustain the rudiments of mental life being tried out. No formula dictated from outside and no amount of cold analysis can enable the adult to find the exact way to adjust the supporting props and set the limits. This can be done only through a personal commitment nourished by the individual's participation in exchanges within the caring group, which is a source of mutual support and revitalization.

In their own way, W. R. Bion's contributions (1967) concerning the concepts of the maternal capacity for reverie and the containing function also provide theoretical elements useful for understanding the psychic work required for an adult to be able to take what comes from the child, transform it, and return it in a form the child can assimilate. What gets back to the child in this way not only acquires meaning but becomes an essential vector in structuring his or her psychic apparatus.

Whether one refers to Winnicott or to Bion, the emphasis is on the functions of supporting, maintaining, and containing, all of which are ideas that concur with the nature of the pathological factors in institutional treatment. But despite the importance of what is played out again in a primordial function as far as the earliest flaws and distortions are concerned, attention is not distracted from the anchor-points and openings where there is a hint of access to the depressive position and triangulation. These elements are present in the way the caring staff express themselves as well as in exchanges with the child, even before the latter is able to absorb them. In this anticipatory illusion, we find that each member of the team holds a unique place in an approach to problems that is wide open to the symbolic and the imaginary without neglecting the basic supporting structure.

3. Two different components can be distinguished in the treatment process. One puts greater emphasis on support and setting up a milieu favorable to education and treatment, and the other on the facilitation of the treatment alliance, particularly through team meetings. This does not mean, however, that the former should be associated exclusively with educational support and the latter solely with psychotherapeutic functions.

In this context, children are not all systematically given individual psychotherapy in its traditional form; it is used only for certain children and at whatever point it is judged to be appropriate. When it is utilized, the individual psychotherapy is articulated with the other components of the therapeutic process, and helps to unify the partial cathexes in a clearly defined space where transference and countertransference issues are more easily handled.

Our insistence on the interaction between educational and therapeutic components led us to highlight the importance of psychotherapeutic activities carried out by each member of the team. This is no way detracts from the importance of the specifically educational functions exercised in everyday life or in formally structured activities such as clubs, classes, and language or psychomotor remediation. Care is taken at every level to ensure that the child acquires the learning necessary and recognizes the demands inherent in life within society.

Current deficiencies of whatever origin are taken into consideration, which means that on admission, and at intervals from then onward, children are given comprehensive evaluations. Besides uncovering any neurobiological factors, these assessments have the advantage of providing detailed information on the current symptoms of cognitive disorders, which are often present in severe childhood pathology. This helps staff members adapt educational activities with a view to avoiding repetition of failure situations and making more emphatic use of methods based on the child's abilities in certain areas, even if they are uneven. This is not an exclusive focus, however, and it does not necessarily mean adopting the hypothesis of a purely cognitive impairment. On the contrary, in our view the development of intelligence cannot be considered in isolation from the overall process of organization of mental life. Backwardness, uneven development, and learning disorders are invariably present in a multifactorial process, and the particular form symptoms take at any given moment requires a multidimensional response, taking special care that the educational measures do not bring in any harmful simplifications. For this reason, rigidly structured programs are discarded in favor of flexibility. This permits adaptation to the needs of each child and modification according to his or her development. It is a process in which, although educators respond by utilizing specific instruments, they nonetheless also mobilize their own creative abilities.

More often than not, the child's deficits are varied and embedded in a complex configuration. Defensive refusals are common and knowledge already acquired cannot be integrated into ensembles that would facilitate subsequent learning. Varied means of communication or interaction therefore have to be adopted by balancing individual contacts and attempts to return the child to the group. While doing this, teachers face the danger of too close a relationship becoming either intrusive or fusional, bringing with it the risk of again producing submission of the child to an externally imposed constraint—which, moreover, he tends to provoke. Elsewhere, the child withdraws from notice to the point of reexperiencing situations of abandonment, where primitive threats of becoming nonexistent are reactivated. Special attention is therefore given to maintaining a presence that counters the threatened danger while at the same time proposing activities capable of encouraging exploratory initiatives from the subject himself, so that he begins to try out the resources already available to him.

We know that the child has to acquire for herself the instruments of mental life that cannot be given from outside sources. This is particularly important in the school context, where learning is based not on one-way teacher-pupil transmission but on an exchange between two people. Here, the teacher has to understand, and conceptualize, the nature and meaning of the child's failures in such a way as to leave her a personal choice, as well as the opportunity to launch into experiences that are likely to reactivate deep-seated anxieties.

Some children raise a different problem: although they take part in class, they confine themselves to repeating stereotyped activities, as though their sole aim were to maintain a state of equilibrium where constant repetition of identical patterns brings confirmation. Without prohibiting behavior of this kind, it is sometimes preferable in these cases to return to educational tasks that offer a more creative dimension, even if the means used seem to depart from traditional school objectives. Under flexible arrangements like this, a link can be maintained between teacher and child that could lead to resumption of more conventional forms of learning.

This is often a difficult path to follow, particularly, as J. Hochmann (1984) has convincingly shown, with psychotics who resist the integration of didactic facts into the network of meanings in which school learning takes place. These children remain immovably attached to private codes that the teacher initially has to learn to recognize and follow. The breadth of understanding and receptiveness required of the primary school teacher does not exclude the authority and ability to apply requirements essential in teaching of any kind.

For all these reasons, and despite the qualities of adaptability expected of anyone teaching in such an educational context, the classroom remains a unique area because of the activities proper to it, its objectives, and the image the children and the adults have of it. The gradual progress achieved in these conditions sometimes enables a child to attend a nearby school without interrupting treatment. This presupposes the establishment of close links between the institution's team and the schoolteacher in the new class so that the latter's educational activities will fit in with those of the specialized center. A similar cooperation is established from the outset in part-time treatment arrangements, which by definition include the continuation of school in a normal environment.

Specialists in language and psychomotor remediation can be included in this structure at the appropriate moment; at this point they reinforce the positive movement triggered by the basic educational and psychotherapeutic groundwork. These specialists also avoid techniques that are rapidly determined in advance and applied with the aim of simply repairing an instrumental function seen in isolation. On the contrary, they maintain an open perspective, making use of spontaneous expressions of the child, whose regressive movements are tolerated in order to make up the time lost because of the wider-based reconstruction anticipated. In this way efforts are directed at sustaining the child's awakening, and his newfound pleasure derived from access to increasingly advanced means of communication, rather than trying to achieve a veneer of new acquisitions. Alongside this, narcissistic cathexis is reinstated and feelings of inadequacy or low self-esteem are left behind.

These psychotherapeutic principles by no means diminish the importance attributed to the results obtained: acquisition of knowledge, access to new patterns of performance, and improved social adjustment. All along the way, remediation specialists make every effort to adjust their actions in harmony with those of the other participants. Speech therapists often work in close collaboration with teachers, for example, when progress in language acquisition can release capacities for symbolization, broadening the range of potential that can be applied in school.

Relations with parents have an important role, which is impossible to describe in detail here. It should simply be noted that extreme measures are not used, from systematic treatment of parents considered to be mentally disturbed to total separation from the family. The basic approach is formed around flexible arrangements adapted to the personality of each individual, without losing sight of the sociofamilial network seen as a whole. The essential thing is to bring about, and then sustain, an alliance that will (if necessary) be able to provide an opening for various forms of more or less systematic approaches. It is preferable for the whole team to be involved in these exchanges, including those that take place with children who have been admitted as residential boarders. On these foundations, which combine the recognition of individual attitudes and the inclusion of all the protagonists, it is easier to acquire a better understanding of the mechanisms at work in the sociofamilial network and their effects on the institutional fabric. This sometimes gives rise to interventions that make it possible to give new impetus to the treatment process, through work done with the parents.

The theoretical stances outlined here need to be applied in a flexible manner, in such a way that from his or her specific viewpoint each individual has sufficient personal freedom to make a contribution to the construction of the institutional fabric while continuing to ensure a satisfactory balance between the psychotherapeutic and educational approaches. Throughout the treatment process the lines of force are modified by interactions among the people involved; at times this leads to very productive points of convergence but at others is liable to provoke confrontations or the danger of stagnation. When this happens, it often points up the damaging effects of an imbalance between the educational and the therapeutic components. Encroachments are inevitable, in fact, and this is why trial readjustments are an inherent part of the dynamics of institutional work.

REFERENCES

Bion, W. R. (1967). *Second Thoughts*. New York: Jason Aronson.
Hochmann, J. (1984). *Pour soigner l'enfant psychotique*. Toulouse: Privat.
Winnicott, D. W. (1971). *Playing and Reality*. London: Tavistock.

42

Training Family Therapists to Work with Low-Income Families

JUAN M. SAUCEDA

The psychological treatment of low-income families requires an understanding of the unique characteristics of this social class as well as the use of special psychotherapeutic techniques. The teaching of these aspects constitutes an important part of the training program offered by the Instituto Nacional de Salud Mental in Mexico City. There we give a course in family psychotherapy for psychiatrists, psychologists, social workers, and psychiatric nurses. The course entails theoretical as well as clinical activities over a period of two years, and the patients come mainly from a population with limited economic resources.

The conclusions derived from the study and treatment of low-income families in Mexico can be, to some extent, generalized to poor families in the rest of Latin America. This does not imply that there are not significant differences among Latin American countries, or even among the various regions into which each country is subdivided. But to understand the vast similarities among the Latin American peoples, it is sufficient to remember that for more than three centuries the countries located south of the Rio Grande were under Spanish domination and influence; therefore, we share our language, religious beliefs, customs, and an indigenous heritage of great importance.

COMMON FAMILY DYNAMICS IN POOR MEXICAN FAMILIES

There are some psychosocial conditions common to low-income families in Mexico. It is essential that the therapist planning to treat this type of family be acquainted with these traits. In some measure, the following concepts are related to the strategic and structural parameters amply explained by Haley and Minuchin in their papers (White, 1979). These are guidelines that we frequently utilize in our work with poor families, as we deem them particularly effective in this setting. These guidelines are the concepts of hierarchy, boundaries or limits, alliances, centrality, and a map of the family (Barragan, 1975).

Hierarchy. As in any other system, the family has members with varying degrees of authority according to the particular personality and developmental stage. It is considered desirable that the highest authority be shared by both parents and that they exercise mutual support in the establishment of the rules that are to organize their children's lives and their family system (Haley, 1977).

Boundaries or limits. These are imaginary borders that define the rights of each individual and of each subsystem within the family. There are individual limits, generational limits, sexual limits, and so on. A well-defined limit is an indispensable requirement for a well-functioning family (Minuchin and Fishman, 1981).

Alliances. This is the open or concealed but implicit association that exists between two or more members within the family. Alliances can be based on personal affinities (age, sex, interests, personality traits) or the desire to establish a united front opposed to another member or family subsystem. When the alliance has the objective of harming a third person, it is called a coalition (Haley, 1975).

Centrality. This term refers to the amount of attention given to each member of the family. The family dynamics are upset when one member gets so much attention it is a detriment to the attention due the others. The identified patient is frequently the most central family member, and the least central member is usually the one least involved in family life (Barragan, 1976).

Map of the family. This is a layout that represents, in a graphic and simple way, the family structure; it can render clues for a therapeutic intervention. For example, it might designate the distribution of the family members during the interview, at the table, at bedtime, or when traveling in their car (Minuchin, 1974).

In Mexico, particularly in rural and poor urban areas, an extremely intense mother-son alliance is common. As pointed out by Santiago Ramirez (1977), there is a very significant sociocultural atmosphere surrounding the image of the female. The world of the Mexican includes a double sexual standard of morality, as well as contrasting characteristics of the roles played by the male and the female because the male is allowed rights denied to the female. The father is feared and his absence is frequent, both physically and emotionally. Thus, we could say that his position in family life tends to be peripheral.

The poor urban family consists of a group of relatives in which one key member is usually missing, frequently the father, either temporarily or permanently. The older children are pressured by these circumstances to mature prematurely and to carry out parental functions with the younger siblings. Mother's work prevents her from fulfilling her parental role during most of the day (Nolasco, 1978). Approximately 16 percent of Mexican families are organized around this woman who is without her companion. At least one-third of poor, urban families are matricentered, as the woman supports the family, sometimes by herself, sometimes helped by her companion or relatives. Two-thirds of poor urban families require the woman to hold a job to help the family economically. But the official breadwinner continues to be the father, and usually the mother receives no recognition for or release from household work.

It is not unusual for the wife to take on the martyr's role in poor families where the father abuses his authority. She manipulates her children through this attitude while undermining her husband's authority with passive-aggressive behavior. As a result of his identification with an aggressive and absent father, the son tends to repeat this model later in his adult life, in spite of the suffering caused in his own family of origin.

An authentic cult of the maternal figure is expressed in diverse forms. Mother's Day, for instance, is a national holiday with a cultural significance equal to that of a religious festival. There are sayings and songs with an unequivocal oedipal content, which reflect the primacy of mother over wife, since the former love is considered to be "purer."

Grandparents also play a very important role in the family. The practice of sending old people to nursing homes to spend their last days almost never occurs in Mexico. Their presence at home can cause confusion as to where the authority in the family hierarchy resides, especially when they exert greater authority than the parents in the upbringing of children. This situation is even more likely when the father is an alcoholic or the mother is a single parent.

When a member of the family marries and has children, there is a tendency to preserve the extended family ties, forming an enmeshed unit. It is not customary for the young adults in the family to live separately from their parents before marrying. The young couple makes the transition from their parents' home to their own home, which is usually built on the same piece of land where one of the parents live. Very often difficulties arise because of the excessive interventions of the parents or because of the couple's inability to acquire their own identity away from their original families. In many cases, economic hardship forces the newlyweds to live with their parents, and this makes the definition of intergenerational limits extremely difficult.

In regard to marital fidelity, masculine centrality is more than evident. A husband's affairs are often tolerated. According to a poll, approximately one out of every six Mexicans lives with two women at the same time and probably has children with both.

In Mexico, then, the culture fundamentally revolves around the relationship with mother. Father is frequently absent and mother looks for compensation in her motherhood, accepting the limitations she suffers as a wife. It cannot be denied that Ramirez has pinpointed a truth when he states that the basic problem in Mexican family structure is an excess of mother, lack of father, and abundance of children.

This view of poor Mexican families does not pretend to be exhaustive or applicable in all cases, but it is imperative for family therapists in training to be acquainted with it and take it into account in their therapeutic interventions.

RELEVANT ISSUES IN THE TRAINING PROCESS

Aponte (1966) concludes that, from a purely psychological point of view, there is nothing particularly peculiar about families of limited economic resources. Yet it is known that there are more behavioral disturbances in children from these families, such as delinquency, drug addiction, prostitution, and conversion disorders. One of the social consequences of being poor can be the lack of access to helping services. But the heterogeneous nature of poor people should not be forgotten. What may function for one group may not necessarily function for another (Minuchin et al., 1967).

Poor people are prone to present certain verbal and conceptual deficiencies, a lack of introspection in their approach toward life, a greater tendency toward action, and little motivation to participate in a prolonged psychotherapy situation (Riessman et al., 1964). The poor have different expectations from those patients coming from the middle and higher classes. Frequently, they expect the therapist to pay attention to their physical ailments and to give them directives, advice, and support, in the context of a firm structured authority.

Psychotherapists in training usually come from a middle-class setting and need to make an extra effort to apply the principles of the family approach to patients who live in a sociocultural setting different from their own. Many of them are not successful in their attempt to understand the context of their patients of humble extraction.

Following are important guidelines for students training to conduct family therapy among lower-class families.

1. *Break away from previous approaches.*

The majority of students have had previous training with emphasis on individual and intrapsychic dynamics, giving little consideration to context as a determinant of human conduct. The mind of each family member is one of the most important elements in the family system, but it in no way constitutes the only one. Family therapy operates with the view that the individual is part of his or her environment. Each family's context is unique: the ecology is neither standard nor unchangeable (Auerswald, 1968). The exploration of pathology is carried out mainly in the area made up of the individual and the social context. When the therapist joins the family, he or she becomes a part of that environment, a necessary condition in order to help the family overcome their conflicts and achieve a more functional organization. To reach certain therapeutic goals, the therapist must first explore the family context and then attempt to modify it.

Students who have been individual therapists find it difficult to follow the customary steps in this approach: first, to join the family in order to understand its structure without attempting to modify it and, subsequently, to create a therapeutic alliance that ensures that the family returns for additional sessions (the engagement process). Later, techniques aimed at restructuring the family dynamics are implemented (e.g., establishing more adequate measures of authority, defining limits, neutralizing the excessive centrality of certain members, encouraging more functional alliances), and these techniques ultimately introduce maneuvers that help maintain the change.

A certain degree of departure from previous therapeutic approaches might be necessary in order to facilitate the understanding of a new and different one. This departure should not be drastic, because once the new approach has been assimilated, one finds that the traditional psychodynamic skills not only are not obstacles but instead contribute significantly to both the understanding of the family and its treatment.

2. *Emphasize the here and now.*

At first, students find it difficult to observe and to promote interaction among the family members during a session; they get lost in an endless, purposeless exploration of past factors or in trying to stimulate the expression of emotions within the family. This technique runs the risk of becoming a distorted form of an individual session in front of the rest of the family. During the evaluation of family dynamics it is much more important to first ascertain who apparently has greatest authority, who speaks to whom, who is allowed to speak and who is not, who is validated and who is invalidated, where the alliances exist, in what manner limits are imposed, who assumes or is assigned idiosyncratic roles, what types of affective involvement prevail, and what the particular patterns of communication in the family are (Hoffman, 1981; Chagoya, 1975; Sauceda, 1981).

This does not mean that exploration into the past of the family is not an important step in therapy, but sometimes the beginning therapist tends to overlook interactional factors in the present that are essential in order to understand the family dynamics. Moreover, the relevant patterns of the past tend to manifest themselves in the interactive patterns of the present. It is the present manifestation that should be treated, especially in the case of poor families.

3. *Adopt directive strategies in therapy.*

One of the characteristics of symptomatic families in the low-income range is their loosely bound structure, their disorganization, and their lack of stability (Minuchin, 1974). For this reason one of the functions of the therapist consists in intervening actively in order to establish a more functional family structure. If it is considered common in family therapy for the therapist to assume a directive position, it is absolutely necessary to do so in the treatment of families of humble extraction.

The focus on the present, rather than on the exploration of the past, also favors the use of directive tactics over the implementation of interpretive techniques and the attainment of insight as a precondition to change. The assignment of concrete directives as a sort of homework is particularly effective in the treatment of low-income families because their members are more inclined toward action than are people with greater intellectual sophistication.

Making modifications in the map of the family (changing the seating arrangement during the session or the sleeping arrangement at home, or assigning different tasks) may seem to the orthodox therapist aberrations of the therapeutic process. On one occasion I had a student who, after the first few weeks, abandoned the program because she disagreed with the techniques, which she deemed excessively directive and manipulative. This student, brilliant in other areas, was not flexible enough to depart from the traditional therapeutic stance, and she abruptly withdrew from the course, exclaiming, "May Freud forgive them!"

When we follow this approach, we assume a greater responsibility in regard to the attainment of results in comparison to traditional therapies. The therapeutic work is directed toward producing an observable change by means of the application of simple directive strategies or as a result of paradoxical suggestions (Watzlawick et al., 1974). A paradoxical communication suggests an action with the intention of provoking the opposite response.

4. *Stop trying to do too much.*

Even though a fundamental part of the therapeutic process consists of giving support and orientation in the instrumental aspects of daily life, some students are carried away by a paternalistic eagerness that leads them to behave too generously with their patients. I remember a student who, occasionally, would take to her own home a young girl who was the identified patient in a very poor family. She gave her additional help in schoolwork, good meals, and a small amount of money. This attitude, even though well intentioned, independent of her unconscious motives, produced a certain dissonance between the patient and her family. The girl's parents began to hold a hierarchical position inferior to that of the therapist. In addition, her siblings viewed her with jealousy and envy. In this way, the image of the therapist was distorted, so that they saw her more as a provider to be seduced and exploited.

5. *Avoid assuming defeatist attitudes.*

In the face of the many deficiencies these families suffer (unemployment or underemployment, lack of decent dwellings, lack of public services, malnutrition, ignorance, illness), the student can fall into the throes of defeatism and demoralization, becoming convinced that nothing can be done if socioeconomic conditions are not radically modified first. In well-developed countries a lack of coordination among the various helping agencies can constitute a serious problem, reinforcing an indolent and cynical attitude in members of poor families. This is definitely not the case in Latin American countries, given their limited social resources. At times, the intervention of government-sponsored agencies represents a problem in itself. Sometimes one might fight against the bureaucratic system or the corruption of those who try to take a personal political advantage and, far from helping people, exploit them. Equally disheartening for the therapist in training is the existence of laws that theoretically protect the family but when put into practice are not applied as they should be, and so might as well not exist. Under such circumstances, perhaps the best action is to intervene as far as one's own possibilities and limitations allow, trying to use whatever benefits can be found in these agencies without assuming a defeatist attitude. Some families may undergo surprising improvements as a result of the therapist's conveyance of confidence in their capabilities and the effect of positive relabeling, directives, paradoxical suggestions, and so on.

6. *Encourage adequate communication.*

It is of special importance that therapists be careful not to use an overly elaborate language that is not attuned to people whose schooling is very limited or nonexistent. Poor people tend to rely less on verbal expression than those who belong to higher social classes. The therapist cannot expect these patients to reach a level of verbal expression similar to those of the middle class, just as he cannot expect them to achieve insight into their problems, as could be anticipated for those who have greater psychological sophistication.

7. *Do not exclude the extended family.*

A common mistake is to exclude members of the extended family from the nuclear family in an attempt to establish limits when they are not well defined. Without the presence of significant members of the extended family, the therapist will fail to get the full picture of the family group as it truly functions.

The presence of grandparents, uncles, and other relatives could favor coalitions against the authority of the parents. This can occur particularly in the case where the mother is without a husband or companion and the grandmother tries to compensate the child for the absence of a father by being overly indulgent. If the mother attempts to correct the child, the grandmother might undermine her authority, which can lead to the child's becoming omnipotent. When the therapist becomes aware of the inadequate interventions of the grandmother, he or she may respond with unchecked countertransference, trying to promote abrupt changes in the family with the intention of excluding the grandmother. As a consequence, the advantages of having grandparents and other relatives in the family system may be lost. The family may not return to therapy, as the threatened family system would prefer to cancel the outside help that is abruptly trying to break the homeostasis. The therapeutic zeal must be moderated in order to help the family achieve more functional dynamics without performing painful amputations.

8. *Do not encourage dependence or violate the hierarchy.*

The novice therapist intent on giving order to a disorganized family might achieve success, but at the same time encourage the family's dependence on him in an excessive way. It is important for the members of the family, especially the authority figures, to exercise what they have learned from the therapist as a model. Dependence, although necessary in the beginning of therapy, can be harmful if prolonged in the therapeutic process. The therapist must allow the family to make its own decisions and reject the temptation to establish an omnipotent attitude. At the termination of therapy the family should feel that the solution of their problems was more the result of their own work than that of the therapist (Haley, 1980). This requires ego strength on the part of the therapist, so that he will not need excessive recognition from his patients for his work.

9. *Do not ignore intrapsychic factors.*

One of the risks confronted when one is enthralled with the systems perspective in family therapy is that of underestimating the individual factors, especially those related to affect. The therapist is often tempted to become what has been called a "behavioral engineer." This refers not only to strict adherence to postulates of behavior modification but also to the view that interpersonal relations are the only important elements within a family system. Therefore, the therapist may employ maneuvers far too drastic in order to modify interaction and achieve an amelioration of symptoms. One therapist who took this stand considered it justifiable to insult and even to lie in order to achieve his goal. To exclusively follow the "black box" approach means that one sacrifices a wealth of resources available through a psychodynamic approach. It is difficult to integrate individual psychodynamic factors with those from the systems view, but to ignore intrapsychic factors limits the therapeutic arsenal and favors the emergence of an omnipotent and intrusive attitude on the part of the therapist.

10. *Do not attempt to achieve mastery of family therapy techniques in a short period of time.*

Even though strategic structural techniques are apparently easy to learn and simple to apply, their understanding and utilization are not, requiring continual study and supervision in order to master them

(Chagoya, 1981). Traditional psychodynamic concepts can facilitate this learning process. In psychotherapy one cannot ignore the lasting contributions of psychoanalysis, such as the concepts of the dynamics of the unconscious, repression, transference, and so on.

11. *Be aware of the possible negative connotations of this approach.*

It is not unusual for these ideas to be considered, by orthodox therapists, as excessively directive and manipulative. But the therapist who follows this approach plans a strategy only after understanding the family structure and is directive as the case requires without ceasing to be respectful. We could label these techniques "manipulation," but we must not become confused by the negative connotations attached to this term. Manipulation is a working tool in psychotherapy, whether we like it or not, and as such it can be used in a legitimate way for the sake of the family. It is not good or bad in itself; that depends on how it is used, on whether the therapist is honest or dishonest. Even the most orthodox technique can have negative results in the hands of a dishonest or untrained therapist. A good therapist will not exclude positive manipulation from the arsenal of therapeutic resources, as long as it produces benefits for the patient and promotes positive changes within the family group and its members (Sauceda, 1981).

REFERENCES

Aponte, H. (1976). "Underorganization in the Poor Family." In P. J. Guerin, ed., *Family Therapy: Theory and Practice*. New York: Gardner Press.

Auerswald, E. H. (1968). "Interdisciplinary versus Ecological Approach." *Family Process* 7:205-215.

Barragan, M. (1975). "Structural Diagnosis." Conference presented at Hospital Infantil de Mexico.

———. (1976). "The Child-Centered Family." In P. J. Guerin, ed., *Family Therapy: Theory and Practice*. New York: Gardner Press.

Chagoya, L. (1975). "Dinamica familiar y patologia." In H. Dulanto, ed., *La familia: Medio propiciador o inhibidor del desarrollo humano*. Mexico: Ediciones Medicas del Hospital Infantil de Mexico.

———. (1981). "Conclusion." In Instituto de la Familia, *Primer Symposium sobre la Dinamica y Psicoterapia de la Familia*. Mexico.

Haley, J. (1975). "Toward a Theory of Pathological Systems." In G. H. Zuk and I. Boszormenyi-Nagy, eds., *Family Therapy and Disturbed Families*. Ben Lomond, Calif.: Science and Behavior Books.

———. (1977). *Problem-Solving Therapy.* San Francisco: Jossey Bass.

———. (1980). *Leaving Home.* New York: McGraw-Hill.

Hoffman, L. (1981). *Foundations of Family Therapy.* New York: Basic Books.

Minuchin, S. (1974). *Families and Family Therapy.* Cambridge, Mass.: Harvard University Press.

Minuchin, S., and Fishman, C. (1979). "The Psychosomatic Family in Child Psychiatry." *J. Child Psychiat.* 18:76–90.

———. (1981). *Family Therapy Techniques.* Cambridge, Mass.: Harvard University Press.

Minuchin, S., Montalfo, B., Guerney, B., Rosman, B., and Schumer, F. (1967). *Families of the Slums.* New York: Basic Books.

Nolasco, M. (1978). "La familia mexicana." *Revista FEM* 2:14–19.

Ramirez, S. (1977). *El mexicano: Psicologia de sus motivaciones.* Mexico: Grijalbo.

Riessman, F., Cohen, J., and Peral, A. (1964). *Mental Health of the Poor.* New York: Free Press of Glencoe.

Sauceda, J. (1981). "Psicoterapia familiar: El enfoque estrategico-estructural." In Instituto de la Familia, *Primer Simposium sobre la Dinamica y Psicoterapia de la Familia.* Mexico.

Sauceda, J., and Foncerrada, M. (1981). "La exploracion de la familia: Aspectos medicos, psicologicos y sociales." *Rev. Med. IMSS* 19:155–163.

Watzlawick, P., Weakland, C., and Fisch, R. (1974). *Change.* New York: Norton.

White, M. (1979). "Structural and Strategic Approaches to Psychosomatic Families." *Family Process* 18:303–314.

43

An Integrated Treatment Approach to Child Sexual Abuse in the Family

TILMAN H. FURNISS

In recent years child sexual abuse has increasingly come to the attention of all professionals involved in child health and mental health. The focus in present research and clinical practice has shifted from primarily forensic and individual aspects to epidemiological approaches and treatment projects with a family perspective.

The first research in the fifties, which assumed that incest occurs in one case in a million per year (Weinberg, 1955), has been followed by more recent data that suggest that child sexual abuse is a common phenomenon. Hard data about the prevalence and incidence of sexual abuse and incest are scarce, however. A study of 796 American college students found that 90 percent of the women and 9 percent of the men had had some experience of sexual abuse as children (Finkelhor, 1979). Another study using more rigid criteria found 38 percent of women reporting at least one experience before the age of eighteen and 28 percent before the age of fourteen (Russell, 1983). A British survey of a nationally representative sample revealed a 10 percent reporting rate of sexual abuse before the age of sixteen, with 1.4 percent of the total sample reporting having been abused within the family context (Baker and Duncan, 1985).

In the mid-1980s, there were shifts in the sex distribution of victims and the reported age of abused children. The percentage of male victims increased and reached to a quarter or a third of all victims (Finkelhor, 1979; Baker and Duncan, 1985; De Jong et al., 1983). The age of disclosure shifted from adolescence to onset in much earlier childhood—between two and five years (Creighton, 1984; Mrazek et al., 1983).

SAMPLE FOR A BRITISH STUDY

An analysis of the first fifty-six cases of the first British treatment project for sexually abused children at the Hospital for Sick Children, Great Ormond Street, confirms these trends of epidemiological data.

1. Of the fifty-six patients, forty-six (82 percent) were girls, but the percentage of boys seems to increase with an increasing rate of disclosure.

2. Child sexual abuse was not primarily an issue of adolescence. The distinction between the age of disclosure of the abuse and the age of onset shows a very different picture. The age range at referral varied from fourteen months to nineteen years. The age group between eleven and fifteen years had by far the greatest number of cases, with thirty-one (56 percent), followed by the six-to-ten-year group with ten cases. The age of onset ranged from thirteen months to fourteen years, but twenty-four (45 percent) of the children were six to ten years old. Most significantly, with fifteen (28 percent) of the cases, the second largest group was aged under five years at the time of onset.

3. The duration of the abuse varied between a single incident and eleven years. Twenty-four (43 percent) children were abused for two to four years, and in eleven (20 percent) of the cases the abuse lasted for more than five years.

4. When compared to epidemiological data there was a clear skew in our group with regard to perpetrators: 37.5 percent were fathers, 66.1 percent fathers and stepfathers, and 8.93 percent relatives and father figures. In only one case was the perpetrator a stranger (Furniss et al., 1984).

A THERAPEUTIC APPROACH TO SEXUAL ABUSE OF CHILDREN

Mrazek et al. (1983), in a survey in the United Kingdom, showed that traditionally, sexual abuse in children was overwhelmingly responded to with denial or, when it came to light, in a punitive fashion. Prosecution of perpetrators was the major intervention; in only 11 percent of the cases was a referral made to a child psychiatrist.

Although *incest* is defined legally as intercourse between biological family members, in relation to treatment the term is often used to describe any form of long-standing sexual abuse between any adult in a parental role and a child within the family context. Therefore I use the term *father* here for any male adult in a parental position within the family. When we planned a treatment project on sexual abuse of children, we based our approach on the following presuppositions (Furniss et al., 1984):

1. Like physical abuse of children, sexual abuse in the family is seen as an expression of severe relationship problems, which may lead to physical and psychological damage of the child. The damaging aspect of long-standing sexual abuse is not only the child's negative experience of being forced into compliance with the abuse. The abuse often takes place in the context of an otherwise caring and trusting parental relationship. Despite the negative aspects, the relationship may be intense and include the experience of positive sexual sensations. These are all ingredients for confusion and difficulty in future sexual relationships, with a high risk of a reduced ability to be a partner and a parent in adulthood (Bentovim and Okell Jones, 1984).

2. The removal of the child from the family without therapeutic help often means an escalation of some aspects of the original traumatic experience. The child not only loses her siblings, her friends, and her social environment in a period of crisis, but she often experiences foster placements and residential placements as punishment and feels guilty and responsible for the abuse as well. In addition, the child may be blamed openly by the parents (Furniss, 1983a).

3. Imprisonment of perpetrators without therapeutic help leads to a danger of the person repeating the abuse, either when returning to the family or by abusing a child in a newly created family. Conversely, comprehensive treatment for abusers can lead to family rehabilitation and the prevention of further abuse (Groth, 1982).

4. The quality of the relationship between mother and daughter is one of the most important risk factors accounting for child sexual abuse in the family (Finkelhor, 1980). The presence of a nonprotective mother-child relationship is an important aspect that may contribute to and maintain a sexually abusive relationship.

5. It should be noted that although I am describing our approach to understanding child sexual abuse between father figures and daughters, the family processes are similar whether the child is a boy or girl.

FAMILY PATTERNS AND APPROACHES TO SEXUAL ABUSE OF CHILDREN

The motivation for the sexual abuse of children is rooted in the experience of the perpetrators. Regressed and fixated individual psychopathology has been described (Groth, 1982). Understanding individual psychopathology, although helpful, is not enough to explain the occurrence and continuation of child sexual abuse. Any simplistic family typology of child sexual abuse must necessarily distort reality. It has, however, been helpful clinically to distinguish between cases where sexual abuse seems to have the function of either avoiding sexual conflicts in the marriage or limiting open sexual conflict in the marriage at a level that avoids the breakup of the family (Furniss, 1984a).

Fathers turn to children for sexual satisfaction because of their inability to resolve sexual conflict within the marriage or to cope with sexual dissatisfactions by seeking help, by resorting to extramarital relationships, or by obtaining a divorce. Although on an interactional level some abusing fathers seem to dominate and control their families, we have found that they are, in fact, usually emotionally dependent, immature, and weak. The inability to separate, individuate, and take appropriate responsibility as fathers and partners keeps the abusers in the family and influences them to turn toward the child. These fathers more often fall into Groth's (1982) category of "regressed" perpetrators, in contrast to the abusive tendency in "fixated" perpetrators, who may be more impulsive, often abusing more than one child, both girls and boys, in intra- and extrafamilial situations.

Mothers often fit into the interlocking marital pattern by taking on the role of an emotional caretaker for their husbands. A punitive attitude toward sexuality ensures that talking about sexual conflicts is taboo, so that they remain unresolved. In addition, the distance between mother and daughter may mean that the mother is insensitive to her daughter's emotional needs or may not believe the child when she tries to confide in her and turn to her for help. This has the effect of reinforcing a nonprotective relationship between mother and daughter, which may make the daughter turn to her father for emotional parenting. The child is then even more vulnerable and liable to comply with paternal sexual demands (Furniss, 1984a).

FAMILY-ORIENTED TREATMENT

In families where sexual abuse serves to avoid marital conflict, the discrepancy between the self-image of family members and the actual facts of family relationships may be so large that the disclosure leads to a major crisis for all family members. In any therapy, children need from their parents permission to speak, and in child sexual abuse, viewed as a syndrome of secrecy, they also need permission to communicate.

Therapeutic work, therefore, has to include both the child and the child's family. Family-oriented work is indicated both to free the child emotionally, as a precondition for treatment in her own right, and to prevent the perpetrator from offending again. In all cases where the parents have dropped out of treatment, the child's therapy has also been interrupted.

The aims of family work are (Furniss, 1983b):

1. For the father (perpetrator) to take sole responsibility for the sexual act.
2. For both parents to take personal responsibility for the emotional care and well-being of the daughter.
3. To work on the mother-daughter relationship to enable mother to become a more central, emotionally caring parent for the child.
4. To deal with the sexual and emotional conflicts in the marriage as a basis for abuse of the child by the father.
5. To deal with the special relationship that exists between fathers and daughters in order to assist the girl's future ability to relate appropriately to men in her life.

I want to emphasize that a therapeutic approach does not exclude legal measures or intervention by statutory agencies. On the contrary, experience with our project, as well as American and Dutch examples (Giaretto, 1981; Furniss, 1983a), shows that successful therapeutic programs often have to be supported by statutory procedures. In a primary therapeutic approach, police action and prosecution may be necessary. Legal interventions, however, should principally be a way of facilitating therapeutic work rather than having primary punitive effects.

Any intervention for sexual abuse of children has to center on helping the child as a victim, but this may also mean having to help the perpetrator and the family. We find it essential to convene a family meeting at the onset of the work to spell out the aims of treatment as listed above. In our approach, we offer group therapy in continuation with family sessions. Group treatment for the children is preferred to individual work because individual therapy can be experienced as a repetition of the highly secret and isolated one-to-one abusive situation that has traumatized the child. Sexually abused children often define themselves totally through the experience of the abuse. In specific groups for sexually abused children the patients are all abused and therefore "normal" in the context of the group. This gives the children the opportunity to see that other children have had the same experience. It also helps them discover their strengths and the positive aspects of their personality. We divide the groups according to sex and age, with separate groups for girls, boys, and parents.

During the initial phase of disclosure it has been helpful to distinguish between the frequent initial crisis of the professionals who learn about the abuse, and the crisis that is induced in the family when the abuse comes to light. Immediate unplanned action by professionals has often led to a failure to establish the fact of the abuse, resulting in nontherapeutic responses by professionals without clear aims or goals; this has often resulted in failure to intervene at all or in secondary victimization of the children involved. The crisis among professionals is often related to the following three factors: (1) child sexual abuse is a crime, and legal and therapeutic interventions often seem to be incompatible; (2) the wish of professionals who want to avoid confrontation with child sexual abuse leads to denial that the abuse exists at all; and (3) the lack of clear concepts about how to intervene and the paucity of resources lead to a tendency to try not to see what otherwise would be obvious.

In our therapeutic approach to child sexual abuse, the first aim is therefore to avoid secondary damage through inappropriate professional interventions. Only then can we concentrate on primary therapeutic steps to deal with psychological damage through the abuse itself.

The legal aspects of child sexual abuse, the fact that child sexual abuse is a syndrome of secrecy, and the addictive nature of the abuse for the perpetrator made it necessary for our treatment approach to include both therapeutic and legal components. The overall therapeutic intervention for the child and the family is firmly embedded in a framework of legal and statutory procedures (Furniss, 1983a).

The term *therapeutic,* applied in the context of child sexual abuse, cannot be used in its traditional meaning. Essential therapeutic ingredients include the framework of the intervention itself, the basic perspective of the professional work, and the way in which the intervention is organized, and these components can either have disastrous effects or be highly therapeutic. Contradictory positions, which seem to arise between statutory and therapeutic approaches, turn into complementary perspectives if the therapeutic potential of a statutory intervention is seen and used and, on the other side, the need for legal backup of a therapeutic intervention is acknowledged.

THE CRISIS INTERVENTION

In order to avoid secondary damage and to achieve initial primary therapeutic effects, we have found it helpful during the crisis intervention to orient ourselves along the lines of the following six steps.

Believing the Child's Communication

First, we have to take the communications and symptoms of the child seriously. Children report time and again that they tried to talk about the abuse, but that they were not believed. Their attempt to disclose was often labeled as fantasy or as lying, and they were punished. In addition, the abuse sometimes has continued for many years. The first step in crisis intervention is, therefore, to listen to the children and take their communication seriously without resorting to immediate and panic-ridden action.

From a Vague to a Well-Founded Suspicion

Any suspicion of abuse first has to be followed up and clarified with the child on her own. We talk to the child in the presence of the person to whom she first disclosed, in order to assess the likelihood and degree of abuse. The presence of a person the child knows and trusts can be of great help if this leads to reduction of anxiety and fosters the child's trust. However, the presence, especially, of mothers, can prevent a full disclosure when the child receives verbal or nonverbal messages not to disclose or when the disclosure leads to acute stress reactions in the mother.

Planning the Intervention

In sexual abuse, even more than in physical abuse, we usually have time to plan the intervention and determine the point of disclosure to the family. The initial crisis in the disclosure is primarily a crisis of professionals. The child may have experienced abuse for many years. A well-planned intervention, one or two days or even weeks after the initial suspicion, is more important than immediate and confusing action responses to first suspicions or part-disclosures of children. The planning of the intervention should from the outset include all groups of professionals who may be involved, including child protection services and, if necessary, police. In a case conference or over the phone we try to establish the role each professional will play in the context of an overall therapeutic intervention. The coordination of professionals prior to disclosure to the family is essential in order to prevent the intervention of legal institutions and child protective services in an uncoordinated fashion, which may lead to secondary damage.

Physical Investigation

During the crisis intervention it may be necessary to conduct a physical examination, both to assess possible injury and to collect evidence. It is important that the physical examination be well prepared and conducted by doctors who are specially trained. The danger is that an insensitive and incompetent procedure may not only bring no results in terms of evidence but also lead to additional psychological trauma. If the history reveals no indication of sexual abuse within forty-eight hours prior to disclosure, the physical checkup does not have to take place immediately during the crisis of disclosure.

The planning stage is used to develop clear plans that answer basic practical questions: Who will talk to the child, in a full disclosure interview, about the abuse and about further procedures? Where will the child go if disclosure in the family makes it necessary that the child leave home? Which role will be taken by legal and child protective services and who will coordinate the overall therapeutic approach?

Crisis of Disclosure in the Family

After the coordination of professionals, the crisis of disclosure in the family can be used effectively to gain the necessary information and put the confusion of the crisis to therapeutic use.

The rate of admissions of perpetrators increases when the intervention with the family is better prepared by the professionals involved. Good preparation and documentation and the confrontation of the perpetrator with as many facts as possible, in combination with a certain surprise effect, can often help perpetrators admit to the abuse. At this point therapists may not be the best people to confront perpetrators and obtain the facts of the abuse. In our interdisciplinary approach, trained police officers often have been able to gain vital information as a basis for further therapeutic procedures.

A careful assessment of the child on her own and good documentation prior to disclosure to the perpetrator are also important. Because of fear of the consequences, children often later withdraw their initial statements and deny that abuse has taken place. This happens mainly for three reasons: the child becomes afraid of paternal threats, the child realizes the possible consequences of her disclosures for herself and for the family, and the reaction of fathers and other family members is often openly hostile toward the child, blaming her for the abuse and burdening her with the responsibility for the consequences of disclosure.

The Family Meeting

Because child sexual abuse is a syndrome of secrecy within the family, a high priority in our therapeutic approach is to bring together all involved family members in one or two conjoint meetings with three aims: (1) to give the abused child permission to perceive the abuse as reality, (2) to get permission for the child to talk about the abuse, and (3) to get implicit or explicit permission from the parents for the child to make use of the treatment. We try to achieve clarification in five areas (Furniss, 1984b).

The first task of the family meeting is to establish the facts and clarify what really has happened. This can be forgotten or even actively avoided in most approaches at present. Each family member may have made separate statements to professionals, police, social workers, doctors, or others. These statements may be of considerable length, and it may have taken hours or days to collect them. In addition, different professionals or agencies involved often have talked about the facts of the abuse at length and may have exchanged lengthy written reports. Despite all these activities, in terms of family relationships, the sexual abuse usually is still a family secret. It has never been talked about openly between the persons most concerned: father, mother, and the children directly or indirectly involved. Furthermore, the child may have indicated that the abuse was happening; she may even have told the mother and other family members and nobody believed her. In the family meeting everything written down beforehand has to be repeated. No facts should be taken as known or shared, least of all the fact of the sexual abuse itself, even if the father has been to court and has admitted to it. The family meeting has to establish first the fact of the sexual abuse and the circumstances, such as where it took place and where everybody was at the time. Words like "sexual relationship" between father and child should be explicitly used to help the family find any open way to approach a subject for which most families do not have the words and language to communicate. The content should be explicit, but emotionally as neutral as possible. The aim is to establish facts in a nonper-secuting and accepting manner.

The second task for the meeting is to help the father take sole respon-sibility for the sexual act itself in a way that is outspoken and that in the presence of other family members (especially the mother) takes any responsibility for the abuse away from the child. The father's responsi-bility has to be very clear; it is known from clinical experience that children often get blamed either for the abuse itself or for the secondary damage following family breakup. If children do not get blamed by oth-ers, they often hold themselves responsible for the sexual relationship as well as the consequences after family breakdown.

The third task is to help both parents—mother and father—to come to an agreement about the degree of their involvement as equal parents who are both responsible for the emotional care of the children. On the father's side, one of the most caring actions may be for him to agree to allow the child to remain away from him and not participate in the child's daily care. In that case, a father who agrees to move out for a while may be taking the most caring paternal action possible. On the other hand, a mother who does not immediately file for a divorce, even if she wants to, but gives the children time to cope with the trauma and to adapt to the new situation with a father who is still involved may be providing the most beneficial maternal care.

The fourth task of a family meeting is therefore to talk openly, in front of everybody, about any separation in the family. This is done in order to make sure that the therapeutic and positive implications of the child's placement are understood by the child, who may otherwise experience her removal as punishment. Even if no forced legal and statutory separa-tion of family members takes place, temporary separation will often occur in response to the developing, often intense family dynamics. This may involve marital separation as well as placement of the child when the child does not want to return home. If the father leaves, it is impor-tant to convey unambiguously to the child involved and especially to any sibling that the father's departure is not the child's fault. On the other hand, a child leaving the family should not be given the impression that she is leaving because no one in the family wants her and that she is being pushed out of the family as punishment for the abuse or for sec-ondary problems arising from disclosure.

Finally, the fifth task is to make a therapeutic contract that contains agreements about the degree of contact between family members and visiting arrangements in cases of separation. The contract should also clearly define for everybody in the family which professionals will be involved in what capacity and to what degree and intensity, and it should specify the possible long-term plans for the family.

The five practical tasks of a conjoint family meeting are described here in detail because of their fundamental therapeutic effect in the short and long term. The family meeting can be conducted effectively by any professional who dares to confront sexual abuse with an open mind, rather than with preconceived notions or revenge feelings. These emotions understandably interfere only too easily with attempts to find a positive solution to child sexual abuse. The greatest danger is that a professional will identify too closely with either the child or the mother. Signs of professionals beginning to mirror family conflict and starting to take up "conflicts by proxy" (Furniss, 1983b) should alert all professionals involved and lead to immediate clarification of aims and means.

GROUP TREATMENT

The increase in the number of identified child sexual abuse victims with psychological disturbances makes the development of effective specific treatment increasingly urgent. Giaretto (1981, 1982) pioneered group treatment for sexually abused children as a cornerstone of an integrated treatment approach. He uses a professional approach combined with a strong self-help component, in which both therapeutic and educational elements are integrated. Mrazek, Lynch, and Bentovim (1983) describe group therapy for young children as helpful if it takes place in the context of other changes in the immediate environment of the children.

In our own approach, group work is a core element of the overall treatment and is combined with family sessions in relation to the aims and goals described above. The group provides a forum within which the abused children may be able to resolve some problems not easily tackled in direct work with the family. The peer group contact and self-help components of the group work enhances the development of self-esteem and the assertiveness of the group members. The group work has specific goals aimed at the girls as individuals, as family members, and as members of peer groups (Furniss et al., 1987).

Because of the specific problems of child sexual abuse, we use a range of techniques in group treatment. First, interpretations center on the process both within the group and between the girls and therapists. Second, we are prepared to intervene actively, if required, even going so

far as to restrain children physically in situations of potentially dangerous acting out. This is therapeutically appropriate, in order to give the
children an experience of firm limit setting in the face of the very blurred
boundaries inevitably involved in the experience of child sexual abuse.
Third, teaching is used to provide information about matters important
to the girls, such as sexual development and child care issues. Fourth,
drawing materials are provided to help the girls express themselves
nonverbally when verbal communication proves problematic. Finally,
role play and videotape feedback are used to increase social skills and
self-assertiveness. Successful group treatment requires not only family
involvement but also close cooperation with all professionals involved
(Furniss, 1983b).

Repercussions from legal and statutory procedures and reverbera-
tions from family conflicts and crises often lead to nonattendance of the
children or to threats to leave the group. In these circumstances, the
local social worker with statutory involvement has a crucial role in ensuring the child's attendance and thus safeguarding the treatment.

CONCLUSION

A therapeutic crisis intervention that follows the path described for diagnosis and disclosure can not only minimize secondary
damage but have a primary therapeutic effect as well. As long as clarity
exists in the aims and the structure of cooperation among all professionals involved, therapeutic effects can be achieved on all levels of
professional intervention. It may be helpful here to remind ourselves of
the following six points:

1. Any crisis intervention has to be planned as carefully as possible. Often there is more time available for preparation than one
   realizes; what is important is that none of the professionals involved resorts to premature actions.
2. Prior to disclosure with the family, the diagnosis should be established with the child alone, preferably in the presence of a
   trusted adult or the adults to whom the child tried to disclose
   first. This may not necessarily be the mother.
3. Secondary psychological damage through professional intervention or through failure to intervene may be as grave as the
   effects of the abuse itself.
4. Intervening in child sexual abuse, when viewed as a syndrome

of secrecy, requires that a family meeting be held as soon as possible in order to break the secrecy within the family as a basis for further therapeutic work.

5. Any help for the child in the absence of at least minimal family involvement of the mother and father will most likely lead to a breakdown of any specific treatment for the child.

6. Therapeutic effects are achieved, in the first instance, not by highly specialized therapy but through the form of the intervention itself. This includes the clarification of aims and goals and good coordination of all professionals involved. A case conference approach can help clarify the relationship between legal interventions and an overall treatment approach.

REFERENCES

Baker, A. W., and Duncan, S. P. (1985). "Child Sexual Abuse: A Study of Prevalence in Great Britain." *Child Abuse and Neglect* 9, no. 4:457–467.

Beezley Mrazek, P. (1981). "Group Psychotherapy with Sexually Abused Children." In P. Beezley Mrazek and C. H. Kempe, eds., *Sexually Abused Children and Their Families*. Oxford: Pergamon Press.

Bentovim, A., and Okell Jones, C. (1984). "Sexual Abuse of Children: Fleeting Trauma or Lasting Disaster." In J. Anthony, ed., *Year Book of the International Association for Child Psychiatry and Allied Professions*. New York: Wiley.

Creighton, S. J. (1984). *Trends in Child Abuse*. London: National Society for the Prevention of Cruelty to Children.

De Jong, A. R., Harvada, A. A., and Emmett, G. A. (1983). "Epidemiological Variations in Childhood and Sexual Abuse." *Child Abuse and Neglect* 7, no. 2:155–162.

Finkelhor, D. (1979). *Sexually Victimized Children*. New York: Free Press.

——— (1980). "Risk Factors in the Sexual Victimization of Children." *Child Abuse and Neglect* 4:265–273.

Furniss, T. (1983a). "Family Process in the Treatment of Interfamilial Child Sexual Abuse." *Journal of Family Therapy* 5:263–278.

——— (1983b). "Mutual Influence and Interlocking Professional Family Process in the Treatment of Child Sexual Abuse and Incest." *Child Abuse and Neglect* 7:207–223.

——— (1984a). "Conflict-Avoiding and Conflict-Regulating Pattern in Incest and Child Sexual Abuse." *Acta Paedopsychiatrica* 50:299–313.

——— (1984b). "Organizing a Therapeutic Approach to Interfamilial Child Sexual Abuse." *Journal of Adolescence* 7:309–317.

Furniss, T., Bingley-Miller, E., and Bentovim, A. (1984). "Therapeutic

Approach to Sexual Abuse." *Archives of Disease in Childhood* 59:865–870.

Furniss, T., Bingley-Miller, L., and Van Elburg, A. (1987). "Goal-oriented Group Treatment for Sexually Abused Adolescent Girls." *British Journal of Psychiatry* 152:97–106.

Giaretto, H. (1981). "A Comprehensive Child Sexual Abuse Treatment Programme." In P. Beezley Mrazek and C. H. Kempe, eds., *Sexually Abused Children and Their Families*. Oxford: Pergamon Press.

——— (1982). *Integrated Treatment of Child Sexual Abuse: A Treatment and Training Manual*, Palo Alto: Science and Behavior Books.

Groth, N. (1982). "The Incest Offender." In S. M. Sgroi, ed., *Handbook on Clinical Intervention in Child Sexual Abuse*. Lexington, Mass.

Mrazek, P. B., Lynch, M. A., and Bentovim, A. (1983). "Sexual Abuse of Children in the United Kingdom." *Child Abuse and Neglect* 7, no. 2:147–154.

Russell, D. E. H. (1983). "The Incidence and Prevalence of Intrafamilial and Extrafamilial Sexual Abuse of Female Children." *Child Abuse and Neglect* 7, no. 2:133–146.

Weinberg, S. K. (1955). *Incest Behavior*. New York: Citadel.

44

Psychotropic Drugs in Pediatric Practice: Their Place in the Dynamics of the Parent-Child-Physician Relationship

ROLAND LAZAROVICI

BLANCHE MÉLIARENNE

Psychiatric work in a pediatric department encounters the importance attached by both physicians and families to the use of psychotropic drugs.

There is little literature on the subject. The uncertainties and difficulties of giving a rational prescription of psychotropic drugs for children are underlined in a work by P. Simon written over a decade ago (1978). As a rule they are prescribed with a symptomatic therapeutic goal in certain typical clinical situations, such as sleep disorders, agitation and hyperkinesia, depression, and psychotic manifestations (including self-aggressive behaviors, stereotypies, and dissociative syndromes). Adolescent anorexia, school phobias, tics, enuresis, and certain functional symptoms (abdominal pains and headaches) are also important disorders for which they are prescribed.

Apart from research describing their pharmacological parameters (how to regulate plasma levels to avoid under- or overdosing), articles on psychotropic drugs are usually written by psychiatrists, whereas they are prescribed to a large extent by pediatricians and general practitioners. Most authors emphasize the symptom-oriented character of psychotropic drug treatment and insist on the necessity of maintaining a psychotherapeutic relationship and keeping the use of psychotropic medication within this perspective. Descriptions are given of the undesirable side effects of these drugs, but there is little examination either of the place these drugs occupy in the conscious or unconscious dynamics of families or pediatricians or of the ideology underlying their increasingly wide use.

We begin by studying the use of psychotropic drugs for hospital patients in a number of different situations: somatic illnesses with a high potential for mortality, surgery, so-called psychosomatic diseases, and the aftermath of accidental drug poisoning or attempted suicide by overdose. This is followed by an examination of the prescription of psychotropic drugs by pediatricians, and finally, we examine the place of the psychotropic drug as a real object in the physician-parent-child relationship.

SITUATIONS OF DRUG USE

Life-Threatening Illnesses

A number of severe somatic illnesses require treatment in a hospital, the only place where the necessary advanced technology is available. Some children are regularly admitted to the hospital at predetermined intervals; others are long-term inpatients. All of them go through a separation experience.

In some cases, the use of psychotropic medication is considered to be a means of enabling the child to bear the harrowing experience of the terminal phase of an illness. An example of this is the case of S., fifteen years old when the pediatric team brought her to our attention. She had been followed by the hospital service for many years for mucoviscidosis, and her condition had considerably worsened in the previous few weeks. She remained perfectly lucid. Seeing the ineffectiveness of physiotherapy, her difficulty in breathing, and the hypoxia shown in the blood gas analyses, the team felt they should do something to alleviate S.'s "anxiety." In view of their own state of acute anxiety, nighttime medication was first prescribed; although only a small dose was administered, she plunged into a protracted state of lethargy, accompanied by sleepiness linked with hypercapnia. S. later gave an anxiety-ridden account of this induced state of somnolence, and her talks with members of the nursing team and the psychologist revealed what she had felt through the muscle relaxant and sedative effects of the tranquilizer.

The fear of death is difficult to put into words, even for a medical team. This powerlessness in the face of a somatic impairment with no possibility of cure brings reflections concerning therapeutic management to a standstill. Falling back on psychotropic drugs seems justified, but each of their effects has to be taken into account; instead of alleviating anxiety, they can have the opposite effect and reactivate it, as occurred with S., by causing too sudden a change in the adolescent's vigilance.

Some illnesses with a high potential for mortality require a course of chemotherapy in specialized units, followed by a period of treatment elsewhere in nonspecialized pediatric care. Immigrant children who are ill may suffer repeated hospitalizations and frequent separations from their parents, who may be in another country. This may erode their defenses, induce regressive attitudes and narcissistic withdrawal, and sometimes lead to severe depression. The need to maintain adequate nutrition means having, for example, to prescribe antidepressants in conjunction with tube feeding. The depression associated with the whole situation is seen as a symptom to be treated by psychotropic drugs. What should be considered, however, is the totality of the elements that can be adjusted in the general framework of the nursing environment—everything that should be *put into words* and talked about with the patient and among the team responsible for looking after the child. In this way the patient can be helped to fight his or her way out of the depression and bear more easily the tremendous, unremitting ordeals and suffering the person has to undergo. What too often happens instead is that hospital personnel wall themselves up in silence, having no faith in the possibilities of the spoken word as an agent of psychic transformation.

Surgery

Anesthesiologists' crucial function in a surgical department means that it often falls to them to determine whether or not psychotropic medication should be prescribed.

F., aged three when admitted to a postoperative intensive care unit, reacted to hospitalization by refusing to eat. The psychiatric team was indeed called in, but before their arrival, sedative anxiolytics were administered in order to create conditions more favorable to the patient's treatment. Once again, greater faith was accorded to the tranquilizing effect of medication, which has a concrete and immediate reality, than to the effect of anything that could be said to the child or among members of the team.

Psychotropic drugs are often administered as emergency medication in sometimes dramatic situations and discontinued once the crisis is over. Their prescription can be precipitated by traumatic circumstances, as in the case of M., a girl of ten admitted to the hospital after severe multiple dog-bites. Her parents were worried by the fact that their daughter, who was still terrified of dogs and suffering intense anxiety, refused to consider the idea of leaving the hospital and was afraid of having nightmares. Before there was any suggestion of seeing a psychologist, the child was given tranquilizers. The surgeon responsible wanted the patient to "forget" this traumatic event "as quickly as possible."

Psychosomatic Illness

Nonpsychiatric physicians are usually willing to work in collaboration with psychiatric teams in the field of so-called psychosomatic illness. Psychological factors are integrated into the conceptualization of the illness, and, similarly, psychotropic medication is included as "background treatment" in the therapeutic strategy.

J., a boy of eleven, was hospitalized for severe asthma. The presence of decisive psychological factors in the onset and evolution of the child's crises was obvious to both the physician and the family. The crises began when the parents separated, increasing in frequency when the father decided to remarry; additional crises were probably instigated by irritations and difficulties in school. Talks with the child and the family enabled a psychotherapeutic approach to these problems to be established, and a meeting was scheduled with the medical team. The anxiety observed in the child by the psychologists, however, was assimilated by the pediatrician into a physiological schema: his intention was to use pharmacological means to raise the child's reactivity threshold and, at all costs, to prevent the onset of bouts of asthma. There was no awareness of the role these crises played in the patient's psychic economy, and the potential long-term beneficial effects of the psychotherapeutic approach were short-circuited. Articulating conjoint psychotherapeutic and somatic medical intervention invariably produces problems, to which we shall return later.

M., aged nine, suffering from a hemorrhagic rectocolitis, had been hospitalized for a month and a half in the gastroenterology department because of his deficient state of nutrition. He passed a great number of stools, indicating an aggravation of the illness, which could not be controlled by intensive steroid treatment. M. seemed depressed. He spoke little, refused all activities suggested to him by his teacher, and remained completely withdrawn in a regressive attitude that worried the medical team. Despite regular talks with the departmental psychologist, no improvement could be seen. On the contrary, M. set the whole team jumping into action by acting out: he had to have a central catheter and tried to get rid of his perfusion by smashing the I.V. bottle, resorting to violence to express his despair and his desire to leave the hospital and be with his family. After this episode, the medical team decided to administer tranquilizers. A few days later, there was a recurrence of M.'s violence, with the child threatening to commit suicide unless he was transferred to a hospital near his home.

At a meeting between physicians and the psychiatric team, it emerged that the child had not been told that he was shortly to undergo a hemicolectomy. The failure to mention it was justified in terms of the child's precarious state of mind. The nurse was discouraged by her inability to alleviate his distress; sometimes becoming aggressive, she could not accept the patient's lack of recognition of their concern. Some of the physicians emphasized that M. "wouldn't listen" to their repeated explanations as to why he had to stay in the hospital. Not only were their explanations given at too late a stage and related essentially to the constraints imposed by the steroid therapy, but they were incomplete since no mention was made of any surgery being planned. This was the context in which they had recourse to psychotropic medication, with some indecision as to whether to use neuroleptics to diminish the patient's aggressivity, the tranquilizers already administered, or antidepressants, which take some time to produce an effect.

The apparent powerlessness of language led to medication, which could make it easier to modify the therapeutic framework and provide more intensive mothering, but which was also liable to obscure the necessity for talking and to be substituted for psychological treatment.

Accidental and Intentional Drug Poisoning

Accidental drug poisoning is a frequent cause for the hospitalization of children. A survey done in the emergency service at the Trousseau Hospital bears this out and demonstrates the prevalence of tranquilizer use. Prevention of this type of accident would require an investigation into the role of psychotropic medications in family life. The medication making such accidents possible is usually a drug being used by parents. The parents themselves often seem "difficult" to nurses, who see the underlying anxiety or depression that breaks through in the form of aggression. Sometimes they are drugs prescribed for the child herself because of behavior or conduct disorders.

Deliberate self-poisonings also involve the use of easily available drugs. Davidson and Choquet (1981) have shown the high frequency of previous prescription of psychotropic drugs to suicidal adolescents (42 percent) and members of their families (51 percent).

This is further evidence that the conscious and unconscious attitudes leading to the prescription of psychotropic medication for children merit further study. Instructional guidelines such as "Keep medicines out of the reach of children" are not enough.

THE PEDIATRICIAN AND BEHAVIOR DISORDERS

The pediatrician is often the first to be consulted about behavior disorders. Parents see the pediatrician as having power over what they themselves are unable to deal with and are distressed about, and this idea reassures them. The doctor's evaluation of the symptoms is colored by the classification of psychotropic drugs into antidepressants, tranquilizers, and neuroleptics. A concern for efficiency causes him to concentrate on taking stock of the symptoms and trying to put a stop to them. An "unconscious conspiracy" is thereby set up between the pediatrician seeking efficiency and the parents who prefer to have a "good" child to one who gives verbal expression to crude or aggressive fantasies. This "dialogue" among parents, physician, and child can be reduced to the prescription of medication, and the "chemical object" supplants a relationship among them.

The medication (muscle relaxants, stimulant drugs, and sedatives, for example) can also be used, however, to achieve effects that will improve the child's ability to think and express himself. Here the consultation work will be focused not on the prescription of medication but on understanding what is happening to the child and also what is going on between the child and his parents, within the couple and in the family. The child's behavior problems are viewed in the context of their relation to the parents' difficulties in establishing and maintaining a way of life and in carrying out their function as parents, and especially their relation to the father's failure to fulfill his specific paternal role.

The pediatrician's prescription is designed to restore a lost balance: homeostasis, harmony, and the absence of conflict are the ideals imposed. The medication is used as an agent to reduce pathology and as a means of "repression": a disagreeable or inconvenient content has to be removed from conscious awareness.

The parents' request often follows a similar pattern. It is one that enables them to avoid a more searching interrogation as to their conscious and unconscious feelings and attitudes, and this explains why parents are more willing to consult a pediatrician than a psychiatrist. The psychiatrist will ask them to "talk," whereas, as they see it, the pediatrician will prescribe medicine to which they attribute a "magical" value all the more easily if the exchange is limited to this object.

Yet, when the pediatrician's prescription has no effect or its initial success later disappears, he or she advises the parents to consult a psychologist.

THE DRUG/OBJECT IN A DYNAMIC PERSPECTIVE

Several factors are involved in this perspective. First, the very young infant receives nutritive substances and physical care. The child is caught up in a "world of meaning and communication that everywhere exceeds his ability to grasp and master them" (Laplanche, 1984). Messages emanating from the adult are enigmatic; primal and "traumatic," they belong to a world permeated with unconscious sexual meanings, of which not even the adult holds the code. The child has neither the physiological nor the emotional responses to the sexually charged messages tendered to him. These messages produce in the erogenous zones the feeling of desire, which can lead to autoerotic activity. Autoerotism arises from the intrusion, and subsequent repression, of the enigmatic signs introduced by the adult, which constitute "thing-images."

Medication can be one of such messages received by the child. The pharmacological effect of drugs given at too early an age—for sleeping problems, for example—alters the place given to going to sleep and sleeping in the psychic economy. The work that should bring the child toward the construction of a psychic object enabling her to think absence through and get over the distress of loss is short-circuited and cut out. This could contribute to the installation of structures that will later lead to drug addiction.

Second, hospital practice considerably reduces the emphasis given to the psychotherapeutic dimension of the medical relationship. Medical training stresses the importance of the anatomical and physiological body to the detriment of the libidinal and fantasy dimension. Even if physicians recognize the complexity of psychic functioning, they usually tend to think in reductionist terms, whereby psychological disturbance is linked to a physiological "disorganization" that ignores the complexity of the living being (Atlan, 1979). Thinking in reductionist physiological terms is reassuring to physicians; it protects them against the anxiety they would be subjected to if they were to take a patient's psychic functioning into account. This type of defense is useful in emergency situations where the appropriate medical prescription or surgical intervention has to be decided upon immediately. The question is whether the medical model is applicable to a child's psychological disturbances, expressed by anxiety symptoms, behavior disorders, or functional somatic symptoms. The logic of the medical discourse is organized with a view to "banishing the unknown" (G. Rosolato, 1978). This is a technological, operational form of language that maintains a metonymic coherence and, as Rosolato demonstrates, is directed at putting aside unconscious formations: "the manifestation of the subject, affective participation and the free play of metaphor."[1] "The relationship of the unknown is channelled," the interhuman relationship is stripped of anything equivocal or strange, and stability and security are ensured for the physician, the parents, and the child.

Third, the psychotropic drug, a real, chemical object, is contrasted to what G. Rosolato calls the "perspective object," the "missing object," denoted by the "maternal penis."

1. One has to go back to Ferdinand de Saussure for an understanding of the metonymy-metaphor opposition, quoted here as used by G. Rosolato, who borrowed it from Jacques Lacan. In the study of language, Saussure distinguished the syntagmatic (horizontal) axis—that of syntax, the formation and organization of the chain of speech—and the paradigmatic (vertical) axis, which governs the arrangement of the terms that can be substituted for the various links in the syntagmatic chain. In other words, syntagmatic contiguity is compared to paradigmatic similarity.

In his *Essays on General Linguistics:Two Aspects of Language and Two Types of Aphasia,* Roman Jakobson refers to this distinction and gives the names of these figures of speech to the two aspects or poles of language he discerns: metonymy (the syntagmatic axis) and metaphor (the paradigmatic axis). He also refers to Freud's *Interpretation of Dreams* and puts displacement (metonymy) and condensation (synecdoche) on the side of contiguity; on the similarity side he sets identification and symbolism (metaphor), which according to Freud are among the mechanisms at work in dreams. Lacan goes back to Jakobson's terminology, but although he does not specify the fact, he uses it in a different way: metonymy is identified with displacement and metaphor with condensation. In metonymy one term is used for another with which it is necessarily associated (for example, container-contents). Metaphor brings in the symbolic element. The child's carnal link with the mother is metonymic, as opposed to the paternal metaphor, the name of the Father, paternal Law. The mother fills up her "openness" by trying to turn her child into a phallus and, failing the intervention of the Symbolic Father, would precipitate him into psychosis.

The purpose of this footnote is not to discuss the legitimacy of Lacan's or Rosolato's ideas but to clarify the meaning of the terms and their connotations. When two perpendicular axes are used as a "figure" of representation rather than of speech, the horizontal axis refers to immanence, materiality, and the vertical axis to transcendence.—*C. Chiland.*

The role physicians attribute to drugs depends on their attitude toward absence. In a pediatrician's everyday practice the question of medication usually comes up in connection with a limited number of differentiated symptoms such as sleep disorders, agitation, and depression; psychotic problems are very quickly addressed to a psychiatrist. Instead of exploring the fantasies underlying these symptoms and trying to understand what they mean, the pediatrician gives a description of behavior, which is the basis for all the categories listed in D.S.M. III. Greater importance is attached to what is externalized and visualized than to the enigma of meaning and psychic functioning, and this is the kind of thinking that leads to medication being substituted for dialogue, instead of being used where necessary to make dialogue possible.

And fourth, the medication alters the structure of the family group. For parents it denotes the child's "pathology," which gives it a function of assuaging guilt feelings. Nonetheless, the underlying ambivalence is not diminished; it is often displaced onto the medication, whose effects are then in doubt. Other physicians are consulted, and other drugs requested.

Recourse to psychotropic drugs has to be considered in the context of a general assessment of family dynamics and the unconscious dynamics of each member separately. Medications can give valuable assistance as long as they do not short-circuit dialogue among the physician, the parents, and the child and are not detrimental to the understanding of the symptoms' significance.

In the short run, the drug can appear as a reassuring, concrete object providing an effective means of eliminating symptoms. From the long-term point of view, however, it can contribute to the genesis of later drug addiction. Of itself, it has no enriching effect on psychic functioning and produces no improvement of the child's capacities for psychic self-control.

REFERENCES

Atlan, H. (1979). *Entre le crystal et le fumée*. Paris: Le Seuil.
Beverina, M. (1983). "Traitement médicamenteux des troubles psychiques de l'adolescent." *Semaine des hôpitaux de Paris* 59, no. 33:2297–2303
Dalery, J., Beaufrere, B., Maillet, J., and de Villard, R. (1980). "Les neuroleptiques chez l'enfant." *Pédiatrie* 25, no. 1:89–94.
Davidson, F., and Choquet, M. (1981). *Le suicide de l'adolescent*. Paris: E.S.F.

Delay, J. D. (1961). *Méthodes chimiothérapiques en psychiatrie: Les nouveaux médicaments psychotropes*. Paris: Masson.

Dugas, M., Zarifian, E., Le Heuzey, M. F., Regnier, N., Durand, G., Bianchetti, G., and Morselli, P. L. (1982). "Surveillance des taux plasmatiques de psychotropes chez l'enfant. 1, Taux plasmatiques de l'halopéridol." *La nouvelle presse médicale* 11, no. 29:2201–2204.

Dugas, M., Zarifian, E., Le Heuzey, M. F., Regnier, N., Durand, G., Rovei, V., and Morselli, P. L. (1982). Surveillance des taux plasmatiques de psychotropes chez l'enfant. 2, Taux plasmatiques d'anti-dépresseurs. *La nouvelle presse médicale* 11, no. 30:2275–2279.

Esman-Aaron, K. (1981). "Appropriate Use of Psychotropics in Adolescents." *Hospital Drug Therapy* 6 no. 3:49–60.

Garoux, R., Roche, J. F., and Bourrat, M. M. (1983). "De l'apport de quelques données pharmacocinétiques à la prescription des psychotropes chez l'enfant. *Revue française de psychiatrie* 1, no. 8:19–24.

Laplanche, J. (1984). *Le pulsion et son objet source, son destin dans le transfert: La pulsion pour quoi faire?* Paris: Association Psychoanalytique de France.

Rosolato, G. (1978). *La relacion d'inconnu*. Paris: Gallimard.

Simon, P. (1978). "Pharmacologie et psychiatrie de l'enfant." *La psychiatrie de l'enfant* 21, no. 1:319–325.

Steru, D., and Simon, P. (1982). *Des essais thérapeutiques en psychiatrie de l'enfant*. Paris: Journées d'études sur le médicament en pédo-psychiatrie.

Werry, J. H. (1978). *The Use of Behavior-Modifying Drugs in Children: Pediatric Psychopharmacology*. New York: Brunner/Mazel.

Whits, J. H. (1977). *Pediatric Psychopharmacology: Practical Guide to Clinical Application*. Baltimore: Williams and Wilkins.

Winnicot, D. W. (1958). *Through Pediatrics to Psychoanalysis*. London: Tavistock.

XI

Conclusion

45

Trends in Child Psychiatry around the World

PHILIPPE JEAMMET

The twenty years following the end of World War II were characterized by the development of child psychiatry and the recognition of its specificity within the wider framework of general psychiatry. This evolution resulted in the genesis of appropriate education and the establishment of centers specializing in the treatment of child and adolescent mental pathology. The existence and expansion of the International Association for Child and Adolescent Psychiatry and Allied Professions demonstrate the autonomy and importance this discipline has acquired.

This part of the history of child psychiatry was heavily stamped by a variety of trends in thinking and research that, although relating to areas not strictly concerned with the child as such, had considerable influence on the understanding of disorders and on therapeutic attitudes in that field. These elements came from psychoanalysis, as well as from familial, biological, behavioral, and cognitive approaches. Of course, none of these constituted a sole and unique mode of reference, and theoretical tendencies have always been overlapping and in competition with one another. But there have undeniably been periods over the past thirty years when one outlook or another has been predominant in the field of child psychiatry. An impact of this kind was not innocent of a bid for hegemony and the exclusion of other approaches. This was regrettable, because such attitudes derive from emotional convictions rather than from a scientifically determined position and risk being detrimental to the therapeutic approach. Even if this is unacceptable, however, it is nonetheless understandable. It is probably impossible for a research effort and new directions of thought to develop, and explore the limits of their potential, without sacrificing themselves to a certain initial rigidity. This involves a forceful demonstration of their views that, for a time at least, cannot afford to be burdened with too many subtleties or doubts.

Such a state of mind is by no means confined to psychiatry, but in this particular discipline it is reinforced by the difficulty of establishing easily objectifiable scientific measures. This difficulty arises from the importance attached to one-to-one conversations and the variable criteria for recovery (which can differ according to what is considered important)—but also the unavoidable necessity for belief in the value of what one is doing, which is an essential part of any therapeutic action where a relationship is involved. The therapeutic commitment has to be so great in this field, even if it is only in order to maintain therapeutic continuity, that here more than in any other area of medicine, it implies the therapist's personal involvement along lines that have to be controlled but cannot be avoided.

The mutual competition among the various approaches is nourished by parents and the media, who have a need to idealize a new therapeutic method whose newfound prestige derives from the limitations—now presented as failings—of earlier methods. Only too often the result of these fads is a break in the continuity essential to treatment, which is all the more crucial in cases of deep-seated personality disorders that can only be modified, whatever method is used, by action carried out over the long term. Therapeutic inconsistency is a brake on any progress and gives ground for skepticism with regard to psychiatry and a fatalistic attitude to pathology. These points of view are easily adopted by parents because they protect them from otherwise inevitable feelings of guilt.

Such controversies are constant occurrences, and the recent arguments surrounding etiologic and therapeutic concepts regarding autism are one illustration. These controversies are now out of date, however, and belong to a period, perhaps still current for some, when it could be thought that a single approach can provide the key to understanding mental disorders and the therapeutic changes possible. We now know that this is not so. Here, as in other fields of medicine, simple linear causality is not acceptable, and the multiplicity of factors at work justifies approaches on different levels. The very number of theoretical models mentioned above has facilitated this discovery by showing the value but also (after their initial promise) the limitations of each one. The limitations relate to each method's capacity for adaptation and come up against the complexity of mental pathology, as well as the varying levels of action at which each can be applied. This indicates the possible complementarity of different types of therapeutic action not only according to the nature of the pathology involved but also according to the particular stage and the prior duration of the disorder. Each of these factors modifies the possibilities for change and readjusts the therapeutic objectives.

A whole new set of combinations of possibilities in the field of mental pathology is taking shape, and it excludes any restrictive one-sided approach. The innate and the acquired are no longer conceived in terms of a juxtaposition of autonomous fields; they are seen as potentialities with a flexibly open future, though they are given form only by their more or less random contact with the propitious environment. Similarly, at whatever level it is organized, the weight of any structure can be evaluated only in relation to the response to it from the entourage, or in other words, to events and particular conjunctures. All the relationships of body and mind need to be reevaluated according to these parameters. In dealing with any behavior, whether psychopathological or not, and whatever angle they are approached from (physiological, neurochemical, and so on), elements that belong to the cerebral-effector level and that are an indispensable adjunct to information can no longer be thrown in together with the elements belonging to the category of the meaning of this information and the communication of it.

Nursing teams seem to be increasingly aware of the limitations (and hence the necessary complementarity) of each model and approach to pathological behaviors in terms of concrete therapeutic action rather than on the research level. This indicates that a new approach to mental health is beginning to take shape, particularly with regard to children and adolescents. Here, pathology is less fixed and there are greater possibilities for prevention, which means that a wide variety of approaches are more necessary and more feasible than in adults.

I would also put this new approach in the context both of authors' widespread concern for finding practical answers to the problems encountered in their specific fields and of their frequent reference to "a working team." Among those who try to communicate their experience, there is an increasingly apparent desire to give an account of a practice as well as a concern for improving on it by taking advantage of the possibilities opened up by our knowledge and the therapeutic actions that are available. Authors appear to have abandoned theoretical confrontations in favor of seeking out what each of these various options has to offer that can be used in the particular circumstances encountered in the work of each individual.

Despite the enormous diversity of training, theoretical models of refer-

ence, and material conditions of work found in the countries of participants (whether psychiatrists, psychologists, social workers, or repre-
sentatives of related fields), this drive to take what is most applicable to
the problems encountered in a given set of circumstances is an attitude
found everywhere. Pragmatism, theoretical flexibility, and teamwork
have become the new values in child and adolescent psychiatry.

So long as it does not get bogged down in indiscriminate eclecticism
or a jumbled amalgam that can cause incoherence in therapeutic action, this search for a pragmatism, whereby the best each concept has to
offer is used in concrete working situations, seems to me to be a good
thing.

There are a number of examples to illustrate this process of maturation and enrichment of therapeutic procedures. It is becoming increasingly obvious that as far as parents are concerned, attitudes can no
longer swing between the Scylla of guilt-loading and the Charybdis of
taking the irresponsible spectator's seat. What has to be done now is to
acquire a better understanding of the mechanisms of interaction and
exchange that are necessary and inevitable. But precisely because they
are essential, they may present a certain number of distortions that can
contribute to freezing such exchanges and transform the response,
through a symptom, into stabilized behavior and illness. Having a responsibility means being an active partner, which is not synonymous
with being a cause, and even less of being guilty. What parents, after all,
would accept being considered as having no responsibility in the formation of their child's personality? Recognizing the importance of creating
a therapeutic alliance with the family in order to give full scope to the
child's treatment, however specific the latter may be, cannot be honestly
seen as putting anyone on trial.

Similarly, whatever the importance of biological determinants and
responses from the various neurochemical-neuronal circuits, the extreme plasticity of children shows a greater dependence on psychological parameters and environmental responses than in adults. Considering children or adolescents from the sole angle of their pathological
conduct simply imprisons them within it.

This brings us to a characteristic specific to the psychological field. It
is well known that in any science the conditions of observation invariably modify the object of observation, but nowhere as much as in our
discipline does the method of study create its own object. The idea we
have of our mental functioning and of what governs our interests and
relationships partly determines our responses. The idea that mental
functioning and relational and affective life can be objectified in the

same way as the physiology of the organs ignores the fact that the distinctive characteristic of human beings is their capacity to think about themselves and therefore about where they belong in the world of values. From the starting point of their genetic endowments, the human young are formed not only by the concrete interactions that take place but also by other people's vision of them, as well as their ability to internalize this vision and see themselves.

This is not just an academic debate, and it can be thought of as philosophical only if philosophy is defined as the study of the systems of values that contribute to shaping our lives. In this respect, there are certain attitudes that, though not new, are making themselves felt within our discipline and that insofar as they are a possible source of danger, should be examined. I shall mention three of them.

- The importance given to longitudinal studies is justified as long as a number of precautions are taken. It is essential to be aware of the risks involved in the evolution of pathological states, but only on condition that such awareness does not aggravate them by discouraging patient and therapist alike, thereby giving confirmation to what at the outset was no more than a potentiality. Knowing that anorexic conduct is in danger of settling into chronicity once its course has gone past the four-year mark is a matter of realism, since it is borne out by fact. But this also increases the risk of diminishing therapists' motivation and giving them absolution in advance for being inadequate or for carrying out the treatment badly.
- This is where the second point lies: the value of epidemiological studies, which cover large numbers, should not overshadow the importance of case studies on the pretext that the latter are less scientific. It can, after all, be asked whether it is of greater interest to be familiar with all the risk factors or to understand, through an in-depth case study, what has enabled even one person to escape the general pathological development despite these factors, thereby giving an indication of what might make it possible to counterbalance the weight of determinism. This is an important way to avoid the frequent confusion between correlated, possibly contributing, factors and cause.
- This touches on an essential subject that is my third point. This book gives a good deal of room to the evaluation of conditions external to the individual as pathogenic risk factors. Mention has rightly been made of concrete measures that could ensure that

the call for health for all by the year 2000 does not end up a dead letter as far as mental health is concerned. This brought the temptation to contrast the reality of the weight of these external factors with the sophistication of certain approaches, particularly those with a psychodynamic orientation that take into account the mental functioning of the individual. This contrast is intensified by the comparison between developed and developing countries.

Here again, however, it would be a mistake to set the two perspectives in opposition to each other. Whatever the importance of creating environmental conditions more favorable to health and of being able to fall back on medication when necessary, it would be both illusory and dangerous to ignore the fundamental importance to the individual of being able to give meaning to his or her existence and to integrate it in relation to parents, family organization, and cultural milieu, which are the points of reference essential to the formation of identity. Internalization of these reference points in the course of one's concrete personal history and their articulation with the organizers of psychic life constituted by the differences between the sexes and generations, the taboo on incest, and the links that govern culture are an integral part of the parameters of mental health. They cannot be dissociated from any health action in this field with impunity.

The evolution of mental health in the developed countries proves this. Can it be claimed that health improvement has been carried out at the same pace for both mental and somatic health? This is doubtful, despite the considerable efforts made. The abundance of psychiatric supply has even been accused of being responsible for the inflation of demand for it. Although it may be true that the improvement in the quality of life and the increase in social and professional requirements make individuals themselves more demanding with regard to their own mental well-being, it is unfortunately an oversimplification—and an essentially false one—to hold psychiatry responsible for this situation.

It is easy enough to agree with this, if only by taking a look at the present increase of behavior disorders in adolescence, which can serve as an illustration. The growing numbers of adolescents brought to psychiatrists following a suicide attempt, academic failure, or social withdrawal accompanied by loss of all interests, or because they have developed drug addictions, compulsive bulimia, or anorexia, constitute a different kind of patient from those psychiatrists used to have. Consultation is usually sought at a late stage, when the patients are already solidly organized in their pathological conduct; they certainly cannot be considered the victims of excessive psychiatrization. On the other hand, two observations have to be made. First, these behavioral disorders have been increasing regularly, particularly in Western countries, over the last thirty years. Even more interesting, the spread of these pathologies has followed the Westernization of life-styles, as is illustrated, for example, by their development in southeast Asian countries. Second, our therapeutic arsenal, especially in the biochemical area, is woefully inadequate to face up to these disorders.

All these adolescents share the common denominator of being difficult to classify within the traditional psychiatric nosology, which reveals its limitations. These adolescents can be understood only by putting them back in the context of their system of relationships, on the intrapsychic level as well as within the various systems and subgroups to which they belong. They have remained very dependent on their entourage and are, in their overwhelming majority, still in search of the self-image reflected back to them from others. They have a great deal of difficulty in setting secure limits, with regard both to limiting their desires and to accepting the limits imposed by reality. They can neither guarantee their own independence nor accept the attachments that indicate their affective dependence. Caught in a stranglehold between the anxieties of abandonment and intrusion, they are unable to regulate their relational distances in any way other than by acting out.

It is hardly feasible to hope for any change in these adolescents without drawing on these facts and attempting to articulate the elements of their psychic life—their mental functioning, their intrafamilial relationships, and their place in the social unit and surrounding culture. Deviant conduct is the expression of a complex conflict situation reflected in various forms of self-sabotage, the results of an adolescent development unable to ensure either the subject's achievement of autonomy or the development of the processes of regulation of pleasures and self-esteem. These conflicts are not in themselves an illness, but they spawn illness through a deviant conduct that becomes pathological and pathogenic insofar as it ties up the adolescent in repetition, impoverishes his attachments, and cuts him off from exchanges that could sustain him and open up the possibility of exercising his potential.

The psychiatric symptom conceals as much as it discloses, to an extent that varies with the factors involved in its etiology. It conceals everything that the subject is unable to accept about himself: his conflicts, weaknesses, shames, and fears, but also his most secret links with his immediate entourage, which he rejects and preserves at the same time. With his symptom or symptoms the adolescent is rejecting a whole part of himself that is feared and refused; the symptom is turn walls him in and helps forge a negative image of himself—what Erikson calls the "negative identity." The risk of adhering to this image is all the greater because he dislikes the self-image he already has and his self-esteem is impaired.

Any symptom, especially in adolescence, very quickly comes to have an organizing power over the formation of personality. It confers an identity, installs a neo-language, serves as a means of expression of conflicts, and becomes a way of handling anxiety and regulating plea-sures and unpleasures. As it persists and settles in, the psychiatric symptom loses its connections with the conflicts initially associated with it. It becomes increasingly stereotyped in expression and un-differentiated in its significance. In other words, it becomes foolish.

Active, diversified, and potentially conflictual relational exchanges, open to change and discovery, are replaced by withdrawal into the self and substitutive objects (drugs, food, dysmorphophobic anxieties, the symptom) whose common feature is that they lend themselves to a relationship of control, but one that becomes increasingly mechanical and stereotyped. This impoverishment is apparent even in autoerotic withdrawal, which gradually becomes detached from the fantasy ob-jects originally linked with it. In this way, active, mobile relationships are replaced by relationships of control; human attachments are trans-formed into a hypercathexis of mechanical bodily functioning, and thought is cut off from its affective nourishment. We know, however, that whatever the help provided by the therapeutic methods applied, these adolescents can achieve a favorable outcome only when they manage to reconstitute a more positive self-image. Otherwise, we are only too well aware of the extraordinary fascination their self-destructive actions hold over them. In this respect, the observation made in the preface to Tolstoy's *Kreutzer Sonata* seems particularly apt: "When one's own weakness is taken as an ideal, one can no longer see the milestones showing where to stop." And where can this ideal be found other than in their culture and through the mediation of the people they value and are valued by?

We live in a world that tends to take the machine, with the computer in the lead, as a model. In this context, perhaps the response of adoles-cents is not surprising: emotions, characterized by attachment to people who can exist either in actual outer reality or on a pure fantasy level, are replaced by the search for sensations. Such sensations give the feeling of existing and provide the minimum stimulus necessary for keeping psychic life going, with these being tied not to relationships but to mechanical experience instead. Their quintessence is expressed in drug addiction or confirmed food-related disorders.

It would be a disaster if psychiatric responses were to be organized solely in this category, and that efforts focused too exclusively on objectifying the symptom were to follow the same direction as this movement of depersonalization and isolation of the conflictual context that is part of the symptom's defensive dynamics. The machine-body of the anorexic, whose only sign of life is the unending action of filling and emptying and its headlong rush to physical exhaustion, would be comparable to a mirror image of mental functioning running along the same lines as a computer, stripped of everything reminiscent of affect or reference to a system of values and ideals.

How we see the child or the adolescent's pathology is never neutral in its effect. A greater or lesser part of her response is determined by it, and what we emphasize in our approach contributes to determining the organization of her personality. Child psychiatry cannot easily be confined to a purely symptomatic response: even more than is the case with adults, it necessarily has to be put at the point of confluence of individual, familial, and social factors.

The diversity of the areas approached—including divorce, new procreation techniques, new forms of paternity, and the impact of modern techniques of somatic treatment—also illustrates this. In every field it has become obviously impossible to reduce problems to a matter of pathology or to "psychiatrize"; what has to be done is to identify and make known the risks and stakes involved in what is going on in the child. This is very difficult to do without having in mind a model of every aspect and angle of personality development. This model must not fail to take account of present-day demands with regard to autonomy, fulfillment, and development on the level of learning of all kinds, as well as the quality of affective life. It is a complex field and one that is difficult to tackle, but it is impossible to sidestep in a society of individual fulfillment such as ours. Treatment is not a luxury but a necessity without which there will be a relentless increase in the negative behaviors that are the sores of the modern world. What use would technical progress, and the horizons it opens up, be if we were incapable of finding a response to these appalling self-sabotaging behaviors on the part of a considerable proportion of today's youth?

INDEX

ADD. *See* Attention-deficit disorder (ADD)

Adolescents: attention-deficit disorder and, 156–58, 159; autistic, 258–59; early maternal deprivation and, 88–102; increase in behavior disturbances in, 470–73; parental loss and, 315–22; psychotic states in, 294–310; in twentieth century, 26–27

Adoption. *See* Maternal deprivation

Adults: autistic, 254–57; childhood school refusal and, 53; gender disorder and, 83–85

Africa. *See* Nigeria

Allen, D. A., 112

Almeida-Filho, N. de, 404

Anatomical-clinical model, 9–12

Anna Freud Centre, 181–90

Aponte, H., 430

Attachment: cognitive approach and, 214–15; early institutionalization of children and, 88–89, 96–98; gene-behavior relationship and, 64–65

Attention-deficit disorder (ADD): cognitive deficit and, 224–25; minimal brain dysfunction and, 153–59; Tourette's syndrome and, 124–25, 144

Australian Outback, 392–402; effects of isolation and, 394–96; living conditions in, 392–94; social services and, 396–402

Autism. *See* Infantile autism

Autosomal recessive conditions, 62–63

Báasher, T. A., 404

Baker, D. J., 114

Bandura, A., 217

Baron-Cohen, S., 226

Beck, A. T., 209

Behavior disturbances: early maternal deprivation and, 93–96; increase in, in adolescents, 470–73; as mental health concern, 31; in Nigerian children, 404–13; psychotropic drugs and, 457–58. *See also* Health-damaging behavior; Neurosis; School refusal; Tourette's syndrome (TS)

Behavior therapy, 48–49

Bentzen, F., 322

Bergmann, A., 247–48

Biological approaches, 9–12; autism and, 70, 250; brain-imaging and, 105–06; China and, 370; gender identity and, 79; meaning and, 235; Tourette's syndrome and, 134–35. *See also* Gene-behavior relationship; Neurobiology; Pharmacotherapy

Bion, W. R., 421

Blum, H. P., 194–95

Bowlby, J., 209

Brain-imaging techniques, 105–06

Broadwin, I. T., 44–45

Brown, G. W., 209, 332

Bruhn, P., 115